Childhood and Adolescence

A Psychology of the Growing Person

Childhood
and
Adolescence

A Psychology of the Growing Person

by L. Joseph Stone *and* Joseph Church

Department of Child Study, Vassar College

 RANDOM HOUSE, NEW YORK

Foreword

by Otto Klineberg

Columbia University

This book really needs no introduction by me, or by anyone else. The authors speak for themselves—and for children—clearly, soundly, constructively. They are men of recognized competence in the field of child study; I am just a little embarrassed at being asked to present to the reading public the work of two specialists who know much more about this subject than I do. By contrast, however, I can perform a pleasant function which would have been just a little embarrassing for them. I can tell everyone else that this is an excellent book.

It is rare in my experience to encounter a book which satisfies the scientific canons of sound and rigorous scholarship and at the same time makes such good reading. The subject matter may be responsible in part, since there are few of us who are not interested in children, but I have read too many dull books about them to feel that this is an adequate explanation. I think that what has happened in this case is that the authors not only know children but are genuinely fond of them, and that their warmth and enthusiasm somehow become clothed in clear and readable prose that delights the reader even as it instructs him.

On the theoretical side, the authors are frankly and explicitly eclectic. They are neither Freudian nor anti-Freudian, for example; they apply Freudian principles of explanation when appropriate, but not otherwise. They deal with learning theory, but they do not force all the data into that or any other psychological system. They obtain their material from many sources—from observation and experimentation with children, of course, but also from animal psychology (with reference to the effects of isolation on development), from sociology (in the excellent discussion of the part played by peer cultures), from cultural anthropology (for the purpose of cross-cultural comparisons). They are not extremist; in the long-standing quarrel between traditional and so-called progressive schools, they take their stand in favor of a "liberal" school which builds on the contributions and avoids the excesses of both. I for one find this general standpoint very palatable, since in my judgment truth is not the exclusive property of any one system or viewpoint, and a constructive eclecticism gives us a sounder and more complete picture of the complex reality of child behavior.

There are many different groups of readers to whom this book should bring both pleasure and profit. I think first of teachers and students of child psychology (or child study) who should find this a suitable and attractive textbook. It seems to me to be appropriate also as a text or at least as required reading in courses on educational psychology, in which knowledge of the child must surely be a major preoccupation. It should be helpful to others who deal professionally with children, for example, teachers and school administrators, social workers, pediatricians. Cultural anthropologists and other social scientists who do field work outside our society will find in it a clear picture of what is known about American children, which should serve as a sound basis for comparisons with child development under different social conditions.

Finally, but far from least important, the book has much to offer the reader who is sometimes identified as the "intelligent layman," and more particularly the fathers and mothers who are looking for guidance in understanding their own children. It has been suggested that Americans are so insecure in this respect that they become eager disciples of the so-called experts, and our comic magazines are filled with unflattering references to the "techniques" of the child psychologist. It is true that in the fairly recent past many people followed rather slavishly the rules which such experts laid down, only to discover a little later that new experts had developed new rules. This book helps us all to put those rules in proper perspective. It sees the parent not as a slave to the child, or to the expert, but as a partner in the process of adaptation and socialization. It offers no blueprint for child-rearing, but it does provide something more important, a clear and readable and sound guide to child understanding.

It gives me great satisfaction to write this word of introduction to a book which I have enjoyed so much.

Table of Contents

Preface

For most adults, children are a relatively little understood—although sometimes enchanting or baffling or exasperating—sub-species of humanity. This lack of understanding is often concealed by an attitude that there is little to understand beyond the fact that children are childish, or by a feeling that the meaning of children's behavior is "obvious" —that is, that children's behavior means the same thing that like behavior would in an adult. To convey a more accurate understanding of children, we will, in part, describe—like a naturalist reporting on a strange species—the shape, size, nature, haunts, and activities of the breed, from conception to the point at maturity when it merges with mankind at large. Our description, however, seeks to be a systematic, integrated, and interpretive one, rather than a compilation and summary of all the facts of childhood. The facts are there, either explicitly or implicitly, but ordered and organized about our central concern with the flow of personality development and subordinated to a set of concepts of how people behave and develop. We have discussed in some detail only those specific researches whose conclusions seem to us especially illuminating or which serve to illustrate the methods by which scientists find out about children. Other sources and findings appear in the notes grouped at the end of each chapter. We feel that our system of presentation is desirable, first, because it makes the material meaningful and graspable, and, second, because there exists a need for an integration of the huge body of facts that has been accumulated, not only by psychologists but by zoölogists, physicians, psychiatrists, sociologists, and just plain people with a sharp eye for the doings of children.

To the authors, as they look back, and to the reader, as he looks ahead, the title and subtitle of this book try to suggest that the book is concerned with all aspects of childhood: as something worthy of study in its own right, as the period on which adulthood is founded, and as the embodiment of principles of behavior and development. Our focus is on the child as a person, with his various special functions in the service of his human way of being. To maintain this focus, we have used an organization that follows him through the major phases of growth: infancy, toddlerhood, the preschool years, the school years, adolescence, and, in a forecast, into maturity. This does not mean, however, that we subscribe to a theory of rigid stages. This plan of organization seems to us less artificial than one that subdivides the child into arbitrary topical segments such as emotion, motivation, perception, and motor behavior.

Our plan of organization furthermore seems to us a suitable one for presenting the child to the various kinds of readers we have tried to keep in mind. Both authors are parents as well as teachers and psychologists, and both share clinical as well as experimental interests. Thus, while our primary emphasis has been on depicting and explaining the child, we have inescapably been concerned with the applications of knowledge about children to child rearing, education, clinical practice, and social action. Indeed, as will become clear in the course of the book, it is our contention that it is impossible to understand child development apart from the physical, personal, and cultural context in which the child develops. Therefore, we have tried to write a book that would be interesting and useful for students, teachers (teachers *of* children as well as those who teach *about* children in colleges and universities), parents and parents-to-be, clinicians, and researchers. Although we have been concerned at every point with the practical implications of our facts and concepts for child rearing, we have not attempted to spell them all out in detail. This is not because we feel that applied child psychology is unimportant, but because the most successful applications derive from an understanding of how the child functions rather than from a list of prescriptions, no matter how well-founded these may be. In short, we hope that this book will be useful as an introduction both to the systematic study of childhood and to the art of dealing with children. Obviously, each reader will approach the book in a way in keeping with his or her own interests. But this does not mean that such-and-such chapters and sections are addressed only to particular kinds of readers. The more practice-oriented passages are rooted in theoretical ones, and indeed contain much of the factual and theoretical material of the book.

The organization of the book into age-level chapters follows, as we have said, from our desire to depict the details of the child's functioning in the context of his overall functioning. The reader who wishes to follow the development of any particular topic should not find it difficult to pick it up in the chapters dealing with successive ages. But, in doing so, he will become aware of why the authors object to a basically topical arrangement of chapters. First of all, such topics are to us necessarily arbitrary abstractions from the functioning of the child as a whole —even more arbitrary than age divisions (which, it might be added, we have felt free to violate when they became too confining). The child, after all, really does pass through infancy, toddlerhood, and the rest, but at no point is he ever pure emotion, pure intelligence, or pure motor skills. Even though we have divided age-level chapters into topical sections, we have felt obligated not to keep these topics too separate. For instance, insofar as this book has a central topic, or theme, it is the awareness of self in relation to the world. In the chapters on infancy, however, the infant's self—or lack of one—is not accorded a section of its own, but is discussed in relation to basic trust, perceptual processes, and the first acquisition of culture. In toddlerhood, the self is discussed in relation to autonomy, language development, and discipline. In the chapter on the preschool years, selfhood is related to play patterns, is allotted a separate section, and recurs in discussions of sexuality and of thinking. In the middle years, the self is taken up in connection with friendship patterns, sex roles and sex differences, and thinking. In adolescence, the self again occupies a section of its own, but is also an important element in discussions of relationships with parents and with contemporaries, of sexuality, and of idealism.

Another objection to the alternative topical analysis of behavior is that the categories themselves change their nature in the course of development. One can, to be sure, speak of changing social relationships in terms of the number and variety of people who exist for the child at different ages. But "social relationships" seen in their living context are qualitatively quite different things from one age to the next. The infant's attachment to his mother is hardly a social relationship in the same sense as the school-age child's loyalty to his gang, or the adolescent's sense of kinship with an idealized humanity. Yet another objection is that the changing relative importance of each aspect of behavior at successive ages is likely to be lost in a topical arrangement. Thus, the perfection of motor skills is crucial in the earliest years, remains important through the middle years, but thereafter is an issue only for athletes.

So, with a bit of labor, the reader might reconstitute this book topically in terms of physical growth, motor development, psychosexual development, intellectual functioning, social relationships, moral development, or almost any other categories he wished to invoke. But he will find that not all of the categories continue throughout the book, while those that do have a way of becoming something else as they go along. Most important, he will find all these aspects of development blending in and out of each other, not quite to the extent or in the way that they do in real life, but in a way that acknowledges their functional kinship.

Anticipating a few of the key notions used in this book may help to convey to the reader how the authors have organized the facts of development. We are concerned with *levels,* both of functioning and of analysis; with *field* relationships binding the organism to his environment; with the shift during the course of development from a predominantly *biological* level of functioning to a more nearly *psychological* one; with the individual's increasing and changing *involvement with other people;* with the growing importance of *learned behavior* as contrasted to *autogenous* behavior; with the transition from *stimulus-determined* behavior to *self-determined* behavior. We have also tried to suggest, partly following Freud and Erikson, some of the crucial adjustments between child and environment characteristic of certain ages.

All this suggests that the authors have a point of view. (To be strictly accurate, they have two points of view, but they have, they feel, done a successful job of compromising their differences without damage either to their theoretical integrity or to the unity of their presentation.) This point of view may not be wholly consistent or wholly novel, and it exists largely in the background of the book. In our explicit statements about theories, we have been at some pains to feature those of other people, even where they do not entirely represent our point of view. We have, for instance, given considerable space to psychoanalytic thinking throughout the book. This is not only because a number of Freud's ideas are helpful and thought-provoking, but also because they have of late taken on respectability and become influential even in the more academic areas of psychology, and the reader deserves the opportunity to hear about them in more detail than is usually given in comparable books. But though this book has a point of view, it is intended to be eclectic, not in the sense of lacking a theory or of simply juxtaposing a number of theories, but in the sense of translating facts and ideas from a variety of sources into a common language which, we hope, gives them all a meaning. Although the authors, as always, must take full responsibility for their formulations, they would like to make clear their indebtedness to the teachers with whom they have worked. These teachers have influenced us not only by their scholarly wisdom but by their warm humanity and humanism. Their teaching has been of a kind that fosters independent equality in their students, making them fellow-searchers after knowledge and understanding, rather than meek disciples. Particularly important for the authors (either jointly or singly) and their thinking in the field of development are Heinz Werner, Gardner Murphy, Otto Klineberg, and L. K. Frank. Among those who have enriched our thinking as scientists, even though their influence may be less immediately visible in the present work, are Karl M. Dallenbach, R. B. MacLeod, and the late Max Wertheimer. Many of our insights have come from the people we have been proud to call colleagues, including, among many others, Lois B. Murphy, Bruno Klopfer, Margaret Mead, Benjamin Spock, Mary Langmuir Essex, Eveline Omwake, Barbara Biber, and the late Eugene Lerner. Special acknowledgment is due Professor Otto Klineberg for his critical reading of the manuscript and his many valuable suggestions, and to Professor Anne Selley McKillop for her review of Chapters 8 and 9. We have a considerable debt to our students, several of whom, along with a number of our colleagues, have read and criticized portions of this book. We think it does no injustice to our teachers and associates to say that we have learned most from the children we have known (in the Sarah Lawrence College and Vassar College nursery schools and elsewhere), including our own. Some of our fond indebtedness to our own families is better expressed privately, but each of us owes his own children special gratitude for the bits of their lives that we have watched and enjoyed and which they have allowed us to smuggle into these pages. Each at her own level of sophistication has contributed information on the inner workings of childhood, and they and their mothers have made not a few critical suggestions for improving the book. We must mention, too, the services of our friend and editor at Random House, Charles D. Lieber, who, in addition to instigating the book, has been more nearly a collaborator than an editor. He has mediated the authors' disputes, kept them working with a nice blend of discipline and indulgence, maintained their spirits in times of crisis, and supplied many pertinent suggestions. Finally, we should like to say that this collaboration has been a thoroughly rewarding experience for both of us.

Childhood and Adolescence

A Psychology of the Growing Person

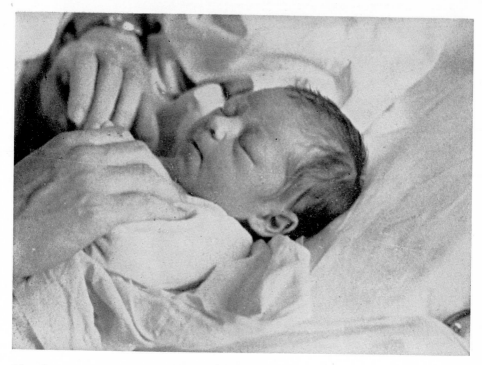

The tiny, often red and wizened creature (note this two-day-old's size in relation to the mother's hands).

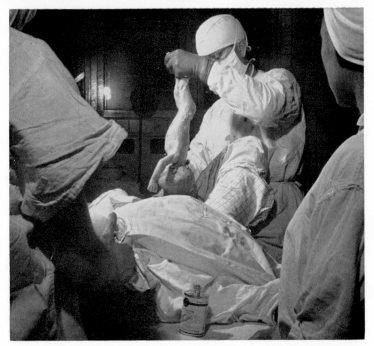

In our society, where 70% of babies are born in hospitals, the birth process is a secret veiled from all but the professional workers who officiate. Even the mother, often heavily anesthetized, may be present only in body, and may not get a good look at her baby for a day or more.[1]

In many societies, childbirth is a public event: everybody knows what a new baby looks like. Here, in New Guinea, Iatmul children—and animals—welcome a new arrival to the village, twenty minutes old (pigmentation will not develop for some days).[2]

CHAPTER 1

The Birth of
the Baby

The Appearance of the Newborn Baby

A moment after he has emerged from his mother's body, the newborn baby (*neonate*) is dangling by his heels from the doctor's upraised hand, a trickle of fluid draining from his nose and mouth. A smart slap on the bottom (almost any sort of stimulation will do), and he gives a thin, reedy wail. The birth cry marks the baby's first breath and serves as a boundary between his former water-borne, parasitic existence and his new status as an air-breathing, separate organism. He is still attached to his mother by his umbilical cord, but this has ceased to function as a life line and will shortly be tied off and severed—an operation no more painful than having one's nails clipped. In another twenty minutes, more or less, the placenta in which the umbilical cord terminates, having separated from the wall of the mother's womb, will be delivered as the afterbirth. The neonate immediately has drops of silver nitrate solution put in his eyes (the *crédé*) as insurance against infection. The nurse ties a string of lettered beads spelling out the family name around his wrist or ankle, as insurance that his parents will get the right baby. He is then set aside while the doctor and nurse devote themselves to his mother.

Many people, whose ideas, unlike those of the Iatmul, of what a newborn baby looks like are based on pictures that appear in advertising addressed to new parents, are surprised by their first actual view of a neonate. The idealized "newborn" babies shown in such advertising are probably two or three months old.

Truth to tell, exciting though his newness may be, many a neonate begins on the unattractive side. Even for eager parents, there is often a

3

discrepancy between the tiny, wet, sticky, often red and wizened creature of the first few days and the images formed in the months of hopeful, anxious waiting. He is coated with a cheese-like substance (*vernix caseosa*) which, when it dries, lends a chalky, velvety coat to his skin. (At one time, the vernix was carefully cleaned off right after birth; it is now thought to provide a protective coating which is better left to wear off in a few days.) His chinless, lolling head seems too big for his body. His nose may have been flattened and his head squeezed out of shape (*molded*) in his arduous passage through the birth canal. (The molding disappears within a week or two.) If he is held vertical, his bowed legs will hang helplessly.

A roomful of newborn babies at first glance all seem to look alike. This is because their countenances share a fetal quality which, until one comes to know them better, obscures their very real individualities. The "feel" of a neonate is something to experience. For one thing, he is incredibly small: average weight seven pounds, average length twenty inches (although, since he is likely to stay curled up in the fetal posture he maintained before birth, he looks even shorter). A skilled adult can hold him easily in one hand: fingertips supporting the back of his head, the heel of the palm holding his shoulders, the lower forearm bracing his skimpy buttocks. Apart from their smallness, however, all neonates do not feel the same to hold. Some remain compactly and comfortably curled, like a kitten, others sprawl like a bundle of loosely joined sticks, still others hold themselves tense and stiff.

There are various striking ways in which the details of the neonate's appearance may differ from that of even slightly older children. He often starts off with dark, coarse hair, not only on his head but sometimes elsewhere on his body: far down his back or low across his brows, for instance. This hair will soon be replaced by a more normal crop, perhaps after an intervening period of baldness.

The genitals of the newborn are at first surprisingly large and prominent. New babies—both boys and girls—often have enlarged breasts, which sometimes secrete milk, and girls occasionally have a brief "menstrual" flow shortly after birth. These phenomena, known as the *genital crisis,* are due to chemicals absorbed from the mother's system and subside rapidly.

Most newborn babies have not yet fully developed their layers of body fat, except for the fat pads that fill out their cheeks. *Postmature* babies (those who arrive a little late) are more likely to be well filled out and pink, and so more closely resemble advertising babies. The fat pads play an important part in sucking and, incidentally, keep the child's mouth from having the withered look of a toothless old person's. In premature babies, the cheek pads have not yet developed, and such babies tend to look remarkably senile, as does the *fetus,* or unborn infant.

We should not, however, be deceived. Unprepossessing as many neonates may be, they are real human beings complete in almost every detail, down to the last eyelash and the miniature nails on tightly clenched fingers and outstretched toes. There remain certain structural deficiencies, of course. All newborn babies, of whatever parentage, have smoky blue eyes: the pigments in the iris that make for brown or green or hazel eyes will come later. The neonate's skull is not yet completely formed, there being six soft spots, or *fontanels,* openings covered with a tough, resilient membrane; the most conspicuous of these is at the very top of the head. The baby's nervous system, although present in all its rudiments, has not yet attained mature form.

Basic Life Processes in the Neonate

Now that we have a picture of the newborn's appearance, let us see how he functions in his earliest days of postnatal life.[3] Although our concern in this book is not primarily with the physiological processes that maintain life, these are so central in the existence of the newborn baby that we must see how they settle down to dependable operation before we go on to examine the rudiments of behavior in the neonate.

It takes between two weeks and a month for the newborn baby's physiological processes to complete the transition from fetal to postnatal functioning; it is at this point that we cease to refer to him as a *neonate* and call him an *infant.* However, the baby's adjustment to his new way of life begins immediately with the birth cry; and when we consider the drastic change of environment he has undergone, we see that he does a remarkable job of adapting. His various body mechanisms may work unevenly and inharmoniously, but in a very short time they are ready to operate, and he is a lot tougher than he looks.

For nine months he has been living in total darkness, suspended in a fluid bath at a constant temperature, and cushioned against physical buffetings. He has been receiving oxygen, water, and foodstuffs directly into his bloodstream through the cord that joins him by his navel to the placenta, and discharging body wastes on the return trip of blood through the cord. Now that he is air-borne, he must begin to depend on his own mechanisms for respiration, digestion, and temperature control.

As far as *circulation* is concerned, as soon as the neonate draws his first breath, circulation through the umbilical cord slows down, stopping completely within a few minutes. Also, the special patterns of internal circulation, geared to the fetus's way of obtaining oxygen and nourishment, begin at once to shift to mature channels; the entire change-over takes about two weeks. The oxygen level in the blood reaches 90 percent of normal in about three hours after birth. Blood pressure is normal within ten days. The acid-alkaline balance of the blood is normal in a week or so.

As for *digestion,* a major feature of the shift from prenatal to postnatal functioning is that now the baby must take in sustenance through his mouth, digest it in his alimentary canal, and eliminate waste products by defecation and urination. From birth, the neonate's digestive tract is equipped with enzymes to handle all the simple foods except starches. It is usually assumed in our hospitals that babies cannot eat for a day or two after they are born. Certainly their mothers' milk does not ordinarily "come in" until eighteen or twenty-four hours later. However, Mead's observations of Iatmul babies, who are fed by wet-nurses immediately after birth, would indicate that neonates are capable of managing food almost at once.[4] Whenever he begins, the newborn baby's eating is likely to be somewhat uncertain. Initially, he will take fluids in one-ounce doses of which a good part may be promptly regurgitated, and he tends to lose weight for the first few days of life. Even in the uterus, he may have begun to urinate and defecate in the regular way. Soon after birth, and before taking food, he will have bowel movements of a greenish-black tarry substance called *meconium.* This consists of glandular secretions, mucus, wastes shed by his body tissues, and some of the amniotic fluid which surrounded him in the uterus and which he has swallowed.

Respiration is a new activity for the neonate. Now he begins to breathe with his own lungs, aerating his blood with the oxygen thus taken in. The neonate's lungs are at first congested with mucus and amniotic fluid, and many babies have to spend their first day or two with their heads lower than their feet, to facilitate draining. The muscle groups used in breathing are poorly synchronized, and the neonate's breathing may be noisy, shallow, and irregular. This is especially true when something upsets him.

In terms of *temperature control,* the newborn is not yet ready to adapt to wide changes of external temperature, and easily becomes chilled. His sweat glands will not be working for another month, which makes it easier for him to conserve heat and body fluids.

The neonate, incidentally, has acquired from his mother a resistance to many diseases that lasts for several months. He is, however, very susceptible to infections of the gastro-intestinal tract, of the respiratory system, and of the skin. All in all, it will take him some years to build up the usual pattern of immunities—particularly if his parents labor unduly to keep him in an antiseptic state.

The Rudiments of Behavior

When we remember that the neonate has just emerged from a passive, almost vegetable existence in the womb, it is not surprising that he spends most of his time sleeping. During the neonatal period of approximately a month after birth, he rarely appears fully awake except when hungry, startled, or otherwise distressed. Apart from the fact that torpor is a more familiar way of life than mobile alertness, the neonate may be made especially groggy his first few days by exhaustion due to the arduous passage through the birth canal or by the effects of anesthetics, if they were given to his mother during labor. Asleep or awake, he is subject to fitful starts and shudders reflecting a spread of stimulation in his immature nervous system. During his first postnatal month, despite the variety of actions of which he is occasionally capable and which we shall describe in a moment, the baby for the most part lies inert with his head turned to one, favored side. Many babies assume the *tonic neck reflex* position: one hand is thrust out in the direction the head is turned, the other arm is bent up behind the head, the knees are drawn high, and the toes point outwards, so that the baby resembles a fencer executing a leap.[5]

Gradually, during the first few weeks, the baby comes to spend more time awake. When awake and in reasonable physiological balance, he lies staring blankly in whatever direction his head is turned. Under ordinary conditions, his mobility is limited to feeble, awkward, symmetrical waving of his arms and legs, which move as undifferentiated units. They may move all at once, but in an unsynchronized fashion. He can do better in his bath, of course, where the water helps support his weight. He does not yet respond to faces or voices. This blankness, it should be emphasized, is characteristic of the neonate only when he is awake and satisfied. When he is hungry, by contrast, he expresses his distress with violent, all-over crying; his whole body turns bright red, and he twists and squirms and flails his limbs. When he is picked up and held close, he may momentarily become calm. Then he may suddenly become active in

a new, more purposeful-seeming way. He squirms busily about, pro-
pelling himself with trunk and legs and arms, rooting with his mouth as
though, it appears, in search of a nipple, clutching firmly at whatever
handholds are available—clothing, skin, hair—until the adult begins to
wonder if he isn't, like the Duchess' baby in *Alice in Wonderland,* changing into a small pig. This transformation from a diffuse to a seemingly
directed pattern of behavior when the hungry baby is picked up illustrates how wholly dependent he is on direct, substantial contact with
his environment—especially his human environment—for cues to activity.

Now let us look in more detail at the neonate's capacities.[6] The neonate's senses, especially the so-called distance senses (sight and hearing),
do not convey to him very much about what is going on in the environment—indeed, for the neonate, there is no distinction at all between what
is outside himself and what is inside. Nevertheless, he does respond to
certain changes in the environment. His reactions to external stimuli are
built-in and automatic, and often are diffuse. They are usually called
"reflexes," although this term must be used with some caution. For one
thing, they cannot be elicited except under special conditions: for instance, the sucking response will usually not appear unless the baby is
hungry. Although the neonate's reflexes are innate, they still have to be
practiced in order to be skillfully performed: there is evidence that the
baby even before birth practices "breathing" and swallowing, in both
instances taking in some of the surrounding amniotic fluid, and the
movements of walking. Also, the neonate's reflexes are not fixed: he can
perform the same act using different combinations of muscles, and later
on he will learn to inhibit his reflexes and substitute new kinds of responses.

In any case, the neonate is capable of a broad variety of responses to
a broad variety of stimuli. Before we go on to catalogue his repertory,
let us point out that some of the responses we shall describe, like the
sucking response, have immediate biological value; others, like grasping,
seem vestigial—the baby chimpanzee needs to cling to his mother's fur
for support, while the human child can count on someone's holding him;
still others, like the "walking reflex," seem to be crude anticipations of
behavior still to come.

One of the most striking reflexes in the neonate is the *Moro* response,
or infantile startle pattern, involving intense activity of the entire body.
The Moro response can be set off by any strong stimulus, commonly a
loud noise, a flash of bright light, or sudden loss of support. The baby

reacts by stretching wide his arms and legs and then hugging himself together again, often crying at the same time. Other, more localized, reflexes, such as those looked for in a neurological examination, can also be elicited. Among these is the familiar *knee jerk* (*patellar*) response. Another is the *plantar* response, produced by stroking the sole of the foot. This reflex undergoes an interesting change as the baby's nervous system matures: at first, the reaction takes the form of a fanning upward of the toes (the *Babinski* response); after a few months, the mature reaction, a downward curling of the toes, appears.

The *sucking* response appears within a day or two of birth, and sometimes immediately. Tactile stimulation of the lips or cheek will cause the infant to turn his head toward the source of stimulation—a nipple is the normal stimulus, but an experimenter's finger will work as well—try to take it into his mouth, and begin to suck. As we said above, the sucking response appears most readily when the infant is hungry—which is not usually a hard condition to meet. In this connection, it is worth noting that the newborn infant cannot voluntarily turn his head from side to side, but does so easily as part of the sucking response. Furthermore, if one tries to turn a neonate's head, he resists strongly, but he can be induced to turn it himself if one simply strokes the cheek on the side toward which one wants him to turn.

Hunger, indigestion, pain, and other conditions hidden from the observer will produce tearless crying which stops abruptly when the condition is remedied. Although the tear glands play no part in the newborn baby's crying, they act to bathe his eyeballs continuously and will step up their activity to wash away irritants from the eye. Apropos of pain, it is worth noting that babies up to a few months of age are apparently oblivious to some sources of pain as long as they have something to suck on.[7] For instance, the only anesthetic used in circumcision (removal of the fold of skin that covers the head of the penis) is a sugar ball in the baby's mouth.

The *grasp reflex* appears when the inner surface of his hand or fingers is stimulated. He reacts by taking a firm grip—in some babies so firm that they can hang by their hands. The grasp reflex reaches maximum strength at about four months of age and then gradually disappears. If the newborn baby is supported horizontally on his belly, he may perform "swimming" movements (*swimming reflex*). If he is held erect with his feet lightly touching a surface, he may move his legs as though walking (*stepping reflex*). These last two reflexes vanish shortly after birth, reappearing later in more mature form. In addition, the newborn baby in his very first hour can, under the right conditions, swallow, vomit, sneeze, blink, and yawn. Boy babies may have an erection of the penis.

We might at this point review some of the things the neonate cannot yet do. The only sounds he makes are those of crying and the noises incidental to digestion. He usually cannot raise his head, he cannot yet roll over, it will be weeks or months before he can move his thumbs and fingers separately. He cannot smile (except the false, one-sided smile of the oncoming "burp"). He cannot recognize people. He cannot cope with solid food. He cannot control his sphincters, grab his toes, or fix his eyes on an object. For the time being, his life is very simple. He wants only sleep, nourishment, oxygen, scope for movement, and to keep warm. Few neonates are disturbed by wet or soiled diapers. Mostly, the neonate is not much involved in what goes on around him. This indifference will not last for long, but for the moment he alternates between the blank, near-sleeping tranquillity of physiological equilibrium and the all-out distress of disequilibrium. His expressions of feelings—and presumably his actual feelings—are confined to the narrow range of neutrality-displeasure.

We have spoken mostly so far of "newbornness" in general. Right from the beginning, however, neonates also manifest their uniqueness and individuality. We have already spoken of how different babies feel when one picks them up—some are wiry, some are soft, some squirming, and some placid. Some startle at a noise, others at a light, others are blandly oblivious to both. They differ in the kinds and intensities of stimuli to which they react: some babies seem primarily visual, others auditory; some require strong stimulation, others seem very sensitive. It has been possible to classify neonates according to apparently reliable categories of fast, moderate, and slow tempo.[8] A child's tempo is consistent from one activity to another, and some authors believe it is likely to determine his later characteristics. We shall return in a later chapter to some of the practical implications of differences in tempo for personality development.

Prenatal Development

Birth, of course, is not really the beginning of life. The neonate at birth already has a personal career nine months long. Before we follow him into the future, we shall go back and look at his past, how he has grown from the union of two germ cells into a full-fledged baby.

The father and the mother of a baby each contribute one germ cell to his initial constitution. The father's germ cell is called a *sperm* or *spermatozoön,* a microscopic free-swimming cell with a whip-like tail. Spermatozoa are produced in the *testes,* bodies which are also endocrine glands for the male sex hormones. The two testes are contained in a pouch of skin, the *scrotum,* which forms part of the male external genitalia. The mother's germ cell is called an *ovum,* a tiny speck barely visible to the naked eye—even so, an ovum looms overwhelmingly large by comparison with a sperm. Ova are formed in the *ovaries,* bodies corresponding to the testes in the production of both germ cells and hormones, but located within the abdomen above and to each side of the uterus. The father has on tap a continual supply of millions of sperm cells, so that he is almost always fertile, that is, capable of siring a child. The mother, on the other hand, usually produces only one mature ovum each *lunar* month (four weeks). The ovum survives only about a day, and actual conception can take place only during this period. Nevertheless, since sperm cells can live several days within a woman's body, sexual intercourse within roughly seventy-two hours prior to ovulation may lead to pregnancy.

The mother produces her monthly ovum (*ovulates*) as a part of the intricate, recurring pattern of fertility known as the *menstrual cycle,* manifested by the flow of blood that appears every twenty-eight days, on the average, in healthy adult human females. Ovulation takes place toward the middle of the cycle, which is measured from the beginning of one menstrual flow to the beginning of the next. At ovulation, a blister-like structure on the surface of the ovary breaks open, releasing the ovum into the abdominal cavity, near the mouth of the Fallopian tube which leads into the uterus. The ovum is drawn into the Fallopian tube and during the next three or four days is carried along it. As we have said, the ovum can be fertilized by a sperm only during its first day in the Fallopian tube. The woman is not aware of the changes that take place during the period of ovulation.

To see the fertilization of the ovum in its proper perspective, we must return for a moment to the menstrual flow and its relation to the fertility cycle. The menstrual blood consists largely of material that lined the womb, ready to receive and nourish a fertilized egg. When the material is not utilized—that is, if the woman does not become pregnant—it breaks down and is shed during menstruation. Immediately after menstruation, the uterus again begins to get ready to receive a fertilized egg: the uterine lining begins to thicken and become engorged with blood. It is shortly before the womb reaches its peak of readiness that ovulation occurs.

If sexual intercourse occurs, about a teaspoonful or less of male fluid, *semen,* bearing some 300,000,000 spermatozoa, is released into the woman's vaginal canal. Unlike the ovum, which drifts passively downstream in the Fallopian currents, the spermatozoa can swim by lashing their tails. Some succeed in working their way in the vagina toward and through the *cervix*—the entrance to the uterus—through the uterus and upstream into the Fallopian tube. The whole journey takes one or two hours. The casualties among the sperm cells are enormous, but even so a goodly number enter the tube which contains that month's ovum, and there lie in wait. When the ovum appears, the spermatozoa are drawn toward it and surround it; however, only one can penetrate the ovum. As soon as one sperm has entered the ovum, the surface of the ovum

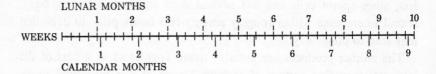

Scale showing the relationship between lunar and calendar months.

becomes impenetrable by any other sperm. The cell structures of the joined sperm and ovum break down and recombine to form a single cell, or *zygote,* and a new individual is on his way to maturity.

This newly formed person will have several names, corresponding to significant stages in his development, before he emerges as a neonate. During the *germinal period* of pregnancy, lasting about two weeks from conception (or approximately until the time when menstruation would normally occur), he will continue to be known as a zygote, even though he is now multicellular. During the next six weeks, when all his body parts are taking rudimentary shape, he will be called an *embryo.* Thereafter, from the age of eight weeks until birth, he will be a *fetus.* His total intra-uterine existence lasts about forty weeks, or ten lunar months, corresponding to the more familiar nine calendar months. Since it is standard practice to describe prenatal development in terms of lunar rather than calendar months, the table above is provided to help the reader translate these time divisions into the more familiar scheme.

The Zygote

During these first two weeks of pregnancy, the mother has no awareness of the events that are going on, and they are virtually undetectable by biochemical means. Almost immediately after fertilization, the zygote, as it travels down the Fallopian tube, divides and becomes two linked cells, these subdivide and become four, and so on. The reader might try carrying out this multiplication by two a few times: 8, 16, 32, 64, 128, 256, 512, 1024, 2048, 4096, 8192, etc.; this will give some notion of the astronomical number of cells (estimated at twenty-six billion) that eventually go to make up the human body. The process of cell division goes on in spurts, with interludes of rest lasting several hours. The new cells which are formed do not, of course, go their own ways like the two halves of an amoeba, each of which is a complete organism. Rather, they remain together in an organized way; they are subordinated to the organism as a whole and operate in relation to a "master plan" of the growing person.

By the time the zygote is about seven days old and has come to rest within the uterus, it consists of a cluster of cells grouped into an inner and an outer layer. Secretions from the outer layer eat a recess in the uterine lining and the zygote embeds itself in this recess, sending out tendrils which take root in the lining's blood-filled spaces. Nutritive material—oxygen, water, blood, sugar, etc.—is absorbed from, and wastes discharged into, the mother's blood through the walls of these projections. Note that normally there is never any intermingling of *blood* between mother and child. The walls of the blood vessels act as a fine screen which admits only certain substances while preventing the passage of the blood itself.

After this embedding process, the germinal period of prenatal development is devoted mostly to the construction of the housing in which the baby will spend his life within the womb; the child himself meanwhile remains largely implicit in an interior bulge of the zygote called the *germinal disk*. The disk plus housing constitute the zygote. For this reason, let us describe the form this housing will assume before we go on to trace the growth of the baby. First of all, there is the *placenta,* a disk-shaped, fleshy slab which is an elaboration of the junction of infant and maternal tissues formed when the zygote embedded itself. One of the placenta's flat sides is closely attached by its root-like blood vessels to the uterine lining, but is distinct from it. The child is attached to the other side of the placenta by his umbilical cord, an extension of his circulatory system. In the cord are two arteries carrying blood from the fetus to the placenta, and a single vein carrying blood back to the fetus. The umbilical arteries carry blood loaded with waste products and carbon dioxide, while the vein returns the renewed blood to the fetal circulation from the placenta, which acts, among other things, as a substitute lung. From around the edge of the placental disk there swells a double-walled membrane forming a balloon-like sac filled with the amniotic fluid in which the child floats.

The Embryo

And now to the child-to-be. Because it is one of the very best and most vivid accounts of prenatal development, and because the authors do not pretend to be specialists in this field, we have elected to quote Arnold Gesell's *The Embryology of Behavior**[9] at some length, interpolating summaries of Gesell and other sources here and there.[10] We begin with his discussion of the embryo that emerges from the germinal disk of the zygote stage.

> Prodigious developments take place between the second and third weeks. These are suggested in . . . a beautifully well-preserved specimen [removed surgically at the age of eighteen days].
> . . . Its form and features are clearly revealed through the transparent amnion. It is a pear-shaped disk . . . 1.53 mm. in length and 0.75 mm. in its greatest breadth [there are about 25 mm. in an inch].
> . . . The ground plan of the prospective child is already discernible. The longitudinal axis has been laid down; the embryo has a left and right side [a front and back, and head and tail ends]. . . . Almost three-fourths of the disk is already set aside for the formation of the head. . . . In the fetus, the head is one-half of the total height; in the newborn infant it is one-quarter; in the adult, only one-tenth. . . .
> Microscopic sections of the embryo show the cells to be arranged in three thin germinal layers, from which all tissues and organs are derived:
> 1. The *ectoderm* (outer layer): [the future skin and nervous system].
> 2. The *entoderm* (inner layer): [the future mouth, throat, and digestive system].
> 3. The *mesoderm* (middle layer): [the future] supporting tissues, skeleton, and muscles.
> . . . Even in the extremely young embryo . . . a median furrow in the head region is faintly discernible . . . from which brain, spinal cord, and ultimately the nerves themselves are formed. The nervous

---

* Arnold Gesell, in collaboration with Catherine S. Amatruda, *The Embryology of Behavior. The Beginnings of the Human Mind.* Copyright, 1945, by Arnold Gesell.

A

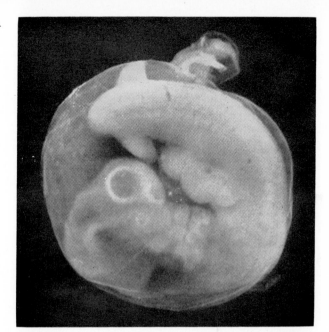

Stages in prenatal
development: A. Embryo
at about five weeks.
B. Embryo at about
nine weeks.

(From Potter, Edith L.,
*Fundamentals of Human
Reproduction,* New York:
McGraw-Hill, 1948)

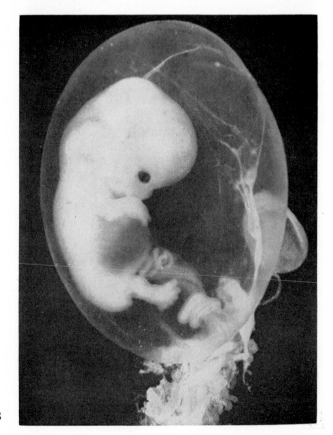

B

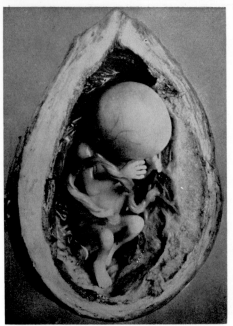

A

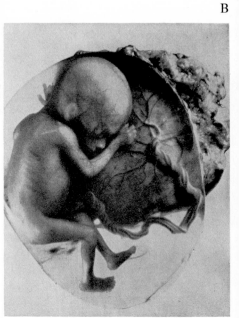

B

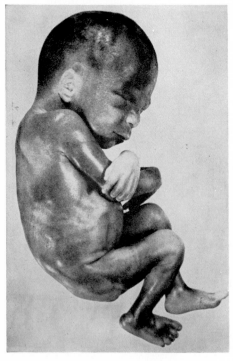

C

Stages in prenatal development:
A. Fetus at about fifteen weeks. This photograph shows the normal relationship of the umbilical cord and placenta.
B. Fetus and placenta at about sixteen weeks.
C. Fetus at about twenty-two weeks.

(From Potter, Edith L., *Fundamentals of Human Reproduction,* New York: McGraw-Hill, 1948) system is developmentally precocious. The spinal cord is laid down to its full extent prior to the middle of the second month.

The heart, likewise, is precocious. By the eighteenth day . . . an isolated space [has formed] to make room for the heart. The heart is at first a single tube. By looping and infolding, it develops two and then four chambers. By the end of the third week, it begins to beat. . . .[11]

By the end of the *first lunar month,* the embryo is equipped with microscopic arteries and blood to flow through them. There are the beginnings of a gastro-intestinal tract. Crude limb buds mark the place of

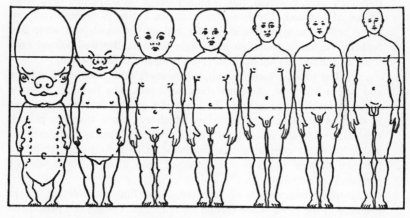

2 mo. (fetal) 5 mo. Newborn 2 yr. 6 yr. 12 yr. 25 yr.

Changes in form and proportion of the human body during fetal and postnatal life. (From Robbins, W. J., et al., Growth. *New Haven: Yale University Press, 1928.)*

the arms and legs. The embryo is a quarter of an inch or less long from head to tail—he does have a tail.

By this time, the mother herself may have become aware of being pregnant. Menstruation will be two weeks overdue. In addition, she may feel a heaviness and fullness of the breasts, and observe an enlargement and darkening of the nipples and surrounding areas. She may find that she has to urinate more frequently than usual. She may have morning sickness, the nausea to which about two-thirds of women are prone in the early months of pregnancy. As specialists in psychosomatic medicine have shown, the mother's experience of the physical changes that come with pregnancy is influenced to a large extent by her emotional attitudes. This is by no means a simple relationship, however. Some mothers feel physically ill during most of pregnancy but are cheered by the thought of the baby to come; others are in robust good health but live in dread of motherhood. For most women, pregnancy, like the rest of life, is a mixed bag of discomforts and rewards, hopes and fears, pain and elation.

During the *second lunar month,* the embryo's face becomes definitely human, his arms and legs begin to develop, and his tail reaches its maximum and then dwindles away. According to Gesell:

> This very growthsome month is notably a period of structural organization. The basic equipment for future behavior is being prepared in bones, muscles, nerves, and sensory end organs. The internal organs—intestines, liver, pancreas, lungs, kidney—take on shape and even some degree of function. The liver, for example, begins to manufacture red blood cells. The sympathetic ganglia and nerves which will some day regulate vegetative functions also begin to form. But well-defined neuromotor activity has not been observed prior to the fetal period.
>
> . . . The arms, which first appear as mere limb buds, now enlarge and divide into two and then three segments. The terminal segment which forms the hand assumes the shape of a paddle; short ridges appear in the paddle foretelling the fingers which are, for a transient period, webbed. The fingers elongate, the thumb projects laterally and separates widely from the conjoint digits, prophetic of its mobile opposability, a behavior pattern which is not perfected until after a whole year of postnatal development. . . .
>
> The major components of both trunk and limb musculature are in evidence at the close of the second lunar month. During this period the embryo floats in a fluid sphere . . . presumably . . . quiescently. Muscles, however, are peculiarly sensitive to environing influences. They tend to twitch at an early stage when the ions in the surrounding medium are unbalanced . . . without the stimulus of nerve impulses. In the heart . . . this contraction becomes a peristaltic sweep and settles into a rhythmic beat before nerve connections are established. Smooth muscles of intestine, stomach, and blood vessels are capable of similar [spontaneous] activity.[12]
>
> . . . At the post-conception age of eight weeks [the end of the embryonic period and the start of the fetal period] the amniotic sac measures about two inches in its longer diameter, and its tiny inhabitant about an inch in length. Loosely moored to the placenta by the delicate umbilical strand, the fetus floats freely in the surrounding fluid. In such an aquatic environment, the soft and almost buoyant fetal tissues are protected from rude shocks and from distorting stresses. Ceaselessly and evenly, gravity exerts its molding influence.[13]

The Fetus

During the *third lunar month,* the fetus (as it is now called) grows to a length of three inches and comes to weigh an ounce. Even at this early stage, the fetus has a distinctly human look:

[The uterus contains] in sculptured miniature the prefigurement of the ultimate human form, soft alabaster in hue, the head strangely massive, not yet childlike in proportion, but already suggestive of the infant-to-be.[14]

It is during this period that the sex of the child can first be surely determined—although it still takes an expert eye to see the difference. Initially, both sexes have almost identical genital structures, which become differentiated according to the appropriate pattern during the first eight or nine lunar months. The male fetus is slightly advanced over the female in sexual development; in the male fetus of three lunar months, long years before he can become a father, primitive sperm cells are already forming. In the female, comparable development is still a month away. At this time, the child's fingernails and toenails begin to emerge, his baby teeth (which will not erupt from his gums until months after he is born) now start to take shape, nerve cells are appearing throughout his body and starting to form connections, and a rudimentary kidney capable of secreting small amounts of urine develops. There are small beginning movements at this time, although the mother will not yet be able to feel them. Indeed, the baby will be evident to her only as a small bulge above the pubic bone. Gesell describes the baby's beginning movement patterns:

> Gradually [the fetus] builds up capacities to flex trunk and neck, to rotate rump, to retract the head, to move the bent arms backwards. . . . During this period, he has a fairly generous Lebensraum. [Even later] when his bulk has vastly increased . . . he still has scope for bodily movements. . . .[15]

During the *fourth lunar month,* the fetus reaches a length of six inches or more and a weight of some four ounces. A downy coat of hair covers his skin. Activity is growing apace:

> [This month] is in many respects the most remarkable in the embryology of behavior; because the fetus exhibits (even though he does not yet command) an extremely varied repertoire of elementary movement patterns. Almost his entire skin is sensitive to stimulation. Crude generalized responses [begin to] give way to specific reactions. Arms and legs show more motility at every joint and make excursions into new sectors of space. . . . These movements are probably mild, and vary from twitches to variably prolonged tonic contractions which wax and then wane into nothingness. . . .
> [The fetus] moves his upper lip. When a little more mature, he moves his lower lip. Later he moves both lips in unison. Still later he opens and closes his mouth. He swallows with closed mouth, but at times he also swallows amniotic fluid. His tongue moves. . . . He may also

rotate his head in association with the "oral [feeding] reflex"; for complex patterns of feeding are in the making. Peristaltic waves sweep over
his lengthening digestive tube.

Arms and legs occasionally move . . . in a manner which suggests
locomotion, whether aquatic or terrestrial. . . . [In addition] the fetus
. . . foreshadows long in advance the [manipulation] patterns of a
higher order. [He moves and bends his arms.] He opens and closes his
hands. He moves his thumb independently, or curls it fistlike under the
conjoint digits, a token of later opposability.[16]

During the *fifth lunar month,* as he approaches the halfway mark in
prenatal development, the fetus grows to a length of ten inches and a
weight of half a pound. Although the fetus has been active for a month
or more, it is usually not until the end of the fifth lunar month that the
mother can first feel his movements. These first perceptible movements
are known as the "quickening" and at one time were thought to mark the
point at which the fetus "came to life." The first movements are felt as
a mild fluttering; later, they are good solid kicks. It may be still another
month before the child's father can feel the quickening by putting his
hand against the mother's belly. By now, any morning sickness that the
mother experienced will probably be past, and she will be in a stage of
pregnancy that many women have described as a time of unparalleled
well-being. Also, her pregnancy will now be obvious to other people, and
she will probably be wearing maternity clothes. During the fifth lunar
month, the physician, with the help of a stethoscope, can hear the fetus's
heart beating. The baby goes through the complicated motions of "eating" and performs quite mature grasping movements—more mature, in
fact, than they will be for several months after birth. There are primitive, widely spaced breathing movements. A fetus born at this time may
try to breathe, but will invariably succumb. At the prenatal mid-point
of twenty weeks, according to Gesell, the fetus

affords a very presentable preliminary picture of what he will be as a
newborn twenty weeks hence. . . . His head is set remarkably straight
on his shoulders. His countenance has taken on an individual and not
unpleasing appearance. . . . Although by no means "finished," he is in
possession of his full quota of [nerve cells, many of them still immature]
—some 12,000,000,000 or more in number. The cortex of his brain has
differentiated into the several layers which will undergo endless organization in the years to come.[17]

During the *sixth lunar month,* the fetus becomes a foot in length and
increases in weight to a pound and a half. His skin is red and wrinkled,

the underlying layer of fat not yet having developed. He can now open and close his eyes, and his lashes and brows may develop. The cheesy coating of the skin, the *vernix caseosa,* appears during the sixth month, when his sebaceous glands begin to operate. He makes slight but regular breathing movements, and sometimes he hiccups. His digestive system is beginning to "work." His stomach muscles are motile, enzymes have formed, liver and kidney are partly functional, and meconium is gathering in the small intestine. His endocrine system, particularly the pituitary, thyroid, and pancreas, is coming into action.

By the end of the sixth lunar month, all the baby's essential anatomy and physiology have been established, although he is not yet ready to operate outside the uterus. Growth after the sixth lunar month is largely a matter of increase in size, complexity, and organization; no new organs emerge.

Although the last four lunar months of gestation are comparatively uneventful from the fetus's point of view, the mother is vividly aware of his final growth. Now, in addition to the numerous physiological adjustments she has had to make to pregnancy, she has to make anatomical ones as well. Her inner organs become crowded by the expanding fetus. She must make postural adjustments to a new distribution of weight. By the last month of pregnancy, many women feel that their bodies are awkward and cumbersome, and are beginning to anticipate the birth as a blessed deliverance.

By the end of the *seventh lunar month* (twenty-eight weeks, or six calendar months plus two weeks), the fetus has grown to fifteen inches and comes to weigh two and a half pounds. He stands about a 10 percent chance of surviving birth at this time. At *eight lunar months,* the fetus, now sixteen and a half inches long and weighing four pounds, has a fifty-fifty chance of survival. It is about this time—although sometimes not until years after birth—that the male testes descend from within the body into the scrotum. During the *ninth* and *tenth lunar months,* the fetus fills out rapidly, gaining close to half a pound a week; as he does so, his red skin fades to a pleasing pink. He begins to shed his prenatal body hair. An occasional fetus may even suck his thumb in the womb. At *nine lunar months* (eight and a fraction calendar months), the fetus has an excellent chance of surviving birth, although the more time he has to "ripen," the less wizened and fetal will be his appearance. However, since the normal range of gestation may be anywhere from 240 to 300 days, and since it is not always possible to date conception exactly, an unexpectedly early arrival does not necessarily imply prematurity and a fetal look. Usually, however, large and well-formed babies are the so-called postmature.

Prenatal Environmental Influences

The normal course of prenatal development is contingent on particular conditions, within the uterus, of temperature, chemical balance, electrical potential, gravity, and so forth. These conditions of the intra-uterine environment vary only within extremely narrow limits. We do not know what effect greater variation would have on the young organism, but evidence from studies made on lower animals suggests that even minor variations in, say, intra-uterine temperature can have drastic consequences for development.[18] At the human level, our knowledge of disturbances of normal prenatal development has to do mainly with the effect of specific injurious agents introduced into the unborn child by way of the placental bloodstream.

Many superstitious people used to believe that the fate of an unborn child could be influenced by the mother's experiences and emotions. This could even be done deliberately, by thinking happy thoughts, the mother could produce a cheerful disposition in her baby. A great deal of the folklore of prenatal influence centered about practices that would guarantee a child of one sex or the other, although, in fact, sex is determined at conception. In addition to influences exerted intentionally, there were those that came about by accident and that might "mark" the infant: if the mother were frightened by a bear, her child might be born with a shaggy coat of fur; if by thunder, he might have a deep, rumbling voice; injuries, such as cuts and bruises, received by the mother might appear in the child as birthmarks in corresponding locations. Physicians, aware of the sheltered life led by the unborn baby, and of the indirect nature of the connections between mother and child, fought such superstitions with considerable success.

Lately, however, the doctrine of "prenatal influence" has been revived in a new form and with scientific blessing. The latter-day version of prenatal influence focuses on the transmission of chemical substances from the mother's blood across the placental barrier to the blood of the embryo or fetus. As we have said, the mother's blood does not mix with the child's, but various materials—notably oxygen, water, and nutrients—are absorbed back and forth. And, as we might have guessed a long time ago, other substances in the maternal bloodstream (such as hormones and viruses) can find their way into the bloodstream of the child. Certain of these may be innocuous, some are even beneficial, while others are demonstrably deleterious. We have already mentioned how the mother lends her baby some of the immunities she has acquired. This of course is accomplished by the passage of antibodies into the baby's bloodstream. On the other hand, the mother on occasion may also transmit her allergies via the same route.

Another source of prenatal influence is relevant to one of the teachings of ancient superstition: in a modified and limited form, the prenatal psychological influence of the mother's emotional states has once more been accepted into decent scientific society. Since strong emotional states involve marked changes in our body's chemical balance, there is good reason to believe that when a pregnant woman becomes severely upset, the emotion-produced chemicals in her blood can find their way to the fetus. Sontag and others have shown that there is a sharp increase in fetal activity rates following prolonged emotional stress in the mother, and have some evidence of higher activity rates and somewhat leaner build in such children at birth.[19] We still do not know at this point what later effects the mother's emotional upsets during pregnancy may have, and it does not seem necessary to resurrect the former injunction about thinking beautiful thoughts during pregnancy. Although the evidence is less well defined, the fetus apparently reacts, too, to his mother's fatigue (which also has its chemical concomitants), to nicotine, and to alcohol —there is even a case on record where a morphine-addicted mother gave birth to a morphine-addicted baby.[20]

Clearly established are the effects of two non-psychological sources of prenatal developmental disturbance, the Rh factor and German measles. The Rh factor is an inherited component of the blood and is found in some 85 percent of white Americans (and 100 percent of rhesus monkeys—hence, "Rh" factor). When Rh factor is introduced into the blood of someone who was born without it—as sometimes used to happen in blood transfusions before it was recognized that Rh factor as well as blood type had to be matched—it has a pernicious effect, and the Rh negative blood produces *antibodies* (special proteins formed to ward off an invasion of the blood by alien substances) which combat the Rh factor. If a man with Rh positive blood mates with an Rh negative woman, she may carry an Rh positive child. (If the father is Rh negative or the mother is Rh positive, there is no danger.) During pregnancy, when an Rh negative mother is carrying an Rh positive baby, some of the child's Rh factor may get into the mother's bloodstream.

When this happens, the mother's Rh negative blood produces antibodies, but usually too slowly to have much effect during a first pregnancy. If, however, the mother has been previously sensitized by a transfusion of Rh positive blood, or if she is carrying a second Rh positive child, the production of antibodies is likely to be accelerated, and her antibodies may enter the child's bloodstream. As one might expect, Rh antibodies in his Rh positive bloodstream work great havoc, in that the blood is fighting itself. Such a situation can lead to miscarriage or to later defects in development. Happily, great strides have been made both in anticipating and in overcoming the consequences to the babies of matings between Rh positive fathers and Rh negative mothers, and the 15 percent of potential mothers who are Rh negative need feel little concern about pregnancy, provided they receive adequate prenatal care.[21]

Another serious source of prenatal injury is maternal German measles (*rubella*) during early pregnancy, particularly in the first two months (period of the embryo). In Australia, early in World War II, when as elsewhere a great many babies were being born, some alert physicians thought to notice the coincidence between a rubella epidemic and the appearance some months later of an unusual number of anomalies in newborn babies: blindness, deafness, motor difficulties, mental deficit.[22] The particular organ system impaired seems to be the one which was at its peak of growth during the invasion of the virus.

In general, the peak of growth brings acute vulnerability. Each organ system in the embryo has its appointed time to develop. If some disrupting factor intrudes, the organ that is undergoing development is the one that suffers. That is, it is not the kind of disease but its *timing* which determines the site of damage. Meanwhile, the schedule moves relentlessly ahead, and the damaged organ has no time to recoup. Depending on how central to overall structure an impaired sub-structure is, those that follow are in turn more or less disturbed in their development: they have to accommodate themselves, in keeping with organizational laws, to the total pattern in which they arise. So when toxins or viruses from the mother's blood enter the embryo just as the hearing mechanisms, for example, are at their critical stage, there is danger that the child may be born with impaired hearing. In the fetal period—when, in general, the child is less vulnerable than in the embryonic period—the pattern of critical stages is not so clear-cut.

Knowledge about such specific factors in prenatal development as those described in the last few paragraphs has helped clarify our understanding of *congenital* anomalies—those present at birth—that were formerly thought to be obscurely hereditary and is a source of reassurance to many mothers of handicapped children, who had felt guilty about passing on what they considered innate constitutional defects. Actually, birth anomalies of all kinds are so unusual that they need not occasion active concern.

The Elements of Childbirth

By now, our fetus is ready to be born for the second time in these pages, and it is time to discuss the general sequence of events that make up the birth process. Toward the end of pregnancy, the baby turns head down and comes to rest with his head in the pelvic basin. When this happens, pressure is removed from the mother's upper abdomen, making her breathing easier, whence the name of "lightening" given to this change. The mother's high-prowed profile now undergoes a marked change as the baby moves into position for his headfirst passage to freedom. Lightening may precede actual delivery by as much as four weeks, or it may not occur until after the start of actual *labor,* the process by which the baby is expelled from the uterus. The mother is made aware of the onset of labor by any one of three signs. One sign is labor pains, produced by recurrent contractions of the uterus, initially of mild intensity and spaced fifteen or twenty minutes apart, then of increasing duration, frequency, and sharpness. Labor pains may begin in the back, but move forward into the abdomen as they progress. (False labor pains, which cannot always be distinguished from genuine ones, may sometimes send a woman on a futile trip to the hospital.) Another sign may be a "showing," the appearance of a small clot of mucus brightly spotted with blood—this is a plug that had formed in the cervix and now is loosened as the cervix begins to dilate. Yet another sign may be a gush of clear fluid from the vagina; this is due to the so-called "bursting of the bag of waters," the rupturing of the amniotic sac that enclosed the fetus. The actual trigger for labor is unknown, but seems to be a chemical interaction between mother and child. Once started, labor consists of contractions of the uterus which, aided by the abdominal musculature, gradually expel the child from his mother's body.

Labor is divided into three stages. The first lasts during the period that the cervix is being dilated to accommodate the baby's head. This is the longest part of labor, and the mother usually remains ambulatory during most of it. Its duration varies greatly, averaging about fourteen hours for first babies and much less for later ones. During dilatation, the pains increase in frequency until they are occurring at four- or five-minute intervals. Although the cervix is normally very small and muscular, at the very beginning of pregnancy it takes on a spongy consistency (this change is one of the signs used by the obstetrician in diagnosing pregnancy) and at delivery stretches easily. Similarly, the pelvic girdle has widened to facilitate birth.

The second stage of labor consists of the passage of the fetus down the vaginal canal. This lasts about an hour and a half for first children and about half an hour for later ones. During this stage the mother can actively help speed the birth process by "bearing down," straining with her abdominal muscles as each pain, or uterine contraction, reaches a peak. This participation by the mother also helps reduce her pain. Like the cervix, the entrance to the vagina has softened during pregnancy and is able to distend enough to permit passage of the baby's head— tiny as it is, the broadest part of his anatomy. The second stage ends with delivery, the actual birth. At one moment, there is visible only the protruding back of the baby's skull. Suddenly the baby's head is free, face down and draining. The doctor supports the head with one hand and draws gently on the baby, following the automatic rotation of the baby's body through a quarter turn until the shoulders are vertical, in line with the long axis of the vulva, and the baby slips quickly out.

The third and final stage of labor consists of the delivery of the *after-birth*—the placenta and the amniotic sac. This usually takes less than twenty minutes and is virtually painless. The doctor carefully inspects the placenta to make sure there are no abnormalities and that none of it has remained in the uterus. Then, for the next hour, he or the nurse rubs and kneads the mother's abdominal wall, massaging the now shrunken uterus. This massage, together with hormone injections, causes the uterine muscles to squeeze tight and shut off bleeding from broken capillaries. All in all, the mother has lost perhaps a pint of blood—about what she would give to a blood bank. During the next ten days or two weeks, she will experience a sort of menstruation, the *lochia,* in which the uterine lining disintegrates and is cast off.

Psychological Considerations in the Management of Childbirth

Thanks to advances in medical knowledge, the past half century has seen a phenomenal decline in the number of maternal and infant deaths during and following childbirth. A good part of this improvement is due to hygienic measures which prevent the spread of infections. The utmost in sanitary conditions and medical facilities is to be found, of course, in modern hospitals; and women, understandably eager to benefit from modern techniques, have come to take it for granted that they will have their babies in hospitals, which is where 70 percent of American births take place. It should be noted that hospital facilities are important in the unusual instances when something goes wrong. A normal birth does not require any particular setting or assistance, as shown by the many accounts of quite successful births taking place in taxicabs, with driver, policeman, or fireman acting as midwife, or even at home when the mother is alone. In England, it has been customary to have the baby at home, usually with the help of a trained midwife, who summons a physician or arranges for hospitalization in the event of complications. American obstetricians in general have come to prefer the familiar and dependable resources of the hospital delivery room.

As is often the case, some of the very real advantages of a hospital setting are bought at the cost of certain unforeseen disadvantages. In this instance, the price, as we have begun to recognize in recent years, is a psychological one. In their well-founded zeal for medical sterility, hospitals have brought about a certain emotional sterility as well. Fathers and siblings are regarded as hotbeds of contagion and are rigorously kept away from the baby until he has left the hospital. Although the mother cannot be wholly excluded, she too is suspect. The stringency of hospital regulations may have two consequences. First, it contributes to the idea that birth is somehow a pathological process rather than a normal physiological function. Second, a point we shall return to in a moment, it induces in some parents an uneasy feeling that the baby belongs to the hospital rather than to them.

In the opinion of many observers, the trend toward hospital deliveries brought with it a parallel trend of excessive medical intervention in the birth process. There has been criticism of the excessive use of forceps to hasten delivery and of overgenerous use of anesthetics to relieve pain. Too early or too profound anesthesia prevents the mother from cooperating and may prolong active labor. It may have the additional effect of partially anesthetizing the baby, making more difficult his first adjustment to the world. To many mothers, being shut off from the birth process by anesthetics is a deprivation. All in all, a number of hospitals succeeded in making fathers and mothers feel like intruders whose emotions stood in the way of efficient medical procedures: the procedures had begun to take precedence over the patient. The last ten or fifteen years, however, have seen a reaction in certain quarters against this extreme of sterility and administrative mechanization. Not only mothers, but fathers, too, are gradually coming once again to be recognized as central figures in the birth process, which is increasingly viewed as a human event as well as an obstetrical problem. Not many American hospitals are likely to emulate the practice of one British physician who routinely invites the father to help him at the birth and then, immediately afterwards, rouses the other children in the family and brings them in for a good look at the new baby and the reassurance of seeing their mother. Nevertheless, a trend to a more human approach can be seen both in the management of childbirth and in the care of the newborn in the hospital.

Modified delivery procedures, sometimes called "natural" childbirth, include restricting anesthetics to sparing use during actual delivery or omitting them altogether. Essentially, this approach rests on the assumption that birth is not intrinsically as strenuous or pathological a process as it has sometimes been made out to be, and that the fear of childbirth instilled in many women is worse than the pain itself, and helps intensify the pain. To combat these fears, pregnant women are given a full understanding of pregnancy and birth, and sometimes are taught special exercises believed to help them at the time of delivery. Just how "natural" a delivery should be must be decided in terms of the mother's temperament and her obstetrician's recommendations made in the light of his knowledge of her, and in terms of his accustomed procedures. For some women, there are intense emotional rewards in experiencing the birth process in its entirety and in "being there" when the baby is born. Sometimes these modified procedures also permit the father to be present, if he and the mother wish it. However, no potential mother need feel guilty about preferring "painless" childbirth. Nor should it be surprising if she feels fear of childbirth in a society where so many terrors of childbirth have been expressed or hinted at and further enhanced by secrecy about the birth process.

A recent general trend in the care of the mother after delivery has been in the direction of reducing the former two-week "lying-in" period to half this time or less. Instead of being allowed to dangle her legs gingerly on the ninth or tenth day, a mother is now kept on her feet part of every day, in an extension of the "early ambulation" procedures developed in surgery during World War II.

Hospital Care of the Newborn

As a part of the shift from home to hospital deliveries that began early in the century, and as a part of the relentless drive to eliminate some of the hazards of childbirth through asepsis, there developed procedures in the care of the newborn which also have taken their psychological toll. It was assumed that it was hygienically unsound to let anyone near a newborn baby except under conditions of total asepsis—ideally, the mother should be kept away, too, but since this was not completely feasible, she was allowed to have the baby at its mealtimes, the rest of its day being spent in a glass-walled central nursery shared with the other newborn babies on the ward, safe from germs, drafts, and people, including fathers. Incidentally, it came to be felt that having all the babies in a centralized nursery made for more efficient administrative procedures. Partly for administrative reasons, and partly in keeping with a trend we shall discuss later, the babies were fed and cared for on a rigid, unvarying schedule. At fixed times, usually every three or four hours, they were trundled out of the nursery and distributed to their various mothers' beds for nursing or bottle-feeding (although bottle-fed babies might be fed in the nursery by the nurse). After their allotted time, they were once more collected and trundled back. This coming and going, and the burping and changing in between, constituted a major logistical problem for the hospitals.

The recently developed *rooming-in* program appears to be a system that takes advantage of hospital delivery facilities and at the same time restores some of the closeness between mother and child that used to be characteristic of home deliveries. Each baby sleeps in a crib in his mother's room, and she begins early to assume responsibility for his care. Under the old program, many mothers reported that their babies seemed like strangers when they took them home. Under the rooming-in program, on the other hand, the mother has a chance to get to know her baby and to develop some skill in caring for it before she finds herself at home and on her own. She is no longer obliged to lie helpless wondering if that can be her baby she hears crying in the nursery down the corridor. The father, subject to reasonable sanitary regulations, is allowed to have some contact with his child. All other visitors are excluded. As it works out, babies, mothers, and fathers thrive under rooming-in. Interestingly enough, it has simplified hospital administration and cut costs. In all fairness, it should be added that not every mother takes enthusiastically to a full-fledged rooming-in arrangement. Some, particularly mothers of several children, would like nothing better than a bit of rest, with no responsibilities, at this time. But for those who want rooming-in, it gives mothers and fathers a new chance to feel that the baby is theirs and not the hospital's. In addition, the release of the baby from the platoon system of feeding makes it possible to start early with a flexible ("self-demand") schedule, the value of which we shall discuss in a later chapter.

NOTES   (Starred items are recommended as further readings in addition to those so listed.)

[1] Spock, Benjamin, Reinhart, John, and Miller, Wayne, *A Baby's First Year,* New York: Duell, Sloan and Pearce, 1955. Courtesy Wayne Miller.

[2] Photograph from Bateson, Gregory and Mead, Margaret, *First Days in the Life of a New Guinea Baby* (Film. New York University Film Library.) Courtesy Margaret Mead.

[3] An excellent summary of the physiological status of the newborn is given in Pinneau, S. R., "A critique on the articles by Margaret Ribble," *Child Development,* 1950, 21, 203-228. See also Gesell, Arnold, *The Embryology of Behavior,* New York: Harper, 1945, pp. 136-143.

[4] Mead, Margaret, *Growing Up in New Guinea,* New York: Morrow, 1930.

[5] Gesell, A., and Halverson, H. M., "The daily maturation of infant behavior: A cinema study of postures, movements, and laterality," *Journal of Genetic Psychology,* 1942, 61, 3-32.

[6] The classic study of behavior in the neonate is given in Pratt, K. C., Nelson, A. K., and Sun, K. H., "The behavior of the newborn infant," *Ohio State University Studies, Contributions to Psychology,* 1930, 10. See also the review by *Pratt in

Carmichael, Leonard (ed.), *Manual of Child Psychology,* New York: Wiley, second edition 1954, pp. 215-291.

[7] Conel, L. J., *The Postnatal Development of the Human Cerebral Cortex,* Cambridge: Harvard University Press, 1947, Volume III, p. 147.

[8] Fries, M. E., "Factors in character development, neuroses, psychoses, and delinquency," *American Journal of Orthopsychiatry,* 1937, 7, 142-181.

[9] New York: Harper, 1945.

*[10] Especially useful are Eastman, N. J., *Expectant Motherhood,* Boston: Little, Brown, second edition 1947, pp. 17-38; and Gilbert, M. S., *Biography of the Unborn,* Baltimore: Williams and Wilkins, 1938.

[11] Gesell, pp. 24-27.

[12] Gesell, pp. 28-30.

[13] Gesell, p. 62.

[14] *Ibid.*

[15] Gesell, pp. 62-63.

[16] Gesell, pp. 68-69.

[17] Gesell, p. 71.

[18] See, for instance, Hsu, C. Y., "Influence of temperature on development

of rat embryos," *Anatomical Research*, 1948, **100**, 79-90.

[19] Sontag, L. W., "The significance of fetal environmental differences," *American Journal of Obstetrics and Gynecology*, 1941, **42**, 996-1003; Sontag, L. W., "Differences in modifiability of fetal behavior and physiology," *Psychosomatic Medicine*, 1944, **6**, 151-154.

[20] Harsh, C. M., and Schrickel, H. G., *Personality: Development and Assessment*, New York: Ronald, 1950, p. 30.

[21] "Toward saving babies," *Newsweek*, August 6, 1956, p. 86.

[22] Swan, C., "Rubella in pregnancy as an aetiological factor in congenital malformation, stillbirth, miscarriage, and abortion," *Journal of Obstetrics and Gynaecology of the British Empire*, 1949, **56**, 341-363 and 591-605.

FOR FURTHER READING

Dickinson, R. L., and Belskie, Abram, *Birth Atlas*, New York: Maternity Center Association, 1940. Stages of pregnancy and birth clearly depicted in photographs of sculptured models.

U. S. Children's Bureau, *Prenatal Care*, Washington 25: U. S. Government Printing Office. A guide for parents, brought up to date at frequent intervals.

Carmichael, Leonard, "The onset and early development of behavior," in Carmichael, L. (ed.), *Manual of Child Psychology*, New York: Wiley, second edition 1954, pp. 60-185. A somewhat technical review of human and animal embryonic behavior. Especially valuable for its attention to issues of theory.

Montagu, M. F. A., "Constitutional and prenatal factors in infant and child health," in Martin, W. E., and Stendler, C. B., *Readings in Child Development*, New York: Harcourt, Brace, 1954, pp. 15-29. Up-to-date information on prenatal influence.

CHAPTER 2

From Organism
to Person

Introduction

Now that we have a picture of the newborn baby and of his development from before birth until a few weeks after, it is time to look at him
systematically, in terms of certain principles. These principles are of two
kinds: those that govern his functioning at any given point in development, and those that govern development itself, the way in which he
changes over time. Furthermore, these principles apply on two levels:
the primarily biological level on which the child begins life, and the psychological level in terms of which an ever greater portion of his existence
is defined as he grows older.

On the biological level, we speak of the *organism;* on the psychological
level, of the *person.* There are also other levels at which the individual
might be described: the biochemical or molecular as "lower" levels,
the sociological as a "higher" one. If we are concerned with the atomic
particles of which people are ultimately composed, we have to apply the
laws of nuclear physics; but if we want to know how the circulatory
system functions, we have to turn to a complete new set of laws, those
governing hydrodynamics, which are not contained in the laws holding
good at a lower level of analysis. In other words, to shift from one level
of analysis to another does not mean merely to look at the same
phenomena from a greater or lesser distance; it means to look in a
different way at a different set of phenomena. Moreover, while all these
levels of complexity at which people can be described exist, the events
on each level must be treated in their own right, and not be "reduced"
to a lower level. This idea is summed up in the principle of *emergence:*

the new and emergent phenomena at each level must be accounted for in terms of new, emergent principles.

The Neonate as a Biological Organism

Although, in this section, we shall speak in terms of organisms in general, we shall be doing so only with a view to helping us understand how *children* function and grow. Therefore, we shall not discuss all the characteristics of organisms—or all the varieties of organisms—that the biologist is concerned with, but only those that are relevant to our purpose. Like all organisms, the baby, prenatally and postnatally, is equipped to survive, grow, and function. It is important to see, however, that he does these things in an environmental context from which he can never be entirely separated. An organism at all times maintains a basic communion with its surroundings, and without these surroundings it would cease to exist as an organism. The environment is important both biologically and psychologically. From our momentary standpoint in biology, we can see that the organism must breathe, exchanging the carbon dioxide produced in the course of metabolism for a fresh supply of oxygen. It must radiate excess heat into or absorb heat from the environment. It must make adjustments to the pull of gravity. At least periodically, it must take in food to fuel the metabolic furnace. The organism's biological context is not, of course, always benign or even neutral. Human beings are bombarded by cosmic and man-made radiation, the air swarms with allergens, chemicals, microbes, and viruses. Moreover, all the human environment does not lie outside the skin. The biologist considers everything contained in the digestive tract, and not yet absorbed through its walls, as "outside" the organism and as an intimate part of its environment. But while we are accustomed to thinking of the organism—even though in relationship to its environment—as quite separate from it, biologists in recent years have recognized that in its functioning the organism is not set off from the environment by clear-cut boundaries, and speak of organism-environment *fields* in which patterned life processes go on.[1] (Later, we shall see how it is often helpful to conceive of psychological fields analogous to biological fields.) Therefore, when we talk about the general characteristics of biological organisms, we are holding them apart from the environment only by an act of abstraction.

One of the most important organismic characteristics in our consideration of the baby, both before and after he is born, is defined by

Cannon's concept of *homeostasis,* or maintenance of stability in the physiological functioning of the organism.[2] Again, although homeostasis is attributed to the organism, it is an excellent illustration of the working of field principles. Body temperature regulation and the maintenance of the oxygen content of the blood are two of the many ways in which the organism preserves its homeostatic equilibrium. Both are maintained within very narrow and precise limits, regardless of relatively wide variations in outside conditions. But in maintaining this balance, the organism must adjust to changes around it. The rate and depth of breathing increase as the oxygen supply diminishes; as the outside temperature goes down, the capillaries near the skin shrink, sweat production decreases, and so forth. Thus by a variety of systematic adjustments to changes in the surroundings, the organism preserves a homeostatic relationship with them. In the same way, internal chemical changes quickly set off the activities needed to arrive at a satisfactory equilibrium. In other words, organisms are *stable*.

Organisms are *sensitive*. That is, as we have seen in the case of homeostasis, they respond to internal or external energy changes. This responsiveness to stimulation exists on several levels, depending on the degree to which the central nervous system is involved. It may be independent of neural activity, as when our skin tans in response to ultra-violet light or an amoeba recognizes food. At a much higher level, it may involve specialized sense organs—eyes, ears, skin receptors—attuned to particular kinds of energies—light, sound, heat, etc. It is through its sensitivities that the organism "knows" what is going on in itself and in the environment and adjusts itself or its environment accordingly.

Organisms are *active*. Even when an organism is not moving from place to place, it is in a state of perpetual activity consisting at the very least of minimal respiration, circulation, metabolism, and muscle tension, or of fine or gross overt movements. Sometimes activity is set off by the organism's inner states, sometimes by external stimulation.

Organisms, as we might suppose from the name, are *organized*. Even the simplest of organisms has a number of different parts that act together so that every part is always in some way in communication with every other part. The neonate, as we have seen, is still diffusely organized. His different sub-systems are both poorly separated and poorly tied together. As a result, there may be a considerable spill-over of energy, as we noted in connection with his twitchings; or he may not be able to mobilize himself, so that what looks like a beginning activity, such as sucking, may get no further than a trembling of the lips.

Organisms *develop*. They grow in both size and complexity. It is important to see that, even while an organism is changing, it somehow remains the same—it has *continuity*. The caterpillar may metamorphose into a moth, Cinderella may become a princess, but at each step of the way there is some carry-over of what was there before. This book, of course, is largely about the way a certain kind of organism, the young human being, changes, so we shall have a great deal more to say about processes of development. Everything about an organism changes: not only its size and its shape, but its way of establishing field relationships, and the very nature of its sensitivity, its activity, and its organization.

The Principles of Development

Every biological organism, given suitable environmental support, shows a systematic pattern of change from its beginning to its maturity. The process of growth, with predictable characteristics for all the members of each species, is called *maturation*. As the organism's structures are maturationally elaborated, new behavioral functions become possible—until he becomes a butterfly and has wings, the caterpillar cannot fly. Bearing in mind what we have seen of prenatal development, we may now abstract some general principles of the growth of organisms. Five of these (leaving out of account the most obvious one of increase in size) seem to us of particular importance in understanding human growth, and we shall refer to them again in later chapters in their application to behavioral as well as anatomical development. We shall first define these five principles briefly, and then consider the significance of each in more detail.

> *1. Differentiation.*   Development proceeds from the simple to the complex, from the homogeneous to the heterogeneous, from the general to the specific. As regards both structure and activity, development is in the direction of complexity and variety.
>
> *2. Functional subordination.*   Differentiated structures and functions become organized in new, more inclusive patterns. (The other terms employed in this section are part of standard usage. However, the authors have chosen to substitute "functional subordination" for the even more tongue-twisting terms of "hierarchization" and "hierarchic integration" used by other writers.[3])
>
> *3. Asynchronous growth.*   The organism never grows uniformly or all at the same time. Its various parts and systems grow at various rates and at different times.
>
> *4. Discontinuity of growth rate.*   Growth does not always go on at

the same rate, but shows characteristic spurts or peaks and then slows down to periods of relative quiescence or latency.

5. *Growth gradients.* In higher organisms, there are two laws of the directional sequence of growth, referred to as the *cephalo-caudal* and the *proximo-distal* gradients. The first describes the fact that in structure and function growth proceeds down the body, with the head end taking priority over the tail end. The second points to the fact that development proceeds from near to far, outward from the central axis of the body toward the extremities.

Now let us look at these principles in more detail.

DIFFERENTIATION   We have already had abundant opportunity to see the principle of differentiation at work, and we shall have a great deal more in chapters to come. From a single-celled zygote there develop by differentiation an immense number of cells of highly varied structure and function. The first cells formed by division of the zygote are all of the same kind, differing only in their position with respect to each other. As differentiation proceeds, the cells change in character, forming different kinds of tissues with *specialized* functions: nerves, skin, bone, blood, muscle, etc. Early in the game, when cells are less differentiated—more *plastic*—they can be transplanted from one part of an experimental animal (and in theory, of a human being) to another, where they take on the form and function of the area to which they have been moved. Thus a bit of primitive eye tissue may blend indistinguishably into a limb bud. Beyond a certain point of specialization, however, this is no longer possible; the transplanted eye tissue will develop into a misplaced eye. The specialization process seems to be governed by the species characteristics represented in the cell nuclei, by the positional relationships of the cells to one another, and by their position in the electro-chemical patterns of the zygote-uterus field. In later chapters, we shall see how differentiation applies as well at the psychological level, to learning motor skills, to finding out where the self leaves off and the environment begins, to distinguishing between fantasy and reality and between objects and their names, and to perceiving diversities within a group whose members at first glance "all look alike," such as a racial group (or a roomful of neonates) encountered for the first time. It is worth noting that much of the newborn baby's behavior, which we have already seen, is of an undifferentiated sort called *mass action:* when the baby cries, for example, he cries with his whole body.[4]

FUNCTIONAL SUBORDINATION   This principle governs the reintegration of differentiated structures or activities into larger units with emergent characteristics of their own. In the fetus, for instance, we have seen how the liver, the stomach, and the pancreas function before birth, but with little reference to each other. Once the baby begins to take in food through his mouth, however, these hitherto independent units are rapidly subordinated in the service of the new, emergent function of eating. In other words, formerly self-contained functions become part-functions of larger activities. At a slightly later age, eating, in addition to being a function in itself, can also undergo a functional subordination to the still higher-level activity of testing parental authority. We shall see in later chapters how activities which to begin with are pleasant or absorbing for their own sake—hammering for the two-year-old, for instance—are later worked into larger patterns—perhaps driving nails; driving nails, after being for a time a satisfying activity in its own right, becomes in turn a part-function of carpentry. In general, as the organism becomes more differentiated, it also becomes organized in broader and broader units; it would be ridiculous to try to describe peristaltic action in terms of what happens to individual cells in the intestines, just as we could never fully describe metabolism in terms of the digestive tract, or sex in terms of the genitals. (See pictures facing page 62.)

ASYNCHRONOUS GROWTH In tracing prenatal development, we described how during the germinal period the baby's placental structures came first, while the child himself lay dormant in the germinal disk. Later, there was an interval devoted mainly to a preliminary formation of cranial structures, while the other body parts marked time. Thereafter, now the heart, now the limbs, now the respiratory system took the lead. This ever-shifting focus of development expresses the principle of asynchronous growth. Later on, we shall see how asynchrony plays an important part in the body changes that take place at puberty.

DISCONTINUITY OF GROWTH RATE We shall have occasion, in future chapters, to point out the ways in which physical and psychological development proceeds in spurts separated by plateaus of much slower growth. We should note that discontinuity of growth rate applies equally to the body's sub-systems. In our discussion of prenatal development, we indicated that the various body parts had growth peaks which were also their critical periods, the times at which they were most vulnerable to damage.

GROWTH GRADIENTS We have seen the *cephalo-caudal* trend in development in the way the head takes the lead in growth, with the trunk and limbs growing at a slower rate. The pictures facing page 14 show how the young embryo consists largely of a head, with a rudimentary body and still more rudimentary limb buds. In terms of cephalo-caudal trends in motor development, we shall see later on how the infant can control his head before his arms, and his arms before his legs. It is possible, too, that self-awareness begins with the head and later extends downward to the rest of the body. As a matter of fact, young children validate the legend about the ostrich who hides his head in the sand. As shown in the age-old game of peek-a-boo, the child at first has only to cover his eyes, and later his whole head, in order to feel that he is invisible.

The *proximo-distal* direction of growth is most conspicuously shown in the sequence of development of the arm buds from the trunk and, in turn, of the still more remote hands and fingers from the arm buds. Functionally, the child will be able to use his arms before his hands, and his hands as a unit before his several fingers. Less visibly, the nerves in the spinal cord appear before the formation of the more peripheral nerves, while the digestive tract starts as a simple central tube, outgrowths like the liver emerging later on. (It may well be that cephalo-caudal and proximo-distal gradients are two aspects of the same law. If we think of the body as growing like an inverted tree, starting with the head, we can see the whole directional trend of development in terms of the proximo-distal gradient.)

It is interesting to note that the principles of differentiation and functional subordination characterize not only individual development (*ontogenesis*) but evolutionary development (*phylogenesis*) as well. At one time it was believed that each individual in his development recapitulated the entire evolutionary history of his species. This is known as the *recapitulation theory,* summed up in the statement that "ontogeny recapitulates phylogeny." While it is now recognized that a human being is never literally an amoeba, a salamander, a fish, a chicken, or a rabbit, there are striking resemblances if not recapitulations at various stages of development between human embryos and the embryos of lower orders. And the process of embryonic differentiation by which a human individual begins life as a one-celled animal and evolves through a number of stages into mature form, gaining and losing such features as gills and a tail along the way, closely parallels the pattern of evolutionary differentiation. Similarly, we shall see that in terms of psychological development the human being proceeds from a primitive, undifferentiated, homeostasis-centered stage, where eating, sleeping, and other simple rhythms are the whole of existence, to more complex, mature ways of behaving.

But in keeping with the principle of functional subordination, those functions that human beings share with their lesser animal brethren have a different meaning in a human context—they are functional parts of the human being's peculiarly human projects and aspirations. It is essential to understand that a human being always evolves according to a strictly human scheme; already built into the zygote is a system of human potentialities, so that even at this early stage he has branched off the evolutionary tree and is following a course that can only end in humanity or death.

From Organism to Person

It is now time to return to the starting point of this chapter and begin our consideration of the individual from the psychological as well as the biological viewpoint. As the individual becomes older, more and more of his behavior and development becomes comprehensible only on the psychological level. Now, instead of talking about an organism in an *environment,* we must talk about a person living in, aware of, and behaving toward a *world.* At the biological level, the relevant environment is defined by metabolic and homeostatic needs and by physical vulnerabilities. On the psychological level, the relevant world that takes shape for the individual is defined by a whole new set of emerging needs and ways of functioning. As a neonate, on the level of the organism, the individual requires milk—or, more precisely, various nutrients. As he begins to function as a person during infancy, although his biological need for food continues, he needs a personal relationship with his mother as well. At the new level, we shall encounter new emergents: values, desires, feelings, purposes, ideas. We shall see how development includes the way the person perceives, feels about, thinks about, and behaves toward his world. In all of us, even during sleep, there flows a steady stream of consciousness—or, as the case may be, unconsciousness. In the neonate, we should guess that consciousness is little more than vague, undirected images that emerge and vanish like clothes seen tumbling in a washing machine. Later on, his mind will be constantly at work, watching, wondering, planning, remembering, enjoying, regretting, deploring, dreaming, and attempting to review and order and rationalize his experience.

A major aspect of the psychological growth of the person is the development and elaboration of new activities and ways of behaving. Although it may be an oversimplification and an overseparation of concepts, we generally speak of two ways in which new modes of functioning are acquired, *maturation* and *learning*.

Needless to say, behavioral growth depends to a considerable extent on physical growth. This is particularly true in the earliest years of life. In infancy, as in the prenatal period, most new behaviors are the product of maturation, the regular, predictable, biological growth pattern, the changes and refinements in anatomy and physiological functioning. Muscles get larger and stronger; bones lengthen, and their cartilage is replaced by true bone; motor and sensory nerves acquire insulating sheaths that permit more differentiated action; the brain develops new patterns of structural organization. As a form of linguistic shortcut, we often say that activities mature. What we really mean is that at each of the child's stages of maturation, new forms of action are possible: he lifts his head, he smiles, he creeps, he walks. Such functions, which are "ready to go" upon completion of their anatomical and physiological underpinnings, Dennis has named *autogenous* (self-initiating) activities.[5] This term points to the fact that they appear quite independent of training, even though they may require environmental signals (as the face of an adult may elicit a smile) or need some exercise and practice for their perfection (as in walking).

It is important to see, however, in terms of the distinction we are drawing between maturation and learning, that in one sense learned activities depend on maturation just as much as do autogenous ones: after certain capacities are present, then, and only then, are certain kinds of learning possible. Thus an autogenous activity, like walking, appears spontaneously as a result of maturation, while a learned activity, such as speaking English, which we usually think of as requiring instruction by exposure to English-speaking people, demands in addition maturation of the underlying speech mechanisms. In short, two kinds of capacities mature: (1) the ability to *do,* and (2) the ability to *learn* to do (which educators know as "readiness").

As we move up the phylogenetic and ontogenetic scales, we become less and less able to account for the individual's behavioral acquisitions in terms of maturation, and are increasingly obliged to invoke the concept of learning. This will be evident in our description of human development in ensuing chapters.

The term "learning" is used to designate new behavioral acquisitions based on the organism's experience rather than its structure.[6] Under the head of learning have been classified an array of phenomena of tremen-

dously varying complexity. Perhaps the simplest of these is the attachment of an activity to a new signal which did not originally elicit it, as in
classical *conditioning* (illustrated by Pavlov's famous experiment, where
a dog learns to salivate at the sound of a bell or to some other *conditioned stimulus;* modern learning theories have considerably elaborated
the original stimulus-response sequence to include the state of the
organism). Another form of learning is the rearrangement of activities
into new, smoothly functioning combinations known as *skills,* such as
speaking, or riding a bicycle. Still another is the absorbing (and the
ability to recount) of new *experiences* (knowledge, ideas)—as in studying this book or exploring a new city—and their organization into new
patterns as in the case of motor skills. In both skill-learning and knowledge-learning, the principle of functional subordination can be seen
operating. Simple skills are organized into more elaborate wholes; a
child learns to utter many words before he orchestrates them into
sentences. Depending on whether the emphasis is placed on the new
sequence of responses or on the new sequence of experienced cues,
maze-learning (or city-learning) may be viewed as either skill-learning
or knowledge-learning. Still more complex is the kind of learning involved in *problem-solving,* where we may find either *trial-and-error*
fumbling until the correct response is chanced upon, or perceptual or
verbal analysis leading to sudden recognition of the appropriate response,
to *insight.* The availability to the individual of the data necessary for a
solution, and his ability to utilize them, seem to determine which of these
takes place, as in solving a mathematical problem or trying to figure out
the solution of a detective story.

For many psychologists, some of these phenomena are to be thought
of as *remembering* or *thinking* rather than as learning. Also, there is
considerable disagreement over the extent to which all these learning
processes can be treated as subject to the same laws, or whether, at
higher levels of complexity, new principles must be applied. Since there
is general disagreement on the facts of learning, and utter disagreement
as to the systematic principles needed to organize and explain them, we
shall speak throughout this book of "learning" in what will appear to the
specialists a loose fashion. In terms of our task of describing development, it will suffice to distinguish as clearly as we can between what is
acquired on the basis of experience and what is brought about by
maturation, and to leave to the specialists the discovery of the underlying mechanisms. In point of fact, these specialists, who are in the forefront of American psychological research, have gone far in such investi-

gations and in bringing them to bear on more complex problems of behavior than were involved in early studies of conditioning. Much of what we have to say about learning could be rephrased according to their formulae, but from our point of view, the focus is on the person rather than on the laws of learning, on what is learned rather than on the details of its acquisition. We are concerned with the accumulation and consolidation of experience, and the new meanings, ideas, organizations, and capacities that emerge out of past learning.

This consolidation of experience includes the process emphasized by Murphy, following Janet and others, called *canalization*. This concept points to the differentiation and specification of those aspects of experience which, under selective cultural influences, become habitual and familiar. For example, hunger, in its more primitive forms, is similar for people in all societies. But from among the theoretically edible substances available, each society selects what is to be regarded as food and what as not-food. As Murphy puts it, "Children all over the world are hungry; their hunger may be satisfied by bread, by ice cream, by peanuts, by raw eggs, by rice, or by whale blubber. Eventually they develop, when hungry, not a demand for food in general, but a demand for what they are used to; in one part of the world peanuts are good food, whale blubber disgusting, and vice versa." [7] The concept of canalization seems to account for many of the acquired tastes characteristic of a culture or an individual, but which are selected from among many potential satisfiers of drives rather than—as in conditioning—attaching the drive to a previously meaningless signal that indicates a satisfier is forthcoming.

Thus, psychological development involves changes in the person, in his world, and, of course, in their relationship to each other. That is, when a person learns something, he learns to see some new feature, meaning, or relationship in his world, and, at the same time, he learns a new way of acting toward the world. Some psychological changes take place gradually, others are abrupt. Some are minor, others seem to entail whole new ways of looking at the world. As we shall see, the world a person lives in undergoes a number of drastic revisions as he grows older, while his ways of behaving toward the world change correspondingly.

When we speak of personality, then, we shall be referring not only to a child, but also to the kind of psychological world that the child lives in, with its necessary implications of how he sees himself in relation to his world. In keeping with the way our language is built, we may talk about personality characteristics as though they were something *in* a person; but, in accordance with the field concept, we will always mean by a personality "trait" a particular way of being related to the world.

Heredity—The Big Gamble

The line of development that an individual follows depends on two main interacting sets of factors: first, the structural potentialities he inherits from his parents, and second, the environment in which he grows up. The outer limits of an individual's hereditary potentialities—although not the precise form they will take—are fixed at the instant of conception. We have already noted in the last chapter that environmental forces begin to operate at the very same moment, and not nine months later as we are often inclined to think. We must now examine the way in which a child inherits a unique biological make-up within the framework of a general human biological design—for even the lowly zygote is already uniquely individual, unlike any other zygote in the great wide world. Some of what the child inherits will be evident at birth, while some will be present only as raw potentials that will later take shape in the course of maturation.

We begin our review of heredity with a word of warning. Our coverage of hereditary mechanisms cannot begin to do justice to so broad a field, and might well set a geneticist's teeth on edge. Those readers who would like to pursue this subject in more detail are referred to the list of readings at the end of this chapter.

The science of *genetics*—biological inheritance—sheds some light on several different issues. One of these is how an individual can be so uniquely and unmistakably himself, and at the same time be so much like everybody else. Second, knowing what two individuals are like, and what their parents were like, geneticists can make certain limited predictions about what their children will be like. Third, genetics is often able to make a sort of backward prediction: given such and such characteristics in an individual, the geneticist can often reconstruct his genealogical history. A fourth kind of problem to which geneticists address themselves is called *eugenics,* ways in which a species—human, animal, or plant—can be improved by selective breeding, by matching parents so as to produce certain kinds of offspring. Eugenics is sometimes contrasted with *euthenics,* a term coined to describe improving the species by manipulating the environment.

What Is Inherited

It might be well to say at the outset that genetics encounters certain difficulties at the human level. It is hampered by the difficulty of collecting pedigrees, the genetic histories of families, if only because human generations are spaced so far apart in relation to the geneticist's own life span. Also, on the human level, genetics has to take its data where it finds them. People—unlike fruit flies and rats—cannot be made to live and reproduce in a laboratory setting, where mating choices and environmental conditions can be controlled according to a predetermined plan. Again, human beings are more plastic than their lesser animal brethren, particularly as regards their psychological functioning, so that it is often difficult with any given human being to trace out the effect of a particular genetic factor. Finally, particularly at the psychological level, there is the difficulty of isolating factors in order to study their inheritance: are such human "traits" as generosity, ill temper, and sociability single, unitary characteristics or are they compounds of various subordinate functions?

Nevertheless, genetics can tell us a good deal about the hereditary transmission of anatomical and physiological characteristics, and a fair amount about psychological characteristics. Even when there is no direct evidence bearing on human affairs, we can often make some inferences from studies of animals. Tryon, for instance, was able by selective inbreeding of the best and of the poorest maze-runners in successive generations to develop two distinct strains of rats: one consisting entirely of "bright" maze-learners and the other of "dull" maze-learners.[8] Hall, working on the problem of temperament, was able in the same way to breed consistent strains of inherently aggressive and of inherently timid rats.[9] Such studies show clearly the hereditary basis of these traits, although without further research, largely blocked by the difficulties we have mentioned, we cannot be sure how far hereditary factors determine intelligence or temperament on the human level.

It should be made explicit that a person's biological make-up, including his potentialities for psychological development, is wholly inherited. However, he inherits characteristics in two ways. First of all, there is the inheritance of relatively *specific* features: brown eyes or blue eyes, straight hair or curly hair, long bones or short bones, and so forth. Second, he inherits *complex* features which depend on combinations of single factors, on how they are connected anatomically and function together physiologically—and psychologically—as an organized system.

Some inherited characteristics are relatively immune to environmental influence, while others appear only under particular environmental conditions. But no hereditary characteristic is completely independent of environmental support. Because the physical environment is comparatively unchanging, we are likely to overlook the fact that it is there, and without the proper environmental support no hereditary trait can reach fulfillment. Over and above the general environmental conditions necessary to survival and development, there are particular ones necessary to the appearance of particular traits. For instance, a person might be destined by his heredity to be tall, but unless he lives under favorable conditions of diet, exercise, hygiene, and so forth, he may end up quite short. Susceptibility to cancer is inherited in mice, but cancer-susceptible mice who are not exposed to cancer-producing agents do not develop cancer. A fish-like creature called the axolotl adopts one or another of two courses, both fixed by heredity, depending on environmental circumstances. In times of drought, he abandons his fish pattern, loses his gills, sprouts legs, and becomes an air-breathing salamander. In the same way, a potential genius may find inspiration for immense achievement, but if not given proper stimulation he may end up in intellectual mediocrity.

It is difficult to be sure exactly what the geneticist means by a unitary trait or "character." The term may refer to some distinguishable anatomical feature, such as eyes, nose, brain, toes, or fingers. It may refer to a particular way an organ functions—the sensitivity of the retina to color differences (as in color-blindness), for instance. Or it may refer to some generalized property of the organism as a whole, or to some major aspect of its functioning—aggressiveness, stature, intelligence, co-ordination. Whatever these hereditary traits may be, they represent inborn variations in size, shape, color, efficiency, and so forth. Virtually all human beings possess the trait of a pair of eyes; some eyes, however, are blue, others are brown, others hazel. Or hereditary variation in the shape and elasticity of the lens of the eye may render some people near-sighted and others far-sighted. At the psychological level, traits are all the harder to pin down, simply because we have never arrived at a satisfactory classification of psychological functions. Even where we do feel that we have succeeded in isolating a psychological trait, it seems to be inherited as limits on the ways it can develop, rather than as something one does or does not have. The different forms in which a trait can manifest itself are known as the *variants* of that trait. Individual uniqueness is a product of the particular variants of general human traits that a person possesses. A list of some common human trait variants is given in Table 1.

A freshly created zygote contains in potential form a combination of trait variants unlike that of any other human being past, present, or

TABLE 1   Some Examples of Human
Hereditary Characteristics

(Adapted from Colin, *Elements of Genetics*[10])

DOMINANT CHARACTERISTICS	RECESSIVE CHARACTERISTICS
(Trait variants which are always visible when the proper gene is present. These are not necessarily transmitted to the next generation.)	(Trait variants which are visibly manifested only when both parents contribute the same kind of gene for the trait. They can be transmitted even though not visible in the parents.)
Black skin (partially dominant)	White skin
Non-red hair	Red hair
Curly hair (partially dominant)	Straight hair
Baldness in men	Baldness in women
Color-blindness in men	Color-blindness in women
Free ear lobes	Adherent ear lobes
Brown eyes	Blue or gray eyes
Hazel or green eyes	Blue or gray eyes
Farsightedness and nearsightedness	Normal vision
Short stature	Tall stature
Blood types A, B, AB	Blood type O
High blood pressure	Normal blood pressure
Allergy	No allergy
Susceptibility to tuberculosis	Resistance to tuberculosis

UNCERTAIN INHERITANCE PATTERN

Schizophrenia	Feeble-mindedness	Artistic talent
Manic-depressive psychosis	Musical talent	Mathematical ability

future. Since the zygote's hereditary make-up is the result of the shuffling together, the reselection, and the recombination of thousands of specific factors, the odds are astronomically high against any two persons' ever coming out with exactly the same combination of factors. Nonetheless, family resemblances do exist because children of the same parents are drawing on a common pool of traits. This uniqueness does not apply, however, to identical twins, triplets, etc., who grow from a splitting of one zygote and so have identical heredities. *Identical* twins are to be distinguished from *fraternal* twins, who come from the separate fertilization of *two* ova.

Hereditary Mechanisms

The traits which the zygote receives from its parents are somehow contained, it is believed, in actual bits of protoplasm called *chromosomes*. The chromosomes, visible under the microscope, are rod-like structures present in the nucleus of each living cell in the entire organism, and not just in its germ cells. Each species has its characteristic, invariable number of chromosomes; in human cells there are forty-eight.

Each chromosome is believed to contain still smaller particles known as *genes,* which are thought to be the direct vehicles for hereditary transmission. There are one or more genes for every trait. Depending on differences between genes governing the same trait, the trait may show up as one variant or another. That is, everybody has genes for a nose; some nose genes, however, produce straight noses, some hooked noses, some turned-up noses.

Now let us see how the concepts of gene and chromosome help us understand the tremendous individual variety possible within the stable limits of the human constitution, and the extent to which a person's uniqueness is dictated by the hand he draws after repeated shufflings, discards, and deals of a prodigiously huge deck of cards—traits.

The combination of trait variants the zygote receives depends first of all on the kinds of genes each of his parents has at his disposal. The first gamble by which the zygote's hereditary equipment is decided comes about when these two unique individuals, out of the two billion or more people in the world, mate together. A different mating for either parent would mean a vast difference in the potential heredity of their children. The second gamble occurs because of a peculiarity of the human germ cells (sperm and ovum). Unlike the other cells of the human body, the germ cells at one stage of maturing (called *reduction division*) come out with only twenty-four instead of forty-eight chromosomes. Each single germ cell, with its particular set of twenty-four chromosomes, has a different combination of the multitudinous genes, which have been shuffled about and recombined in the course of the cell's formation. A given germ cell, then, carries only half of the parent's hereditary potentialities, and is incapable of carrying the other half. Hence, each parent is potentially many parents, since each of his germ cells carries a different combination of trait variants. The third and final gamble comes about when one particular sperm cell with its specific, unique combination of trait variants unites with one particular ovum and its specific, unique combination of trait variants, since it is the interaction of these that finally determines the zygote's hereditary potential. It should be pointed out that the zygote's genetic composition may not be entirely expressed in his future make-up, since some genes carry (*recessive*) traits which show up only when a matching gene is present (*see* Table 1, page 44). However, as a parent, he may still pass a recessive gene along to his offspring, in whom the trait variant will be overtly manifested if it is paired with a corresponding gene from the other parent.

To understand how the sex of a child is determined, we must first make explicit that the forty-eight chromosomes in human cells are arranged in twenty-four pairs, each pair splitting up at the stage of reduction division in the germ cells. In women, the members of each pair are essentially alike, although each may carry different trait variants. In men, on the other hand, one chromosome, called the X-chromosome, is paired with an under-sized one called the Y-chromosome. When the male germ cell splits, one of the resulting cells receives an X and the other a Y. If a sperm cell carrying an X joins with an ovum (which always has an X), the result is a girl. If, however, a Y-bearing sperm joins with an X-bearing ovum, the result is a boy. Because the Y-chromosome is relatively inactive, it has been possible to identify a number of traits carried by the X-chromosome. These are known as the *sex-linked recessives*—color blindness, hemophilia ("bleeder's disease"), and so forth—which appear predominantly in men. In women, since these traits are recessive, they are usually overshadowed by a dominant trait variant carried on the second X-chromosome. It is interesting to note, however, that sex-linked recessive traits, although they are found most commonly in men, are transmitted by women: a boy inherits his color blindness from his mother, not from his father.

To describe the predictions that geneticists can make would require a more technical discussion than is appropriate here. It is sufficient to say that, given information about trait variants present in two parents, plus whatever information can be obtained about those of their ancestors, the geneticist can give the probability of the appearance of any simple trait in the parents' offspring. He can say, that is, what the chances are that a particular child will display a particular parental trait, or, more accurately, how parental traits are likely to be distributed among a number of children. Sometimes the probability that a child will inherit a given trait is zero (negative certainty), sometimes 100 percent (positive certainty), and sometimes in between. If, on the other hand, the geneticist wants to predict the appearance of a given *combination* of traits, he must first calculate the probabilities for the individual traits and then multiply these probabilities together. Thus, if a child has a 50 percent chance of inheriting blue eyes, and a 50 percent chance of inheriting wavy hair, he has only a 25 percent chance (.50 x .50) of inheriting them both.

Eugenics

Another application of the science of genetics is to be found in the field of *eugenics,* which advocates the betterment of mankind through planned selective breeding. Farmers for centuries have had great success with selective breeding in producing animals and plants to almost any specification or group of specifications. Corn, for instance, can be bred for color, for flavor, for resistance to rot, for size of ears, etc. The popular broad-breasted midget turkeys on sale in the local market are a product of selective breeding, as are Jersey cattle, noted for the high butterfat content of their milk. The whole train of evolution, in fact, might be thought of as a process of selective breeding (Darwin's "natural selection") by impersonal forces, the "better" variants surviving and the less serviceable ones dying out. While it was formerly thought that the genes dwelt inviolate in the cell nucleus and were passed on intact from one generation to the next, it is now recognized that the genes within a species are constantly subject to *mutation,* changes in structure which produce new versions of old traits, to be proved or found wanting in the environmental competition. Many mutations appear, of course, without ever being transmitted to offspring. Such mutations as were formerly observed were thought to represent spontaneous, unprovoked changes in gene structure. In recent years, however, scientists have identified a number of agents that will modify gene structure, notably forms of nuclear radiation and such chemicals as mustard gas. Nowadays, "spontaneous" mutations are thought to be caused by the action of cosmic rays which constantly bombard us from outer space. So while it is true that the genes have a sort of immortality, and while it is true that we can trace the genes in our bodies right back to our first ancestors, they have undergone changes along the way. Presumably it is the accumulation of viable mutations which accounts for the evolutionary appearance of a whole new species. Selective breeding fosters the preservation of desirable new mutations as well as the preferred variants of existing traits.

But in human beings, selective breeding is another story. There have been attempts to legislate various eugenic measures of a somewhat negative sort, to eliminate unwanted and presumably hereditary traits. In some states, habitual criminals or the feeble-minded can be sterilized, with a view to preventing the propagation of their kind. However, few responsible geneticists today are willing to support such programs, because the hereditary contribution to these complex conditions may be very limited or obscure—or even where it is clear, its manner of transmission is uncertain. Geneticists will occasionally recommend that particular people not have children. For instance, the unusual degenerative disease of the nervous system known as Huntington's chorea may not appear until middle life, and can be transmitted genetically before a person knows he has it; therefore, if one's father or mother had Huntington's, it might be wise to consider the risk to one's children. In other cases, however, recommendations that certain people not procreate are more validly based on the poor sort of environment they can provide for their children. On the positive side, rather than selective breeding designed to cultivate a limited number of desirable traits, as with dairy cattle, some geneticists recommend the most heterogeneous human matings possible, across as many social and geographic barriers as possible, with a view to fostering the occurrence of every kind of diversity in gene combinations. Needless to say, some of these combinations would work out badly and some well, but the odds for producing favorable combinations would be increased, while natural selection in the long run would counter the perpetuation of the unfit. (This does not mean, of course, that marriages within the same family stock are necessarily inadvisable.) Thus, instead of trying to homogenize mankind according to somebody's eugenic ideal—as Hitler wanted to do—these geneticists advocate a maximum of variety, and are as much concerned with improving the environment as with improving the species. And in any case, human customs and personal tastes run very deep, and are likely to conflict with the projects of the eugenic planners. Meanwhile, of course, the possibility that the development of ways to release atomic energy will significantly increase the radiation rate, and hence the mutation rate, has aroused speculation over an unplanned and unpredictable program of eugenics—or dysgenics—that might well change the entire face of nature.

In closing this discussion of heredity, it would be well to repeat and make explicit what we have said above. A person's physical and psychological development is by no means fixed by his biological inheritance. The final shape his heritage takes is determined to a large extent by the life experiences he encounters from conception onward. It is an unfortunate fact that we have few if any means for raising the ceilings imposed by heredity on development in given areas, but there seem to be infinite possibilities for lowering them. Since, at this stage in history, most people live far below their potentialities anyway, it seems to be less important for the present to try to raise their developmental ceilings than to find ways that will enable them to reach them. In other words, there is still much to be learned about how we as parents and teachers and policy-makers can best treat children so as to help them attain optimal development.

It should further be stressed that the environment in which human hereditary potentials find their fulfillment is not merely a physical environment, but even more a social and cultural environment. What shape a child's endowment will take is not determined only by how well he is nourished and protected against illness and injury. It is at least as much determined by the nation, region, socio-economic position, ethnic setting, and family pattern into which he is born at a particular moment in history. As we shall see in a later chapter, included in the human being's biological make-up are the ability to use speech and symbols; to absorb a culture—a way of looking at and understanding and transforming his surroundings; a sensitivity to dimensions of experience that are forever closed to lesser species; and an ability within certain limits even to transform himself. Although the gulf between culture and biology, between body and mind and spirit, may seem hopelessly wide, we are obliged to think of all of these as rooted in the human being's biological constitution. At the same time, the individual's biological development must be nourished on his culture. Just as the biologist has had to redefine the "obvious" boundaries between the living creature and its environment in his concept of *organism,* so the psychologist, dealing with the *person,* sees him as an integration of biology and culture, shaped by the people and events he encounters in the course of growing up.

NOTES (Starred items are recommended as further readings.)

*[1] A comprehensive treatment of the concepts of "field" and "level" can be found in Murphy, G., *Personality,* New York: Harper, 1947, pp. 1-26.

[2] Cannon, W. B., *Wisdom of the Body,* New York: Norton, 1939.

[*3] For a detailed exposition of the concept of "hierarchization," see Werner, H., *Comparative Psychology of Mental Development,* Chicago: Follett, revised edition 1948, p. 41 and passim.

[4] Irwin, O. C., and Weiss, A. P., "A note on mass activity in newborn infants," *Journal of Genetic Psychology,* 1930, 38, 20-30.

[5] Dennis, W. "Infant development under conditions of restricted practice and of minimum social stimulation," *Genetic Psychology Monographs,* 1941, 23, 143-190.

[6] Probably the most complete statement on the subject of learning is to be found in Hilgard, E. R., *Theories of Learning,* New York: Appleton-Century-Crofts, second edition 1956.

[7] Murphy, *op. cit.,* p. 161.

[8] Tryon, R. C., "Genetic differences in maze-learning ability in rats," *Thirty-Ninth Yearbook of the National Society for the Study of Education,* 1940, 111-119.

[9] Hall, C. S., "The inheritance of emotionality," *Sigma Xi Quarterly,* 1938, 26, 17-27, 37 (reprinted in Martin and Stendler, *Readings in Child Development,* pp. 59-68); also, "The genetics of behavior," in Stevens, S. S. (ed.)., *Handbook of Experimental Psychology,* New York: Wiley, 1951, pp. 308-309.

[10] Colin, E. C., *Elements of Genetics,* New York: Blakiston Division, McGraw-Hill Book Co., copyright, 1941, pp. 118 and 162. By permission.

FOR FURTHER READING

Dunn, L. C., and Dobzhansky, Th., *Heredity, Race and Society,* New York: Mentor, revised edition 1952. An excellent popular account of hereditary mechanisms and the social implications of genetics.

Scheinfeld, Amram, *The New You and Heredity,* Philadelphia: Lippincott, 1950. An authoritative popular account, with special emphasis on psychological inheritance.

CHAPTER 3

The Infant: 1

Introduction

Growth in infancy—from the age of a few weeks until the baby is walking securely—is a dramatic thing to watch. In the early months of life, striking and radical changes take place within a brief span of time. During his first twelve or fifteen months outside the womb, the baby changes from a helpless if vocal neonate lying flat as he has been placed on his back or stomach to a high-powered pedestrian investigating and mastering everything within reach in the most active way possible, tasting, chewing, fondling, probing, tugging, pushing, pounding, and tearing. As a child's activity increases, his sleeping time decreases: many newborn babies spend all their time sleeping except when they are hungry or being fed; by the end of infancy, a child may sleep as little as ten hours at night, with one or two naps during the day—there are, of course, great individual differences in this respect. During infancy, a child adds almost twelve inches to his stature and gains fifteen pounds or more. He acquires half a dozen temporary teeth and a full head of hair. His face loses its neonatal look and becomes the smooth, chubby face of a baby.

Socially and emotionally he begins with an alternation between self-contained indifference when he is satisfied and grief-stricken but undirected rage when he is not. In a little while, he begins to study people's faces; before he is two months old, he begins to smile when people approach him; then he actively demands company; then he laughs and wants to play; after midyear, he will know that some people are strangers, and may shriek with dismay when they come near. By fifteen months, he is able to understand a great many words, listens attentively even to those he does not understand, and may (again there are marked individual differences) use a few words of his own. The simple, scarcely differentiated emotions he began with elaborate into half a dozen distinguishable ones: anger, fear, disgust, distress, elation, affection, and perhaps others.[1]

From a baby wrapped up in his own volatile inner processes, responding only to those external events which had a direct bearing on his physiology, he becomes a child with a rudimentary awareness of a world outside himself. It becomes a world full of countless possibilities for action; but in becoming so, it is first a world of emotional meanings that will dictate the child's most basic attitudes of optimism and pessimism.

We shall begin this chapter with a description of the baby's behavioral capacities and how these develop month by month. Then we shall discuss in more detail the environmental conditions favorable to sound development, and the ways attitudes toward child rearing have changed in the present century.

Landmarks in the Baby's Behavioral Growth

Growth has two visible aspects: first, the change in the size, shape, proportions, and complexity of the body; second, the new, emerging forms of behavior. Since our concern is primarily with behavior and personality development, we shall say little about physical growth except in this context. In describing new behaviors, we shall present development month by month, based on the *average* times at which particular responses appear. *These averages must always be seen as midpoints in the broad normal range of times at which an activity may first become possible for the baby.* The accompanying table shows why. It gives several illustrations of published norms (averages) of development, together with the data (from another source) on which they are based and which are not ordinarily presented. It will be clear that the norm conceals as much information as it reveals. While the source from which the norms are drawn warns the reader that there are many normal departures from this timetable, the failure to give its authors' own data on the actual range of variation makes it difficult to know how to apply this qualification. Parents who compare their children to tables of norms would be spared much anxiety if they could bear in mind the difference between an average and a baby. It should further be pointed out that most norms are concerned with the appearance of motor skills; it is only recently, in the work of such students as Griffiths, Yarrow, and Spitz, that the infant's psychological and social functioning has come in for major consideration.[2] But if norms do not tell us accurately about the timing of new developments in individual cases, they can still serve

T A B L E 2   Some Examples of How the Simple Norm May Mask the Actualities of Development:

(A comparison of selected developmental norms[3] with the range of ages at which corresponding activities first appear[4])

	NORM (AGE IN WEEKS)	CUMULATIVE PERCENTAGE OF CHILDREN SHOWING BEHAVIOR AT SUCCESSIVE AGES (IN WEEKS)									
BEHAVIOR		4	6	8	12	16	20	24	28	32	36
Head predominantly in midline	16	0	4	7	15	67	*(the remaining 33 percent, although normal, are unaccounted for)*				
Rotates head from side to side	16	38	32	29	38	57	*(43 percent unaccounted for)*				
Grasps dangling ring	16	0	0	0	8	22	73	96	100		
Pulls foot to mouth	28	0	0	0	0	4	10	24	31	44	8
		(some children do not display this behavior)									
Sits unsupported	36	0	0	0	12	11	34	62	88	100	

a worth-while purpose in giving us the fairly fixed *sequence* of normal development, regardless of timing.

Before going on with us here to the new behaviors that appear in infancy, the reader may wish to refer back to Chapter 1 and the behavior repertory the neonate brings with him into the world. Our present description begins at the end of the neonatal period, or approximately one month of age.

In his second month, the baby is awake more than he was as a neonate, and begins to perceive the world through sight and hearing as well as his contact senses—touch, taste, etc. He now looks at objects (although it would probably be going too far to say that he *sees* them) and follows them with his eyes (but not his head). Many babies can now raise their heads slightly to look at things or to take the nipple (some postmature ones could do so at birth), although others may not be able to for a month or more; here we see the cephalic beginnings of a cephalo-caudal sequence. The baby will stop crying when his mother comes near, or when other people caress him. Sometime during the month he will respond to a moving human face with a smile. When he cries, he sheds tears for the first time; before this his crying was real enough but dry. Whereas formerly the baby was either crying or silent, he now makes what Gesell describes as "small throaty sounds." [5] He is still largely immobile; his legs are more active than before, but he generally holds them flexed, as though squatting. He eats at frequent intervals, and takes two or more night feedings.

During the third month, he no longer loses objects he is looking at, and can follow them by moving his head. However, if an object moves out of sight, he acts as though it had suddenly gone out of existence and shows no awareness that it can be found again by turning his head or looking around the edge of something. His eyes are becoming better co-ordinated, and will converge on an object as it approaches his nose. The baby is becoming more social-minded, even to the point of enjoying mild roughhousing. His vocalizations have become gurgles and coos, which he utters either in response to people or spontaneously. This is the time when people often say that the baby is "becoming human."

By the fourth month, the baby may enjoy the playful fright that comes when a parent says "Boo!" and then smiles or tickles him. It may give him hiccups, but he enjoys these, too, as often as not. During this month, he will occasionally laugh or chuckle when people play with him, and look around to see where a voice is coming from. He takes active pleasure in his bath. He recognizes his mother from among people in general, as shown by the especially warm welcome he gives her. He can be propped sitting for a few minutes at a time, and may begin to eat "solid" foods—more accurately, strained, mushy solids. At first, this entails a fair amount of spluttering, coughing, and spilling, but it is usually easy to tell, each time it is attempted, whether the baby is now favorably inclined to food in this novel form. When he is on his back, his head is now habitually in the midline—aimed at the ceiling—although he moves it freely when he wants to look at something. He picks things up by corralling them with his forearm and hand and scooping them against his body.

During his first four months, the baby has been taking hold of the world in ever bigger pieces as his physiological rhythms have become stabilized. By the beginning of the fifth month, he will consume generous quantities of milk and solids and go four or five hours between meals. Many babies at this age sleep the night through, or wake up to be fed only once, and take a couple of well-defined naps during the day. During the fifth month, the baby may be able to wake up and entertain himself for a while before yelling for food and attention—earlier, he could, as a rule, be content only after he had been changed and fed. He plays with and studies his fingers, and whatever they hold goes into his mouth for sampling. Although he can pick things up, he cannot intentionally let go of them: they get knocked out of his hand as he moves it, or are dropped unnoticed when his attention strays to something new; if he wants to get rid of something he is holding, he rubs it against his body until it is pulled loose from his grip. During the day, he can play contentedly alone at least long enough for his mother to finish a few household tasks uninterrupted. His mother still has to sit him up and brace him against a pillow, but he can stay sitting for longer periods, enjoying his broadened horizons, before his head begins to loll and his body to slump. If he is comfortable, he can sit or lie quietly and seems to enjoy his parents' conversation or music on the radio. He now makes crowing sounds, either because he is pleased or simply for the sake of making them. At this time, his ankles begin to straighten; formerly they were bent so that even with his legs extended the soles of his feet stared each other in the face.

In the sixth month, he will be able to grasp, hold on to, and let go of rings and rattles and rags. Letting go is the biggest advance: it shows that his grasping reflex is being subordinated to higher level functions, in that stimulation of his palm does not force his fingers closed. The same tendency to functional subordination is seen in his new ability to use both hands together in handling things, as in stretching out a piece of cloth while he explores its intricacies, or even transferring things from one hand to another. He still puts things into his mouth, although now it may be with a view to chewing (rather than sucking or mouthing) on them—his teeth are beginning to push through the gums, and chewing relieves the discomfort. This is the time when a baby is often weaned from the breast, sometimes to protect the mother against the infant's new need to bite. The baby discovers his feet about now; he likes to grasp them and pull them up to his eyes for inspection and, although he may not manage it for another month or more, to his mouth for tasting and chewing. As he becomes convinced that his feet are his own, he begins to use them as assistant hands, fetching objects that his hands cannot reach or supporting an object while his hands manipulate it. He will often be able to roll completely over, and when on his stomach will push himself up by his hands until his chest is clear—the typical pose in the photograph of the nude baby on the rug. His walking reflex—set in action by holding him upright and supporting his weight while his feet touch a flat surface—returns about now, having disappeared shortly after birth. His growing awareness is seen in the fear or uncertainty he may show in the presence of strangers—this "strangeness" is at its peak between the ages of six and eight months—and in his increasing sensitivity to his parents' moods. On the other hand, his world is becoming more stable and reliable. He begins to wait, at first tensely and fretfully, later calmly, secure that relief is on the way. He likes to hide his face with the corner of a blanket, peering out from time to time as though to see whether anything has changed. His vocalizations are becoming more mature and differentiated: cooing sounds give way to gurgles, and gurgling to babbling, where the child tries out every speech sound known to man. Later, of course, these sounds will be patterned selectively according to the structure of the child's native language.

The baby's first teeth are likely to make their appearance during the seventh month. Usually, these are the two center lowers. Teething may be preceded by some discomfort, and almost always is marked by a compelling urge to chew on things. The child will begin to sit without support during the month, although he will have to be helped into a sitting position. He will now be content to play in his playpen, provided he is not left there too long. In his feeding table, he will amuse himself by banging objects together or on the table top. He may even begin the delightful (to him) game of dropping objects overboard from his table so that his parents can retrieve them for him. Here his skill at letting go is being assimilated—functionally subordinated—to the social interchange that becomes increasingly important for him. He may have to be given a spoon to hold while he is eating, or else—after his first ravenous hunger has been appeased—he will be more interested in the one his mother has than in the food it contains. When lying on his stomach, the baby will make abortive crawling movements and perhaps even make some progress—forwards, sidewards, or backwards, as chance dictates. He may begin to play peek-a-boo, although he will not be able to stand the suspense for more than a few seconds at a time.

During his eighth month, the baby will learn to pull himself into a sitting position, and he will probably begin to crawl. He will insist on trying to feed himself and will make a splendid mess of his food, himself, and his surroundings. One or two more teeth may come through in the course of the month, and for the remaining months of infancy. Before he is eight months old, he will become aware of and interested in his image in the mirror. It will probably not be much before the age of ten months, though, that he becomes curious about the source of the image, trying to look behind the mirror, and interested in playing with it.

In the ninth month, the baby's thumb becomes fully opposed, and he now grasps with great accuracy. Earlier, he was likely to have to grope for an object, and could not always tell until he actually tried whether or not it was within reach. He will enjoy and laugh over give-and-take games, passing a toy back and forth with an adult. Here adults may get their first inkling of the baby's love for repetitive activities. At the same time, he will begin to show active resentment when something he wants is taken away from him. Before, his reaction—if any—probably did not go beyond mild perplexity. His new resentment indicates two things: he has some awareness of his ability to control what happens, and objects are taking on stability for him, so that they continue to exist and can be recaptured even after they have disappeared. Similarly, the baby may now enjoy games where his parents hide things from him and challenge him to find them. He may be able to find a toy hidden, while he was looking, under a box; but he will not know which of *two* boxes to look under. Long after an adult has grown bored, the baby will go on enjoying a game, while the adult must get his enjoyment from watching the baby. The baby will be able to raise himself on hands and knees and creep. Now he will feel severely frustrated if left too long in his playpen. He wants to be out exploring the wonders of the house, and parents have to begin imposing the first simple taboos on dangerous locations.

During the next three months, the final quarter of his first year, he will be busy getting onto his feet, by stages we shall describe in a moment. He may gain control over his bowel movements during this period, perhaps only to lose it again in the new adventure of becoming a biped or in the face of other stresses. By ten months, he is usually extremely sociable with adults and plays advanced games like pat-a-cake. He may even know a few words, although his vocabulary is not likely to go much beyond "mama" and "dada." These first words probably have little meaning beyond the fact that adults react enthusiastically to them. "Dada" is easier to say and hence may appear first, much to mama's chagrin. Apart from the words the baby himself can use, he seems to understand quite a few, responding to simple commands such as "give me. . . ." By eleven months, he can stand up with help, and may even take a few steps supported by a parent. By the end of the year, he can pull himself to his feet; to get down again, he lets go of whatever he is holding on to and sits down hard. He can probably "cruise"—side-stepping while he supports himself on furniture or playpen railing—or even take a few steps on his own. As his body becomes more familiar to him, he may discover and play with his genitals. His growing skill in manipulation is shown by his ability to pile one small block, somewhat precariously, atop another. He understands a great many words, although he still may not be able to use any, and he can wave bye-bye— usually by closing and opening his fist.

During the final months of infancy—approximately the first quarter of the second year—little emerges in the way of new, separate skills, but there is a great deal of consolidation to be done, particularly in achieving a stable biped stance and locomotion, and in perfecting and combining his manipulatory skills. He begins to anticipate his interests as a toddler when walking and grasping are united in lugging, shoving, and hauling out-sized objects. Now, he enjoys his herculean efforts for their own sake, although later they will be functionally subordinated in the service of other goals such as building projects. Typically, he will often want to push his stroller instead of riding in it. He can sometimes get food from plate to mouth aboard a spoon, although the spoon usually arrives at his mouth upside down; he does much better using his fingers. He can drink from a glass. Now, he not only enjoys receiving affection but is able to return it with hugs and very wet kisses. He tries to sing, and enjoys listening to simple songs, rhymes, and jingles. He knows his own name. As his language skills develop and he becomes aware of his contemporaries, he prepares for his next great step in socialization.

The Foundations of Basic Trust

In outlining the development of behavior in infancy, we have largely disregarded the environment, particularly the human environment, in which this development took place. It is now time to examine the physical and emotional conditions necessary to the seemingly automatic, maturational growth we have described. Underlying the specific development we have spoken of is a more general kind of learning that pervades all the baby's emerging relationships with his environment. This is the learning not of specific skills or acts but of basic attitudes of trust or distrust toward the whole world, which Erikson postulates as the first of a series of critical alternatives arising during development.[6] The infant first becomes aware of the environment in terms of the way it meets his physical and emotional needs. If his needs are attended to fully and dependably, he becomes aware of the world as a good, stable, safe, encouraging place to be—a place to be trusted. When his needs are not met, the world comes within his ken as a frustrating, threatening place where no trust is possible. This essential learning exists in a pervasive awareness which is largely implicit in, and gives its color and meaning to, other things, and occurs on an emotional rather than a verbal or motor basis. This makes it all the more fundamental and resistant to change than much of the learning of facts and skills that takes place later. Nevertheless, as we shall see, the learning of trust or distrust is not absolute and final, and can be modified by later events.

In the baby's first few weeks, his needs are mainly physical. As we pointed out in the first chapter, these are few but vitally important. Apart from the more general needs, as for air and warmth, which we may largely take for granted, the central need in infancy is the recurring need to be fed. Babies sometimes seem all mouth. Feeding is important from the standpoint not only of maintaining physiological equlibrium but also of psychological development. Freud, on whose work Erikson's theories are based, describes infancy as the *oral stage* of development.[7] The child's primary contact with the world is by way of his mouth, which can be thought of, apart from its motor functions in eating, as a sense region through which the infant receives information about objects and their emotional meanings. Thus, the way in which the baby's most urgent and frequent need is met by feeding goes a long way toward determining his basic attitude of trust or of distrust. Pleasant feeding experiences nourish both the baby's body and his sense of emotional well-being and security.

Early in infancy, the baby comes fully awake only at times of crisis, such as hunger. At these times, he is on the verge of what the adult would call panic; the baby has no time perspective, for him the crisis drags on interminably, and he is helpless to do anything about it. If relief is delayed, he becomes even more upset or exhausts himself with crying; already a tiny seed of distrust has been planted, and next time the panic is a little closer, the crisis more exigent. Eventually, of course, he always is fed. His panic subsides, but it leaves a residue of suspicion and distrust. If his equilibrium is promptly restored, on the other hand, his existence is secure.

After a few weeks, as the baby becomes more a person and less an organism, the *process* of satisfying his physical needs becomes as important to him as their actual satisfaction. In other words, the baby's psychological needs become more prominent. At this time, still early in infancy, there arises a fugitive self-awareness which, unless it is nourished and supported by the comforting contact and sensory stimulation of fondling, rocking, and sucking, is touched with the chill of isolation. Thus, in responding to the baby's cry of distress, it is the quality of the parent's touch, and not just physiological relief, that conveys stability, security, warmth, and affection, that tells the baby the world can be trusted. As the baby comes to spend more time awake, he wants cuddling and stimulation apart from that connected with feeding.

But just as the sheer satiation of physical needs is not enough to instill a sense of trust, neither is sensory stimulation as such: in various ways, babies sense the quality of the attention they receive. If parents are grudging, if they are hostile or impatient, their movements may be jerky and abrupt. If they feel anxious, their movements may be hesitant, fumbling, and erratic. Handling which lacks the definite, tenderly firm quality of a self-assured, loving parent seems to disorient and frighten a baby. An infant needs the kind of mothering that expresses love and confidence. Without it, his very being is threatened; with it, he will be able to build new forms of experience on the solid foundation of trust. The baby's responsiveness to parental emotions can readily be verified by informal observation; support for the generality of this phenomenon is to be found in reports by Bateson and Mead, among others.[8]

Lest the reader interpret what we have said to mean that he is bound to traumatize his young infant if he handles him awkwardly at first, or if he occasionally makes him wait a few minutes for a feeding, it should be stressed that babies are not that vulnerable. For several weeks the neonate will care very little about anything as long as his discomfort is relieved in a reasonable time, and even what may look to the uninitiated like rough handling—although it is really only casual and direct—by an experienced mother or nurse does not seem to harm him a bit. In fact, it would be rather surprising if a new parent did not go through a clumsy period where he was not quite sure what the baby's crying betokened, just how to take hold of this elusive creature, or what to do with it once he had it safely in his grip. These are passing things which a sensitive person learns quickly. Evidence from observations of lower species suggests that there may even be virtues for the mother-child relationship in an initial period of fumbling: the mother goat, for instance, keeps the newborn kid circling about her searching for the teat for a prolonged period; if she should be distracted, so that the kid is allowed to nurse too soon, his emotional relationship with the mother is weakened, and he may display "neurotic" behavior.[9] On the human level, it is the quality of the day-by-day adjustments and the parent's more or less permanent disposition that are communicated to the baby and which color his outlook on life.

We should also make clear that there is no one way to love a baby.

Babies are individuals and need different amounts and kinds of affection. Parents, too, are individuals and have different ways of showing it. Some are lavish with physical demonstrations of their feelings; others are not, but still manage to get them across. Some parents are soft and tender, some are bluff and hearty, some are sober, some ironic. Furthermore, no one can love his baby equally at all times and under all conditions. Babies are sometimes cranky and sometimes exasperating, they can destroy the parents' sleep or a favorite treasure. What is important in terms of the baby's sense of trust is the reliability of his parents' love, the clearness with which it shows through transient vicissitudes, through the inevitable anxieties and irritations.

The satisfaction of needs and the establishment of trust are sometimes made difficult by parent-child differences in activity rates, or tempos. Some people are presto, some andante, some largo. Some are staccato, some legato. Some babies drain their bottles in a single rush, others remain unhurried and even indifferent during a feeding. Some babies can hardly wait to become mobile, others seem content to stay comfortably in one place. Even though there is probably an hereditary basis for tempo, parents and their children do not always move at the same pace, any more than they necessarily match in other hereditary traits. And a fast-moving mother paired with a slow-moving child, or vice versa, can spell mutual frustration, exasperation, and conflict. Tempo can be modified, but only slowly, and it is usually the parent—provided he is aware of what is going on—who has to make the initial shift, slowing down or speeding up as required. This adjustment is made easier if the parent realizes that, in time, the child will make reciprocal adjustments as he goes along. If friction develops over differences in tempos, the effect is often first to make the child antagonistic and then to give him a weapon—the exaggeration of his natural pace—with which to vent his antagonism. This consequence is not likely to appear during infancy, but in toddlerhood the spectacle is all too common of a super-charged baby running his frazzled mother off her feet, or of a small, imperturbable monolith dawdling endlessly over meals or dressing while his mother's full head of steam builds up to the danger point.

What we have said so far about building trust by meeting the infant's physical and psychological needs is, in most circumstances, a matter of more or less. Few children grow up with total confidence that the world will take care of their needs, and those who do come in for some rude shocks. On the other hand, few acquire an attitude of total pessimism and distrust. There are, however, well-documented cases which show the devastating effects of not meeting the infant's emotional needs for support and stability and affection, even when his physical needs for food, sleep, shelter, and protection against disease are adequately taken care of. Bowlby and a number of others have observed that shallowness of feeling and inability to form good human relationships could often be traced back to conditions of insufficient or interrupted mothering.[10]

Studies by Spitz suggest that babies given first-rate physical care but deprived of frequent, consistent mothering by the same adult (who need not be the baby's own mother, or even necessarily a woman) become damaged in the very core of their functioning.[11] At first they cry for long periods. After a few days, weeping ceases, and the babies seem to fall into a mood of hopeless but silent grief. After another month, their grief gives way to dull apathy. A few more months, and they begin to show signs of behavior resembling that of adult psychotics, such as odd grimaces and gestural mannerisms. This condition becomes progressively worse and is all but irreversible. If at any time during the first three months or so of separation from the mother, the mother should return, the infant shows an amazingly rapid recovery. If separation is too long continued, the baby's total development lags. New behavior fails to appear on schedule, so that a two-year-old may still lie helpless in his crib. Such babies become retarded intellectually, and their language development is severely if not totally crippled. They become physically run down, so that what would normally be regarded as mild infections suddenly become lethal. According to Spitz, these effects are most severe when separation occurs in the second half of the baby's first year, suggesting that this is a critical period in emotional development, analogous to those critical periods we have spoken of in connection with prenatal growth. These grief reactions were first systematically studied in hospitals, foundling homes, and similar institutions, and have been given the name of *hospitalism*. Comparable effects had previously been observed in so-called *feral* children, those supposed (usually on inconclusive evidence) to have been raised by wild animals but in any case obviously neglected; in orphanage children; and in children raised at home under conditions of serious deprivation.[12] We might also mention Anna Freud's observations of British children in wartime.[13] Children who were able to be with their mothers withstood bombings and other stress quite easily, while children separated from their mothers broke down under minor trials.

The essential part that mothering plays in every aspect of normal de-

Functional
subordination:
Hammering for its
own sake becomes
hammering for a
purpose.
(See page 34.)

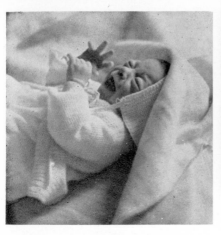

A helpless if vocal neonate

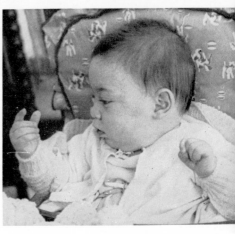

Self-discovery at six months

Early smiling

A two-month-old tackles solid food.

A six-month-old finds relief from the discomfort of teething by chewing on things.

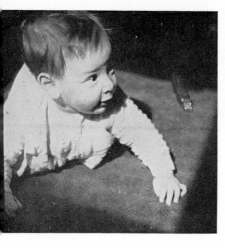

At five months, the baby can push his chest clear of the surface on which he is lying.

At eight months, this baby wants to feed herself.

At eleven months, some babies can walk holding an adult's hand.

A one-year-old waves bye-bye.

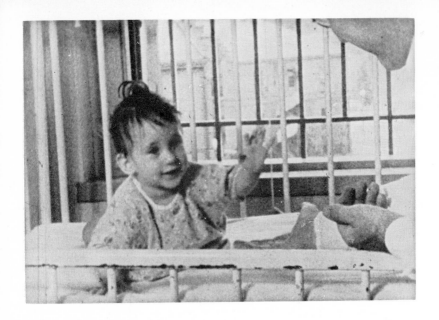

Maternal deprivation: The same child prior to and following separation from his mother.

(From *Grief;* photographs courtesy of Rene A. Spitz)

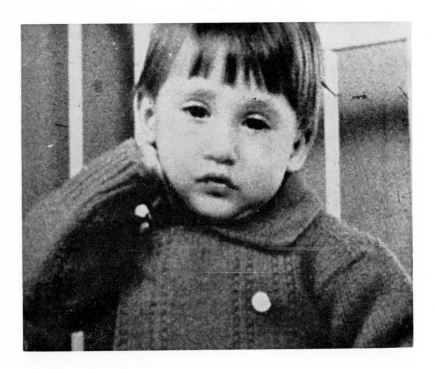

velopment is not a modern discovery, as shown by a quotation from Salimbene, describing the unlooked-for side effects of an experiment conducted in the thirteenth century by Frederick II:

> . . . He wanted to find out what kind of speech and what manner of speech children would have when they grew up if they spoke to no one beforehand. So he bade foster mothers and nurses to suckle the children, to bathe and wash them, but in no way to prattle with them, or to speak to them, for he wanted to learn whether they would speak the Hebrew language, which was the oldest, or Greek, or Latin, or Arabic, or perhaps the language of their parents, of whom they had been born. But he laboured in vain because the children all died. For they could not live without the petting and joyful faces and loving words of their foster mothers. And so the songs are called "swaddling songs" which a woman sings while she is rocking the cradle, to put a child to sleep, and without them a child sleeps badly and has no rest.[14]

Modern studies, like those of Spitz and Ribble,[15] pointing to much the same conclusion as Salimbene's, have met with considerable skepticism in some quarters.[16] While the experimental design in such pioneer studies may have been faulty, and while assumptions about the importance of such detailed specifics of maternal behavior as rocking or handling are not well supported, it is hardly appropriate to discard the basic observation that adequate "mothering" or "parenting" has vital significance for development. Very recent studies, such as those of Rheingold and of Yarrow, describing the effects of much less drastic variations in mothering, provide eloquent support for the basic proposition.[17] Yarrow's data suggest that the human infant's attachment to the mother is a gradual process which takes some months to complete. A group of European zoologists ("ethologists") who study animal behavior in naturalistic settings, rather than in the arbitrary, man-made laboratory situations of most psychological research, have demonstrated in such creatures as the goose that the attachment to the mother, which appears to be instantaneous and fixed, actually depends on a process of "imprinting" during the first hours of life outside the shell. By establishing himself as the first significant stimulus (meeting certain criteria) in the lives of goslings, Lorenz became to all intents and purposes their mother, whose cues they followed with unswerving filial devotion.[18] Whether attachment takes place rapidly, as in imprinting, or gradually, as on the human level, the process can be described as one of canalization.

Studies of sub-human animal species also lend support to hypotheses about the importance of mothering. That is, apart from specific learnings

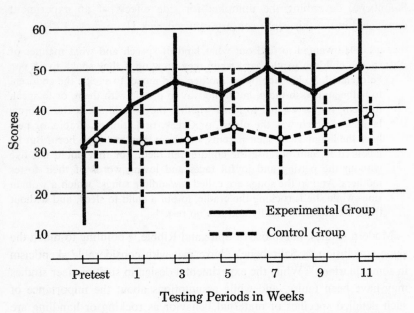

Social response of institutional children to a "mother-figure" (experimental group) and to the same person as one of many attending to their care (control group). (From Rheingold, Harriet L.,
"The modification of social responsiveness in institutional babies,"
Monographs of the Society for Research in Child Development,
1956, 21, No. 2.)

and teachings, an experience of warm nurturance appears to free the
infant animal for optimal development and range of performance. As
one instance among many, Thompson reports that white laboratory rats
given regular handling ("gentling") by the experimenter are healthier
and actually learn to run mazes better than those not given such stimulation.[19] Cathy Hayes's charming account of one of several attempts
that have been made to raise chimpanzees in the same manner as human
babies makes very clear the difference between their "Viki" and chimpanzees raised in the chimpanzee nursery, differences similar to those observed by Spitz between socially isolated babies and babies with adequate
mothering.[20] (Hayes's book is also of interest in terms of the recurrent
and consistent parallels between Viki's emotional and social behavior
and that of human infants, suggesting the simian—if not, indeed, the
mammalian—generality of these basic tendencies.) Liddell, in the course

of a series of careful studies on the experimental production of neurotic behavior, showed that conditions which regularly produced neurosis when the lamb or kid was by itself failed to have this traumatic effect when the mother animal was present.[21] Pronounced differences between the mother-protected and isolated animals were still evident under retest two years later.

In connection with studies of extreme deprivation, a word should be said about recent investigations which suggest that not only lack of social contact but sheer deprivation of stimulation may be involved. The babies in Spitz's studies who suffered most experienced not only relative social isolation but virtual stimulus starvation in their toyless, walled-in cubicles. Recent research shows that adults, if cut off experimentally from the steady shower of visual, auditory, tactual, and kinesthetic stimuli which are usually a part of the unnoticed background of experience become seriously disoriented and remain so for some time.[22] (There have been hints that such sensory deprivation may play a part in the procedures known as "brainwashing." [23]) Here we see dramatically demonstrated the way our psychological existence is a part of a field situation and tends to disintegrate when cut off from environmental communication.

In general, then, a fundamental attitude of trust or of distrust is not learned in the same way that specific skills and knowledge are acquired. Nor is its expression and effect as highly localized. Trust exists implicitly in the normal development of the infant's full range of potentialities for action, thought, feeling, and learning; and mistrust is implicit in the inhibition of development. In other words, the conditions that foster trust may be compared to the normal environmental conditions that are so essential to prenatal maturation, but which we take for granted until they are disturbed.

Severe though the consequences of maternal deprivation may be, they are not always hopeless, as shown by the work of Aubry, who has had a limited but encouraging success in psychotherapy with such children.[24] Recognition of the possible ill effects of extended separation from the mother has led to preventive measures as well as curative ones. The recent shift to the earliest possible age of adoption, from institutional to foster home care, and the so-called cottage plans used by some institutions in an attempt to establish a home-like atmosphere for inmates, are measures of this sort. Many hospitals are now developing special volunteer and professional programs on their pediatric wards, so that children can be given needed emotional support as well as the usual medical care, or are making it possible for mothers to be with their children during much or all of their hospital stay.

It should be emphasized that we have been discussing extreme cases and are in no wise suggesting that mothers should spend all the hours of their days hovering solicitously over their babies lest a grief reaction set in, or that a baby whose mother has to leave him with grandma for a week or two is thereby doomed. Young babies are quite elastic and can tolerate a fair amount of mishandling. Trust does not develop out of parental anxiety, but in a sustained emotional climate that stimulates and nourishes the infant's inherent capacity to become a secure personality. Such stimulation includes frustrations and upsets the child can handle and grow on. A healthful emotional climate is not tepid but temperate, with hot spells and cold spells and storms and seasons, where a child can experience the variety as well as the stability of being a secure human being.

Trends in Child Care

The things we have been saying about children's needs, individual differences, and maturational readiness converge in a new concept of child-rearing practices that has been gaining ground over the past two decades. It should be pointed out that what we think of as the modern needs-oriented point of view is less a new development than a partial return to practices that were long taken for granted. People always had given considerable thought to the best way of rearing children—note the biblical maxim about sparing the rod—but, remarkably enough, it was only in recent years that they became concerned with the raw material, the child, rather than with the manufacturing process which was to convert this raw material into a finished product. Once people really started to look at children, especially early in the present century when there was much questioning of established adult values, a great many doubts arose about the old ways of child rearing. This widespread doubting ushered in the era of "self-conscious parenthood." Parents found themselves at a loss, and numerous self-appointed experts stepped in to tell them what to do. The expert spoke in the name of Science, and many parents listened. Dominant from about 1915 to about 1935 was behaviorist psychology, which played a major part in the era of self-conscious parenthood. One manifestation of this era was the tendency for parents —and babies—to get lost in the maze of dictates handed down by the obstetricians, pediatricians, nurses, and psychologists to whom parents surrendered much of their initiative. According to the then "scientific" precepts that parents were supposed to follow, child rearing was to be regarded as a matter of instilling in the child a certain number of desirable "habits," as though he were some sort of automaton in which one had only to set a few switches and dials properly in order to insure smooth operation according to any desired plan. In 1928 John B. Watson, one of the leaders of American behaviorism, offered the following general prescription to parents:

> There is a sensible way of treating children. Treat them as though they were young adults. Dress them, bathe them with care and circumspection. Let your behavior always be objective and kindly firm. Never hug and kiss them, never let them sit in your lap. If you must, kiss them once on the forehead when they say good night. Shake hands with them in the morning. Give them a pat on the head if they have made an extraordinarily good job of a difficult task. Try it out. In a week's time you will find how easy it is to be perfectly objective with your child and at the same time kindly. You will be utterly ashamed of the mawkish, sentimental way you have been handling it.[25]

Strangely enough, however, this mechanistic view somehow managed to incorporate a Victorian or perhaps medieval moralism according to which the child was a greedy, scheming, power-mad creature in whom nasty, filthy, disgusting habits could and would crop up without warning. Perhaps something of the rigor of the habit-training way of thinking can be conveyed by a quotation from the U. S. Children's Bureau pamphlet *Infant Care* in an edition as late as 1938, by which time this view was already considered by many to be obsolete:

> . . . Immediately after birth he will begin to form habits, which if they are the right kind will be useful to him all his life. Regularity from birth on is of first importance.
> Through training in regularity of feeding, sleeping, and elimination . . . the tiny baby will receive his first lessons in character building. He should learn that hunger will be satisfied only so often, that when he is put into his bed he must go to sleep, that crying will not result in his being picked up or played with whenever he likes. He will begin to learn that he is part of a world bigger than that of his own desires.[26]

The habits approach, for all the weight of its prestige, almost from the beginning ran into obstacles. First of all, there was the spontaneous humanitarianism of parents, for whom "letting the baby cry it out" went against the grain of every sympathetic feeling. Equally important, as now seems obvious, it ran counter to the facts of what children are like.

It took no account of readiness—assuming as it apparently did that the baby could learn anything at any time. It laid great stress on meeting the baby's physical needs, but took no account of his needs for mothering and nurturance. Moreover, behaviorism behaved as if it assumed that all babies were the same, and overlooked individual differences in activity rhythms and rates of growth, which often fail to coincide with clock and calendar schedules based on group averages. If drastically imposed, instead of teaching the child desirable habits, the habits approach taught the incidental lesson that the world was an unfriendly place and if the child knew what was good for him he would knuckle under quickly. This lesson, although incidental, was not altogether unintentional; it followed logically from the undercurrent of belief that if parents failed to take over immediately, the baby would soon get the upper hand.

As habit-training proved more and more clearly unsatisfactory and unworkable, there was a second shift which took account of the needs and individuality of children and, somewhat later, of parents. Although the change of climate was not as abrupt as the juxtaposition may indicate, a quotation from the more needs-oriented 1942 edition of *Infant Care* may illustrate the striking contrast:

> . . . Suppose a very young baby becomes hungry. He becomes vaguely conscious of discomfort, begins to wiggle and twist, and finally to cry. Soon after he is thoroughly aware of his discomfort his mother appears, with a cheerful, quiet voice, a warm bosom, and firm arms. The baby responds by nuzzling about until he finds the nipple and sucks it, and then warm milk flows into his stomach. Not only the milk, but also the warmth, the sense of being held firmly, and probably even the sound of his mother's voice all help to give that baby a sense of comfort. Through many repetitions of this experience the baby responds with pleasure, not only to food but to friendly human contact. Such experiences help him [later] become a likable, friendly person.
>
> On the other hand, to take an extreme example [which would not have sounded extreme in the 1938 version], suppose another baby becomes hungry, and he wiggles, twists, and finally cries as did the first baby described. Instead of having his needs for food and affection satisfied soon, this baby is [consistently] allowed to cry on and on, and finally a bottle is put into his mouth. . . . He may have so exhausted himself that he is too tired to obtain much pleasure from the food [or even to eat it]. . . . Eventually . . . the baby may develop an attitude of dislike toward the world and instead of responding in a friendly way he remains withdrawn, fearful and a little suspicious—an attitude that will make his ultimate adjustment to life difficult.[27]

In effect, the contemporary rejection of behaviorist rigidity, the shift from habit-training to a needs-satisfaction viewpoint, involves a recognition that parenthood is not a matter of blanket regulations which apply to all babies in all situations. Instead, if parents know what they can reasonably expect of a child at various ages, and how their expectations fit in with his needs and capacities, they can devise their own system of operation. Needless to say, even so broad and benign a stricture has not solved the problem of self-conscious parenthood overnight. Parents, in becoming very much aware of the importance of their conduct for the welfare of their children, can see the unspoken threat of dire outcomes for their baby's future adjustment lurking behind even the gentlest dictum. After the behaviorists, and the early nursery school teachers and parent educators who learned from the behaviorists and were ready to tell parents how to train their young, came discordant but no less authoritative voices. Some, under a psychoanalytic banner, but completely misunderstanding Freud, taught that one must never inhibit the child's spontaneous impulses or frustrate his self-expression. This led many timid parents, in avoiding overwhelming their children with the demands of habit-training, to the opposite extreme of inviting the baby to tyrannize over the family with a whim of iron. This submissive and frightened version of self-conscious parenthood ("permissiveness") was reinforced by misunderstandings of other findings as well. Many, without comprehending the inter-relationships among all the ways of behaving which make up a culture, advocated the adoption of child-rearing practices of one or another primitive society. Another trend, which, although undoubtedly not new, has been aggravated by parental self-consciousness, is the tendency to compare children's development competitively. This is one reason for the intense preoccupation with norms which we mentioned earlier. For the behavioristically oriented parent, the motto seemed to be "try harder and do it earlier." For the pseudo-Freudian parent, the developmental timetable offered new cues for guilt feelings about parental failures, and for renewed resolutions *never* to be angry.

Actually, and fortunately, many parents were quite unaffected by the opposing doctrines that raged about them, particularly in the transition period of the thirties. Parents who did seize upon one or the other of the extremes probably found in it rationalizations for their own attitudes. People do not don new attitudes and practices like articles of clothing. Ways of dealing with children are not merely procedures to be followed as in baking a cake: they involve human situations in which the parents' own emotions are deeply involved and are not easily altered.

In the long run, the extremist views have tended to cancel each other out, and the more balanced and sober students of human development have found that there is much to agree on. Basically, it would appear that the parents' chief task is to comprehend their child's needs and his changing capacities, and to balance these against the needs of the rest of the family—including their own adult needs. Parents, in the modern view, need neither to impose inappropriate demands nor to surrender to a baby's passing whims. They need not browbeat their infants, but neither do they abdicate as adults, and they are not afraid to take the responsibility that goes with being bigger, stronger, older, and wiser than their infant. Part of the wisdom comes in the ability actually to comprehend needs and to distinguish them from whims. This means that parents first of all have to know what the baby wants. The word "infant," after all, comes from a Latin root meaning "unspeaking." Instead of spoken language, parents—or anyone dealing with babies—must, as Langmuir has put it, recognize a "language of behavior," of tones and intensities of crying, of posture, tension, coloring, distractibility, and so forth.[28] Given a relaxed attitude on the parents' part, no harm will ensue from occasional misinterpretations of the baby's state of mind.

In the sections that follow, we shall discuss a few of the central issues in child rearing, not so much for the purpose of supplying parents with a manual as to provide an understanding of some of the baby's critical encounters with the environment and their implications for personality development. We cannot cover exhaustively all the specific implications for child-rearing practices entailed in a needs-oriented philosophy. However, we shall try to show briefly how each of the customary "problem" areas appears from this viewpoint. Our discussion will bear in mind, where they are applicable, four main points. First, good parental practice takes account of the vast variety of *individual differences* in both daily rhythms and tempos and in long-range growth rates and patterns. Second, there is the approximate age range at which the parent may expect *readiness* for new learning of a particular kind; we might repeat that the peak of readiness is often a critical period when a function is most susceptible either to cultivation or to damage. Third, there are the *behavioral cues* a child gives his parents—if they are observant—about his individual needs and rhythms and readinesses for something new. Finally, there is the matter of *mutual trust and affection* between parent and child, which determines whether the parents can try things out from time to time—is he ready for solids?—just to see if they work, without setting up a surge of resistance in the child or feeling thwarted themselves if the experiment falls through.

Crying, Attention, Spoiling

To a number of parents, a needs-centered approach to child care still, perhaps as a carry-over from the "habits" orientation, seems to be flirting with disaster. Their qualms may be summed up in several recurring questions: Should he have so much attention? Won't he get the best of us if we give him what he wants? Won't he be spoiled?

When babies cry, it is because they need something—not that they (or we) always know what. Among the things they need is attention, and in great abundance. What is "attention," after all, but the closeness and stimulation and love that we have been talking about and to which the baby is entitled? As we said earlier, the very young infant needs the reassurance of active contact with the environment to forestall the panic of isolation. Such contact convinces him of the solidity and reliability of the environment. Once this conviction has been formed, he will not have to ask constant reassurance—"seek attention." He will ask for it from time to time, but his need will not stem from panic. He will then be able to enjoy his parents' company on a more mature basis, in a spirit of social interchange. He will also be able to do without it for brief periods while he pursues his primitive researches in physics, mechanics, and gastronomy. When he is tired or sick, when strangers come to visit, or he is otherwise out of sorts, of course, he needs even more to be reassured and bolstered by parental attention. But if his need for attention is met at the right times, it becomes satiated, liberating both parent and child. If it is not satisfied, on the other hand, it increases instead of decreasing. Worse yet, it may, like neurotic needs of adults, become essentially insatiable. Thus, premature efforts to develop the child's "powers of self-reliance" may have exactly the opposite effect.

Furthermore, very young babies are not interested in getting the best of anybody; even when they are older, they are not unless they have somehow been taught that their needs are gratified only when they have worn somebody down. Children are egocentric, in that they are tied to a single viewpoint, their own, and take a long time to develop an ability to see the world through other people's eyes; but they are not inherently selfish. They have wants and needs, but most of these are quite reasonable in the child's own terms. If a baby gets the essential things, and has developed basic trust in the people about him, he can tolerate denials.

In infancy, of course, children have little sense of wanting to own things; rather, they want access to them so they can feel and taste them. The baby who has lots of opportunity to poke into things does not feel more than momentarily aggrieved when some things are forbidden to him.

During infancy, at least, children do not become spoiled by a maximum of affection and attention. There seem to be three main sets of conditions which lead to spoiling. First, there is the well-meaning but oversolicitous kind of mothering that hurries to do something about every discomfort before either the baby or the mother has had a chance to find what he really wants. In this way, the wrong need often gets gratified, leaving the baby with a vague, restless, but unformed dissatisfaction, and a combination of wanting and resenting his mother, which may later express itself in spoiled behavior. Second, there is a similar pattern arising from parental insecurity: the mother is so afraid of losing the baby's love, or feels so guilty about a lack of genuine affection for him that she gratifies his needs blindly. Third, there is the spoiling that results from teasing, capricious, or inconsistent meeting of the child's needs, leaving him fearful that he may never really get what he wants, and dissatisfied when he does get it.

A needs-centered approach does not advocate that parents become doormats. We assume that parents are reasonably mature human beings with independent interests, attitudes, and opinions, who have a strong affection for and enjoyment of their children, a serious concern for their well-being, and a decent respect for their own needs and those of the rest of the family. The present thesis is that affection is not incompatible with discipline. A concern for a child's present and future welfare often obliges his parents to make demands and impose restrictions on him— when he is able to handle them—that may not coincide with what he wants. Parents soon learn to distinguish between a child's needs and his wants, between short- and long-term goals; and before the child can do so, they begin to balance his wants against the needs of others in the family, including themselves.

Feeding and Scheduling

Current doctrine concerning feeding meets likewise with a certain amount of worried opposition, even though it is essentially what everybody always did until the habit-formers came along and spread confusion. In their day, it was heretical to say that the best time to feed a baby is when he is hungry. Going further, however, current doctrine says that mothers can safely leave it almost entirely to the baby to decide when, and how much, and what to eat. The naturalistic doctrine—whose impact we saw earlier in the hospital rooming-in programs for the new-born—has occasionally been pushed to the extreme of condemning all bottle feeding. Apart from the superior nutritive value of breast milk, and its convenience (no formula to be mixed and no sterilization routine to be followed), it has an emotional advantage in that it automatically provides a "time out" period for the mother and baby to be together, a time when the baby can stare at and learn to know his mother's face and feel close and warm and supported. But it is possible to give a bottle under similar conditions, if the baby is held, rather than left to his own devices with a bottle propped up somewhere near his mouth. Incidentally, older babies—after six or eight months—who can hold things easily and are able to maintain contact with their mothers from a distance may sometimes prefer to hold the bottle; but we are speaking here of early infancy.

The habits approach, basing its dicta on how long it takes the average baby's stomach to empty, required a strict schedule of feeding every four hours on the dot (some physicians prescribed three-hour intervals for very young babies), whether the baby had been shrieking with hunger for an hour past or was so soundly asleep that he had to be awakened by snapping one's fingernail against the sole of his foot. Moreover, besides the daily timetable to which the mother had rigidly to adhere, the authorities plotted out well in advance a complete calendar schedule telling when to wean the baby and what new foods to give him.

But if mothers do not depend on the clock to tell them when their babies are hungry, they are free to respond to and increase their understanding of the baby's expressive language, learning the terms by which he announces his hunger, as opposed to sickness or chilling or overheating or fatigue or pain. When a healthy baby shows distress during the neonatal period of a month or less, it is probably because he is hungry—even though he ate only an hour before: some babies, because of the small size of their stomachs or because their stomachs empty rapidly, become hungry at intervals much shorter than the standard three or four hours. The baby's distress might be due to colic, but colic and other sources of internal pain usually cause his body to double up, while hunger causes him to stretch out and make feeding movements with his mouth. If the baby becomes tranquil after he has been picked up and burped, he is probably not hungry. If he engages in "rooting" behavior, searching for the nipple, he probably is. After a month or so, parents learn to recognize a particular note in the baby's cry, or some other behavioral cue, that tells when he is hungry rather than tired or in pain or in need of fondling. It should be noted that babies are not always in very good communication with their own bodies and can be misled about what is ailing them. They may try to eat and then decide that they do not want to; they may fret through the most tender mothering. It goes without saying that parents have to learn to be front-line diagnosticians able to recognize the physical upsets that call for something more than food and affection.

But self-demand feeding, as it is called, becomes self-scheduling; it does not imply that the baby will go on indefinitely eating odd amounts at odd hours. Simply by virtue of increasing physiological stability, he will begin after a few months to take larger feedings at longer intervals. Combined with the stabilization of his sleeping patterns, this means that he can be led quite easily by the time he is five or six months old into a routine where an alarm clock will go off in his stomach three times a day, no more and no less, as though the three-meals-a-day convention of our culture had been built into his genes. The self-scheduling tendency of babies in their first six months has been amply demonstrated by Gesell's observations,[29] not to mention those of numerous mothers.

That babies are equally competent to decide *what* to eat was shown in a classic study by Davis in which newly weaned infants eight to nine months of age were allowed to select the foodstuffs they wanted from a large array of dishes placed in front of them at each meal.[30] These babies of their own accord ate the proper proportions of the right food components: proteins, starches, fats, vitamins, minerals. Two of Davis's subsidiary findings are quite striking. First, the babies did not adjust their choices in terms of each meal or even of the daily requirements of a dietician's chart; it was only in the long run that their diets balanced out. Along the way, the children sometimes went on "jags," sticking to one food, such as bananas, for days at a time. Second, the babies made sure they got essential foodstuffs even when these were patently disagreeable, as in the case of salt, which some of the children took straight, grimacing all the while. In general, the subjects paid no attention to adult standards of what "goes with" what, or of the sequence in which foods "should" be eaten. They might very well start with dessert and work their way back to the appetizers. Because of its fundamental importance, Davis's study badly needs repetition with a larger sample of babies and including more elaborate foodstuffs—candy and caviar, for instance—in addition to the staples her original subjects were offered.

Davis's findings illustrate the principle called by Cannon the "wisdom of the body" (a form of homeostatic mechanism), whose relevance for food selection was first observed in cases of pathology.[31] People suffering from Addison's disease, which interferes with salt metabolism because of damage to the adrenal glands, spontaneously increase their salt consumption to compensate. In the same way, rats with their adrenal glands removed develop a highly increased sensitivity to salt and can detect extremely minute quantities dissolved in water. Again, children who eat (calcium-rich) plaster from the walls are sometimes found to be suffering from calcium deficiency. It is possible that children's traditional resistance to spinach is due, although they do not know it, to the free oxalic acid in spinach, which interferes with calcium metabolism and makes it an inappropriate foodstuff for the very young.

There are two ways, however, in which the wisdom of the body is less than absolute. First, although it steers us toward nourishing foods, it cannot be counted on to steer us away from toxic ones. Children do not hesitate to sample the contents of medicine bottles and soap boxes, nor do our tissue needs signal which is the delectable mushroom and which the deadly toadstool. Second, culturally defined eating habits tend to corrupt the body's wisdom. In many cultures with subnormal diets, vital nutritional supplements are ready to hand but ignored. In wartime, many Americans preferred to reduce their meat consumption drastically rather than turn to strange or "inferior," but perfectly nourishing, cuts. Tomatoes, a valuable source of vitamins and minerals, were long eschewed as poisonous.

It is seldom practical for parents to offer their babies cafeteria service of the kind used in Davis's experiment, but this does not mean that they cannot benefit from her findings. They can learn not to be upset by a baby's aversions to specific foods or to be taken aback when he goes on food jags; they can, in other words, learn to respect the wisdom of the body.

In summary, then, parents can rely on cues from their baby's behavior to help them decide when and what and how much to feed him. If they are secure in the knowledge that he will not demand food needlessly—unless he has experienced physical or emotional starvation—and that he will come around to eating at reasonable hours with a minimum of prodding as soon as he is ready, then the child in turn can feel secure in the trustworthiness of an environment that does not make arbitrary demands on him long before he is able to comply.

Weaning

Nowadays the doctrine of gradualism in introducing new foods has found such wide acceptance that it is often hard to realize what bitter battles once took place between mother and child over weaning. Some mothers felt it necessary to drive home the fact that a new era was in effect by making the baby witness a ceremonial smashing of his precious bottles. Weaning, of course, means two things: first, a transition from breast or bottle to cup, and second, a transition from milk to solid foods. Modern pediatric practice makes both of these transitions gradual, on a try-and-see basis, and allows for long periods of overlapping, so that the introduction of the new and the withdrawal of the old are both made as unstressful as possible. From the age of three or four months until toward the end of his first year, the baby gradually learns to take it for granted that food comes in a variety of flavors, consistencies, textures, temperatures, and containers. His long-range readiness for something new is taken into account in starting the process: his security; absence of physical upsets, particularly digestive; and such outward signs as an increase of drooling, indicating stepped-up activity of the salivary glands. There are also short-range readinesses to be considered: the baby is most amenable to feeding innovations when he is wide awake and after his hunger has been partly satisfied; when he is tired or very hungry, his urge to suck is strong, and he will be impatient with spoons and cups.

Before gradualism became the rule, when weaning was a matter of days rather than of weeks or months, the abrupt transition was liable to produce various untoward consequences. The baby, finding his accustomed patterns, with all their implications of emotional support, suddenly and inexplicably disrupted, sometimes developed feeding problems or showed generalized distress. It should be mentioned that abrupt weaning often took place just at the time Spitz has pointed to as critical in the formation of basic trust (see page 62).

Needless to say, some babies take to the transitions of weaning with great gusto, others are cautious and skeptical; some are ready sooner, others later. Again, a confident parent senses what his child needs and acts accordingly, trying out his intuitions as he goes along.

Thumb-Sucking and Comfort Devices

Thumb-sucking is a "problem" closely related to eating and weaning. Sucking is an essential element in the neonate's mechanisms for survival. In addition, it soon becomes a need which demands gratification in its own right. When the sucking need does not become satiated in the course of nursing, the baby compensates by sucking on other things: his thumb, a corner of his blanket, toys, etc. Levy has demonstrated comparable phenomena in puppies and chicks.[32] Puppies bottle-fed from a free-flowing nipple, which gratified their hunger so quickly that they failed to satisfy their need to suck, sucked avidly at themselves, each other, curtain fringes, and human fingers. Similarly, chicks given only a limited opportunity to peck, although adequately fed, pecked at each other's bodies until the feathers came out. On the other hand, chicks fed but deprived of any opportunity to peck during the first two weeks of life starved to death when later obliged to eat in this normal way; pecking, and perhaps sucking as well, have critical periods in which they must be stimulated in order to appear at all, and when they must be satiated if they are not to take inappropriate forms.

To understand the importance of satiating the sucking function, we must expand on what we said earlier concerning Freud's conception of the oral stage. According to Freud, if the baby is not given sufficient oral gratification, he will not be able to move on to more mature modes of experience. That is, he will become *fixated* at the oral level, and continue to seek the gratification he has missed out on long after it has ceased to be appropriate. In adults, this fixation takes the form of the "oral character." One has only to look at the crowds in the streets or in a football stadium to be convinced that few if any adults suck their thumbs (perhaps a comforting thought to the parents of a thumb-sucker). There are, however, many adult mannerisms and "habits" that have been interpreted by Freudians as analogous to thumb-sucking and as residuals of the sucking and biting behavior of the oral stage of infant development: smoking, nail-biting, pencil-chewing, gum-chewing, drinking, etc. One form of the oral character consists of a clinging, dependent approach to the world that seems to be a symbolic plea for the effortless nurturance of infancy. Moreover, even if there is adequate sucking experience during feeding, the baby will still want to put everything that comes his way into his mouth. The mouth in infancy serves as an important exploratory and sensory region, which works in concert with hands and eyes to tell the baby what things are like. He cannot properly know an object until he has looked at it, manipulated it, and sucked on it. His most vivid awareness of objects comes to him through his mouth, and it is only later that this mode of perception can be subordinated first to the experience of objects that comes from handling them and then, eventually, just from looking at them.

Viewed from these standpoints, thumb-sucking in infancy takes on a new meaning. It is not something dirty and disgusting which threatens to remain with the child for all time and which is to be cured with splints and cuffs and bitter medicines, as in the habit-training approach. During infancy, it is not even a problem, and almost all thumb-suckers stop of their own accord before the end of the preschool period. It may also be remarked here that, according to the best current authority, thumb-sucking's threat to the shape of the dental arch has been much exaggerated.[33] Any dislocation of the teeth produced by thumb-sucking usually corrects itself spontaneously when thumb-sucking stops. Returning to infancy, if parents feel that their baby is overdoing thumb-sucking, they can try leaving him at the breast longer, or, if he is bottle-fed, using nipples with smaller holes. If these expedients do not work, then the child has to find extra sucking experience by sucking his thumb, a pacifier, or whatever. If an older child continues indefinitely in a pattern of excessive sucking, it may suggest that he is missing out in other areas, such as parental affection, and that sucking serves as a substitute gratification. Thumb-sucking perhaps occurs most frequently at bedtime (or at moments of tension) and seems to act as a means of closing off the child's communication with the environment, allowing him to withdraw into sleep—he can shut his eyes, but he cannot desensitize his mouth and hand except by incorporating them in a closed circuit of internal activity. Here again, the answer seems to lie in letting the baby have enough sucking experience so that his urge to suck becomes satiated and so is less demanding. At the same time, he needs to have enough variety of experience so that alternative sources of gratification are open to him.

At bedtime, along with thumb-sucking, often go a variety of other comfort rituals: twisting a lock of hair, holding an ear, rubbing a blanket, clutching a rag, or cuddling a favorite—often disreputable—doll. These patterns are not indicative of psychopathology, as they are often regarded by anxious, self-conscious parents who are ever vigilant for signs of something wrong. Late in the first year or early in the second, a new phenomenon may appear—masturbation. This comes when the baby discovers, and finds that he has access to, his own genitals for the first time. Masturbation sometimes follows irritation of the genitals. More often, however, it is a natural outcome of the baby's growing awareness of his own body sensations. Once he (or she) has discovered this fascinating bit of anatomy, he will want to explore all its possibilities, which he will find pleasant. Usually, though, his interest is transient, if recurrent; there are too many other fascinating things in the world, and the sensations arising from genital stimulation are not nearly as definite and intense as in the adult. In general, such stimulation seems to be soothing rather than exciting, as shown by its deliberate use in some cultures, such as Alor, to quiet a crying baby.[34] Doubtless it is for this reason that it occurs most frequently at bedtime, when the baby finds ways to demobilize his forces and go to sleep. Habitual masturbation can become a problem later on, but not in infancy, and the prescriptions for curing it that one encounters are largely irrelevant. A few years ago, child care experts sometimes worked themselves into a dilemma: to prevent thumb-sucking, the baby's hands should be put under the covers at night; to prevent masturbation, they should be put outside. Both sorts of interference with the infant have become obsolete. It now seems more appropriate to allow the baby a certain amount of freedom to find out about the body he is going to live with, without unintentionally giving it an overemphasis the parents hardly wish for.

Toilet-Training

By rights, the topic of toilet-training belongs in the next chapter, dealing with the toddler. However, since it is still commonplace to hear that babies can be "trained" by six months—or four months, or one month—it is perhaps relevant to say a few words about it here. First of all, it sometimes happens that a baby (more often a boy baby) quickly settles down to a predictable pattern of defecation that a parent can capitalize on as soon as the baby is old enough to sit up by himself. When a parent knows that a bowel movement is due, or can see from the baby's expression that one is imminent, the baby can be placed on the toilet or potty chair (the earliest editions of *Infant Care* suggested the "ordinary porcelain cuspidor" as a suitable receptacle). Such a procedure, involving the mother's being in the right place at the right time, is not training. It does not teach the baby to announce his needs or to hold on until he is taken to the toilet; at best, it will save a couple of diapers a day and familiarize him with the toilet as a comfortable place to be, instead of the battleground it too often becomes. If, however, the baby's elimination pattern changes, as it often will, or if he turns against the idea, parents have no wise choice but to adapt to the new schedule or drop the whole program. Stable bowel control, where the baby himself plays the chief role, usually comes after he can walk. True sphincter control is a *learned* function—although contingent on maturation—and when parents think the baby is ready for it, then they can try and see.

Probably a majority of babies have decidedly irregular patterns of elimination during the first year, and for them bowel control is almost out of the question at this time. On the other hand, they too can be acclimatized to the toilet, which obviously must never become a prison. At the height of the habit-training vogue, early training was recommended without a qualm, as evidenced by the following quotation:

> At what age may parents begin to teach good bathroom habits? When the baby is a few weeks old. Many doctors say that there need be no soiled diapers after the eighth week of life [!]. The younger the baby, the more easy it will be to win Nature's cooperation. . . .
> By the end of the first year there should be daily evacuations at eight o'clock sharp every morning and six o'clock every night. These are ideal hours because they can be adhered to later on throughout the school years.
>
> Soon after the child begins to walk [he] should begin to learn to control his bladder. . . . [Set] aside one week or ten days for . . . teaching this habit. Every day, while he is awake, the baby should be put onto his toilet chair at fifteen minute intervals. . . . In a very short while he will discover that telling you of his needs saves him great discomfort, for no child enjoys wearing wet clothing.[35]

Today, however, we know that for almost all babies, bladder control does not come about until between eighteen months and two years by day, and two to three years, or even later, by night. All in all, the views embodied in the preceding quotation have been repudiated by people who have taken the trouble to find out what children's capacities actually are.

Sleeping

Sleeping, like eating, is better left to the baby's discretion, subject to parental wisdom, than to tables showing how much the average baby sleeps. It is sometimes said that one should not play vigorously with a baby just before bedtime, as this will excite him and make it hard for him to sleep. Although this applies to some babies, it does not hold true for others. Some babies like a good romp at bedtime as a means of using up any surplus energy and thus being able to relax. Other babies like to frolic and then have an interlude of soothing before they turn in. Some babies like to sleep right after meals, others feel sociable, still others want to have a period of quiet digestion. Parents soon can learn what pattern their baby follows, and act accordingly. If the baby is allowed to go to sleep when he is tired and to wake up when he wakes up, he will usually get sufficient rest. This may not be so, of course, when there is an undue amount of noise or in very hot weather, but in such circumstances parents have to do what they can to make the baby comfortable. Like his other physiological rhythms, the baby's sleep pattern stabilizes—with a small amount of encouragement from his parents—until he sleeps the whole night through and takes well-defined naps during the daytime. This stable pattern often begins to be evident between the ages of three and five months.

On the other hand, as babies grow older and more sociable, they seem able to put off sleep indefinitely as long as there are other attractions around. It is easy enough to tell when a baby is sleepy and remove him from stimulation. This is one of the points where parents have to have the confidence that *they* know what is best and to go serenely ahead, even if there are squalls. "Meeting needs" does not mean inviting the baby to impose on the rest of the family. It is because the baby would often rather do other things than get the sleep he needs that there is some merit in the stern injunction against picking him up when he cries. Most babies have an interlude of "fussy" crying before they fall asleep; this is easily distinguished from crying due to distress, and does not call for parental action. When the baby is really unhappy at bedtime, then he should be soothed and comforted in a way that does not provoke further wakefulness. In very young babies, this may take the form of rocking, crooning, stroking the head, or patting the back. Somewhat older infants may just like to have a parent stand by the crib for a while, serving as a familiar, reassuring reference point before the baby lets go and falls asleep.

In sum, then, if the baby is sleepy, if his surroundings are conducive to sleep, and if there are no temporary or enduring anxieties to plague him (and if there are, his parents can see him through them), he will sleep. And on the whole, he can safely decide how long he needs to sleep in terms of his own vital capacity.

NOTES   (Starred items are recommended as further readings.)

[1] Bridges, K. M. B., "Emotional development in early infancy," *Child Development,* 1932, 3, 324-341.

[2] Griffiths, Ruth, *The Abilities of Babies,* New York: McGraw-Hill, 1954; Yarrow, Leon J, "The development of object relationships during infancy, and the effects of a disruption of early mother-child relationships" (paper delivered before the American Psychological Association, September, 1956); Spitz, R. A. (with the assistance of Wolf, K. M.), "The smiling response: A contribution to the ontogenesis of social relations," *Genetic Psychology Monographs,* 1946, 34, 57-125.

[3] Gesell, Arnold, and Amatruda, C. S., *Developmental Diagnosis,* New York: Paul B. Hoeber, second edition 1947.

[4] Gesell, Arnold, and Thompson, Helen, *Infant Behavior,* New York: McGraw-Hill, 1934.

[5] Gesell and Amatruda, p. 30.

*[6] Erikson, E. H., *Childhood and Society,* New York: Norton, 1951.

[7] See, e.g., Freud, Sigmund, *A General Introduction to Psychoanalysis,* New York: Liveright, 1935.

[8] Bateson, Gregory, and Mead, M., *Balinese Character,* New York: New York Academy of Sciences, 1942, p. 31.

[9] Blauvelt, Helen, "Dynamics of the mother-newborn relationship in goats," in Schaffner, Bertram (ed.), *Group Processes: Transactions of the First Conference,* New York: Josiah Macy, Jr., Foundation, 1955, pp. 221-258.

[10] Bowlby, J., *Maternal Care and Mental Health,* Geneva: World Health Organization, 1951.

[11] Spitz, R. A., "Hospitalism: An inquiry into the genesis of psychiatric conditions in early childhood," *Psychoanalytic Study of the Child,* 1945, 1, 53-74; "Hospitalism: A follow-up report," *Psychoanalytic Study of the Child,* 1946, 2, 113-117; "Anaclitic depression," *Psychoanalytic Study of the Child,* 1946, 2, 313-342.

[12] A review of findings in this area is contained in Montagu, M. F. A., *The Direction of Human Development,* New York: Harper, 1955, pp. 199-248 and passim.

[13] Freud, Anna, and Burlingham, Dorothy, *War and Children,* New York: International Universities Press, 1943.

[14] Ross, J. B., and McLaughlin, M. M. (eds.), *A Portable Medieval Reader,* New York: Viking, 1949, p. 366.

[15] Ribble, M. A., *The Rights of Infants: Early Psychological Needs and their Satisfaction,* New York: Columbia University Press, 1943.

[16] Orlansky, Harold, "Infant care and personality," *Psychological Bulletin,* 1949, 46, 1-48 (reprinted in Martin and Stendler, *Readings in Child Development,* pp. 321-336); Pinneau, S. R., "A critique on the articles by Margaret Ribble," *Child Development,* 1950, 21, 203-228; "The infantile disorders of hospitalism and anaclitic depression," *Psychological Bulletin,* 1955, 52, 429-452.

[17] Rheingold, H. L., "The modification of social responsiveness in institutional babies," *Monographs of the Society for Research in Child Development,* 1956, 21, No. 2; Yarrow, *op. cit.*

[18] Lorenz, K. Z., *King Solomon's Ring,* New York: Crowell, 1952, pp. 40-42.

[19] Thompson, W. R., "Early environment—its importance for later behavior" (paper delivered before the American Psychopathological Association, June, 1954); see also Weininger, Otto, "Mortality of albino rats under stress as a function of early handling," *Canadian Journal of Psychology,* 1953, 7, 111-114.

*[20] Hayes, Cathy, *The Ape in Our House,* New York: Harper, 1951.

*[21] Liddell, H. S., "Conditioning and the emotions," in *Twentieth-Century Bestiary,* New York: Simon and Schuster, 1955, pp. 189-208.

[22] Bexton, W. H., Heron, W., and Scott, T. H., "Effects of decreased variation in the sensory environment," *Canadian Journal of Psychology,* 1954, 8, 70-76. The pioneering study in this area is probably Riesen, A. H., "The development of visual perception in man and chimpanzee," *Science,* 1947, 106, 107-108.

[23] *New York Times,* April 21, 1956, p. 49.

[24] Aubry, J. (Roudinesco), "Severe maternal deprivation and personality

development in early childhood," *Understanding the Child*, 1952, **21**, 104-108; *see also* *Freud, Anna, and Dann, Sophie, "An experiment in group upbringing," *Psychoanalytic Study of the Child*, 1951, **6**, 127-168.

[25] Watson, J. B., *Psychological Care of Infant and Child*, New York: Norton, 1928. Cited in Symonds, Percival M., *The Dynamics of Parent-Child Relationships*, New York: Bureau of Publications, Teachers College, Columbia University, 1949, p. 113.

[26] U. S. Children's Bureau, *Infant Care*, Washington 25: U. S. Government Printing Office, 1938, p. 3.

*[27] *Infant Care*, 1942 edition, p. 30. *Infant Care* is revised periodically. Its recent editions provide a humane and psychologically sound guide to parents.

[28] Personal communication.

[29] Gesell, Arnold, "The ontogenesis of infant behavior," in Carmichael, *Manual of Child Psychology*, pp. 335-374.

[30] Davis, C. M., "Results of the self-selection of diets by young children," *Canadian Medical Association Journal*, 1939, **41**, 257-261 (reprinted in Martin and Stendler, *Readings in Child Development*, pp. 69-74).

[31] Cannon, *The Wisdom of the Body*.

[32] Levy, David M., "Experiments on the sucking reflex and social behavior in dogs," *American Journal of Orthopsychiatry*, 1934, **4**, 203-224; "On instinct-satiation: an experiment on the pecking behavior of chickens," *Journal of Genetic Psychology*, 1938, **18**, 327-348.

[33] Dunn, H. Lincoln, *Thumb-sucking* (unpublished manuscript); *The Child and His Thumb* (film), J. H. Sillman, 1954. (Distributed by Film Publishers, Inc.)

[34] Du Bois, Cora, "The Alorese," in *Kardiner, Abram, and associates, *The Psychological Frontiers of Society*, New York: Columbia University Press, 1945, pp. 101-145.

[35] France, Beulah, *Teaching Children Proper Bathroom Habits*, Chester, Pa.: Scott Paper Co., 1940, pp. 4-6. For a contemporary physician's view (perhaps one of those referred to by Miss France), see Kenyon, Josephine H., *Healthy Babies Are Happy Babies*, Boston: Little, Brown, 1935, pp. 116-117.

FOR FURTHER READING

Beach, F. A., and Jaynes, Julian, "Effects of early experience upon the behavior of animals," *Psychological Bulletin*, 1954, **51**, 239-263. A comprehensive review of experiments on the after-effects of particular infantile events in a variety of species.

Spock, Benjamin, *The Common-Sense Book of Baby and Child Care*, New York: Duell, Sloan and Pearce, 1946. (Also available in Pocket Books edition.) An excellent practical guide to child rearing.

Gruenberg, Sidonie M. (ed.), *The Encyclopedia of Child Care and Guidance*, New York: Doubleday, 1954. The facts of child development and their practical implications, arranged by topics.

Bowlby, John, *Child Care and the Growth of Love*, London: Pelican, 1953. The effects and prevention of maternal deprivation.

Aldrich, C. A. and M. M., *Babies are Human Beings*, New York: Macmillan, 1938. One of the pioneer works on the "needs" orientation to child rearing.

Stone, L. J., "A critique of studies of infant isolation," *Child Development*, 1954, **25**, 9-20.

CHAPTER 4

The Infant: 2

Introduction

In the last chapter, we talked about what the infant does and what the world does to him. Except for passing references, we have not had a chance to consider how his experience appears to the baby. In this chapter, we shall begin by discussing how the infant perceives and experiences his world, and go on to a consideration of how different societies and different families shape the baby's experiences, and through them, the development of his personality. As compared to adults, babies are aware of different things organized in a different way. In the first section, we shall attempt to describe what sorts of things the baby is aware of and how he becomes aware of them. First, though, a word of caution about the term "aware." We cannot observe a baby's awareness at first hand, and he cannot tell us about it in words. We can only make inferences from the baby's language of behavior, reconstructing his awareness in crude analogies drawn from adult experience.

How the Infant Perceives His World

The baby's experience of reality is at first global and undifferentiated. It develops, just like embryonic structures and like motor skills, from the general and diffuse to the specific and precise, by a series of differentiations followed by reorganizations and functional subordinations.

Infant and Adult Views of Reality

We can perhaps best make clear the character of infantile experience by contrasting it with the more familiar adult forms. In early, global experience, almost everything is like the adult's perceptual *background,* of which he is almost unaware while he is concentrating on something;

out of this only the vaguest objects come and go and melt into each other. For the adult, this kind of experience—background without foreground—is all but unrecapturable except in dream-like states. Central in adult experience is the distinction between "me" and "rest-of-the-world." This distinction does not exist in early infancy: self and environment are one. For the adult, both the "me" and the "rest-of-the-world" have been still further differentiated. The me of the adult is both a body-me and a person-me which knows about "my" body. The things that happen in the body-me are recognized as "my" aches and pains and pleasures and appetites and needs. The things that happen in the person-me are "my" feelings and ideas and memories and plans. The rest-of-the-world is differentiated into people and not-people; into different kinds of people, into different kinds of things. There is a further differentiation in the adult's world between objects and their settings.

Moreover, when reality becomes differentiated, its newly distinguishable segments become related to each other in new integrations. The adult has a kind of many-dimensioned map or ground plan of the world he moves in, a sense that it exists even if he is not there. For the adult (but not at all for the infant) objects exist in an organized world in which he distinguishes (fairly well) reality and fantasy, as well as up and down and sideways, or past, present, and future. In addition, some objects exist in a social network with countless subtle relationships of blood, respect, duty, affection, envy, role, status, power, etc. Possibly most important for human experience, perceptual reality—and unreality —exists for the adult not only as a theater of action but as something to be talked about and thought about.

In earliest infantile experience, the world is only a diffuse field with objects coming and going but without a fixed framework. To begin with, events or objects come into the baby's awareness in terms of immediate threat or gratification to him. Soon after, there may be connections between things, but the connection is always personal, through the infant. Orange juice may signify that a bath will follow, but these are related as things that happen *to him* in close succession, and not as events in a world which includes his mother's schedule, too. Similarly, the kitchen where he gets his juice and the bathroom where he takes his bath may be tied together in terms of personal relevance, but there is no notion that they have geographical relationships as well. And here is the difficult part for most adults to grasp: although, for the infant, everything is related to "my" immediate needs, wants, and experiences, there is no *me*. There simply *is* Hunger, and Wetness, and Orange-Juice-Followed-by-Warm-

Immersion, all in a context of familiar person and place; but there is *no* "I am" hungry, or "I feel" wet, or "I taste" orange juice, and so forth. The baby's experience is *personal,* as we have said, because, after all, it is only his own hunger and wetness and pleasures that he has any knowledge of. But there is no me until a me (the *self*) has emerged as an entity from the total welter of experience. In effect, the whole world is wet and hungry, because "I" and "rest-of-the-world" are, as yet, one. This state of affairs, where all the child's universe is centered upon him, without his being aware of himself at the center, has been named *ego-centrism* by Piaget.[1] This term is rather misleading because it implies an *ego*—a self—but it is intended to indicate the infant's isolation within his own experience before he knows of a me or of a world with an existence apart from him. This term has occasioned a great deal of controversy, usually based on a misinterpretation of its meaning.

Perceptual Development

Now that we have seen some of the contrasts between infantile and adult perceptual experience, let us concentrate on the way the baby's experience develops. For the first few weeks of his life, the infant is enclosed within the immediacy of his own body (although, it is now clear, he does not recognize it as his own). His eyes and ears are in good working order—he may stare at things or seem to be listening—but the information they bring him is negligible. As we have said, his experiencing is like the adult's background-of-awareness except when there is a sharp, sudden increase in the intensity of light or sound, producing a startle response. In general, the newborn baby seems to be aware only of considerable disruptions of his equilibrium—hunger, pain, loud noise—that is, his first perceptions are identical with a feeling that something is dreadfully wrong. When he is in equilibrium—when his stomach is comfortably full and his digestion working smoothly, when he is warm and snugly wrapped and supported—his awareness seems to fade out, and he drifts into sleep. As both Bridges and Spitz have pointed out, events are either distressing or neutral.[2]

Beginning at the age of a few weeks, he seems to become aware of the process of gratification of his needs as well as of the needs themselves. His feelings and his perceptions, still intimately linked, are becoming differentiated by one further step: instead of the simple distinction between distress and neutrality that marked his experience as a newborn, he now knows distress, neutrality, and pleasure. At the same time, his awareness of threat (will hunger never end?) and gratification (how wonderful the warm flow in my mouth and insides) begins to expand, including now in an ill-formed way the recognition that it is Person (not *a* person, not *people*) who holds and feeds and fondles him. His awareness of pleasure seems still to be centered in his mouth and stomach, but is enhanced by the movements of rocking, by the things that touch his skin, and, after a couple of months, by the sight of the faces that hover over him, and the sound of voices that murmur reassuringly, and somehow includes all these experiences in the initial person-awareness.

What this says is that the baby *first perceives emotional significances.* At the beginning it is the meaning of threat and gratification, and not body states or external objects, that is perceived. Objectively, a cross and a circle should be easier to tell apart than two human faces, or than a smiling face and a frowning one; but long before the baby can differentiate a cross from a circle, he can tell his mother's face from all other women's faces, and his mother's smiling face from his mother's face wearing a frown, because these have emotional significance for him. It is important to see that *meanings* always precede *objects* in perception. We begin to mobilize our responses to objects before we become aware of the objects themselves, and the way we perceive an object is determined as much by our response (that is, what the object *means* to us) as by the object's stimulus properties. In the adult, perceptual processes are highly skilled and almost instantaneous—provided he is not dealing with wholly novel situations—but it can be demonstrated in the laboratory that even adults require a tiny interval of time for their perceptions to take shape from the meaning of an object to the object itself. For instance, adults distinguish the threatening quality of words that have previously been accompanied by an electric shock when these words are again flashed on a screen at speeds too fast to be seen as anything more than a blur.[3] It is as though the baby could not yet go beyond this first stage in adult perception, where only the emotional meanings appear.

The meaning of an object for the baby is defined first of all by what it can do to him; at about three or four months of age, when the baby can grasp and handle objects and bring them to his mouth, objects come to be defined by what he can do with them. In other words, at about the time people often say that the baby is "becoming human," there is a beginning shift from a passive to an active relationship with reality. But it is essential to note that throughout infancy only those objects, and only those aspects of objects, which have some behavioral meaning, some functional relevance, become differentiated for the baby. Infants usually do not discriminate the colors we adults consider vividly obvious. But if six-month-old babies are fed a pleasant-tasting formula from a red bottle and an unpleasant-tasting one from a blue bottle, they quickly learn to accept the red bottle and reject the blue one.[4] In other words, when previously undifferentiated aspects of reality are made functionally important, then they may be differentiated and perceived. That is, the baby perceives only what Werner calls *action-objects* rather than things in themselves.[5] We see the same tendency at work in the preschool child's definition, "a chair is to sit."

In the same way, as the baby becomes able to move around, he comes to inhabit an action-space—differentiated by his activities in it. A stairway is largely meaningless, and essentially nonexistent, to a six-month-old; but for a one-year-old a stairway has strongly appealing action qualities: it is something to be climbed. In other words, with the shift from a passive to an active orientation toward the world, emotional meanings emerge as more elaborate action-meanings, which become as variegated as the behavior of which the baby is capable. The baby is liberated from strictly biological concerns and becomes susceptible to "esthetic" (what does this toy feel like, and sound like, and taste like?) and "intellectual" (what can I do with it?) appeals: he becomes curious. Again we see that earlier psychological views of the independence of perception, of action, and of emotion must be questioned. Perception (the perceived world) grows out of emotions, as we have seen; it grows out of behavior, too.

Although the baby becomes active with regard to objects, he still has to rely on the objects to tell him what to do. What they tell him depends on three things: (1) their action possibilities (stairs are to climb); (2) the baby's general readiness for action of the kind suggested by the object (stairs aren't anything at all if I'm too young to climb them); and (3) his momentary state (stairs mean a lot more to me when I'm not hungry; they're not very attractive when I've been on them ten times in a row). But when an object does tell the baby to act, he cannot refuse. This means that he is highly distractible, and if he is exposed to excessive stimulation—too many new toys, too many new people, too much activity—he may be pulled in all directions at once and start to cry in confusion. Goldstein has given the name "stimulus-bound" to this inability to turn away from the solicitation of objects.[6]

It is worth noting that action-objects, although rich in vitality and meaning, are lacking in continuity and solidity. Up to the age of about four months, when an object breaks contact with the baby, it ceases to exist. If the rattle he is watching disappears behind his carriage top, he may stare for a moment at the point where it vanished and then forget about it. If the bottle from which he is being fed goes out of reach and sight, he will shriek with dismay. After four or five months of age, he will be tense with the expectation that the rattle or bottle will reappear, but he will not look for it. By about six months, he will begin to look to see where something has gone. By this time, certain objects have taken on some degree of permanence and reliability, notably his mother and his own body—although these may not be clearly differentiated from each other. He now counts on the bundle of warm sensations and visual patterns that other people see as his mother to continue existing even when she is absent. Although his mother may now exist for him as a stable identity, he still may not recognize her when she is dressed up to go to a party. He is becoming aware that those two tiny hands tugging at each other under his nose, carrying each other to his mouth, belong to the same intimate complex of feelings as the mouth that chews on them, the eyes that look at them, as the feet that rise up over the horizon of his belly and are quickly held captive by the ever-active fingers. A little later, at seven or eight months, perhaps, he is fascinated by the behavior of objects that he bangs together as though sampling their solidity, but he still cannot understand why *it hurts* (him) when he kicks the bars of his crib. It is at about this time that he seems to begin to know what he wants. His awareness of his own distress is becoming more differentiated, and he has a better idea of what behaviors of his and what objects are necessary for gratification. All in all, he is developing a rudimentary *frame of reference*—although still essentially a "self"-centered one. In terms of this frame of reference, he has expectations. For instance, when he is hungry and his mother carries him past the door of the room where he usually eats, he gives a sudden start, becomes tense, and may begin to cry or whimper.

Along with this increased permanence of objects and growing stability of organization of his world, there goes a shift toward the *dominance of visual perception*—a shift that may not reach completion before adulthood. This shift has two aspects. First, there is the shift from a focus on things with which the baby is in bodily contact—his own physiological states, the movements of his body, the nipple in his mouth, the things that touch his skin—to things perceived at a distance through sight and hearing. During the first six months, the *mouth* is the main channel of perception, with touch, manipulation, and vision playing subordinate roles. Thereafter, until the baby can move around freely, *touching* and *handling* seem to take the lead. Once the baby is fully mobile, overall *body movement* appears to be the central component of his experience. Vision is important in keeping the infant oriented to action-things and action-space, but the reality of things lies in what he can do with them rather than with what they look like. To be able really to *see* an object without touching it or manipulating it is an achievement of a high order.

The second aspect of the visual trend is the shift to a stage where movement is no longer necessary to visual perception. The newborn baby can only perceive things that change. Then, action objects can be perceived in terms of their potential movements. Space is first perceived only in terms of the baby's movements within it. Only much later, perhaps not until the school years, does space become a stable setting for fixed objects with properties and meanings that have little to do with their or the baby's action patterns.

It is important to see that the emergence of action qualities from feeling qualities, and of objective properties from action qualities, does not mean that these earlier components are lost. The meaning of an object always continues to comprise its action qualities and its emotional or esthetic connotations, although adults may be able to resist these or, by intent, exclude them from consideration.

At least during the first six months or so of life, and probably well into toddlerhood, all of the baby's experience is wrapped up in the *present moment*. He has no conception of past or future time. If he has expectations, it is of things that will happen in the present; the present situation points forward, but only as far as the next step, with no intervening ones. Out of this "present future," of course, will emerge the real future of which the toddler starts to be aware. The infant, however, does not remember that the sun set yesterday or anticipate that it will set again today. This does not mean that he does not learn. His past experiences teach him what objects are like, what they can do to him and he to them, but this learning is embedded in the way things exist for him in the new *now*—he also has a "present past"—but he cannot recall the lessons that taught him what he knows. His closest approach to remembering comes, we may speculate, when he is sleeping or near sleep and the attitudes and sensations of past events rise unbidden to awareness; but these are felt as real present experiences and not as recollections. We shall see later how the preschool child attributes to his dreams the same substantial reality as waking events. But although the baby may not see the resemblance between today's sunset and yesterday's, he is not surprised when it occurs, and is able to recognize it as a signal for bedtime; or at a given moment, thanks to internal and external cues, he knows that it is now time to eat.

For the sake of simplicity, we have been talking as though the development of the baby's experience of reality depended solely on his random encounters with the environment. Needless to say, the baby does not meet life alone. Throughout infancy, his feelings are closely tied to the emotional reactions of his parents, which have an immediacy and an impact far transcending the reality of virtually any other experiences, both because of their primacy and because of their importance for him. His experience of himself and of objects, as we have seen, is initially altogether ambiguous, and is shaped to a large extent by what his parents communicate to him about it. The objects he becomes aware of, and how he becomes aware of them, are determined not merely by the action characteristics of the objects and his own readiness to react to them, but also by his parents' reaction or lack of reaction. In addition, of course, the objects the baby does and *does not* meet up with are selected by his parents. Thus, many objects come to be colored with moral and emotional values that for the baby would not have been conveyed by their action qualities. According to signals from the parents, things are exciting, disgusting, mysterious, alarming, pleasant, and so forth. Sometimes, when a baby has been bumped on the head, he does not even know that his head hurts—until he sees and hears and feels his parents' worry. He may be inclined to laugh at his sneezes and hiccups—unless they provoke parental concern. Tension in his mother's manner, a note of anger in her voice, a sudden jerk of the arm in which she holds him, or even strangely loud and prolonged laughter, will set him crying; a word or gesture of affection and reassurance can sometimes transform his discomfort into pleasure.

The Baby's Cultural Heritage

In Chapter 1, we described organism-environment relationships in prenatal development. In Chapter 2, it was pointed out that as the individual's functioning as a person becomes more prominent we would speak of his significant surroundings in terms of his *world*. In Chapter 3, we saw how his parents' handling of the baby influenced his world and made it one that could or could not be trusted. Now we propose to discuss some systematic variations in the possible worlds a child may meet in terms of the diverse patterns of human existence—the *cultures*

—into which he may be born, and whose meaning for him can be understood in the light of what we have said about development in infancy and, in the last section, about the way the infant perceives the world.

It is because of the baby's susceptibility to his parents' feelings, and the fact that these shape and color his perception of reality, that he begins to learn the lessons of his culture long before he has any notion there is such a thing. It is often hard for us to realize that the obvious reality of our experience takes the particular form it does because other people have shaped our perceptions according to a cultural pattern, but even the most intimate and strongest of our feelings are not immune to cultural molding. Even so clearly pleasant an experience as sex can take on a disagreeable quality as a result of our learning—such learning as may be incidental, for example, to overly strict toilet-training. In the same way, such clearly unpleasant experiences as pain can be neutralized or made valuable by what people tell us, explicitly or implicitly, about them.

The child's learning about whether or not he can trustfully count on the world goes hand in hand with learning that there *is* a world, of which he is a part but a separate one. The particular world he learns about, of course, is the one his society defines for him. Just as the child receives a particular anatomical legacy from his forebears, so he receives a specific cultural legacy—out of all the available human possibilities— that tells him what his world is like and what he should do about it. We shall begin our discussion by pointing to the nearly universal ways of humankind, then to those ways shared by large groups or societies of men, then to the more restricted special versions shared by the members of sub-groups, and finally to the particular family and individual specifications of the cultural heritage. A *culture,* then, is a coherent and all-inclusive view of human nature and physical reality, embodied in the explicit beliefs, the implicit assumptions, and the ways and doings of its members.

There are many different human cultures with strikingly divergent sets of beliefs and practices, but they all express a peculiarly human mode of existence of such universality that we cannot be sure whether it is a biological or a learned phenomenon. Perhaps the most essential of the universal ingredients of culture is *language.* As Clarence Day has said, the human world is also a simian world—we live on chatter. But for human beings, chatter becomes languages with elaborate vocabularies of thousands of words. Perhaps because of the way they are built, with the kinds of brains and spines and hands which they have, all human beings use *tools* of some complexity, whether hammers and chisels and plows, or telephones and automobiles. Perhaps because of the much longer time it takes human beings, as compared to other species, to grow to biological maturity, all humans have a highly developed *family life* and a long tutelage in the culture. All human beings share *certain basic emotions,* although the given culture may dictate how these are expressed and toward whom directed. Some of these, it will be noted, are extensions of emotions found in the lower mammals; indeed, the very fact of mammalian child rearing implies certain ways of being related to reality which would be incomprehensible to a fish or a bird or an insect. All human beings share the *basic needs* for emotional nourishment which we spoke of in an earlier section, and every culture provides ways of meeting them; needs become canalized in particular patterns of gratification. Every society, too, has been driven to question its environment and evolve a *conception of reality* with its supporting *mythology,* which in turn implies *codes of morals, ethics,* and *practical skills* (whether ritual or functional). Cultural anthropology has shown us that a culture is a coherent, integrated system of views and customs, rather than the miscellaneous collection of quaint practices which the travelogue recounts. Usually, each culture has a language of its own, unifying its members and shutting them off from other cultures. Until recently, anthropologists were concerned for the most part with primitive (but contemporary) societies, those which have not developed reading and writing, but in recent years they have increasingly applied their methods of analysis to complex, literate societies as well.

A child does not learn about his culture only from what people explicitly tell him. Much of culture is *imparted implicitly,* almost accidentally, in manner and touch and tone of voice, and is *learned incidentally.* Indeed, a great part of any culture exists only implicitly, in the things its members unquestioningly take for granted, the "of courses." It is this fact which makes it so difficult for us to see our culture at a distance rather than from the inside; with respect to the culture, we are often in the same position as the baby with respect to his own body: insofar as it is a means of knowing, it is not something to be known. As Werner says, one cannot, from within, see his own eyes.[7] From the standpoint of our own culture, *of course* dessert comes at the end of the meal, of course the baby is wheeled about in a carriage (not carried on his mother's back), of course the baby uses a toilet (and is not allowed to drop his feces for the pigs and dogs to eat), of course one brushes one's teeth after meals, of course it is cruel to beat animals. But from the perspective of other cultures, *of course* you cannot consider yourself a grown-up young lady until your teeth have been filed to a point or your back has been tattooed, of course you cannot be a man until you have fasted in the wilderness and talked to the spirits, of course it is admirable to stand on one foot for twenty-four years as a mark of spiritual purity, of course the calendar is arranged according to the scents of the trees that bloom at various times of the year, of course a week is four days long, of course beetles are a great delicacy, of course your mother's brother wields authority in your home, of course pregnancy comes about because you have walked where the gods of fertility dwell, of course the mother chews the baby's food and spits it into his mouth.

Different cultures provide different kinds of opportunities and make different kinds of demands. In Russia, for instance, the child may spend his first few months bound stiffly in swaddling clothes; he may go on to a communal day nursery while both his parents are at work; his formal schooling will be an odd mixture of straightforward education and Soviet indoctrination; also, he may have to adjust to two conflicting value systems, that of the formal state doctrines, and that of the Russian Orthodox Church. In the Hopi Indian culture of the American Southwest, the child will likewise be swaddled; he will be weaned and toilet-trained much later than in the neighboring American society, and he must begin early to learn the ways of the evil spirits who play so large a part in his life. An infant in Alor, in the Dutch East Indies, will at an early age be abandoned to his own devices or to the casual attention of siblings or neighbors, while his mother goes to work in the fields and his father haggles over endless financial transactions; the Alorese baby will quickly learn about hunger, and much of his later life will be centered around perpetual discomfort in his mouth and belly. In Japan, the infant comes into an atmosphere where behavior is closely regulated in terms of self-control, honor, duty, and station. Each of these cultures, as well as our own, will present the child with its unique, ready-made version of reality. Each will give him more or less opportunity to think and act creatively in relationship to his surroundings.

Our American culture, to be sure, is not a single, uniform set of beliefs about reality. It includes a number of different versions, or *sub-cultures,* each with certain concepts of its own. Sub-cultures are formed by the clustering together of a group of people who separate themselves, or are separated by external pressures, from other groups. Examples are the tendency of each recent immigrant group to set up enclaves—Chinatown, Little Italy, etc.—based on similarity of language and custom and, in some cases, on rejection by older, established groups. Mountain communities without modern roads and communications likewise cling to and elaborate their own ways while the surrounding culture changes. In general, American culture seems to be moving rapidly toward a blending of sub-cultures, thanks to high geographic and economic mobility, virtual disappearance of isolated areas, decline in immigration, mass production and distribution of food and other goods, and uniformities of experience propagated by television, radio, magazines, and syndicated newspapers. Nevertheless, we can still recognize that the southern version of American culture is not exactly the same as the northern. Rural America has still in many respects a sub-culture different from that of the urban and suburban regions. Many racial, religious, and ethnic minorities have perceptibly different ways of behaving and of viewing the world. Slums breed a kind of culture different from that of middle-class neighborhoods. Rural slums have cultures different from those of urban slums.

A complex culture such as ours not only has simultaneous variations but exhibits historical shifts which we may regard as sub-cultural variants. The more primitive societies, of course, are relatively fixed in their patterns of activity, even though their isolation has now begun to break down. In Western societies, on the other hand, distant events ramify down to the least citizen. It makes an important difference to an American child whether he is born into a world at war or at peace, in the giddy throes of an economic boom or locked in a depression. Not only day-to-day events make a difference, however. The whole complexion of our society has changed in the course of historical evolution. It meant something different, emotionally and practically, to be a child in colonial times, when Puritan precepts prevailed and much of life was a struggle against the rigors of the environment, than it does to be a child of today. One has only to consider the transformation in our attitudes and behavior brought about by the change from an agricultural to an industrial economy, by the shift from rural to urban and suburban living, by widespread ownership of automobiles, by the great depression, by World War II, by myriad advances in technology and medicine, by the arrival of the atomic age.

Within any culture (or sub-culture), individuals play different *roles* determined by their social position along a variety of dimensions. Some of the important dimensions in our own society are income, neighborhood, occupation, prestige, religious affiliation, and so forth. Moreover, each family has its own values, traditions, and history, and provides its own special flavoring of experience. What the child learns is not his whole culture plus a sub-culture, plus a role to play within it, plus a family tradition, but simply his own family's ways which are compounded of all these. More than this, he learns his own special adaptation of these determined by whether he is born at an opportune or inopportune time, is of the desired sex, is first-born or ninth-born, etc. And, of course, the interplay of his own temperament and characteristics with this general and specific array of social and environmental pressures makes for a unique version of the culture he learns. According to the kind of family he is born into, not only in terms of its formal position in the scheme of things but in the concrete terms of its living quarters, its diet, its dress, its patterns of recreation, the intonations of its speech, he will learn a particular view of himself and reality. For in the final analysis, each family can be regarded as a special version of a sub-culture. The cultural values of any given pair of parents (the generally accepted ones of their society, with their special, say, eastern, Protestant, Jones flavor) will be reflected in the emotional climate which structures their baby's awareness of reality. This awareness does not take final form for a number of years, but its emotional groundwork is established during infancy, so subtly and so firmly that it appears to have been there all along, as though this special way of viewing the world were the only conceivable one.

Even more specific than the family's special version of the surrounding culture is the special meaning that a baby—and this particular baby—may have. These specific attitudes are also a part of the heritage which the child must assimilate in the course of development. Some of these attitudes rest on expectations which the child satisfies or disappoints, at birth or at later phases. Obviously, the very fact of being disappointing or satisfying, on whatever grounds, is highly significant in his relationships.

People want children for a variety of reasons. Chief among these is likely to be the pleasure of having a child who will share their triumphs and tribulations, who will be a person of their own creation whom they can love and cherish and watch grow into a life which he will eventually create for himself. Often, of course, people do not stop to think out why they want children, and having them is as natural a part of marriage as the wedding ceremony. Sometimes secondary, accessory motives enter the picture. Less often now than formerly, children are wanted to carry on the family name and fortune. But less obviously, a child may be a means of projecting into the future the realization of one's own frustrated ambitions, or of filling what seems to be a vacancy in one's life but may actually be a vacancy in oneself. Whatever the destined role of the child, unless it is very rigidly defined, his actual coming may demolish all his parents' preconceptions. An honest-to-goodness child on the premises, once they get the hang of how he operates, can often arouse in his parents a fund of tenderness and protectiveness and delight beyond anything they ever dreamed of knowing. However, if the parents' motives are centered primarily about what the child can do for them, rather than about what they and the child can do for each other, his presence is liable to create new problems rather than solve old ones.

Parents sometimes count rather heavily on having a child of one sex rather than the other, although on occasion they may not even realize their bias. This can be carried to the point where they only have one name ready. Or they may betray their implicit expectations by falling into the habit of referring to the unborn baby exclusively as "he" or "she." If a child of the wrong sex arrives, they may have trouble adjusting to reality, and treat the child in ways inappropriate to its future sex role. In other cases, parents automatically expect a second child to be just like the first, and are chagrined to find him manifesting highly individual forms of behavior.

Life for the baby is one thing if he is the first child of a young couple enthusiastic about building a family; another if he is the third or fourth child, whom his parents can take in stride; yet another if he is the unwanted child of parents who are torn by strife or trapped in poverty or illness; yet another if he is the bearer of a proud name, or has blue eyes exactly like grandfather's, or is the final symbol of Americanization for a family of recent immigrants.

Depending on family variations, some children have to learn their manners early, some are valued for their personalities and others as props for the parents' declining years, some are initiated from the outset into a pattern of religious observances, some are pressed to command and others to compete, or to co-operate or obey or passively accept. Some children are just another mouth to feed and another body to clothe. Children may come to see the world as looming and ominous, or fast-moving and bewildering, or lively and exciting, or tranquil and soothing, or dull and deadening. These are some of the prospects children face, in terms of family attitudes, even before they have seen the light of day. The essential point here is that parents have notions, sometimes explicit and often implicit, about what kind of child they want to have and how he will fit into their scheme of life. The more rigid and unrealistic such notions are, and the less aware the parents are of their preconceptions, the more likely parent-child conflict becomes. In some cultures—the ancient Greek and the Eskimo, for instance—socially approved channels have been established for doing away with children who fail to meet parental expectations in terms of sex, health, beauty, etc. Ordinarily, however, parents in our society are obliged to live with the children they beget, and, to live with them successfully, as we suggested in Chapter 3, parents must learn the fine art of flexibility.

Nowadays, with our rising birth rate, there are very likely to be older *siblings* (brothers and sisters) at home waiting for the new baby. Depending on their age, their relationship with their parents, and how the prospect of a new arrival has been presented to them—some parents feel it unnecessary to give any advance notice to the older sibs—they may be more or less resentful of the newcomer. In the currently standard psychological cliché, the second child is seen as dethroning the first, but this obviously need not be the case. Most often, the older children feel *ambivalent* toward a new arrival; that is, they both welcome and resent him at the same time. Ambivalence is sometimes seen when an older child begins to pet his younger sibling, his caresses becoming more vigorous until they are indistinguishable from blows. The new child, however, often finds it an advantage to have older siblings. For one thing, the first child "breaks trail"—that is, the parents learn about children the hard way, by practicing on their first-born. Hence, and because family situations change with time, different children in the same family have different environments as well as different heredities. Subsequent children are handled more casually, since parents by now can avoid repeating their mistakes and, besides, realize that they don't have to intervene at every juncture in the child's development—he can do and learn a surprising lot (sometimes things the parents could do without) by himself. At a later age, older children help initiate younger ones into the ways of childhood, acting as preceptors and models. It goes without saying that a child relies chiefly on his parents for values to grow up to, but supplementary models—siblings, uncles and aunts, corner grocerymen, policemen, door-to-door salesmen—all play their part.

The baby may live in an extended family which includes grandparents and aunts and uncles. Members of the extended family may sometimes be sources of indulgence and petting, or refuges when things get too hot in the immediate family. Or perhaps they will be sources of advice and counsel and financial aid, welcome and unwelcome, to the parents. They may live in the same house, or just down the street, or in another part of town, or a continent away. They may have a strong sense of family unity, or continuity, or reciprocal obligation, or they may function in a way similar to that of good friends.

An Example of Cultural Shaping

We cannot hope to do justice in this section to the whole intricate process of acculturation during infancy. Instead, we shall concentrate on one aspect of the total, both for its own significance and for its value as an example: the ways in which children are made aware of sex differences. (Later in the book, we shall return to this theme in its subsequent development.) In effect, parents begin immediately upon birth to tell a baby, "You are a boy," or, "You are a girl." Learning what it means to be a male or a female is one of the most vital lessons of childhood, and can serve as a model for all cultural learning. Clearly, sex differences are not strictly a matter of anatomy and physiology. Masculinity and femininity are each supposed to carry with them a whole cluster of traits, attitudes, values, and capabilities by which the sexes can presumably be distinguished. But, subject to wide biological limits, the characteristics of each sex are variously defined by various cultures, just as are religious beliefs, beliefs in particular forms of government, or language forms. There are common threads running through the definitions of masculinity or femininity in all cultures, but much that we take for granted as biologically determined turns out to be simply what our own culture tells us the biological differences mean. In our own relatively recent history, as we can see in eighteenth-century paintings, men had long, braided hair and wore ribbons and bows and long silk stockings. It is only in the last two generations that women have been judged competent to vote, to hold office, to own property, and to make legally binding contracts. In some cultures, men are thought to be too flighty and tender-minded to be entrusted with practical affairs. In some cultures, it is always the woman who takes the sexual initiative. Americans are shocked to see photographs of Russian women doing heavy manual labor; the Russians see nothing odd in this, since it apparently does no violence to their definition of sex roles.

In spite of these variations among cultures, within each culture the standards of maleness and femaleness are relatively fixed. Even our culture, which includes more variety than most, prescribes to a considerable extent how boys and girls are expected to behave. Boys are expected to be active, aggressive, rough, unkempt, interested in sports and adventure; they are expected to be manly, that is, essentially stoical. Girls, on the other hand, are expected to be quiet, ladylike, docile, considerate, interested in dolls and miniature versions of domesticity; they are thought to be more sensitive than boys, and their tears are taken for granted.

How, then, are these concepts of masculinity (or femininity) transmitted to an infant who doesn't even know yet that he exists, let alone that he has a body which places him forever in the category of male (or female)? To begin with, these are not concepts that the baby learns, but dispositions, attitudes, feelings. Parents treat a boy differently from a girl because they, the parents, have learned from their culture a set of expectations, of inclinations to respond in certain ways to boys and to girls. Thus, without thinking, they convey their attitudes through their feelings, through the things they do, through the sorts of objects with which they surround the baby and toward which they direct his attention and feelings. In short, they create for the baby a world which tells him—even, as we have seen, in the case of autogenous behavior—what his capacities for action and feeling are.

More specifically, boys get blue things, girls get pink. Friends and relatives give the boy tiny trousers to grow up to, and the girl frilly dresses. Boys get masculine playthings, girls feminine ones. This differentiation is less marked in early infancy, but it exists, and it becomes more pronounced when babies get to the manipulative stage. These tangibles, as we have said, go hand in hand with deep-seated parental attitudes toward boys and girls. It is noteworthy that the parents' first, key question about a new baby is always, "Boy or girl?" When they know the answer, and not before, there is language available to talk about the baby: up to now, it has been an ambiguity, an *it*. As soon as the parents have had this question answered, one or the other of their two waiting sets of expectations is released and begins to fall into place. As we have seen, these expectations immediately shape the parents' manner toward the baby. Boys can be handled boisterously; with girls, one tends to be gentle. One takes pleasure in the delicate contour of a daughter's mouth; in a son one finds delight in how lusty and husky he is. Some mothers have even reported that they find it somehow less disagreeable to change their daughters' soiled diapers than their sons'! It should not be necessary to labor further the point that boys and girls grow up in different emotional atmospheres from an early age. They are reacted to not only in terms of their individual characteristics but also in terms of the values the parents' culture attaches to boy-ness and girl-ness. All the far-reaching implications for feeling and behavior that go with being a part of a man's world or a woman's world will require years of elaboration, but it is as a baby that one receives his first taste of sex differences. Perhaps the strength of parental attitudes toward the sex of their child can be seen in these lines from Ogden Nash's "Song to Be Sung by the Father of Infant Female Children":

> My heart leaps up when I behold
> A rainbow in the sky;
> Contrariwise, my blood runs cold
> When little boys go by.
> For little boys as little boys,
> No special hate I carry,
> But now and then they grow to men,
> And when they do, they marry.
> No matter how they tarry,
> Eventually they marry.
> And, swine among the pearls,
> They marry little girls.*[8]

Implications of Cultural Shaping

The question often arises of what people would be like if we stripped away the veneer of culture and allowed them to exist in a "natural state." Some writers, dating from Rousseau and the romantic naturalists, with their concept of the happy savage, and perhaps currently including Gesell and Montagu,[9] tend to view culture as a system of social restraints upon the smoothly flowering process of development. At the extreme, this anti-cultural viewpoint seems to say that one should just let the child grow, on the assumption that there is a kind of natural mold which is warped and deformed by the artificial demands of society. Another school, while accepting the idea of a natural mold, sees the newborn child not as trailing clouds of glory but as steeped in sin, so that without the restraints of culture people would grow up to depravity. Among the writers of this persuasion would be included such disparate figures as Calvin and, at least implicitly, Freud. Neither of these views seems to fit the facts. It appears, rather, that there can be no human nature without culture. Far from living in a state of nature,

* Copyright, 1933, by Ogden Nash.

the most primitive peoples we know of have highly elaborated cultures, even though these are vastly different from our own and each other's. Man is less well equipped than the lower animals with instinctual mechanisms for behavior and survival—digging wasps, for instance, never see their mother, who dies after laying her eggs, but reproduce the characteristic behavior of their species without ever having had a chance to learn it. Even apart from biological survival, psychological development depends, as Spitz and Salimbene both have said, on mother-child contacts. Given these contacts between sensitive human beings, extending over a long human childhood, it would be impossible to avoid transmitting a culture. As long as a mother is reacting to a child—whom she inevitably perceives in a way partly dictated by her cultural framework—they are linked in a system of interpersonal exchange and she is imparting to him information about himself, herself, and the world in general.

For many people, it is an uncomfortable notion that their reality would be otherwise if they had grown up in a different cultural setting. But there seems little doubt that the world remains largely latent and ambiguous until the "culture-bearers"—parents, siblings, teachers, etc. —bring it into focus for us. However, the mere fact that we now, in our society, can begin to recognize our debt to our culture, instead of taking its teachings for granted, gives us a peculiar advantage. Unlike many primitive cultures, our own fosters an autonomy of thought which permits us to make up individual variations on the central cultural theme, to question reality and approach it in new ways, and even, to a limited extent, to stand off from our own culture and treat it as one more aspect of reality, to be shaped at will like any other plastic material.

A modern view of development asks of parents and teachers that they exercise this opportunity to form their own personal views of reality. If they do, a greater part of their cultural transmission can be conscious and deliberate rather than unformulated and accidental. In this way, culture can be remade to an emerging human ideal instead of remaining in the stage of blind assumptions: we can, in effect, lift the world by our babies' bootstraps. There are, however, certain impediments to cultural change. We can only attain a partial perspective on our own culture, as we said earlier, and it is only at a distance that we can become aware of our assumptions and question them. As a simple instance of the things we take for granted, most Americans think of knitting as a feminine occupation. It is only when we see photographs of indisputably masculine R.A.F. pilots knitting while they await orders for a bombing mission that we become aware of the arbitrariness of our assumptions about men who knit. Yet we do not therefore immediately drop our assumptions. For a second difficulty arises in the feeling that once we have called the obvious into question, we have nothing left. (Not to mention that it is so deeply embedded in us that we are not even aware of all its roots, and it is not easily dug out.) If a mother has always "known" that children should be spanked, and she is told not to spank, what *does* she do? Without a few external verities to cling to, without new goals to substitute for discarded ones, life is in danger of becoming meaningless. We must be sure, in the instance cited, whether we are talking about the simple act of spanking or about the fundamental view of behavior that lies behind it. Perhaps it is fortunate that we are too deeply immersed in our own culture to do a great deal about it all at once. Especially when it comes to transmitting value changes to children, we have to move slowly. Children cannot tolerate ambiguities and relativisms as well as adults do, and it is advisable for adults to be ready with clear-cut, even though tentative, answers. It is usually better for parents to act in error but with certainty, maintaining contact with the child, than to lose themselves in indecision or in the index of Somebody's "Authoritative Book of Child Rearing." However, since our culture includes so many different sub-cultures, and makes available information about other cultures, people growing up in it almost inevitably encounter conflicting ideologies and have a chance to try on new points of view, just to see how they feel. Under these circumstances, some of the most deeply ingrained lessons about reality may yet be altered in the course of growth.

While we have been talking, our infant has pulled himself to his feet and toddled into a new stage of development, where we must make haste to follow him—at this age, he is moving very fast.

NOTES (Starred items are recommended as further readings.)

*[1] See, for instance, Piaget, Jean, *The Construction of Reality in the Child*, New York: Basic Books, 1954, p. 352. One of the most careful studies of the development of perception in infancy.

[2] Bridges, "Emotional development in early infancy"; Spitz, René A., "Diacritic and coenesthetic organizations," the *Psychoanalytic Review*, 1945, 32, 146-162.

[3] See, for instance, Lazarus, R. S., and McCleary, R. A., "Autonomic discrimination without awareness: A study of subception," *Psychological Review,* 1951, 58, 113-122. Some of the theoretical implications of "subception" are brought out sharply in Werner, Heinz, "Microgenesis and aphasia," *Journal of Abnormal and Social Psychology,* 1956, 52, 347-353.

[4] Werner, *Comparative Psychology of Mental Development,* p. 100.

[5] Werner, *op. cit.,* p. 173 and passim.

[6] Goldstein, Kurt, and Scheerer, Martin, "Abstract and concrete behavior," *Psychological Monographs,* 1941, 53, No. 2, p. 3 and passim.

[7] Personal communication.

[8] From *Many Long Years Ago,* by Ogden Nash, by permission of Little, Brown & Co.

[9] Gesell, Arnold, and Ilg, F. L., *Infant and Child in the Culture of Today,* New York: Harper, 1943; Montagu, *The Direction of Human Development.*

FOR FURTHER READING

Balint, Alice, *The Early Years of Life,* New York: Basic Books, 1955. A psychoanalytic account of the infant's subjective experience.

Mead, Margaret, and Wolfenstein, Martha, *Childhood in Contemporary Cultures,* Chicago: University of Chicago Press, 1955. Techniques, with many examples from sophisticated and primitive societies, of cultural research and interpretation.

Soddy, Kenneth (ed.), *Mental Health and Infant Development,* 2 vols., New York: Basic Books, 1956. Descriptions of child development patterns in the United States, France, and Great Britain; the case histories in Volume Two are especially valuable as source material.

Lewis, Claudia, *Children of the Cumberland,* New York: Columbia University Press, 1946. A sensitive depiction of childhood in an isolated mountain region in Tennessee.

Davis, W. A., and Havighurst, R. J., "Social class and color differences in child rearing," *American Sociological Review,* 1946, 11, 698-710 (reprinted in Kuhlen, R. G., and Thompson, G. G., *Psychological Studies of Human Development,* New York: Appleton-Century-Crofts, 1952, pp. 130-137). An examination of some sub-cultural variations in parental practice; a number of the findings no longer hold good (see Maccoby, et al., below), thanks at least in part to changes in our social structure.

Maccoby, E. E., Gibbs, P. K., et al., "Methods of child rearing in two social classes," in Martin and Stendler, *Readings in Child Development,* pp. 380-396. *Cf.* Davis and Havighurst, above.

Mead, Margaret, *Male and Female,* New York: Morrow, 1949. The cultural patterning of sex roles in Western and primitive societies.

Spiro, M. E., "Culture and personality: The natural history of a false dichotomy," *Psychiatry,* 1951, 14, 19-46 (reprinted in Martin and Stendler, *Readings in Child Development,* pp. 117-141). The embeddedness of culture in the individual.

CHAPTER 5

The Toddler

Introduction

Between the ages of fifteen or sixteen months and about two and a half years, the child is a toddler. Although many writers consider the period of infancy as extending well into the second half of the second year, when, for them, the preschool period begins, the authors are among those who believe that toddlerhood is as clearly marked a phase of development as the ones that precede and follow it. Some writers, particularly the English, speak of the toddler as the "runabout baby."

At the outset of this period, while the child may already have been walking for several months, he has probably done so uncertainly, with elbows close and hands held high—he was so involved with balance that his hands could not be used for any other purpose while he walked; when in a real hurry to get some place, he was very likely to revert to the speed and security of travel on all fours. But now he is truly up and away—exuberantly, or doggedly, or timidly, according to his temperament—his feet wide apart but pumping steadily. His legs are still short for his body in comparison with adult proportions, giving him a bottom-heavy look. This is often further enhanced by bulky diapers that will soon give way to the training pants more appropriate to his new estate. In appearance, the toddler is still a baby, although now a walking baby, and it is startling to realize that during this period he will attain half his adult height. Nevertheless, he is still low to the ground, and he sees most of the adult-scale world in terms of the undersides of things. In much of what he does, too, the toddler is still a baby: every new object is seized, inspected, waved aloft as though to sample its heft and the sound it makes, and often stuffed as far as it will go into his mouth; he may be content to sit on the floor for quite some time—for him—banging and tinkering with pots and pans and utensils while his mother goes about her work. He is still a baby, too, in being, usually, far more motor than verbal in his transactions.

In other important respects, however, the toddler is moving rapidly away from babyhood and into childhood. The central theme of development during toddlerhood, as Erikson has pointed out, is *autonomy:* becoming aware of oneself as a person among other people, and wanting to do things for oneself.[1] The toddler demonstrates his beginning autonomy—and his drive for more of it—in every field: in the mastery of his own body (in walking, climbing, jumping, and in controlling his sphincters); in the mastery of objects (the toddler typically wants to push his stroller instead of riding in it, he wants to carry outsized things from place to place and back again, he wants to put on and remove his own clothes—although he is not very adept at doing so); in social relationships (he learns language, he begins to refuse parental commands and requests and offers of help).

The toddler's push toward autonomy is by no means absolute and continuous, however. During toddlerhood, we first see the child vacillating between dependence and independence, a pattern that will persist in various guises well into adolescence. The toddler, out on a walk, may plunge off in pursuit of a pigeon, or go scuttling into a particularly alluring hallway, only to stop short and throw himself into his mother's arms. He may strike out on his own to explore the wonders of the supermarket, then burst into tears when he realizes the hand he is reaching for belongs to a stranger. When trying some new feat such as jumping from a step, he will make a great show of boldness but still cling tightly to an adult hand. In other words, he is only beginning to try himself out, and it will be some time before he can shift his emotional base from parents to contemporaries and, finally, have a secure anchorage in a sense of his own identity.

Motor Behavior in Toddlerhood

Toddlerhood reaches a climax at age two. The characteristic style of action in this period has been beautifully captured by Louise Woodcock in terms which are scarcely to be surpassed in aptness or perceptiveness. We therefore seize the opportunity to quote at length from her *Life and Ways of the Two-Year-Old.*[2] (The reader should note, however, that the year from two to three only partly overlaps with our toddler period.)

His impulses are to move and explore; to react to experience that he meets by some direct, overt behavior; to affect his environment by such changes as he can bring about in it. His attention span is short, his threshold of distractibility is low. His inhibitory apparatus is only slightly developed; he readily takes impulse to action from sights and sounds around him. His tempo is normally slow, and time as a measure means nothing to him. His information is scanty and unorganized. His language is unelaborated and often inadequate to his earnest efforts at communication. He is immature in social awareness and his techniques are primitive to an extreme. . . .

He has attained control of an upright posture and habitually he walks, trots, or runs from place to place instead of creeping or bear-walking, though these he resorts to playfully at will. His balance is still uncertain; turning around still tends to be a studied motion, a rocking from foot to foot as he revolves, more precarious than the quick spinning round of the three-year-old.

His gait, though no longer the baby stagger of his first walking days, is short-stepped and constrained compared with the free-flowing stride he will use at three. His lack of freedom at both ankle and knee leads to his up-and-down tread, in contrast with the long, forward-swinging step of his elders. When he breaks into a run, his arms fly up and wave jerkily as he goes. Similarly they play an active part in his steppings-up and steppings-down.[3]

In this description, the toddler sounds rather clumsy, and so he often is. However, a good deal of his ungainliness is imposed by the bulk of diapers and snowsuits, by the interference of shoes and overshoes. The barefoot toddler, like Tuesday's child, is full of grace. His toes are likely to be spread as he runs—and he is likely to run, and to run trippingly on his toes, far more than he is to walk or to use a sedate heel-and-toe movement. The toddler, rather than the infant, is the model for the cherubim and Cupids of Renaissance paintings.

. . . When he first rides a [kiddy-] kar, he pulls forward or pushes backward with both feet at once before he adopts the pattern of alternating steps of the more mature rider. When he sits on a box and kicks his heels (a favorite pastime of his kind) he swings both legs simultaneously while his three-year-old comrades vary their pattern at will with alternating thumps of one heel, then the other.[4]

The reader should take note of this process of differentiation in the sphere of motor development. The toddler's symmetry of action can also be seen in his need to use two hands for most operations, as when he carries objects. He is not likely to escape from this undifferentiated use of the two sides of his body before entering the preschool period.

He shows a similar dependence of one limb upon the other of the pair when he stretches out both hands toward an object he wants, whose size and weight require no more than one hand to grasp; when he jerks the empty hand as vigorously as the one that shakes the rattle; when the injured finger that he thrusts out for bandaging has a counterpart in the extended corresponding finger of the other hand; when he beats in the air with both arms or pounds with both hands on the table; when he carries around with him two like objects, one in each hand. . . .

Not only in the use of his hands but in many situations during the day he shows his two-year-oldness. He bends up his knee when his teacher tries to stiffen it to press a shoe into place; he steps about un-noticing on her feet when she is trying to button him and walks off unfinished when the impulse takes him; he opens his mouth overwide to insert his spoon; he is inspired to lick out with his tongue at the wash-cloth or another child's person or whatever else passes close to his mouth.[5]

Perhaps one further instance of the toddler's movements through space should be added here. Nothing conveys more vividly his whole-souled —and whole-bodied—but clumsy and roundabout style than his way with a chair. Not a large, grown-up chair that he must clamber into, but a suitable, toddler-sized chair or stool. Despite its small dimensions, the toddler does not sit in it lightly or readily. His approach makes it perfectly clear that our casual and confident plumping down on a seat is a highly practiced skill. For the toddler, the undifferentiated space behind him offers a real challenge. Some toddlers devise elaborate ways of aiming themselves into chairs, edging backwards or sideways, or bending double and sighting between their legs. More usually, the toddler climbs onto the chair almost as if it were a large one, kneels or sprawls on the seat, and twists himself around until, at last facing in the right direction, he gets his feet down and is triumphantly seated. He is still, of course, a frequent lap-sitter, but he is not likely to climb into an adult lap. Rather, he offers himself to be drawn onto the adult's knees. Once he is up there, unless he is tired or out of sorts and reverts to sheer cuddling, he is likely to be a very active occupant: he seeks and delights in jiggling and bouncing and dipping backwards while his hands are firmly held. Although the adult does most of the work, the activity is induced by the toddler.

Play in Toddlerhood

Much of the toddler's pattern of play follows from his style of move-ment and consists of an exploration and exploitation of his capacities for action. He does things less with any intention of objective accomplishment than to see how they feel. It is fascinating—if tiring—to follow him on the playground, if he should be one of the early entrants into nursery school or if his mother takes him to the park. Observations of such children in our own nursery school and others show that the toddler loves the spring of a jumping-board under his feet, the swooping movement of a swing, the tug and jounce of riding in a wagon, the unwieldy weight of big objects that he can lift and push and haul. Notice that he likes to use his big muscles, if not his whole body. He likes to carry things, big and small, and even a length of thread may be gravely tucked between his arm and chest for carrying. The use of small muscles in delicate manipulations, like the sensitive appreciation of textures and consistencies, of sounds and smells and tastes, will not develop to any great extent until the preschool years. His world is still a world of action and is only beginning to emerge as a world to contemplate and think about. Woodcock, again, has graphically depicted the spirit of the toddler's play:

> A group of two-year-olds in nursery school presents a composite picture of behavior that is characteristic for their stage of maturity and different from that of children of other stages. At one moment they are to be seen moiling laboriously in a dense cluster in the sandbox or swarming over the sides of a packing case, clutching at each other for support, their feet scraping past each other's ears and faces, bodies plumping down upon each other's bodies in a general cheerful disregard for the discomforts attending such close proximity. At another moment they are wandering in self-sufficient units each on his own journey of exploration, stopping here and there to bob up and down, to practice a stepping-up on a block and down again, to finger a wall, to close a door that is open or to open a door that is closed. When they meet up with a [kiddy-] kar they climb aboard it and ride. When they stub a toe on a shovel in their path, they pick up the shovel and dig for a little or carry it on with them to drop it soon and seize upon a wagon that meets their eyes.
>
> Certain arrangements of their physical environment serve as unfailing stimuli to their activity. Steps or rungs inspire them to climb, inclines invite them to proceed up on foot or on hands and knees, apertures invariably draw them into their depths and the sight of a tunnel assures their prompt traversing it from entrance to exit and back and forth again and again.
>
> Objects in motion attract them more quickly than objects at rest. They patter after a rolling ball or keg or wagon; they hurl themselves upon a table a comrade is pushing, they determinedly escort the rolling dinner wagon.[6]

When he was a baby, the only people in the toddler's world were familiar adults, and they still have an important part in his play. As a toddler, he continues to enjoy games like peek-a-boo and patty-cake. In addition, he plays a crude form of hide-and-seek with his parents, waiting in delighted terror to be caught. He likes to show off for adults, joining excitedly in their applause or becoming suddenly coy. He likes to look at picture books and listen to simple stories, songs, and nursery rhymes. But for all his attachment to adults, he is becoming aware of people his own age. Although he does not always seem to distinguish too clearly between people and things, there is no doubt that in young toddlerhood other children are beginning to emerge for him as especially intriguing kinds of things with which he senses a certain kinship. Toddlers like to examine each other, poking and tasting and embracing and shoving. Toddlers sometimes even play briefly together, one holding the sand bucket while the other fills it, or handing a toy back and forth. Most characteristic of this age (and extending on into the early preschool years), however, is the phenomenon known as *parallel play*, where children go about their individual activities side by side. There is no overt interchange, but there is every evidence of taking satisfaction in the other's nearness. Toddlers often spend long periods watching other children at play, often participating vicariously in the others' activities or else frankly and unself-consciously copying them. Interspersed with this budding sociability are long intervals of *solitary play* and a tendency to use the other children as convenient objects or pieces of furniture to sit on or climb on. At other times, a toddler will act as if another child simply did not exist at all, walking through him or appropriating his toys.

It is in toddlerhood that we see also the early beginnings of *dramatic play*, the imitation or re-enactment of everyday themes, as though the child could better participate in and understand such activities by acting them out in play. The toddler confines himself to simple, unelaborated themes for his dramatic play: telephoning, ringing the doorbell, going for a walk, going to school, shaving, drinking tea, shining shoes, fixing the car, bathing the baby. In a couple of years, he will weave these themes into more complicated and sustained dramas, but now he is content with one scene or role at a time, with little concern for continuity. His re-enactments tell us much about his selective perception of the world at this age. The emphasis is on common domestic activities, which are recurrent, simple, easily grasped (at least in their externals), and which come to constitute his first notions of grown-up doings.

Most of our descriptions of the toddler at play have been based on his activities as a junior member of the nursery school set. However, most toddlers spend most of their time at home, where, traditionally, they are "into everything." Things that could easily be placed out of reach of a creeping or unsteadily walking baby now have to be moved to new, higher levels. (The high-water mark at which breakable objects are located indicates to the eye of a seasoned visitor the probable age and energy output of a child.) This is the time when the boundaries between permissible and forbidden objects and activities, which first had to be sketched out when the creeping baby was released from his playpen, must now be more firmly and explicitly drawn. The toddler's intense exploratory drive is not very well modulated by considerations of value, weight, danger, and breakability. Outdoors, he is oblivious to the menace of automobiles, excavations, ponds, precipices, and the like. His mother is likely to be very much tied down during this stage of his growth. She is never sure what will happen next, and she learns to expect sudden crashes after periods of unnatural silence. Morever, the toddler may be prey to fits of panic when his mother is out of sight, and he will literally cling to her apron strings or whatever part of her is within reach. We shall discuss in a later section the business of setting limits to the toddler's explorations. At this point, we wish to emphasize the importance for the child's growth, and for his comprehension of his surroundings, of giving him as much scope as is feasible.

The toddler's tastes in activities and playthings are considerably more diversified than when he was an infant. He loves vehicles of all sorts and will labor painfully to master the pedals of a tricycle. He loves doll carriages and dolls, trundling them eternally through the house or about the neighborhood. He cares for, disciplines, hugs, and carries his dolls. He likes containers ranging in size from pillboxes to jars to drawers to closets, and spends a good part of his day opening and closing, emptying and filling them. He takes an interest in the possibilities of raw materials: water in the bathtub or a mudhole, the sand in his sandbox, cloth, paper. He likes to scribble with crayons on paper—or on walls, floors, woodwork, and furniture if he is not restrained. He likes to look at picture books, especially those offering an assortment of easily identifiable things, animals, and people; these have only to sit still for him to look at, since he does not yet perceive the activities they are pursuing. Late in toddlerhood, he will begin to enjoy stories read to him by his parents. Meanwhile he likes listening and dancing to music, especially vocal music, and will chime in with occasional words of familiar songs. He loves to drape himself in odd garments, scarves, blankets, and hats, and to clomp about the house in his parents' shoes. He likes to watch his mother at her work and imitates the gestures of mixing batter, breaking eggs, dusting and sweeping, and sewing. Often, though, he will insist that his mother interrupt her housework to "play," which means only that she keep him company while he goes about his business. He shifts rapidly from one activity to another, in keeping with his brief attention span, and sometimes gives the impression of trying to do half a dozen things at once.

One more facet of the toddler's play is his playing with sounds and words, which we shall discuss in the section on language development. Now it is time to pick up again the thread of autonomy that leads the toddler toward maturity and follow its various ramifications.

The Foundations of Autonomy

Autonomy, in the sense both of the wish and the ability to be independent, appears as the salient trend of development during toddlerhood. Out of his experience, the toddler is becoming aware of himself as a separate person with his own budding sensitivities and capacities. As he becomes aware of his new abilities, he wants to exercise them for himself, without help or hindrance or coercion from other people. But his sense of competence has two sides, his powers—the things that he can do—and his deficiencies—the things he cannot do. The latter tend to remain hidden from us and from the toddler behind his conviction of his omnipotence, but crop up unbidden or in response to overwhelming situations; just as the toddler is most vigorously asserting his autonomy, he may suddenly want to be helped or carried, to be babied and cuddled and protected.

Perhaps the most striking display of the toddler's autonomy is in his intermittent *negativism,* variously expressed by "No!"; going rigid all over; going limp all over; running away, kicking, biting, and scratching; or by temper tantrums. Usually, the toddler does what he is told, automatically and casually, but negativistic behavior springs up abruptly in the midst of his cheerful conformity. Often his protests are little more than play-acting designed to find out how it feels to say no, and a parent who continues unperturbed to dress the child or tuck him into bed will find the child still co-operating through a refrain of vocal resistance. Negativism is a normal, healthy part of development and, unless it is inflated into an issue between parent and child, soon is assimilated to the more positive aspects of autonomy. In general, if the toddler has ample opportunity to practice things on his own, balanced by the support he sometimes needs and by a minimum of necessary prohibitions, he will emerge from toddlerhood with a sound sense of his own abilities and a readiness to tackle the new problems of social adjustment that await him in the preschool years.

There is one area in particular in which the toddler's do-it-myself attitude is liable to run afoul of the demands of society as embodied in his parents. This is the matter of toilet-training (which we shall discuss from the practical point of view in a separate section). In the Freudian theory of development that provides the basis for Erikson's scheme, toddlerhood corresponds rather closely to the *anal stage*.[7] In this view, the focus of the child's gratification and concern has shifted from the mouth, with its connotations of eating, taking in, and absorbing, to the anus and lower digestive tract, with connotations of holding or of releasing; of control over his own functions; of giving or withholding of himself. Since anal functions are likely at times to become a focus of concern for the toddler or his parents, conflicts concerning toilet-training —or other conflicts arising at the toilet-training age—are believed by psychoanalysts to have significant and specific implications for later development. We shall have more to say about these in a later section. It should be stated at once that there is no inherent reason for toilet-training to be a source of warfare between parent and child. In many societies, and increasingly in our own, it is left largely to the workings of maturation plus a small amount of prodding by precept and example. For a number of parents, however, the processes of elimination continue to be "dirty": disgusting, anxiety-producing, and perhaps even tinged with immorality. For these adults, toilet-training is something to be instituted early and rapidly, with no questions asked and with whatever coercive measures seem called for. Unfortunately, such an approach leaves out of account the critical factors of developmental timing and of how the toddler is likely to react.

For the toddler himself, the process of elimination—if he is aware of it at all—is mildly pleasant, and the products of elimination are simply objects of curiosity, something to be felt, played with, smelled, and even tasted. As his neural connections mature, the processes of elimination become conscious, control becomes possible, and the pleasurable nature of the process may even be enhanced—we have the word of one older child who stated, "This is what I go pee-wee with. And it is nice. . . . Oh, how I love it . . . what fun it is . . . like a stream I am rushing. It is really too much for me! Water I drink, then water goes from out of me. . . . It is so nice a feeling, rushing." * [8] If, however, the child's parents display excessive concern over his elimination, he is less able and less willing to control it in the way they want. In short, his parents are trying to usurp his new-found powers. It has been said in psychoanalytic writings that the child may discover he can deliberately withhold or expel his wastes as an expression of resentment against his parents. This seems to attribute too much to the toddler's still amorphous conception of himself and other people. It seems safer to say that he does not understand what it is his parents want, especially in an atmosphere of some agitation. He becomes angry and confused, and either freezes up or loses control altogether. In time, of course, the child may indeed learn to use his eliminations as a weapon.

The important point is that premature or overemotional attempts to make the child control elimination according to a set pattern of time and place exaggerate the importance of control and make the child aware of his body and its functions as something unclean and disgusting and even alien. He is caught in what has been called the "Victorian circle": his parents are perpetuating the attitudes they learned from similar treatment as children, and he can be expected in turn to transmit these attitudes to *his* children. Overemphasis on toilet-training exposes the child to *shame and doubt,* which Erikson has defined as the developmental hazard of this age.[9] The child is made to feel exposed, vulnerable, and impotent rather than capable of autonomous self-direction. In infancy, as we have seen, the child must learn to trust the environment; in toddlerhood, he must learn to trust himself. But his

---

* The child we are quoting here is *Stuart,* who will be heard from frequently in this chapter and the ones on the preschool child. Stuart is a remarkably lucid spokesman for his contemporaries. While his interests, his puzzlements, and his theories were those of most children around his age, his ability to give voice to them was extraordinary. Most four- or five-year-old children, as family lore and collections of bright sayings attest, have occasional flashes of this sort, when their words, their unexpected combinations of ideas suddenly illuminate for the adult their ways of thinking. But Stuart, while spending most of his time at the Vassar College Nursery School at the same occupations as his fellows, had almost daily interludes of thinking out loud, often at nap time or when sharing a new idea with a favorite teacher. Fortunately, Miss Lucretia Williams, Mrs. Dorothy Call, and others, were ready with the ability to listen without interfering and were well skilled in swift recording. It is hoped that a full compilation of Stuart's musings on life can some day be published.

trust in himself depends on the self-picture that the environment reflects back to him.

Central to the development of autonomy, as we have said, is the toddler's growing self-awareness. In early infancy, the child was largely unable to distinguish between what went on in himself and what went on outside. Now, as a toddler, his experience has become differentiated to the point where he has some sense of being a person separate from other people and from the physical environment. He is still not always sure where the boundaries lie: emotions, for instance, are highly contagious among toddlers, and he may find himself laughing, yelling, or crying simply because someone nearby is doing so. Nevertheless, he is strongly aware of a new competence to do things for himself, if necessary in opposition to outside pressures. The child is not, however, aware of himself as a self-contained entity, to be perceived and judged objectively. He has not yet achieved the adult stage of knowing himself critically and abstractly, as such-and-such a kind of person, with certain physical dimensions, with qualities of handsomeness or homeliness, of virtue or wickedness. Instead, his self-awareness is formed of practical competences and emotional meanings. Most important, the child seems to experience himself indirectly, in the way the environment echoes his behavior back to him: he learns to see himself through the world's eyes.

Even his own body states may be incompletely differentiated for the toddler. Especially when he is busy doing something—and this holds true to some extent for older children and adults as well—he may not realize that he is chilled, or feeling sick, or tired, even though it is perfectly obvious to his parents. In the same way, it may take him some time to recognize and respond to the sensations that indicate a need to go to the bathroom. In early toddlerhood, he may not be aware, even while it is happening, that he is wetting or soiling himself—or, afterwards, that he has wet or soiled himself. His body is first represented to him not as a bundle of sensory impressions, needs, and impulses, but as the concrete embodiment of his emotional states relative to his surroundings. When he is interacting smoothly with the environment, we may surmise that his body exists only as a pleasant tingling. When he meets and masters an obstacle, his body feels strong and handsome and good. When he is thwarted or punished, and especially when his behavior provokes storms of moral outrage, he may come to feel that his body and its functioning are cumbersome, unclean, deformed, or, in extreme cases, an alien personality with which he is forced to live but which he cannot control.

Ordinarily, of course, such distortions of body-experience are temporary. As adults, too, we have moments of shame or embarrassment when we feel swollen and lumpy—or, in dreams, when we find ourselves walking agonizedly naked down a crowded street—but such feelings soon pass, leaving us at home with a body which, for all its shortcomings, is not such an unpleasant covering to have. In the same way, the child, triumphant in his growing repertory of skills, making his parents laugh affectionately at his cute sayings, discovering in the world around him the new and fascinating wonders that are the counterparts of his developing capacities, soon forgets his setbacks in a pervasive sense of competence and self-esteem. In this connection, it should be pointed out that it is only when the child esteems himself that he can esteem other people, if only because he follows the universal, naïve, but understandable practice of judging other people by himself. Lest it be feared that the child's self-esteem grow beyond all bounds, or that he become too trustful of others, we might remind the reader that parental restraints and demands do exist, that growing up always entails its share of frustrations, that the child will inevitably encounter enough minor betrayals to season his basic trust in the world with the proper amount of skepticism, and that from the beginning the child's omnipotence is partially balanced by a sense of vulnerability and helplessness. These negative experiences will not damage him. It is only in a climate of constant criticism, reproach, and taboo that the child's experience of himself becomes fixed in a disagreeable self-consciousness, a sense of shame and doubt, quite damaging to his future development.

Language Development

Probably the first great milestone in the development of autonomy is learning to move under one's own power, whether by crawling, creeping, or walking. A second milestone is attained when the toddler learns language. Obviously, toddlerhood is only one period in the acquisition of language. Since, however, it is at this time that speech reaches its first flowering, we have elected to discuss language at some length in the present section.

As the toddler acquires names for things and actions and relationships, he comes to possess his world in a new way: it is always with him, extending beyond the immediate situation in which he used to be

TABLE 3   Some Landmarks in the Development of Passive and Active Language   (Adapted from McCarthy[11])

AGE	ITEM	REPORTED BY
1 mo.	Differential cries for discomfort, pain, and hunger.	Gesell & Thompson
2 mo.	Makes several vocalizations.	Gesell & Thompson
2 mo.	Definite reaction to voices.	Gesell & Thompson; Bühler & Hetzer
2-4 mo.	Coos spontaneously or as response to people or music.	C. Bühler; Bühler & Hetzer; Gesell, Thompson, & Amatruda
6 mo.	Coos or crows to express pleasure.	Bayley; Gesell & Thompson
7-9 mo.	Ma-ma, da-da.	Bayley; Gesell, Thompson, & Amatruda
13-15 mo.	Expressive jargon.	Bayley; Gesell & Thompson
11-17 mo.	Obeys simple commands.	Bayley; Bühler & Hetzer; Gesell & Thompson
12-20 mo.	Obeys prohibitions.	Bühler & Hetzer; Gesell, Thompson, & Amatruda
17-24 mo.	Names one or more objects or pictures.	Bayley; Shirley; Bühler & Hetzer; Gesell & Thompson
21-24 mo.	Combines words.	Gesell & Thompson; Cattell; Shirley
23 mo.	First pronoun.	Shirley
24-28 mo.	Understands two prepositions.	Gesell; Bayley

enclosed; he can talk about it, think about it, and manipulate it, even when it isn't physically there. In addition, language brings him a world that may lie forever outside his perceptions, either because it is over and done with, has not happened yet, never could happen in reality, or exists in regions where he cannot travel. It gives him a new power to communicate his feelings to other people. Without language, he is limited to sheer expression: crying, smiling, laughing, grunting, gesticulating. As the toddler comes to grasp the categories imposed upon experience by adult language, the world becomes more highly differentiated and organized, and he can navigate in it more freely and adeptly. Language helps put the child in touch with his environment and at the same time liberates him from it.[10]

In Table 3, page 117, we have summarized a few of the important steps that mark the child's acquisition of language. We find, condensed in the data of this table, a number of interesting trends. The first thing to note is that language is not altogether new in toddlerhood but grows out of behavior that dates back to early infancy. Throughout, we can see two major aspects of learning language: learning to *understand* it and learning to *speak* it. Understanding, or *passive language,* comes first, when the child learns to sort out language from all the other sounds, sights, smells, pressures, and so forth, that move him to action. Language is first learned in its practical settings and the child has to differentiate it from the facial expressions, tones of voice, gestures, and objects that accompany it. Probably the earliest words he distinguishes are those which always accompany an obvious action, and in time evoke the action when they are used alone: bye-bye, pat-a-cake, and so forth. Then come simple signals and commands to action: "Here's your bottle," "Bath time," "Daddy's coming," "Give Mummy a kiss," "Bring it here," "Hold still," "No!" Even earlier, of course, he will get the sense of expressions of affection, praise, blame, and "watch this."

Speaking, or *active language,* lags slightly behind understanding. This is true at all ages, of course: as adults, we can understand in context a great many words we would never think to use; we find it easier to learn to read a foreign language than to speak it. Words become differentiated out of the vocalizations of infancy in a number of more or less definite stages. However, once the toddler has begun to talk, language bursts out all over him, and it is not always easy to tell these stages apart. The baby's first cries of distress, and later of pleasure, although they may tell parents what the baby is feeling, represent a spilling-over of emotion and cannot be thought of as deliberate expressions. Within a few months, however, the baby seems to realize that he can make sounds at will and takes delight in using his voice. Here we see what has been called the "circular reflex": by making sounds, the baby *stimulates himself* to make more sounds[12]—it is noteworthy that deaf babies begin to babble, too, but soon stop. Later on, the circular reflex becomes social as well: parents, often in the conviction that the baby has said a word, repeat "mama" or "dada" back to him and provide the restimulation signal, until there develops an exchange of babblings resembling conversation in some exotic language. Along the way, the baby has learned that people respond to his voice, and he begins to use it purposefully to call his parents' attention or to initiate an exchange of gibberish. Here we see the beginnings of true communication.

Before expanding on the sequences in learning active language, we shall first present them in summary form. The acquisition of active language proper begins toward the end of the first year, when the child begins to learn simple labels for things and actions and to compile a catalogue of his environment. Within a few months, he begins to use these names for purposes of communication, largely in the form of commands and requests. A little later, the child begins to communicate about matters of fact, as in narration or description. His first efforts along these lines are likely to consist of what Gesell calls "expressive jargon": a flow of gibberish, often punctuated with real words, that imitates the sound of speech with some fidelity and often seems tantalizingly on the verge of being comprehensible, like the comedian's doubletalk. Soon, though, the toddler's speech settles down to the use of real words (but of words which imply whole sentences, and not of isolated words with a single meaning), then phrases, then sentences, and the foundations of language are firmly established.

As might be expected, different children show these patterns at different ages and with different speeds of development. Some children telescope all the stages described above into a brief learning period and then blossom forth with highly advanced speech. In others, language development seems to go underground between babbling and talking, so that the child skips over the intervening stages. Some children are remarkably silent until, late in toddlerhood, they suddenly begin producing full-blown language. Some children seem to be bursting with speech and can hardly wait for the words to come; others seem indifferent to language; still others seem to be biding their time, listening, watching, mulling things over until they are ready to talk in earnest. At about the time when expressive jargon appears, a number of children go through a period of imitation when, by reproducing what adults say, they seem better able to understand it. Other children go through a period of *echolalia,* which again is repeating what adults say, but in this case in a blind, mechanical parroting that may continue over and over. Eventually, language usage becomes one of the best indicators available as to the child's intelligence, but inferences about intelligence may be drawn only with many reservations in the early stages of learning to talk. While it is true that retarded children usually talk late, so, as it happens, do many superior children.

The Functions of Language

In outlining the general sequence of language development, we have already alluded to the numerous uses to which the toddler puts his language. Now let us look at some of these uses in more detail. The first active use of words (leaving out of account the many interjections —bye-bye, hi!, etc.—that a baby learns) is usually in *naming* people, things, and actions: dog, cat, milk, baby, eat, fall, and so forth. Young toddlers often develop a great interest in names. Once they have learned to label a few familiar objects, their parents contribute to this by asking, "What's that?"; and in no time at all the child is insatiably demanding, "Whadda? Whadda?"; often without waiting for an answer. The child frequently appears, in his naming mania, to be seeing the world for the first time, as though names were able to fix and stabilize his experience, and make it really his. It is almost as though the names had greater reality than the objects themselves, as though the objects took on a new existence when fitted into the peculiarly human and intimate framework of language. We see the same tendency at work in later development, where it is unpleasant or not nice to talk about certain things, as though by preserving silence one could prevent facts from existing.

Just as names give shape and identity to the world, they also tell the toddler what is going on inside himself, and enable him to tell other people about it. It is as he acquires words for his wants, urges, pleasures, aches, and pains that his experience becomes clear to him and takes on common properties with that of other people. It is important to see, in this connection, how much communicating the child does *with himself,* first by naming the things he encounters and eventually by telling himself what he is doing, commanding himself, criticizing himself, repeating parental prohibitions and encouragements, etc.

As soon as the toddler begins to ask "Whadda?" or even to look at his parents for agreement when he names something, his language is being assimilated to the process of communicating information. Much of the toddler's early communication, as we have said, is in the form of commands and requests. His first shouts of "Eat!" accompanied by bangings of his spoon on the table top are probably nothing more than recognitions of the fact that being sat at the table and having a bib tied on are indications that food is on its way. Shortly afterwards, however, he does not wait for these specific signals, but toward mealtime sets up an imperative clamor of "Eat! Eat!" perhaps at the same time sitting down expectantly at the table. Gradually, the toddler's speech moves away from feeling and action and toward the exchange of facts: "[My doll is] broke!"; "[Is that] Daddy['s hat]?"

The Structure of Language

In his factual communications, the toddler seems to shift from the fluency of expressive jargon to what have been called *one-word sentences*, such as "Go," "Mama," or, as above, "Broke" and "Daddy." Although such utterances may appear as single words to adults, for the child they are complete statements. Thus, "Go" may variously contain the notion "I want to go," or "Daddy is going," or "Make the car go." Obviously, such highly condensed utterances need a goodly amount of pointing and gesticulating to make their meaning clear. Some one-word sentences appear—in adult terms—to be compounds of two words, as in "awgone," or of parts of words, as in the French toddler's equivalent, "yapu" (*il n'y en a plus*). It would seem that the child seizes on the more prominent features of what is for him a single "glob" of sound, and has no notion of selecting or combining lexical units. Also, of course, most parents cater to this tendency in the toddler by speaking to him themselves in one-word sentences. Gradually, as the toddler's language and experience become more differentiated, we see his one-word sentences become two-word sentences, and then three, and so on until they are highly articulated utterances complete with subject, verb, object, modifiers, prepositions, conjunctions, main clauses and subordinate clauses, and all the other grammatical trappings of adult speech. Even by the age of two, many children can deliver themselves of full-fledged statements. The word order may be slightly scrambled, as in "Audrey's came my shoe off," and the pronunciation obscure—Woodcock cites "Wiffer," "Crissa," and "Crissawa" as versions of Christopher[13]—but the children make themselves understood.

Although there may seem to be a huge gap between the toddler's global, impressionistic approach to language and the refinements of adult speech, this is the "natural" and certainly the most effective way to learn a language. Adults, for instance, who are forced to learn a foreign language catch-as-catch-can, by hearing it spoken, usually pick it up much faster than those who learn it one word at a time, along with rules (consisting mostly of exceptions) for combining words into sentences. Those deaf children who are given an opportunity to learn the natural rhythms of speech, whether visually or tactually or through what little hearing they may have, are able to use language with greater facility and clarity than those who are taught isolated words and speech sounds. The deaf child who can say "Wiffer" is more likely to be understood than the one who produces "Ka-ris-to-fer" in a hollow monotone.

Although grammatical categories do not exist for the toddler, by imposing them on his utterances we can obtain a crude measure of the content and structure of his experience. The toddler's first one-word sentences consist largely of what adults would call nouns—"[There's a] doggie!"—and verbs—"[I want to] eat!"—plus a scattering of adjectives—"[My cereal is] hot!"—and adverbs—"[Let's go] out!" (He also uses interjections—"bye-bye," "no," "hi," "ouch"—liberally; sometimes, of course, these interjections, too, can serve as one-word sentences.) Between the ages of eighteen and thirty months, the toddler's use of noun-like words drops from about 50 percent of what he says to about 20 percent. Verb-like words increase from 15 percent to around 25 percent, and the other parts of speech rise correspondingly.[14] A little thought shows how these grammatical differentiations may reflect differentiations in experience—although it should be pointed out that other languages than our own provide different categories for ordering the world. Adjectives and adverbs, which qualify and specify undifferentiated nouns and verbs—"the *big* wagon," "go *fast*"—help the toddler make comparisons and distinctions. The possessive forms— "mine," "Mommy's," "Daddy's"—sharpen the boundaries of self and other, and express the feelings that go with ownership: power, intimacy, vulnerability, etc. Prepositions—*on, in, under, from,* etc.—help tie the world together in terms of systematic relationships.

As the toddler's language forms become more diversified, he has less need to rely on pointing and physical movement to fill out what he wants to say, although it goes without saying that even adults count very heavily on such non-verbal aspects of speaking as gestures, facial expression, and intonation to convey their full meaning. In other words, the toddler can begin to talk about things that are not present. His earliest utterances always refer to the immediate situation and are couched in the present tense. Then he begins to use the future, and then the past. As in infancy, the toddler's first anticipations of the future and remembrance of things past seem to be a sort of "present future" and "present past," referring to where he is now headed or where he has just been: "Gonna slide," or "Fall down." Next comes an awareness of events lying just beyond the present situation. Although his statements are still couched in the present tense—"Go out?"; "Have nap"—their context clearly shows that the child intends a past or future reference. Then comes an awareness of events lying at one or more removes from the present, until, by late toddlerhood, the child may be able to anticipate *tomorrow* and recall *yesterday* (although he will use the words for them more or less interchangeably);[15] anything more remote is likely to fade off into eternity. It will be a long time before he can grasp the meaning of more formal time concepts or of those embracing a longer span: the days of the week, the hours of the day, weeks, months, seasons, years, Christmas—he has, after all, watched comparatively few of these landmarks go by. It will be even longer before he can comprehend the hypothetical time expressed in the conditional tenses.

The Content of Language

As we can see, the growing variety of the toddler's experience is reflected in the number of words he uses. It is almost impossible to know exactly how many "words" a child has at his disposal, but a good estimate would seem to be that during toddlerhood, while the child is doubling in age, his spoken vocabulary grows from twenty to five hundred words, a twenty-five-fold increase.[16] As we have already suggested, of course, the toddler can understand a great many more words than he uses. Such vocabulary estimates, needless to say, are averages, and do not attempt to take account of individual differences due to differences in intelligence, in the amount of language to which children are exposed, or of severely limiting factors such as deafness.

Which words a child uses tells us something about what he is aware of and concerned about. It is noteworthy, for example, that he learns names for other people before he learns one for himself. This points to the low degree of self-awareness prior to toddlerhood. Sometimes, as we pointed out earlier, an infant learns "dada" before he learns "mama," perhaps because his mother is so close to him that he cannot become aware of her so soon as someone requiring a name. When it comes time to refer to himself, he usually does so by his given name, by the third person "baby," or by the accusative "me." It takes him quite a while to accomplish the miracle of getting straight the notion of "I" as always being the one who is talking rather than a particular person. He is not likely to use pronouns, except "me" and "mine," with any precision until he reaches preschool age. In other words, his thinking is still absolutistic and cannot yet deal with the shifting relativism of personal pronouns. The magnitude of this problem even on into pre-school days is reflected in the following dialogue between our friend Stuart, age four, and his teacher:

> STUART: "Me" is a name, you know. My name.
> TEACHER: "Me" is my name, too.
> STUART: No, it is *mine*. How can it be yours? I am *me*.
> TEACHER: I am, too.
> STUART: No, you are not "me." I am me. You are you. (After a pause for quiet meditation) I am me. You are not me to me, but you are me to you.[17]

It is interesting, too, that the toddler can use "no" long before he can use "yes." Until, at age two and a half or three, he does learn to say "yes," he has two major ways of conveying assent: either he goes ahead and does what has been asked of him, or, in agreeing to questions of fact, he echoes what the adult has said to him. In the realm of quantities, the toddler distinguishes between "one" and "two"—"two" being anything more than one. We often find, when we look into the toddler's vocabulary, that there are unexpected gaps. Leopold, for instance, who tabulated his daughter's speech with great care, lists a number of words for things within her ken which she had not yet found occasion to use by age two, among them: chair, picture, tongue, yard, garden, street, good (although she did make an "m" sound indicating that "it tastes good"), little and small, see, take, jump, hug, like, and look (many two-year-olds know this word well and incessantly command their parents to "yook! yook!").[18] Needless to say, there will be great variation from child to child in which words are learned and which are missing.

Word Meanings

Apart from how many and what words the toddler uses, we must also take a moment to look at the toddler's *word meanings,* that is, the way he forms *concepts.* As we might gather from the one-word sentence, where a single "word" contains a whole set of ideas, the toddler's concepts are often overrich, including as yet undifferentiated, unseparated connotations which an adult might think extraneous. For one thing, the toddler's language is still closely tied to the here and now, it has not yet become abstract and general—indeed, there is evidence that, initially, names do not "stand for" objects but are concretely imbedded in them.[19] This too may go on into the preschool years, as illustrated by Stuart's four-year-old reaction to a friend's comment of "Baloney!": "Baloney is not a word, it is a *thing!* It is a meat. (Pause) Words still do tell about things. The word says what is the thing. It must be, or how would you know what was the thing without it had a word?" [20] Despite this concrete attachment of word to thing, the toddler does generalize the labels he has learned to new situations. When he does so, he may reveal a kind of concept quite different from that of adults. For instance, he may greet any adult male as "Daddy," suggesting that the term is not restricted to his father, but refers to all large trousers-wearing people. In later years, of course, the term will become further differentiated. He will learn to distinguish between Daddy (large *D*), who lives at his house, and daddies (small *d*), who live at other children's houses. He will learn with some amazement that daddies have daddies, too, and, eventually, that one can be simultaneously father and child. Instead of the formal properties which define an adult concept, the child may seize on some striking perceptual feature as the central meaning of a word: he may call a great variety of fuzzy or furry things "kitty"; he may call a grain of sand a "crumb." Parents, of course, in their baby-talk often use words stressing the characteristic sounds things make: moo-cow, bow-wow, choo-choo. It is hard to say to what extent adult baby-talk influences the child's language or to what extent it mirrors it, but children's invented words often have the same characteristics as baby-talk: the onomatopoeia of "choo-choo," the double syllables of all the above examples, the rhyming of "bow-wow," and the alliteration of "kitty-cat."

Part of the confusion of meanings for the toddler, as we have seen, comes from the fact that his experience is not yet clearly differentiated. Another part, however, comes from the oddities of language itself. The toddler, of course, is subject to deception by the vagaries of language without being aware of it. One of Stuart's comments, at the age of four, expresses vividly one way in which such deceptions can occur and go on occurring beyond toddlerhood. Invited by his teacher to go see the puppets, he asked, "Puppies?" His teacher repeated a previous explanation about puppets, but he was not satisfied: "Yes, but those two words are like each other so the things should be like, are they?" "No, not much." "But they should. . . . They sound almost as if they were each other, except the little end, so they should be like one thing. . . ." [21] More than a year later, he was still worrying about such semantic problems and expressing the confusions which other children feel but cannot formulate. In this case he was concerned with the similarities and differences between *hole* and *whole:* "But it is mixing to have words that mean the opposite sound just the same. People hear the sound and what do they think? The opposite! And then they make mistakes but it is not their fault. It is because of the word. . . . It is mixing enough anyhow with words not to have some that sound the same but are opposite." [22] This feeling that words have an existence of their own and are something more than convenient labels for reality does not, of course, stop with childhood. Even as adults, we feel a small thrill of significance or perhaps of resentment when we encounter someone with the same name as ours; when someone misuses a word, we are as annoyed as though he had actually altered our familiar reality.

Language as a Tool and a Toy

It is precisely because words have such power over reality, however, that it is so much fun to play with language. Language play of a sort begins, as we have seen, with the babbling of infancy. In toddlerhood, some of the child's expressive jargon is a more advanced form of word play, where the child spouts nonsense, partly for the sheer pleasure of hearing the sound patterns come out but partly also in a spirit of deliberate silliness, as though recognizing the absurdity of what he says: "Lig a loggie, dig a poggie, a la boggie poggie boggie." [23] Children at this age are not so likely to appreciate adults' verbal humor; if the adult, for instance, changes the wording or the sense of a favorite story with some idea of entertaining the toddler, he will probably encounter fierce indignation. It is not until the child has attained the relative sophistication of the preschool years that he can feel sufficiently master of his language to move on to the next stage, where sense and nonsense are consciously intermingled.

The toddler's language often accompanies and punctuates his other play, as mood music, as narration, as commands to himself and his playthings. As his dramatic play becomes more social and less solitary, true conversation plays an increasing role in it. His jokes are usually amused commentaries on events and incongruities—"Johnny pants off"—and do not yet include the banter, verbal teasing, and deliberate surprises and manufactured incongruities of which the preschooler is capable. When he does happen upon something that is funny, such as getting his overshoes on the wrong feet, he will repeat the joke, including appropriate expressions of mock dismay, until something new intervenes to break the spell. As we can see, the toddler's growing language skills are assimilated to everything he does; in addition, though, they open new

The toddler is the model for the cherubim and cupids of Renaissance painting.

Toddlers are traditionally "into everything."

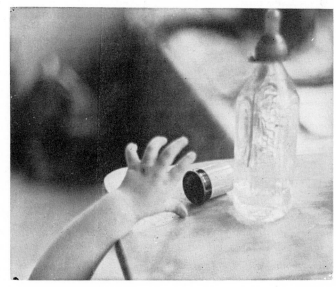

Parallel play

In much of what he does the toddler is still a baby.

Some toddlers devise elaborate ways of aiming themselves into chairs.

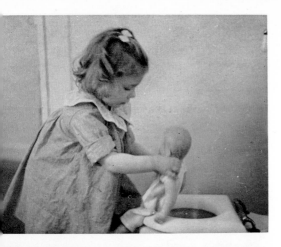

Early dramatic play

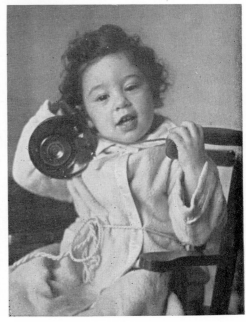

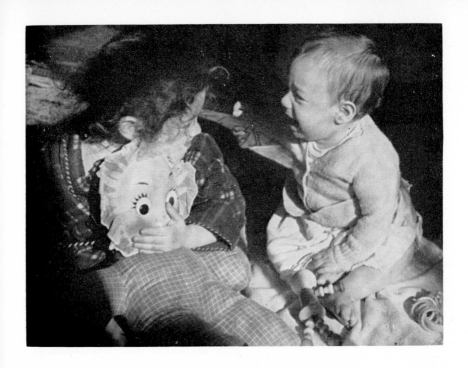

Sibling relations

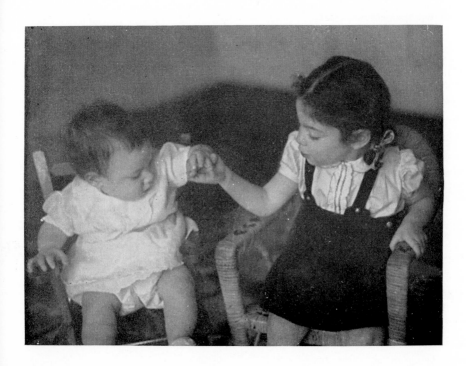

realms of activity to him, in learning and thinking and in the social interchange that will come to occupy an ever-growing part of his still narrow existence. Meanwhile—and to some extent regrettably—he moves from the verbal music of infancy toward the still egocentric poetry of the preschool years and the communicative but often barren prose of adult discourse.

The Regulation of Behavior in Toddlerhood

The theme of toddlerhood, as we have said, is autonomy. In preceding sections, we have seen some of the ways in which the toddler expresses his new independence of thought and action. Now it is time to examine some of the practical issues raised by the growth of autonomy. As we said in Chapter 3, these issues are not merely of importance to the parents who must cope with them, but throw considerable light on the process of personality development. It should be evident that the toddler's autonomy cannot yet be absolute, and that parents have to retain and exercise a generous amount of authority. Later on, we shall discuss specific areas and ways in which parents channel the toddler's freedom of action. In dealing with these specifics, however, a number of general principles should be borne in mind. Some of these were discussed in earlier chapters and some are new to toddlerhood, but all deserve to be reviewed here.

To begin with, there is the matter of *developmental timing*. It is futile, and hence frustrating for parent and child alike, to demand of a child behavior for which he is not maturationally ready. In toddlerhood, however, there is first likely to arise the opposite danger, that of holding a child back from experience for which he is ready, of overprotecting and "babying" him.[24] Next, we might mention the doctrine of *gradualism*. In introducing something new—weaning in infancy, toilet-training in toddlerhood—the transitions should not be unnecessarily abrupt, and we should not expect quick results. Even the most cooperative of children need a little time to get used to new ways of doing things. Then there is the matter of *parental self-confidence*. Parents must be able to act decisively, secure in their own maturity and in their love for their child, without undue concern for what The Neighbors will think. There will be times, too, when parents have to have a certain amount of disregard for what the child himself thinks. We pointed out earlier that there is distinction between *needs,* which have to be met in the interests of sound development, and mere *wants,* which sometimes have to yield to the greater good, whether the child's or his family's. Parents who try to satisfy all a child's wants may soon find themselves at the mercy of a small tyrant who is no happier about his power than they are. There is still another aspect of parental self-confidence that should be mentioned: parents cannot afford to be so afraid of losing a child's love that they hesitate to do anything that might antagonize him. Certain of the demands and restraints we impose upon the toddler inevitably arouse his anger. We must be prepared to recognize the appropriateness of his reaction, without feeling that he has withdrawn his affection and without becoming indignant at his lack of filial respect.

It is important to see that various "problems" confronting the toddler's parents are problems only for those who ignore the factor of developmental timing. A great deal of needless concern has been expended on toddlers' deplorable table manners, their tendencies to exhibitionism, their blunt frankness, their personal sloppiness, their expressive jargon that often accidentally manages to include sounds remarkably like certain disreputable four-letter words. These manifestations are all in keeping with this level of development, will be succeeded in due course by more adult-like forms of behavior, and do not call for specific remedial action during toddlerhood.

Other practical issues, real enough in themselves, may be needlessly complicated by *moralistic attitudes* on the part of parents. This is not to say that parents should be indifferent to morality. But morality, too, develops like other aspects of behavior, and there are inappropriate and appropriate moralities for different ages. The central core of any true morality, awareness of and respect for the feelings of others, has its beginnings early in life in the example of the parents' love for the child and for other creatures in the environment. Toddler morality cannot extend far beyond this beginning stage, and it will be some time before generosity, "selfishness," truthfulness, modesty, and so forth can be matters of moral concern.

With these general principles in mind, let us go on to examine some of the specific practical issues faced by the parents of a toddler. We shall begin with toilet-training, which, though it poses fewer problems now than in recent history, still may be regarded as the crucial adjustment of the toddler period.

Toilet-Training

It is obvious that children in our predominantly middle-class urban society must learn, sooner or later, to use toilets. In some primitive or rural settings, one can go off behind a convenient bush, and even in the city it is customary for lower-class children to relieve themselves in an alley or between two parked cars; but by and large it is mandatory that our children stop soiling and wetting themselves and use the elegant plumbing put at their disposal. Even though maturational readiness is an invariable condition for success, parents cannot count on maturation alone to do the whole job of training. This need not imply, however, a grim struggle for supremacy. Once he is biologically ready, the toddler, for all his occasional negativism, is usually willing to go along with his parents' suggestions about the toilet, if only because he wants to do as Mommy and Daddy do. As we have said before, bowel training and bladder training differ both in their timing and in their methods, and therefore have to be discussed individually.

Bowel control can usually be established soon after the age of one year. The signs of readiness are regularity of movements and advance warnings of which *the child seems to be aware*. Even in late infancy, parents can see by the baby's expression and other signs that a bowel movement is approaching and, tactfully, put the child on the potty-chair in time. (A potty-chair, rather than a seat that fits over the toilet, is recommended: first, the toddler can get into it himself, without help; also, quite a number of children are frightened by the altitude of a toilet-seat or by the turbulence of a flushing toilet.) But voluntary control, which is the goal of training, can come only when the toddler has control over his anal sphincter and can himself recognize the significance of certain interior stirrings. Given the toddler's readiness, further progress is more a matter of parental attitudes than of techniques. A casual, cheerful manner throughout, a concern for the child's comfort, a reasonable amount of praise when he does well, all contribute to the success of a co-operative enterprise. Anxiety, strain, disgust, haste, punishment, and moral outrage when the child falters merely prolong and complicate the process. When the child is able to squat easily, it is sometimes a good idea to let him use his pot without the chair or perhaps try a toilet seat; this is because children sometimes fasten on one particular set of conditions as appropriate to defecation and cannot function when these conditions are changed. There is the case of one well-trained little girl who, on a camping trip with her parents, was quite unable to eliminate, in spite of an obvious need, when held comfortably on her mother's fore-arm.[25] Next time, her parents took along her toilet seat, which, although it had to be held by a parent, was sufficiently familiar to permit her to move her bowels. To forestall such inflexibility, in the interests of being free to travel, it is sound practice to vary toilet conditions.

We pointed out earlier that the issues centering in anal functions—control over elimination, the pleasure of withholding or expelling feces, and conflict over surrender of control to the parents—are for psychoanalysts the crucial issues of the anal phase between infancy and the preschool years. Erikson, with good reason as it seems to us, has broadened the central concepts of orthodox psychoanalysis. For him, the important questions are not only "shall I eliminate at the time I am asked?" or the related one of "shall I assert my power by withholding when I choose and eliminating when I wish?", but a generalization of these in the themes of self-control versus submission to authority, of being the master of one's own body and its powers.

In the orthodox view, the functions of *withholding* or *expelling* (either as a timely "gift" or as an untimely expression of hostility) may become generalized themes in all the individual's behavior if there is excessive pressure in the matter of toilet-training, or if other serious problems arise at this time. In keeping with the principle of *critical periods,* any disturbance in the individual at the time when anal control is developing will have their effects in this area. Specifically, the individual is said to become *fixated* (developmentally arrested) at the anal level. In the adult *anal character* which the psychoanalysts believe results from anal fixation, many of the individual's characteristics can be seen as expressing the persistence of conflict around the two issues of withholding and expelling. Withholding, the guarding of one's own integrity, may be expressed in several ways: most literally, as constipation; more symbolically, as parsimony, emotional constriction, suspiciousness (a fear of invasion or close contact), and so forth. Because defecation is so easily equated with dirtying (as in the term "soiling"), the excessively sloppy and disorderly person can be seen as expressing anal fixation about the issue of expelling. But the opposite characteristics of neatness and fastidiousness can also be seen as manifestations of the same tendency—or, more properly, as vehement denials of the tendency, in accordance with the mechanism of *reaction formation,* or "protesting too much." Apart from such fixations, of course, all children, in the Freudian view, necessarily pass through the periods of orality and anality, and the later phallic, latency, and genital stages which we shall discuss in future chapters.

Bladder training has two aspects, waking control and sleeping control. Waking control comes first, usually around age two or two and a half, while sleeping control may lag a year or more behind. The delay in bladder control by comparison with bowel control can be attributed to three factors. First, maturation seems to come later. Second, the sensations announcing a need to urinate are initially less clear-cut. Third, and perhaps most important, urination is a reflex response to bladder tensions and must be inhibited, whereas defecation, once the stool has become formed, requires an act of expulsion. In other words, control is easier when you have to make something happen than when you have to keep it from happening.

As Gesell has pointed out, bladder control comes in three stages.[26] First, the child becomes aware that he *has* wet himself—parents are often dismayed when the child comes to them proudly with such an after-the-fact announcement instead of letting them know beforehand; they should, rather, recognize this as an important first step and respond accordingly with approval. Somewhat later, as he approaches age two, the child becomes aware that he *is* wetting, and can proclaim the fact. Within a few months, he will begin to anticipate that he *is about to* wet, and then can start to practice holding on until he reaches—or almost reaches—the toilet. It perhaps needs to be said that initially both boys and girls urinate sitting down. It also happens that both boys and girls, when they have a chance to observe their parents in the bathroom, may want to try to urinate standing up, the way Daddy does. Explanations to the boy about his short stature in relation to the height of the toilet, and to girls about anatomical differences, will probably have little effect, and both boys and girls may have to learn from experience before they are willing to sit down again.

As we might expect, bladder control is not usually established once and for all as soon as the child is ready, but will take some time to become stabilized. It might be noted in passing that bladder control appears somewhat earlier in girls than in boys, in keeping with the advanced maturational pace set by females during childhood. There are occasional children who abruptly train themselves. One child, remarking spontaneously of a baby sister that babies certainly wet a lot, thereafter stayed virtually dry. A little girl, on a motor trip with her parents, was fascinated by filling-station rest rooms, and, after insisting for a while on frequent visits to them, became completely trained. These, however, are the exceptions, and do not even provide an ideal. Ordinarily, bladder training has to follow its slow, on-and-off course, giving the child ample opportunity to use the toilet—but without making it the principal feature of his existence—offering mild praise for success

and taking accidents in stride. Even after the child has good control over
his urinary sphincters, he may suffer brief relapses when engrossed in
play or tired, or more prolonged ones if sick or otherwise upset.

Nighttime bladder control can be established only when it has become
second nature for the child to respond to tension in his bladder by
tightening his sphincters. In addition, he has to be able to keep his
sphincters closed without waking up. It is for this reason that techniques
such as cutting down on fluids at bedtime or picking the child up
during the night do not seem to advance the cause of sleeping control.
There are on the market various devices intended to cure bed-wetting
(*enuresis*): when the child begins to wet, the urine bridges an electric
circuit, causing an alarm bell to ring or giving the child a slight electric
shock. Repeated use of such a contrivance supposedly establishes a
"conditioned reflex," with bladder tension as the signal to wake up and
go to the bathroom. Apart from the questionable efficacy of such devices
—human beings have a remarkable and laudable resistance to this kind
of "scientific" manipulation—they are unsound in principle. The goal
is not to get the child to wake up, but to be able to sleep dry. To this
end, a small amount of patience and understanding is worth more than
a great deal of elaborate "technique." Once the child is secure in his
waking control, knows what is expected of him, and *wants* to co-operate,
sleeping control seems to follow largely of its own accord. Too much
stress on the issue upsets the child and makes control more difficult.
Enuresis at times may be a sensitive barometer of emotional changes.
It was noticed that even children of school age separated from their
mothers during the wartime evacuation of London reverted to bed-
wetting in great numbers until, as one observer put it, "half of England
was awash." This does not mean that every instance of persistent bed-
wetting points to an emotional disturbance. If, however, nighttime
control is too long delayed—until age five, say—then it may be necessary
to look for some physical or psychological cause.

Sibling Rivalry

There is now a traditional belief, dating back to the story of Cain
and Abel, and made into a concept in formal psychology by Alfred
Adler,[27] that there necessarily exists among siblings a spirit of competition, jealousy, and hostility. An older sibling, for instance, may feel that
a new baby has deposed him from his reigning position in the parents'
affections. A younger sibling, on the other hand, may feel resentfully
envious of his older sibling's size, strength, and privileges. Adler and

others have plotted out what they believe to be the typical patterns of sibling rivalry attending various positions in birth order ("family constellation") and sex, but for our discussion of toddlerhood we need be concerned only with the situation presented by our first example, the possibility that a toddler may be upset by the arrival of a new brother or sister.

Authorities have proposed various methods of forestalling resentment in an older sibling when a new baby arrives. If he is old enough and mature enough—two and a half rather than one and a half—he should be notified enough in advance so that the baby does not come as a total surprise, but not so far in advance that he forgets about it or that it becomes unreal with the slow passage of time. He should be given, within his restricted competence, a share in the preparations for and care of the newcomer, so that he will feel that the newcomer is in a sense his as well as his parents'. Most important, the parents should not become so engrossed in the new baby that they lose sight of the older child's continuing need for affection and attention. It is doubtful whether these and similar measures, no matter how assiduously and skillfully applied, will altogether prevent the older child from becoming jealous of the new intruder. It is not even certain that all jealousy should be eliminated, since it is something the child will have to learn about eventually.

A toddler may show jealousy of a new sibling in several ways. He may *regress*—that is, turn back to more infantile ways of behaving. He may begin to whine or cry easily, he may cling to his parents, his speech may become more babyish or even disappear, he may lose control over his bladder. Such behavior often indicates that the toddler feels left out; it sometimes looks almost as though he had concluded that the only way to get attention is to be a baby. In these circumstances, it may be necessary to give him an especially generous ration of love, together with whatever hints are possible to the effect that he can safely act his age. Another way in which the toddler can show his jealousy is by trying to hurt or get rid of the unwelcome newcomer. This may take the form of suggestions to the parents that they somehow dispose of it, or that it is now quite time to return it to the hospital. Sometimes the toddler will try to take matters into his own hands, with the sincere intention of doing away with the usurper. When this happens, the toddler will have to be restrained from injuring the baby. On the other hand, there need be no suggestion that the toddler is wicked or depraved; a formal, inflexible, and even angry prohibition can be imposed but in full understanding of how natural the toddler's feelings are. From the fact that one loves the toddler, it need not follow that one must approve of everything he does. Nor in disapproving, does one cease to love him. As in all disciplinary situations, the emphasis must always be on the act, not on the toddler himself, as the object of disapproval. An excessively moral approach to such a situation merely reinforces the toddler's conviction that he has been displaced by an interloper and so serves to increase his resentment of the baby or the parents. There may well be times, as when the new baby is very young or is sick, when the toddler is bound to feel that he takes second place in his parents' affections. Such temporary strains are inevitable and will, in the long run, probably do as much to strengthen as to weaken the bonds between him and his parents. But if they are the rule rather than the exception, the toddler cannot help thinking of love as something to be fought for or earned or stolen rather than as something that is given in a free exchange.

Other manifestations of the brutality of which toddlers are sometimes capable call for similar treatment. When he is angry—or simply unthinking or unknowing—the toddler may abuse pets or parents as well as small babies. In such cases, he has to be restrained—although parents can endure a small amount of pummeling if it makes the child feel better—but, in addition, parents must convey in their behavior toward objects in the environment and toward the child himself the tenderness and respect they want him to feel. It should also be noted that what may appear to adult eyes as brutality is often nothing more than the result of the toddler's clumsiness, his curiosity, or his excitement over some new discovery, combined with his ignorance about how fragile some things are.

Eating

During infancy, especially in the first few months, parents often find it hard to believe that a baby can possibly get as hungry as he does as often as he does, especially if they have been oversold on the notion of feeding schedules. In toddlerhood, they often face the opposite problem. As the child's rate of growth levels off, he requires less food and his appetite declines sharply until, in the view of some mothers, he never seems to want to eat anything. The toddler's loss of appetite can be a source of alarm to parents, particularly if they are not aware of it as a regular, normal part of growth. Practically, they know that he needs nourishment for growth and for energy. But eating is not merely a practical matter; it is closely bound up with cultural attitudes as well.

Some of us are heirs to the Puritan tradition that there must be no waste, that a clean plate is somehow a mark of virtue. In the same tradition, dessert is frivolous and hence permissible only after the grim business of meat and potatoes and spinach has been got through. In the Mediterranean tradition, where food is to be enjoyed, if the child does not eat, either he is seen as unhappy or as bearing a grudge against the provider of food. Moreover, the bulk that comes with heavy eating is a sign of health, of prosperity and hence of prestige, of happiness, and sometimes of beauty, and is taken as proof of good mothering. With factors such as these in the background of their thinking, it is not surprising that parents may become upset when their child shows no enthusiasm for his meals.

However, parental concern in this area is usually groundless and can be quite harmful. If the toddler has ample opportunity to choose from a well-balanced diet, he is almost certain to get enough to eat, even though his intake appears to have dropped off to zero. If, on the other hand, his mother becomes anxious and uses pressure, urging, and cajoling, she can in her agitation create a true feeding problem where none existed. Like the infant, the toddler can generally be relied on to adjust his food consumption to his fluctuating needs, and parents have only to offer him a varied, well-prepared diet. If it is important to parents that the toddler eat at mealtimes rather than at odd moments during the day, or if they feel that between-meal snacks overweight his diet in the direction of starches rather than proteins, he can easily do without snacks. If he then surprises his parents by turning ravenous, he can be given his regular meal a little early.

Setting Limits

The toddler is an active creature with a taste for vigorous, noisy exploration and experimentation. In the interests of his own safety, family comfort, and the preservation of furnishings, certain bounds must be set to his activity. (The problem of setting these bounds is by no means limited to the toddler age. We have already mentioned it in connection with late infancy, and much of what we have to say here applies also to the preschool years.) Limits are particularly necessary at this time because of the toddler's active mobility and poor judgment, as we said in describing his play. If, in imposing limits, the parent allows himself to become trapped in a battle of wills, he may either win, at the expense of the child's curiosity, enthusiasm, and self-esteem, or lose to a determined child's tantrums and negativism. To avoid this grim dilemma, observance of several principles is necessary. First, limits should not be thought of simply as restraints, but as a channeling of the child's behavior from areas of restriction to areas of freedom: he may not be allowed to tear up the collection of first editions, but there is no reason he cannot have his own collection of old telephone books and magazines to do with as he will. Second, a reasonable number of reasonable limits are good for a child. They let him know where he stands, and, in revealing the strength of his parents, show them as people who can be understood and relied on. It is important to see that the toddler (and older children, too) cannot always control his own impulses, and needs and wants protection from them by his parents. Without well-defined, consistent limits, the toddler is obliged to keep probing to see just how far he can go, a necessity that makes him as uncomfortable as it does his parents. Third, limits must not be oversubtle and beyond the toddler's powers of discrimination: if the electric toaster is forbidden, it must— at this early stage—be forbidden at all times and not merely when it is turned on. Fourth, limits have to be as few as is compatible with the child's and other people's welfare. If fragile and precious objects are not needed for frequent use, they are best put safely out of the child's reach, thus obviating some of the need for prohibitions. Insofar as practical, forbidden objects should be grouped together in a small number of locations so that a few wholesale taboos can take the place of many specific ones. A constant stream of "No!" and "Don't touch!" soon loses all impact or bewilders and paralyzes the child. Fifth, the toddler's life has to consist of something more than taboos. There must be places he can go, things he can play with, times and places that he can make a racket and run off steam. Children react in different ways to taboos— some are meek, some bland, some sweetly innocent; some are resentful, some are hurt, some are teasing—but a child who has ample gratification can easily tolerate the frustration of necessary prohibitions. In the same way, parents do not have to become ogres in the course of forbidding things to their child, but can remain as affectionate as ever. Sixth and finally, the toddler must not be so thoroughly protected from harm that he becomes fearful, upset by minor hurts, and clumsy in his behavior. He is entitled to a few wild oats, even if he has to pay for them with an occasional scratch or bruise or abrasion or pain. In other words, the firmness and consistency of the necessary limits must be balanced by a certain amount of flexibility, a willingness to let the child learn for himself.

Provided parents know what limits they want to set—it goes without saying that each parent will have his own particular areas of leniency and strictness—the establishment of taboos need not be difficult. Some taboos (such as those applied to the electric toaster) are best conveyed by a bark of "No!" reinforced, where necessary, by a slap on the hand, although usually the parent's tone of voice is enough. But since toddlers forget easily, and since forbidden fruits are always the most alluring, several repetitions may be needed. Also, it is during toddlerhood that children first learn the fine art of teasing, and they will continue to make passes at taboo objects, watching out of the corner of their eyes for a reaction. Under these circumstances, it may be well to remove the child from the site of temptation and get him started on something more acceptable. As the toddler's vocabulary and understanding increase, other and more relevant words can be substituted for the original "No," words like "Hot," "Ouch," "Break."

It will be noted that in setting limits there is little place for "reasoning with" the toddler, if only because of his insufficient language. He often cannot understand why a given object or activity should be dangerous for himself. There is, for instance, nothing especially lethal in the appearance of an electric wall outlet. Still less can he grasp the notion of monetary or sentimental values which adults attach to objects. The toddler has a strictly utilitarian viewpoint: objects have value in terms of how they behave, not in terms of what they are. Hence taboos at first have to be indisputable. Indeed, "reasoning" may be far less satisfying for the child than is an abrupt command. The latent menace of much of the adult's reasoning is conveyed in a preschool child's tirade against a contemporary: "I'll hit you! I'll cut you up in little pieces! I'll—I'll—I'll *explain* it to you!" [28]

However, the alternative to premature reasoning need not be only the battle of wills. Children of this age, as we know, are highly distractible and have brief attention spans and wide-ranging interests. Hence it is often easiest and most appropriate to side-step the "I want" or the "No" by changing the subject or offering some new attraction. It is not necessary to resolve every issue. Another virtue of distracting the child is that his early pride and sense of self are left intact if he is not made to "lose face" by yielding or submitting. Later in the preschool years, diverting the child becomes less suitable, and the adult must be willing to take a clear stand and use his authority, or to explain—but simply and clearly, within the child's comprehension, and without excessive moralizing. The overexplanatory parent is likely, by the time his child enters the preschool period, to become the victim of the false "Why?" An insistent series of "why's" can be used by the child to keep the parent off balance and to delay resolution of simple matters. Parents should note that "why" is sometimes such an aggressive device, sometimes a real question, and sometimes a device to keep the parent in contact with the child.

Although we can properly expect the toddler to abide by the prohibitions we lay down, we have no right to ask that he like it. As we said earlier, we have to understand and tolerate the toddler's occasional resentments without feeling offended or outraged. Even our mildest requests, of course, may sometimes run up against one of the toddler's sporadic bouts of negativism, which may take the extreme form of tantrums or of hitting, kicking, scratching, and biting at his parents. (As we have pointed out, the toddler's *verbal* negativism need not always be taken literally.) When violent negativism occurs in the particular context of eating or of toilet-training, it may be time to take off the pressure. When it is a matter of dressing or undressing him, of getting him home from the playground, of putting him to bed, and similar situations, the parent can be alert for any of three sources of opposition: pressures that are too steady and too overwhelming, a conflict of tempos between parent and child, or too abrupt a termination of an activity, without adequate notice that gives the child time to get used to the idea of what comes next. In some cases, of course, a parent can only keep his head and carry on with what he wants to do: if necessary, a small and very angry child can be carried under one arm, his legs flailing behind the adult, without injury to either party. Adult excitability tends to breed tantrums, while tantrums that go unrewarded in terms of anger or dismay or surrender—or subsequent moralizing—tend to subside more rapidly.

Toddlerhood can be a turbulent period, but the toddler's strivings for autonomy, to learn the limits between himself and the environment, to see the new and exciting human qualities of which he becomes aware, to learn a language which helps delineate reality and permits him to talk and think about it, are an indispensable prelude to the new sophistication that comes in the preschool years.

NOTES   (Starred items are recommended as further readings.)

[1] Erikson, *Childhood and Society*.

*[2] New York: Dutton, copyright, 1941. Quotations by permission of Basic Books, Inc.

[3] Woodcock, pp. 31-33.

[4] Woodcock, p. 33.

[5] Woodcock, pp. 33-35.

[6] Woodcock, pp. 37-38.

[7] See, for instance, Freud, *A General Introduction to Psychoanalysis*, pp. 276, 279 and passim.

[8] Williams, Lucretia, Observation record, Vassar College Nursery School, 11-13-39, age 4:0.

[9] *Childhood and Society*, pp. 222-224.

[10] Cassirer, Ernst, "Le langage et la construction du monde des objets," *Journal de Psychologie Normale et Pathologique*, 1933, **30**, 18-44.

*[11] McCarthy, Dorothea, "Language development in children," in Carmichael, *Manual of Child Psychology*, pp. 492-630 (our tables are adapted from those on pp. 499-502). By permission of John Wiley & Sons, Inc.

[12] Baldwin, J. M., *Mental Development in the Child and the Race: Methods and Processes*, New York: Macmillan, 1895.

[13] *Life and Ways of the Two-Year-Old*, pp. 121 and 125.

[14] McCarthy (pp. 530-532), summarizing studies of the use of various parts of speech, points out the impossibility of obtaining anything but the crudest estimates of their actual proportions.

[15] Ames, L. B., "The development of the sense of time in the young child," *Journal of Genetic Psychology*, 1946, **68**, 97-125.

[16] McCarthy, pp. 532-536.

[17] Williams, Lucretia, Observation notes, Vassar College Nursery School, 1-26-40.

[18] Leopold, W. F., *Speech Development of a Bilingual Child*, Evanston-Chicago: Northwestern University Studies in the Humanities, **6**, 4 vols., 1939-1949, Vol. 3, p. 168.

[19] Piaget, J., *The Child's Conception of the World*, New York: Harcourt, Brace, 1929. See also Dennis, W., "Piaget's questions applied to a child of known environment," *Journal of Genetic Psychology*, 1942, **60**, 307-320.

[20] Williams, Lucretia, Observation notes, Vassar College Nursery School, 2-8-40.

[21] *Id.*, Observation notes, Vassar College Nursery School, 1-24-40.

[22] *Id.*, Observation record, Vassar College Nursery School, 2-12-41.

[23] Woodcock, *Life and Ways of the Two-Year-Old*, p. 94.

[24] Levy, D. M., *Maternal Overprotection*, New York: Columbia University Press, 1943. (See also abridged version in Kuhlen and Thompson, *Psychological Studies of Human Development*, pp. 387-395.)

[25] *Cf.* Favez-Boutonier, J., "Child development patterns in France (I)," in Soddy, *Mental Health and Infant Development*, Vol. I, pp. 15-24, esp. pp. 19-21.

[26] Gesell and Ilg, *Infant and Child in the Culture of Today*, pp. 122, 128-129, 138-139, 148-149.

[27] Adler, A., *The Practice and Theory of Individual Psychology*, New York: Harcourt, Brace, 1923, p. 321.

[28] Omwake, Eveline, Personal communication.

FOR FURTHER READING

U. S. Children's Bureau, *Your Child from One to Six*, Washington 25: U. S. Government Printing Office. Like other Children's Bureau publications, this periodically revised manual provides an excellent account of modern practices.

Mead, Margaret, "Age patterning in personality development," *American Journal of Orthopsychiatry,* 1947, **17,** 231-240 (reprinted in Martin and Stendler, *Readings in Child Develop-*ment, pp. 170-176). A cross-cultural review of attitudes and practices toward children of different ages.

Davis, W. A., and Havighurst, R. J., *Father of the Man,* Boston: Houghton Mifflin, 1947. Some of the problems of toddlers and their parents.

CHAPTER 6

The Preschool
Child: 1*

Introduction

Some time between the ages of two and three, the child moves out
of toddlerhood and into the preschool period (although some part of
what we have said about toddlerhood applies equally to the preschool
years). The mass of research on childhood, most of it the product of
the past thirty years, has dealt most with this age. There are several
reasons for this: first, for many researchers, this is deemed the "crucial
stage" of development; second, the widespread establishment of nursery
schools has provided ready laboratories for observation and experiment;
and third, children of this age, because they express their feelings so
directly, are particularly accessible to study. It should probably be
further confessed that this period, in the authors' biased view, is the most
delightful of all to observe, to work with, and to know. The charm of
the preschool child may be evident even to harassed parents, for whom
this is a time when children are "cute" but "naughty." For the professional worker, who is not likely to think in such terms, the preschool
child is completely rewarding to be with. He will soon learn, after the
adult manner, to mask his active spirit, but meanwhile he wears his
personality on his sleeve: his thoughts and passions are instantly trans-

* We wish to make clear that we have objections to the term "preschool," which
we nevertheless use because it has become part of the language of child development as a designation for the years between toddlerhood and the time of entering
first grade. The term should carry no implication, however, that a nursery school
or kindergarten is merely "pre" anything else. It has a curriculum and a validity
in its own right. Nor does it mean that a child of this age is necessarily attending
such a school.

lated into words and deeds. His behavior is often colorful and sometimes violent, and always easy to observe and record.

As a toddler, the child became a member of his family. Now, he is beginning the slow process of finding his place in humanity at large— although the family will continue to be his primary frame of reference for several years to come. His individuality is becoming more pronounced. To adopt L. B. Murphy's metaphor, we can even characterize different children as bunnies or tigers or bears, or deer or sloths or chameleons.[1] We can distinguish talkative and reticent children, those who like to use their bodies, those who like to use their hands, those who like to use their eyes and ears. There are beginning to be leaders and followers, participators and lone wolves and onlookers. The preschool child has fewer internal limitations than when he was a toddler and knows fewer external, socially dictated restraints than he will in the future. As a result, these are years of maximum spontaneity. Because of his openness, he often gives us striking insights into his own world and even into our adult world—always provided, of course, that we are prepared in our turn to be openly receptive to what the child can tell us. All too often, as adults, instead of looking and listening and appreciating, we laugh or admonish or shrug off or pass judgment.

The preschool years do not lend themselves to a simple summary in a key phrase such as those we employed for the infant ("trust") and the toddler ("autonomy"), largely because so much development is going on in so many directions. Again, there is the matter of individual differences noted above. For another thing, as Erikson points out, the preschool years are an age of rapid fluctuations, when the child may be both overdependent and eager for independence, at one moment surprisingly mature and the next moment babyish, sometimes boyish and sometimes girlish, sometimes winsomely affectionate and constructive and then abruptly destructive and antisocial.[2] Another obstacle to a simple summary is that the preschool years are not a simple unit, but contain within them several phases of development. Age five is a far cry from age two. Just as the toddler is in many respects still an infant, so is the young preschool child often still a toddler. He may not yet be fully toilet-trained; according to studies by Roberts and Schoellkopf, some 40 percent of two-and-a-half-year-olds have daytime toilet accidents.[3] Especially in sleep, the young preschool child's sphincters are likely to betray him. Half-undressed for a nap, sucking his thumb, clutching a teddy bear or a frayed strip of blanket, he is revealed in all his vulnerable immaturity. Alongside him, the five-year-old appears sophisticated, competent, and self-assured. Socially, from two to six, the child is moving from the parallel play of toddlerhood toward integrated, co-operative play projects. The dramatic play of the early preschool years is episodic and disjointed; by the end of this period, the child will be playing out elaborated, coherent themes. The preschool child's vocabulary grows from 500 to 2,000 words; his piping, often indistinct voice becomes resonant and precise; and his language attains new highs of fluency, expressiveness, and, in many children, creativity.

He is developing a new and acute awareness of his body. He is learning to be a boy or a girl, so that toward the end of the preschool years we can see the first signs of a division into same-sex communities. At the same time, his motor skills are multiplying: the high-stepping toddle of age two becomes a free-swinging stride; his one-foot-at-a-time approach to staircases is yielding to a continuous movement of climbing or descending, and he is learning to scale ladders and trees and jungle gyms; from clutching spoons and banging kitchenware he goes on to manipulate mechanical toys and hammers and saws; the blocks and boxes he likes to carry become building materials to be fitted into intricate and delicately balanced structures. With paint brush or crayon he progresses, successively, to swirls and scribbles, lines, cross-hatchings, and color masses; where first he uses single colors randomly selected, he goes on to single colors chosen with care, to combinations of colors kept well separated, to many colors freely intermingled, and colors used to identify specific areas; and from the welter of his early experiments with pure line and color there emerge in the later preschool years recognizable depictions of familiar objects and activities. Just as his motor skills and scope expand, so he is acquiring, at his own level, the skills of the contemplative philosopher; now he is bringing language to bear on his busy taking in and digesting of the world—its colors and flavors and textures and implications. He is even preparing to branch out into the world of vicarious experience provided by written literature; toward the end of the preschool years, he not only listens to stories but goes through the motions of reading, "saying" the text as he goes.

During this time, the child's growth rate is leveling off from the first spurt of infancy toward the plateau of the early school years. In his first two years, the "average child" added fourteen or fifteen inches to his height; in the three years following, he will grow only nine or ten inches. In his first year, the child gained some fifteen pounds (about twice his birth weight); thereafter, his rate of gain drops off to about five pounds annually at age five. His proportions are changing. His legs grow faster than the rest of him; at age two, they account for 34 percent of his length; at five, 44 percent, which approaches the half-and-half proportions of the adult. By age five, his head will almost have reached adult size, but because his limbs have lengthened, he will have lost the top-heavy look of infancy and toddlerhood. His full set of twenty baby teeth is usually completed at about the age of two and a half —roughly the beginning of the preschool years. Similarly, the end of this period coincides approximately with the loss of his first temporary tooth. As the cartilage and bones of his face develop and the fat pads in his cheeks dwindle, his countenance loses its babyish cast and becomes better defined and more individualized. Throughout the preschool era, sex differences in rate of growth are not very pronounced, although boys and girls are already beginning to follow divergent paths of psychological development.

Meanwhile, beneath the surface, the maturational processes of *differentiation* and *functional subordination* continue working. During the preschool or late toddler years, however, we can see *learning* start to take precedence over maturation. No longer do autogenous behaviors regularly spring fullblown out of anatomical and physiological growth. Now it is primarily the capacities for learning new ways of behavior that mature: the ability to master skills and concepts and values and social relationships. Without nourishment from the human and physical environment, these capacities remain unfulfilled. Given a rich and stimulating environment, on the other hand, the preschooler can perform prodigies of development. We should remember, of course, that the preschool child's central environment is the one provided by his family, even though he may spend three or four or six hours daily at school. Nowadays, however, the preschool child is exposed to a far broader range of stimulation than in years past. Not only is he more likely to begin school at age two or three, but even when with his family more of the outside world is with him than formerly. The automobile lends his family a great deal of physical mobility. They have more money and leisure than ever before, and current mores dictate that the child shall participate to the utmost in family ventures. Perhaps most interesting is the way television has introduced new notions to the preschool child. In pre-television times, cowboys, for instance, belonged to the culture of older children. Now, four- and five-year-old children swagger about wearing broad-brimmed hats and with six-guns strapped low on their thighs. A few dogs wandering across the kindergarten playground may become the occasion for a coyote hunt. Not that the kindergarten child will have any clear idea of what a coyote is—or, for that matter, of what a cowboy is, except for appearance and manner. Regardless of the varied influences working on his development, however, the crucial ones are parental. In the first place, the parents decide to a large extent which experiences he will have and which shall be excluded. More important, they provide the emotional accents and labelings that determine the significance of experience, thus building the framework through which the child views all creation.

Meeting People

In the child's eyes, his parents are the repositories of all wisdom and strength and virtue, but during the preschool years his social horizons slowly broaden to include, on somewhat lower planes, people outside his immediate family. True, he has visited and been visited by numerous people during his first two years, but they have existed for him largely as passing and curious apparitions without the solid identities of the members of his family. Now he amplifies his circle of attachments and forms relationships with new adults such as a teacher; then, through her, with his contemporaries (*peers*); until finally, late in the preschool years, he may be able to operate for fairly extended intervals in the company of his peers—although he will still like to have a familiar adult nearby for ready reference. Of course, children who have been able to spend a good bit of time in the company of siblings close in age, cousins, and child neighbors may be temporarily advanced in social skills.

If the two- or three-year-old goes to nursery school, he ordinarily has to undergo a period of weaning from his mother to his teacher. After a few days, as he becomes convinced that the teacher too is a human being and that his mother will indeed return for him at the end of school, he can safely turn his attention first to the play materials and then to the other children. It is, of course, an individual decision as to when the child is ready for nursery school, and if his separation anxiety becomes too prolonged, the decision may have to be reconsidered.

As was noted in the discussion of toddlerhood, young preschool children may at first treat each other like mere things. Before long, however, a reciprocal curiosity appears, manifested by a staring examination or a tentative reaching out to touch each other's bodies or faces. Once other children have been inspected, identified, and named, there is a fluctuation between overt interchange and parallel play—where, it will be remembered, the other child's presence is important even if unacknowledged. Later on, the children begin to do things in bunches (*associative play*): a flock may collect in the sandbox, or crowd into the rocking boat, or swarm over the climbing structures, shrilling together in a display of shared feeling. There is a growing willingness to look and admire—as when the teacher calls attention to someone's new shoes—without, as yet, a need to compete for the center of the stage. Imitation of other children becomes more pronounced. One child, seeing another swinging or sliding or tricycling or painting, will want to do the same. There may be an epidemic of telephoning, each child speaking into his own instrument, sharing the fun of phoning but not conversing like older children. If one young preschool child produces a peculiar verbalization or vocalization, the others may take it up in an echoing chant. Perhaps this is the place to remark that it is important to hear and see activities of this sort, which the printed page can only dimly suggest. If the student does not have access to a nursery school laboratory, films and tape recordings may convey some of the immediacy we cannot hope to render. (A list of recommended films is appended at the end of the book.)

The same pattern of degrees of social interchange is discernible in the child's language behavior. Initially, except for an occasional cry of "No!" or "Mine!" in case of a property dispute, young preschool children tend not to talk directly to each other, but rather talk at and about each other to themselves or to the teacher. Early attempts at direct intercommunication are often a verbal version of parallel play, known as the *collective monologue*. The children talk in turn, each waiting for the other to finish, and apparently derive great satisfaction from the exchange. However, what one child says bears no relationship to what the other is talking about—their remarks are not even tangential. In the following example, Chris and Jenny are sitting cozily side by side, swinging their feet, politely waiting their turn to speak in "conversational" style, and enjoying, in the words of their teacher, a feeling of "comfortable togetherness" (these two children are about four, somewhat past the age when collective monologue predominates):

JENNY: They wiggle sideways when they kiss.
CHRIS: (vaguely) What?
JENNY: My bunny slippers. They are brown and red and sort of yellow and white. And they have eyes and ears and these noses that wiggle sideways when they kiss.
CHRIS: I have a piece of sugar in a red piece of paper. I'm gonna eat it but maybe it's for a horse.
JENNY: We bought them. My mommy did. We couldn't find the old ones. These are like the old ones. They were not in the trunk.

CHRIS: Can't eat the piece of sugar, not unless you take the paper off.
JENNY: And we found Mother Lamb. Oh, she was in Poughkeepsie in the trunk in the house in the woods where Mrs. Tiddywinkle lives.
CHRIS: Do you like sugar? I do, and so do horses.
JENNY: I play with my bunnies. They are real. We play in the woods. They have eyes. We *all* go in the woods. My teddy bear and the bunnies and the duck, to visit Mrs. Tiddywinkle. We play and play.
CHRIS: I guess I'll eat my sugar at lunch time. I can get more for the horses. Besides, I don't have no horses now.[4]

As the child grows older, he becomes better able to shape his thoughts to those of other people—although, as the misunderstandings, cross-purposes, and confusions of much adult conversation demonstrate, uncluttered communication is an ideal rarely attained. By the time he is four or five, the child will be able to exchange a great deal of information, describe events comprehensibly (although tending to include too many irrelevant details and sometimes to forget essential ones), and use language to co-ordinate group activities in pursuit of some agreed-on goal, lapsing less often into blind self-assertion or egocentric speech. (Incomplete communications in which the child appears to assume that his listener knows—as he himself does—the missing terms. See Jenny's opening statement above.)

There are three other aspects of social relationships that begin to appear during the preschool years and which, though seemingly contradictory, appear most strongly in the same individuals: sympathy, aggression, and leadership.[5] The first signs of sympathy appear when a child pauses in his play to stare at another child who is in distress. He may even, particularly back when he was a toddler, begin to cry himself, but less from a feeling of compassion than from an inability to distinguish the other child's emotions from his own. Such contagion is most likely to occur when some tension or anxiety is already present and ready to be mobilized. Later in the preschool years, we can see behavior akin to mature sympathy. One child will console another who has been hurt, run to call the teacher, or scold someone who has been unkind. Of course, as Murphy points out in her study of sympathy in young children, the child's motives may not be entirely pure, and his sympathy may contain elements of superiority, guilt, hostility, or other feelings.[6]

True sympathy implies understanding of how other people feel—including both positive and negative feelings—and it is perhaps for this reason that sympathy and leadership go hand in hand. In general, at this age, group organization shifts from moment to moment, making sustained leadership difficult. Also, the child acting as leader often loses interest and slips out of his role. In spite of these impediments, a number of preschool children do show traits of leadership in a variety of forms. Some children impose their will on others by sheer force of muscle or character. Some become "bossy," successfully identifying with adult authority; it should be noted, though, that there is also the futile bossiness of the insecure child who is trying vainly to win respect. Some preschool children can play on their fellows like an organ. Some, remaining largely inconspicuous or aloof, can exert a quiet but potent authority as arbiter, advisor, and model.

The relationships between sympathy and leadership and between leadership and aggressiveness are fairly obvious. That between sympathy and aggressiveness is more subtle. It seems likely that they occur together in individuals who have strong feelings, who are highly responsive to the feelings of others, and who are secure enough either to stand in opposition or to yield to others' feelings, as circumstances require. The correlation between sympathy and aggression is, of course, by no means perfect. Some children who feel or display little hostility are capable of considerable sympathy—most especially, perhaps, in situations where they themselves feel imperiled. Other children's aggressions may wholly lack the component of sympathy and appear quite heartless, or may even be expressive of profound psychological disorders.

Regardless of their source, the preschool child's passions run high, although, like summer squalls, they come and go quickly. For a young child, aggressive-appearing behavior may be more of an exploration than an act of hostility. Yet in a flash of anger, if his strength were equal to the job, there is little doubt that he would kill without compunction. But at this age, enmities are as unstable as friendships, so that a moment later, he may be showering endearments on the person he was prepared just now to annihilate.

Dawe has traced the development of children's patterns of quarreling during the preschool years.[7] Like so many studies of this age group, Dawe's was based on nursery school observations; neighborhood patterns may be quite different. Although in most respects we do not have to concern ourselves with sex differences in talking about preschool behavior, in the matter of quarrels such differences appear early in nursery school society. Before age three there is no noticeable difference between boys and girls, but thereafter girls show a decline in frequency of quarreling, while boys become increasingly combative up to age five, when they quickly become more self-contained. There are also marked changes with age in the reasons for children's quarrels. Two-and-a-half-year-olds quarrel mainly over possessions. This source of conflict yields with the passage of time to retaliation for physical attacks, resistance to being thwarted (earlier, undirected rage is the more usual reaction), and —an issue that will predominate in later childhood—difficulties in social adjustment: who will play with whom, what they will play, who will be leader, etc. The form of quarrels likewise changes with the years. The toddler's or young preschooler's grim, wordless tug-of-war over a disputed wagon gives way to physical violence punctuated with angry cries; to violence displaced upon an offender's property, neutral objects, or weaker scapegoats; and these in turn are gradually supplanted by the more "civilized" technique of verbal abuse.

A great deal, however, of what might seem to be aggression is shown by careful observation to be simply part of the preschool child's constant role-playing. In the following lunch-table conversation, there is only a half-playful aggression enhanced by the four-year-old's love of language for language's sake and by a sort of co-operative competition where each child builds on the other's ideas in an attempt to outdo him in fantastic exaggeration:

> JOHN: We'll cut off his arms.
> ELLIE: We'll saw off his legs.
> DON: Let's hang him up in a tree and tickle him.
> JOHN: Let's poke him full of black and blue marks.
> ELLIE: Let's cut off his hair and put it in the sandbox.
> DON: Let's cut out his grunties.
> JOHN: Let's smear him all over with grunties. . . .
> ELLIE: Let's make him eat lots of grunties.
> JOHN: We'll wrap it up in some paper—not cellophane—some
> yellow paper, and then tie some string around it.[8]

We might point out incidentally two other preschool themes evident in the preceding quotation. First, there is the major scatological component. Children very early learn the shock value of certain words. Late in the preschool years, most children become addicted for a while to "toilet talk," generously using words whose meaning they know very well; some of their earlier "bad language" was merely bad but meant little in terms of content. Whether or not the child knows the meaning of these fascinating words, adult outrage only intensifies their value, and they are best dealt with casually. Some restrictions may be necessary, but these can be couched in terms of the times and places and audiences appropriate for such talk. The second theme is that of mutilation. As we shall see when we discuss self-awareness in the preschool child and the psychodynamic conflicts he may have to deal with, body intactness is often of great concern to him. Meanwhile, it is enough to point out that one of the ways the child has of understanding and mastering his doubts and anxieties is to make light of them in his play, just as the medical student affects a tough air or plays macabre jokes to help control his squeamishness about the things he is called on to do.

The preschool child's social behavior, like much of his waking life, revolves around his play. It is now time to examine in more detail what his play consists of, what it means to the child, what it tells us about him and his world, and what it tells us about *us*.

Play, Reality, and Fantasy

Adults are inclined to think of play as recreation, a way of relaxing from the serious business of work. By the same token, although they tolerate the child's play, since it keeps him out from underfoot and since he is not yet ready to undertake anything really productive, they are inclined to dismiss it as unimportant. The preschool child's play, on the contrary, is a serious business, it is his work, his means of finding out what he and his world are like and what they can do to each other.[9] Probably the first form of play in infancy could be called *"sense-pleasure" play,* reveling in or relishing the experience of movements, pressures, flavors, sounds, and so forth. This form of play includes sheer appreciation of sensory experience, the seeking of ways of prolonging or repeating it, and the exploration of his surroundings and of himself as though to discover new sources of sensory experience. Whether the infant is snuggling against his mother's breast, shaking a rattle, playing with his fingers, kicking his legs, shouting, masturbating, or sucking his thumb, he delights in his learning about his capacities for feeling and, to a certain extent, about the external agencies linked to his experiences. Sense-pleasure play continues throughout life, usually in increasingly complex and patterned forms: the toddler bounces on a board; the preschool child swings, he samples the squirming texture of an earthworm or the taste of poster paint; and so on, to the adult who spends an evening in a cloud of music or who likes to explode balloons at parties. Even during infancy, sense-pleasure play branches out into a somewhat less self-contained *skill play,* the exercise of one's capacities for action. It is remarkable how, at the point of near-mastery of a skill, a child will drill himself in it over and over again. Later, once acquired, the skill serves other ends (it is functionally subordinated); at the time of acquisition it is fun for its own sake. The infant creeps and creeps, cruises endlessly from chair to couch to table; the toddler pounds and pounds his pegboard, undoes and recombines his nesting blocks, climbs all the furniture again and again, loads and reloads his wagon with the heaviest things he can pick up; the preschool child confabulates chants and stories to the point of adult distraction; the adult may volley a tennis ball against a fence or do crossword puzzles for hours on end. Late in infancy or early in toddlerhood, when the baby begins to feed his teddy bear, there emerge the first signs of *dramatic play,* the enactment of scenes from everyday life, which, at its peak of evolution, becomes the substance of life itself.

The child has, in effect, two ways of getting to know his world: he can interact with it, or he can act it—in other words, *be* it. In dramatic play, the child tries out concretely (by *identification*) what it feels like to be in the roles of other people and other things. As the child starts to become aware of other people with an existence apart from his own, as he starts to break loose from the shackles of egocentricity, he tries to comprehend the style, the attitudes, the activities of others by putting himself—often literally—in their shoes. We see children dressing up in adult clothes, playing mother or baby or doctor, serving tea, playing fireman or groceryman, pretending to be a rabbit or a tiger, acting simultaneously as airplane and pilot, as steam shovel and operator. Dramatic play does not serve merely as a means of learning about the society of which the child is a part. In play, his feelings of participation and identification afford the sense of power, consummation, and accomplishment that are not yet his in the practical scheme of things.

Roles which involve visible and clearly functional activities appeal most to the child. The jobs of housewife, policeman, carpenter, or roadbuilder can be grasped instantly. Although it may chagrin the white-collar or professional father, it is not surprising that the child finds the role of office worker or attorney dim and unappealing. Moreover, the child's portrayal of the roles he does fasten on depends on a highly literal use of externals, such as words whose meaning he may not understand. One child, for instance, turned to his teacher and announced, "You know, I'm really desperate! Tell me how to play I'm desperate." [10]

At first, the central theme of the preschool-age child's dramatic play is domesticity. Later on, he will branch out in his role-taking into the great but immediate world of filling stations, railroad stations, and garbage collection. Later still, he will go on to the more distant but still active realms of cowboys, ships, or jungles. To begin with, however, he is bound to the situations that are best known and most immediately vital to him. In domestic play, it should be noted, young preschool children feel no need to adhere consistently to the sex roles ordained in their biology. Boys can as easily be Mommy as Daddy, girls can as easily be Little Brother or Grandma. At three, children are a long way from having any stable notion of socially defined sex roles and are only beginning to be aware of physical sex differences. In the same way, the child is willing to be baby, parent, or grandparent—if necessary, all at the same time. When children "play house," i.e., play at being a family, roles change rapidly as the children tire of their parts. Baby may clamber out of his carriage and announce that he is now going to be the Mommy; the erstwhile Mommy may then make herself comfortable in the carriage, or perhaps decide that she will be Daddy, provided a third child will agree to be Baby.

Reflections of the Adult World in Play

Although children are relatively indifferent to considerations of age and sex, they soon develop an acute sensitivity to status values and are likely to compete for the parts with the greatest prestige. It may be painful but illuminating to fathers to note how often the mother, by her decision-making powers in the central areas of the child's life, such as what clothes to put on, when and what to eat, assumes much greater prestige than the father. An example of the behavior of a four-year-old girl with marked leadership qualities toward a boy with low standing in the group shows, incidentally, some of the status attached to particular roles in suburban society. The boy had been persistently trying to intrude on a game of house in which the girl was playing the role of Mommy. Finally, with all the skill of a born leader, she accepted him and disposed of him in one breath: "O.K. You be the Daddy. Finish your breakfast and I must drive you to the station. Here's your briefcase and you must get on the train. G'bye!" [11]

This quotation illustrates how dramatic play sometimes throws our adult characteristics into bold and startling relief. Needless to say, children's enactments of adult behavior often reflect parental tenderness, humor, and good sense. The most striking insights, however, come when we find ourselves projected as a scolding or whining voice, as a monument of pomposity, as a sleeping ogre who if disturbed snarls and gnashes his teeth. Here is a speech by Alice (age four and a half) as she tucks her doll into bed: "We like to have her but I just want her to stop the nonsense. She wets the bed all the time. You *wicket* girl! You bad, *wicket* girl!" [12] On another occasion, Alice (four years, eight months), having been excused from naps, was alone with her teacher in a small room during nap time and decided to play school:

> "I'm going to be the teacher and I'll teach you how to write." Takes pad and scribbles. Goes off across room to discipline a very noisy class (imaginary). Bawls out one child after another, ties them to their desks with long, long ropes so they can't get out, shuts the door firmly on them so she can't hear them crying. Throws arms around teacher's neck, kisses her, says, "You're very, very good. Pretty soon you can go out and play with those recesses. That's really hard. It's really for older children." [13]

In case there is any doubt, this was not Alice's own nursery school teacher she was portraying, but a version of "teacher" she had acquired from older children. We might remark parenthetically that all teachers are viewed in the culture of school-age children as tyrants, even in the case of children who have never been exposed to anything but the most benign of teachers and methods. In the same way, violence such as Alice perpetrated on her pupils need not necessarily be a direct re-enactment of treatment received at home. Even totally unspanked children still talk about and practice spanking in an attempt to fathom what it is like. Caricature of the adult is sometimes more deliberate than in the examples we have just cited, as seen in this conversation between two four-year-old boys perched atop a nursery school jungle gym and convulsed by their own wit:

> JACK: It's *lovely* to see you!
> DANNY: I'm so happy to see you!
> JACK: How *are* you? How have you *been*?
> DANNY: Sorry I have to go so quick.
> JACK: (adding broad strokes of four-year-old slapstick humor) I hope you have a good time falling down and bumping your head. [14]

Some of the most revealing insights into the child's-eye view of the adult world have come from the experimental or therapeutic use of toys (projective play techniques—see Chapter 14) which invite the child to construct scenes from family life. In his dramatizations, and in the very arrangement of the toys, the child may convey his view of the relative significance of children and the various adults in his family, of the things which frighten children or anger adults, or of the weightiness of adult controls and impositions. He may depict himself hemmed in by threatening creatures, or act out the revenge he would like to take against parental discipline.

The Mastery of Materials

In all the preschool child's play, we can see a trend from variable, impulsive play which is largely under the control of external stimulation toward more sustained and deliberately planned activity. As we saw in the last chapter, the child between two and three is still highly distractible and very much subject to the pushes and pulls of the environment. He responds to whatever catches his attention, promptly forgetting the activity he was just engaged in—we must bear in mind, of course, that his world is not so richly furnished as that of the five-year-old, and there are fewer things likely to evoke a response. A sequence from a film on preschool children clearly illustrates how this distractibility is often true even of four-year-olds: in the film, a child starts painting with the evident intention of portraying a horse; as he proceeds, the dripping paint suggests new patterns which he follows until his finished product is a composite of many superimposed inspirations.[15] The three- or four-year-old's pictures seldom represent objects identifiable to adult inspection, partly because he is more concerned with the qualities of the medium itself than with using it as a means of depiction, and partly because they record a chain of successive intentions. The young child's fascination with the sense-pleasure possibilities of paint and paper is worthy of respect in its own right: he is not and need not be concerned with picture-making. At this stage, the tactless adult can ask him no question more embarrassing than "What is it?" By the time he is five, by contrast, the child will often want and be able to plan and execute a recognizable picture of familiar objects. Again, the five-year-old can usually be counted on to find his own subject matter, and nothing is more pointless or stultifying than limiting the child to mass-produced pumpkins or to filling in the outlines of adult-made coloring books.

A similar line of development is visible in the use of other materials, such as building blocks. The three-year-old, in his block play, is more concerned with problems of balance and size and ways of combining blocks than he is with building any *thing*. The four-year-old uses blocks to make things, but his structures are usually sprawling, amorphous, and loosely hung together. The five-year-old can build highly integrated, carefully balanced block structures that often reach to phenomenal heights and are enormously intricate. Such constructions serve as settings for dramatic play which may continue over a period of days. These trends appear most clearly, of course, in nursery school, where simple raw materials like blocks are available in the lavish quantities children seem to need. Homes are generally limited to a small number of too-small blocks, often embellished, to attract adult customers, with alphabets or other irrelevant designs. In general, then, the five-year-old is able to initiate a chain of activities, each a necessary prelude to the next, without getting sidetracked, while younger children go from impulse to impulse.

As usual, of course, we have been talking about middle-class American children. The mastery of materials that we have described would look like mental retardation to many primitive peoples, where a three-year-old may build perfectly effective traps for birds, fish, or small game, as among the Kaffirs,[16] or where the five-year-old may take his own canoe out on the waters of the lagoon, as in Manus.[17] Accelerated learning in the use of materials is possible, but before parents begin a program of intensive training, it should be pointed out that the specific precocities of certain primitive children may be bought only at a price. For reasons that we do not wholly understand, forced growth can lead to early fixation, so that the learning process is arrested and a ceiling placed on development.

As the preschool child becomes better able to shape and dominate raw materials, to subordinate the materials themselves to other uses in play, he somewhat paradoxically begins to demand a greater degree of inherent structure in certain of his playthings. For a three-year-old, a block can be a doll, a train, a building, a cow. For the five-year-old, a block is a building material, and he wants some approximation of a real train to run in and out of the railroad station he makes with his blocks. The three-year-old can people a universe with sticks and stones and paper and rags—which, however, he does not try to shape in representational images. The four-year-old, to be a successful cowboy, wants some outstanding prop—a broad-brimmed hat, a cap pistol, or a neckerchief. For him, one element can stand for the whole configuration "cowboy." The five-year-old, though, is likely to feel dissatisfied in his role-playing unless he can wear the full regalia of his part. At the same time, he himself can often do much to provide the accessories he needs from the materials at his command. He can lay out boxes and blocks in the form of a space ship, cut pieces of wood and nail them together to make boats and airplanes, improvise a costume out of oddments from the rag bag.

Reality and Fantasy

Much of the play we have been discussing can be viewed as a product of the child's fantasy life, of his imagination. Such a view would not, however, be altogether correct. For it assumes that reality and fantasy are two distinct realms, which is only partly true in the preschool child's experience, where fact and fancy are likely to be interchangeable. But the preschool child's growing insistence on realism in his play and playthings points to the fact that he is becoming more sharply aware of a difference between pretending and reality. To the young preschool child, as we have suggested, playing is not play-acting, it is not making believe, it is living the roles he assumes. As he grows older, he finds it harder to believe in his own impersonations and has to bolster his play with more life-like supports. This increasing recognition of limits on his own ability to assume roles at will is nicely expressed in the four-year-old's remark, "Let's pretend we're not playing pretend." [18]

Despite the preschool child's new awareness that not everything he thinks is necessarily so, throughout most of this period we find that the child has not yet developed the adult's sharp boundaries between the world of stubborn facts and the world of imagination and dreams. Certainly the preschool child is in satisfactory contact with our "objective" world: he recognizes people and places and limits, he uses the utensils available to him appropriately, and so forth. But his own feelings and thoughts and wishes flow out into and influence the objective world, animating and coloring and shaping it so that his world includes much that is quite surprising to adults. To the preschool child, dreams are real events taking place in real space—a child may even balk at sleeping in his own room, on the grounds that there are too many dreams in there.[19] Stuart expressed puzzlement on highly realistic grounds: "How can I see the things in dreams unless my eyes are open?" [20] Although it is less true for the preschool child than for the toddler, pictures may have the same reality as the objects they represent; one will occasionally see a three-year-old with his ear glued to a picture of a watch, or trying to pick something off the printed page. It is not unheard of for young preschool children to think that the characters on television programs live inside the set, as in the *New Yorker*'s account of a four-year-old who, seeing his grandmother on a program, insisted that she "come out of that box" and play with him, and who, the following day, told a friend that Grandma was inside the television set but would be out in two weeks, when she was due to visit.[21] The preschool child often nourishes a firm conviction that he can magically influence external events by an application of his will, just as he sees an adult "making" the car go. Professional magicians find that young preschool children make a very unresponsive audience. The children see nothing more remarkable in a rabbit's emerging from a silk hat or a lady's being sawed in half and then reunited than in the everyday magic of their lives. For the same reason, adults are far more likely to be entertained by *Alice in Wonderland* than are very young children.

It is during this period, especially at ages four to five, that imaginary companions appear. Estimates as to the frequency of such manifestations vary. One of the more careful studies, by Ames and Learned, indicates that some 20 percent of children have imaginary companions, identities, or domains, human, animal, or inanimate.[22] Informal inquiries among female college students suggest that the incidence may be much higher, perhaps above 50 percent. Imaginary companions are often experienced with all the vividness and solidity of real objects, and children's families may find themselves obliged to make extravagant adjustments to the invisible (to them) visitor, taking care not to bump into him or to sit on him. Imaginary companions or domains are sometimes born of a special need in the child's life: a friend, a scapegoat, an extra conscience, a model, or a place to get away from it all. Although, at age six, she was beyond the preschool years, Frances Warfield's autobiographical account of her imaginary friend Wrinkel provides an excellent description of one of the many possible functions an imaginary companion may serve. In this case, Wrinkel was the private spokesman for the resentments of a well-behaved hard-of-hearing girl who was afraid to acknowledge her handicap and therefore could not ask people to speak up.

> Wrinkel came along at this time. I wanted a close friend. Also, in my world of aunts and sisters, a boy was interesting.
> Wrinkel was invisible and inaudible, which left him free to do and say whatever he wanted. The first time he entered a room he found the exact center of the ceiling and drove in a large invisible staple. He tossed an invisible rope ladder through the staple, festooning it over the tops of pictures, curtain poles, and chandeliers, and climbed over people's heads, listening to their talk and making nonsense of it.
> Wrinkel was smarter than anybody—smarter than my sister Ann. For one thing, he was a boy. For another thing, though he could hear as

perfectly as Ann could, he didn't care whether he heard perfectly or not.
He chose to hear, and to act on what he heard, strictly as he had a mind
to. . . .[23]

When people talked and talked and Wrinkel didn't make sense of
what they said, that wasn't because he didn't hear it. It was because he
liked to make nonsense by weaving his own name in and out of their
sentences. . . .[24]

He killed people off for me all the time. He killed off all the ones
I didn't like—the ones who cleared their throats pointedly or raised
their voices at me, as if they thought I might not hear them. He killed
off deadpans, when they mumbled some question at me.[25]

Not all imaginary companions, it should be said, are as pleasant for
the host to harbor as was Wrinkel. Sometimes they are distinctly unwelcome, like invading hallucinations, and seem to be the incarnation of
some deep-rooted fear or guilt.[26] In some children, for instance, a
companion who serves as a conscience may be gently reproving to the
child when he errs; in other children, however, it can castigate and
scold the child into a state of terror. Some imaginary companions do not
seem to fill any particular need or express any particular problem. They
simply appear on the scene, do what they do, and leave—sometimes
fading away, sometimes dying a melodramatic death in an automobile
accident or at the hands of pirates. Although the preschool years are the
heyday of the imaginary companion, such phenomena occasionally persist or arrive as late as age ten. Older children, however, sensitive to
adult standards of reality, may be reluctant to talk about their fantasies.

It is because the preschool child's world is a mélange of what to the
adult are fact and fiction, shot through with magical potentialities, that
the child may seem to adults uninstructed in his ways to be playing free
and easy with the truth. During most of this period, however, the very
notion of an untruth is inconceivable to the child. A preschool child will
have a very hard time complying with an adult's request that he repeat a
statement such as "the snow is black," although he could enjoy *pretending* that snow is black. When, however, the child's own wishes conflict
with reality, reality is likely to yield. If the child can make things so
merely by thinking or saying them, then his claim that he has performed
an assigned task or his denial that he has committed a misdeed is sufficient to do or undo the action in question. The young child can create
past history—not to mention a present and a future—by waving the
wand of his tongue. But he is not lying, in the sense of thinking one thing

Associative play

(From *A Long Time to Grow: Part I: Two- and Three-Year-Olds in Nursery School*)

Co-operative group play

Five-year-olds can co-ordinate their activities in sustained group projects.

Preschool combats

(From *Preschool Incidents: When Should Grownups Stop Fights*)

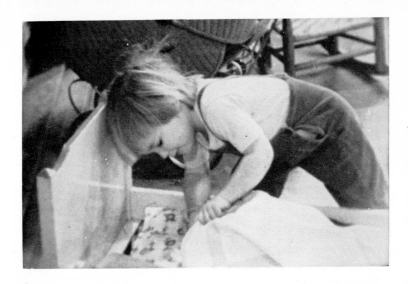

The central theme
of the preschool
child's dramatic
play is domesticity.

(From *A Long Time
to Grow: Part I*)

In dramatic play,
children's roles
are not confined
by considerations
of sex.

The three- or four-year-old's paintings seldom represent objects identifiable to adult inspection.

A four-year-old's block building.

and saying another. It is not much before age five that the child has any notion of keeping his thoughts to himself. Even then, he can only deceive by silence, and even this does not work very well: the child feels that his thoughts, whether spoken or unspoken, are somehow plainly visible to adults. This is one reason why a secret is burdensome to young children—it is only a matter of time before some all-seeing adult will notice it. (A second reason is that young children find the prospect of startling someone with confidential information almost irresistible: "You know what, Daddy? I have a secret. . . .") Since deliberate deception is beyond the preschool child's powers, parental anger at his lies is somewhat misplaced. This does not mean that parents should never impose their reality on him, but they should be able to strike a balance between molding the child's thinking and enjoying it for what it is and for the insights it provides. Of course, when true lying does appear, perhaps at six or seven, it is always well for parents to keep in mind that lying sometimes is the first refuge for a frightened child whose trust must be won anew.

In talking about the preschool child's play behavior, we have necessarily referred to ways of viewing the world peculiar to this age. In the next two sections, we shall look in more detail at some of the ways his world is put together, beginning with his new ways of being aware of his own body and its potentialities for action and experience.

Awareness of Self

In discussing infancy, we were forced to make inferences about the baby's *self-awareness*—or lack of it—from his often vocal but nevertheless wordless behavior. In dealing with the toddler, we were somewhat better off, since his behavior repertory included a fair number of words. The preschool child, by contrast, can often tell us directly about his self-experience—although we are still in many cases obliged to infer it from what he says about other things.[27]

It should be remembered that the child's developing self-awareness is almost a special case of his developing awareness of things around him, particularly other people. His awareness both of himself and of the environment increases as he becomes psychologically more differentiated from his surroundings, as he comes to distinguish between external events and internal ones, and as he learns to suspend action in favor of contemplation, thought, and feeling. In one sense, of course, the child's awareness of other people precedes awareness of himself: he is aware of their capacity to gratify or harm him before he knows that *he* is there to be gratified or harmed. But as his experience begins to add up, as he becomes aware of his own boundaries and strengths and vulnerabilities, he becomes ready to see that other people too share, in differing degrees, his strengths and vulnerabilities, his capacities for joy and sorrow and pain. It is a difficult thing to perceive other people in the round. We have already spoken of how the preschool child's feelings of sympathy develop from direct participation in what happens to other children into a more mature sympathy based on a detached understanding. But even though the preschool child soon learns to appreciate the feelings of other children, the feelings of adults present a much greater problem. To the preschool child, adults—even when he consciously or unconsciously mocks their ways—appear as omniscient, omnipotent beings who order other people and things around and do only what they want to do. How can he suspect that these lordly beings have fears and worries and frailties—not to mention constitutions—like his own? But each discovery about himself tells him something about other people, and vice versa. The following quotations from Stuart's discussions with his teacher at intervals during his fifth year illustrate how the child co-ordinates his experience of himself with his experience of others:

> What is my back like, Miss Williams? (Nice. Like other backs, etc.) NO! Different. MINE! (Yes, but most backs are alike.) Like Mr. Stone's? Wide? (Like his and other people's.) Oh. (He is thoughtful and slightly dashed. . . .) [28]

> You can't see your own face, can you? . . .[29]

> (Inspecting his abdomen as he dresses after nap.) You know a thing? There is something funny about my skin. It fits all smooth mostly, but when I do this, there are extra skin in crumples. What is that for? (It's loose so you can move and stretch, etc.) No, it is not loose or it would show. It would hang down. It would be too big. (Like a rubber band.) Would it break if you pulled it too much? (Can stretch a lot.) I had this same skin when I was a baby. It fits very nice. It is me.[30]

> Why have you a long head, and me a little round one? . . .[31]

> Sometimes I wonder about the blood in me. Inside me it is all wet and blood and moving and lots of insides, but outside is all dry and careful and you would never know about the inside part by looking at the outside part. Not unless you got a hole in you and some of the blood came out. All the people are like that. Their skins keep them in, but underneath their skins is such a lot. . . . Your insides never stops. . . . It is

so funny to think of you being all wet inside and all dry outside. Everybody is like that. I am. Why, Miss Williams, *you* are (laughs). Did you ever think about it? (Teacher offers to show him anatomical picture.) A picture that would be for you would be for me, too? Then we are alike. You and me are alike.[32]

This growing consciousness of common experience is not limited to the human sphere and does not automatically lead to clarification in adult terms. Thus, on other occasions, Stuart wanted to know how it feels to be an earthworm and whether it hurts the ground to have holes dug in it.

Stuart's comments imply another theme which we mentioned briefly earlier and shall return to again, the problem of intactness of the newly discovered self. The more the child becomes aware of his separateness from the environment, the more he is obliged to question his own identity and the more he becomes concerned about staying intact. This concern is not a new development—a toddler, for instance, may be quite distressed at being offered a broken cookie—but it becomes particularly acute late in the preschool years. Stuart, at five, objected strenuously when his teacher appeared without her glasses and hence incomplete or damaged. These further quotations show how a visit to the dentist, coupled with anticipations of a tonsillectomy, seems to have stirred up some of his feelings about being complete:

> Once there was Stuart with a tooth and in it there was a hole. So it was fixed. The man had many little streams there, very nice. There was a pain, a bright pain. It was bright when he pushed with a noise and a bar. But there was no blood. No blood. . . . Can I get a hole in my hand like the hole in my tooth? Will it have to be filled with a loud noise? . . . The queen was in the garden hanging up her clothes, there came along a big thing to snap off her nose. . . . Her nose was not. It bled and bled and she died. Humpty Dumpty did die, too. He fell off and couldn't put together again. . . . When I have my tonsils out— what will happen when I have my tonsils out? Will it bleed? Will I be dead? Being blood is being dead. Why do I have my tonsils out?
> *I do not like myself not to be myself, and that is what will happen if even my littlest tonsils is taken away from me.*
> . . . Sad it was to have a nose taken off. So it will be sad to have a tonsil out. Blood, blood, blood. When the nose—the tonsil is out.[33]

Fears

The vulnerability that comes with self-awareness is often expressed in a sudden outcropping of new fears at ages four and five.[34] At age four, these seem to have less to do with specific damage to the child's integrity than with a menacing cast in his emotional world. He is learning about the real and imaginary dangers that exist—kidnappers, spooks, burglars, giants—but does not see their explicit relationship to himself. It is not uncommon that four-year-olds will need to have the light left on while they sleep; in a dark or half-dark room, it is too easy for the swaying curtains to take on monstrous aspects, for unnamed terrors to lurk under beds or in closets. On the school playground, a child who declares himself a tiger and begins snarling, or who pronounces his undulating arm a snake, may provoke genuine panic in his fellows. Their terror may be tinged with skepticism, but they would rather not take a chance on finding out.

By age five, the child often has a fairly specific sense of the harm he can suffer. Among other things, he may become afraid of dying. This fear is not rooted in a recognition that all men are mortal, and that he himself will some day grow old and die, but simply that people do die and that something could happen to him—not eventually, but now. What "die" means, of course, is likely to be indistinct and variable. In games, death is reversible: "Bang! You're dead! O.K. Now you must be alive again." Children find it very hard to grasp the blank finality of death; one child asks, "If you woke up one morning, and you were dead, would it hurt?" Stuart, in his advanced fashion, draws an analogy to being blind: "Being dead is like being blind, only *all* the time and the same feeling all over, everywhere, like blind in the eye." [35] After a child is misguidedly told that death is like a continuing sleep, his parents, forgetting, may wonder why he has suddenly become terrified of going to bed at night.

Adults, particularly in middle-class society, are inclined to shield young children from the knowledge of death. This may even take the form of pretending there has been no death ("Grandpa's gone on a long trip") or of attempting to deny their own feelings about death (even the devout seldom feel the whole-hearted joy, unmixed with grief, they try to impart to the child when they say, "Grandpa is happy now in Heaven"). The child, however, with his acute emotional sensitivity, will rapidly detect that something is seriously wrong. His perception of adult distress, his awareness of mystery and exclusion and of the macabre atmosphere with which our society surrounds death, and his interior elaborations of fragments of knowledge, are likely to lead to fear and bewilderment far greater than would be produced by simple frankness about what has happened and honesty about adult feelings. The tendency to conceal death from the child rests on the same assumption of childish innocence as other tendencies in our society to insulate the child from the hard realities—sex, money, disagreements and animosities between parents, for instance. In all of these areas, in our view, children benefit from being given as many facts as they can understand, rather than inventions and denials that complicate their feelings.

We shall allude in another section to other sources of fears in preschool children.

Awareness of Growth and Continuity

A further aspect of self-awareness is the child's increasing knowledge of growth and continuity. Time is beginning to move—as we are aware, it seems to slip away with ever greater velocity as we grow older—and the child begins to sense the transitory nature of his experience; as one child remarked, his birthday had come and gone and there was nothing left, but he was older. In addition, the child is now learning about the penalties as well as the gratifications of growing. Along with the power and independence of being big come the responsibilities and the loneliness. Such notions, of course, exist only fleetingly and inarticulately for the preschool child, but they may well underlie otherwise unaccountable spells of babyishness, sulkiness, clinging behavior, weeping and whining. Such feelings and such behavior are often precipitated by the birth of a younger brother or sister, when the child may for the first time be aware of the state of passive bliss he has left behind and the self-reliance that is now demanded of him. Even sib-less children, however, are to some extent ambivalent about growing up: they may play at being a baby, they may ask the adult to "Feed me" and "Dress me." Whatever the cause of such regressive interludes, such ups and downs are a part of normal growth, and parents must be ready to assure the child of their continuing love and support, although on the whole emphasizing the rewards that accompany the—in any case inevitable—process of growing up.

The child's emerging awareness of himself does not yet make for a constant *self-image* or *identity*. The child's identity can shift dramatically in emotionally charged circumstances, in dramatic play, or in the course of being an imaginary personality. Our friend Stuart, for instance, spent a number of months, when he was four, earnestly, skillfully, and doggedly being a particular nine-year-old boy whom he had heard of but never met. While there is no record of his ever having convinced anybody else that he was anyone but Stuart, he nevertheless managed for a time to strike his contemporaries dumb with his patronizing manner

and references to the school he attended, where they had real "lissons."
The identity of other people also lacks fixity. Biber relates the story
(poignantly familiar to nursery school teachers) of the three-year-old
who, meeting his well-loved teacher on the street, totally failed to recognize her. In school the next morning, he gave her his usual affectionate
hug and then, as though struck by a sudden thought, asked her in some
bafflement, "What's your name with your hat on?" [36] It seems that, for
the preschool child, identity may shift beyond recognition when removed from a familiar context. Needless to say, adults are somewhat
prone to the same instability: we may have difficulty recognizing the
corner grocer when we see him away from his customary setting; almost
proverbially, the people who made such stimulating cruise companions
turn out to be utterly commonplace when we meet them again ashore.
We might also take note of the personality changes adults undergo as
they move from situation to situation: having dinner with the boss,
visiting their parents, complaining about the telephone service, and so
forth.

We should mention here Horowitz's study on the *localization of the
self* in preschool children.[37] Having ascertained a child's name, he would
ask him to point to Johnny. It developed that children would consistently
indicate one circumscribed region of the body: a point in the jaw, for
instance, or in the abdomen. Horowitz would then point to other parts
of the body, asking each time, "Is this Johnny?" Parts other than the
one first pointed out were acknowledged as Johnny's, but not as Johnny.
This finding might be contrasted with Claparède's observation that for
adults the center of being comes to rest in the middle of the skull, just
behind the eyes.[38]

It is interesting to note that, although the preschool child is aware of
himself and others, he seldom seems able to entertain both awarenesses
simultaneously. Asked how many people there are in his family, he
forgets, because he is counting them from his standpoint, to count himself. Similarly, if he draws a picture of his family, he himself is not likely
to appear in it. Asked if he has a brother, he will (assuming it is so)
answer yes. Has his brother a brother? No. Is he his brother's brother?
Yes. Has his brother a brother? No.[39]

Psychosexual Development

Early in the preschool years, the child's awareness of his own sex
membership plays little part in his identity. The child can say readily

enough whether he is a boy or a girl, but the designation probably lacks any profound significance or stable anchorage for him. As we have already mentioned, most young children in their play feel free to take on male or female roles as the occasion demands, without reference to their own biological make-up and without the embarrassment a school-age child would feel. At age four, even those children who know about genital differences between boys and girls regard them as secondary to styles of coiffure or dress in determining sex and sex differences.[40] One four-year-old, visiting a family new to the neighborhood, observed their small baby creeping about the sunny lawn in the nude. Reporting on the new family to her mother, she was asked whether the baby was a boy or a girl and replied, "I don't know. It's so hard to tell at that age, especially with their clothes off." The curiosity of three- or four-year-olds about sexual matters, and their ventures into sex play, are likely to be brief. Toward five, children take genital differences more seriously and begin to be aware of personality differences related to sex. In groups of five-year-olds, one can see boys pursuing masculine interests in predominantly masculine company, and girls banding together in feminine activities. Here we have a foreshadowing of the pronounced cleavage of the sexes that takes place during the school years. We should also add that awareness of sexuality and sex roles comes earlier, as Rabban has pointed out,[41] to lower-class (and to most primitive) children than to middle-class children. Not only does the lower-class child tend to lead a less sheltered life, but masculine and feminine roles are more clearly defined for him than in our middle-class society of many overlapping activities for men and women.

Although the social implications of being a boy or a girl seem to outweigh the sexual ones up to the time of puberty, five-year-olds are likely to be quite persistent in their questions and experiments, and seem to be on the threshold of clear-cut sexual experience. Indeed, Kinsey cites evidence to show that some children—it is all but impossible to know how many—are able to attain sexual climax as early as age three.[42] Our discussion of self-awareness thus brings us to a consideration of the psychosexual crisis of the preschool years.

The Freudian View of Sexual Development

Freud's formulations of the role of sexuality in development are accepted in differing degrees by professional people in the fields of psychiatry, social work, and psychology. There can, however, be no doubt that Freud's ideas have been enormously influential, so that even those

workers who reject the general framework of Freudian theory still find
many of his concepts useful, and those who reject his concepts are
obliged to find new ways of accounting for the facts he brought to light.
Because Freud's thinking was so influential, and because his ideas have
become a part of our general culture, we feel that it is necessary to
present, at least in brief outline, something of the original Freudian
doctrine. We have already sketched in Freud's notions about the oral and
anal stages of development. Here we shall deal with what was for him
the most crucial period of all, the *phallic stage,* culminating in the
Oedipus complex.[43]

The term "Oedipus complex" comes from the Greek myth of King
Oedipus, who unwittingly, but in fulfillment of an old prophecy, killed
his father and married his mother. Analogously, the small boy is seen as
falling in love with his mother and turning against his father as a rival
for her affections. Naturally, these strivings are opposed by the realities
of the situation, by the child's sense of danger in competing with an all-
powerful father, and by contradictory impulses of affection for the father
and resentment (as when she disciplines him) against the mother. The
normal outcome of this (in Freud's view) universal *conflict* of opposing
forces is to align and identify oneself with the father, submerging (i.e.,
repressing) the unacceptable wishes. It will be noted that here and in
what is to follow, we speak largely in terms of the boy. In general, it is
safe to say that the girl follows a roughly equivalent sequence, with the
opposite parent substituted in the relationships of attachment and hostility. However, Freud was never quite satisfied with his description of
the female Oedipus complex (sometimes referred to as the "Electra
complex"), and at various times developed its details in different ways.

This view, based originally on work with adult neurotics, has found
some confirmation in—or at least is not inconsistent with—the behavior
of both normal and disturbed children. In regard to turning against the
parents, although adults were long loath to accept the fact, children are
ambivalent about their parents; that is, they blend or alternate hostility
with affection. It likewise seems to be true, as Freud proposed, that
children feel guilty about their anger and conceal or deny it. In regard
to the Oedipus complex itself, we should make explicit that for Freud
the attachment to the mother includes specifically sexual feelings, coin-
ciding with the shift of focus of *erogenous zones* (parts of the body susceptible to sexual stimulation) from oral and anal to genital during the
latter half of the preschool years. Freud calls this stage *phallic,* however,
to distinguish it from the true *genital* stage of adult sexuality. Even

though Freud acknowledged a real difference between infantile and adult sexuality, his ideas were highly repugnant to his contemporaries. Nevertheless, subsequent observations of children have shown the ubiquity of masturbation and other indicators of sexual interest and activity. It is, as we know, commonplace for little boys to announce that they will one day marry their mothers, or little girls their fathers. One little girl, at age five, went through the house systematically turning pictures of her mother to the wall. Such behavior may well reflect Oedipal strivings of the kind Freud postulated.

The repression of dangerous wishes that ends the Oedipal phase was thought by Freud to be a product of threats of castration by the father. (Freud did not use "castration" in the literal sense of removal of the gonads, but in the sense of any implied or actual injury to the genitalia, especially to the penis itself.) Unlike some other societies, ours has placed powerful taboos on masturbation, and there is no doubt that many irrational threats have been made by adults to check its practice, even, according to widespread testimony, to "If you don't stop, I'll cut it off!" Perhaps such threats were more common in Freud's day: they seem to be present in the reports of all his patients. Freud concluded that even if the father did not make such threats openly, they were sensed by the child and associated with sexuality, with yearnings toward the mother, and with guilt for hostility against the father, and hence became one of the major forces in the repression of these unacceptable feelings. In the Freudian view, therefore, the fears of young children that we discussed earlier are seen as *castration anxiety,* open or disguised representations of fear of mutilation at the hands of the potentially angry and vengeful father (often symbolized in dreams or fantasies or dramatic play as a large animal). The underlying threat is always seen as the threat of bodily attack, specifically against the genitals. Thus, alarm like Stuart's over the intactness of his body, "even to the littlest tonsil," would be seen by the Freudian psychologist as veiled castration fear.

According to Freud, the infant is born with primitive desires and rages. Freud called this primitive aspect of the personality the *id,* and conceived of it as wholly wishful, demanding, and wholly uninfluenced by the demands of reality. In another Freudian phrase, the id functions solely in terms of the *pleasure-principle.* In the course of growing up, the id components of the personality are always present in their unmodified state (we may become aware of them in some of our dreams and daydreams), but their expression is limited by two other "sectors" of the personality, labeled *ego* and *superego.* The ego is the reality-oriented part of the person: the person as perceiver, rememberer, reasoner, doer, and mediator of id-impulses in terms of what is realistic and feasible. In Freud's terminology, the ego is governed by the *reality-principle*. As the child becomes more aware of his parents as people whose love is crucial to him, his concerns with their admonitions and rules of behavior become something more than a recognition of reality in terms of what he can get away with. In the process of resolving the Oedipal conflict, the child buries his early overattachment to his mother (if he is a boy) and substitutes for the hostility toward his father a strong identification with him. This is said to involve an actual incorporation of certain aspects of the father's image, including the authority-wielding ones. The internalized paternal authority becames the superego (roughly speaking, the conscience), which influences the kind of behavior the child now allows *himself*. It is as though a bit of the parent were inside him saying—but saying in the child's own voice—"Thou shalt" or "Thou shalt not": these are now *his* standards of good and bad. He is now capable of experiencing *guilt,* the product of self-condemnation, as opposed to the shame produced by parental rebuke or ridicule.

Freud's view that all children normally experience passion, hostility, shame, anxiety, and conflict is surely closer to the mark than the "sweetness and light" viewpoint that he did so much to undermine. At the same time, Freud was an extremely moral man and emphasized the importance of guilt. Conscience, the voice of guilt, is the necessary basis of much of the self-regulation required for sound social relationships. According to Freud, this is the time when one can throw in one's lot with other people or else become alienated from them and, as an inevitable consequence, from oneself. A healthy and complete superego incorporates parental love and dependability as well as threat. The failure to establish close ties of affection may lead to the development of a "psychopathic" personality, a person for whom the feelings of others are important only as something to be manipulated, and for whom right and wrong are measured in terms of personal gain (see Chapter 13). On the other hand, excessive threat by parents, producing excessive guilt in the child, causes different disturbances, including constriction of spontaneity and initiative. Erikson, whose rephrasing of basic Freudian concepts we have drawn on in describing the critical issues of infancy and toddlerhood, makes the key issue of the preschool years development in the direction either of initiative or of guilt. (While we share his view that there is a danger that initiative or spontaneity may be crippled at this period of growth, this single issue, as we stated at the beginning of the chapter, does not seem to take in enough of the developmental phenomena, or even the developmental problems, of the preschool years.)

Freud's views on parental roles may have been influenced by the Middle European family structure of his time, with its emphasis on the father as a powerful, authority-laden figure. Many writers, including psychoanalysts, have pointed out that this picture does not precisely fit the contemporary middle-class American father. We have come a long way since Clarence Day's time, when, according to the image we now hold, Father was a remote, Olympian figure who dispensed counsel, commands, rewards, and punishments (most often the last: "Just wait until your father gets home!"). During the day, he disappeared to a vaguely hallowed place known as The Office. Nowadays, he may still be remote, but he surely cannot be Olympian. There is a distressing trend in some families for father to become a dissociated supernumerary whose life does not really intersect with those of his wife and children. There is yet another trend in which father is, in his off-duty hours, submerged in family activity, playing a much more intimate role in household management, changing diapers and giving bottles, running the appliances that make mother's lot easier, and doing the weekly shopping. He would not think of handing down decrees from on high, as in the Clarence Day era, but shares the decision-making process with his wife and, as they get old enough, the children. The Office has lost its sanctity—indeed, mother has probably done a term of service in an office, too.

Not everyone, however, is totally enthusiastic about this second trend in being a husband. The husband himself may feel somewhat cut off from the masculine world he knew as a soldier or young bachelor. Along with this goes the changed significance of his work, which was at one time a separate compartment of male existence with gratifications quite different from those of having a family; the lessened value of work contributes to the husband's decreased sense of personal worth. Whatever he may be on the job, back home in the suburbs he may be in danger of becoming an assistant mother and of losing his specifically masculine identity. At first glance, studies of unemployed men in Austria during the 1930's might not seem too relevant to today's prosperous young American husbands, but findings by Lazarsfeld and his associates about the loss of prestige these unemployed men suffered in the eyes of their families may be comparable to a loss of prestige because work has low esteem.[44] There is evidence in the content of radio programs and comic strips that father, in descending from his pedestal, has lost his dignity and become a figure of fun, a lovable, well-intentioned incompetent who is more to be tolerated than condemned. Some psychologists feel that the process has already gone too far and that in some versions the modern father does not give his children a sufficiently clear picture of masculinity, that he is not sufficiently differentiated from the mother to provide a model of the manly virtues for his sons to identify with and his daughters to relate to. Needless to say, our description of the contemporary middle-class father is a composite caricature, and the trends we have spoken of are not universal. Besides which, we should not overlook the very real gains for fathers and children in the increase of companionship between them. We are not advocating a return to the stern, Freudian father, but an understanding, participating kind of fatherhood which is nonetheless paternal and masculine, and not a second-rate, part-time motherhood. In any event, fathers are worth having, a view recently reinforced by Stolz's study of children separated from fathers in military service.[45] By comparison with children not so separated, Stolz's children showed a greater number of feeding and similar problems, reduced independence, poorer relations with their age-mates, increased anxiety, and other such indications of maladjustment.

Sex Education

In the light of Freudian theory, of clinical findings, and of careful observations of children's behavior, concerns, and questions, we are likely to be more aware of children's sexual interests and curiosities, and of the unspoken implications in queries about their "insides" or about sex differences. Certainly we have learned the unwisdom, at this vulnerable period, of threat or punishment in dealing with children's sexual concerns. Going further, we have come to appreciate the need to give children simple, accurate sex information. Children of three or four often want to know where babies come from and can be told simply that babies grow inside their mothers. It is well to add that there is a special place for them, or else a child may think that the baby is mixed in with food and feces and other body contents. It is usually not until he is five or older that the child wants to know how the baby got there. At five, it may be enough to say that the father has to help start the baby growing, and perhaps, if the child seeks more information, that the father's body makes sperm cells, one of which joins with the maternal egg cell. Some five-year-olds, and certainly older children, are ready to learn that the sperm cell travels from the father's body through the penis and into a special opening in the mother's body, the vagina. A term like "mating" or "sexual intercourse" may be used. The child will feel more free about raising these and many associated questions, and parents about answering them, if the child's earlier questions about the genitalia were answered frankly. While simple terms may be used, it is wise to avoid those that are confusing. Girls particularly often seem to have been given terms for their bodies which confuse for them urination, defecation, and reproduction, as regards both anatomy and the processes themselves. Such confusion may in some cases seriously affect later attitudes toward and acceptance of sexuality. At the same time, we have learned that children are likely to distort or elaborate in fantasy our explanations and may have to be "told" again and again. Thus, it is wise not to be over-generous with the facts of life, like the mother who deluged her daughter with stored-up explanations only to learn that the trigger question "Where did I come from?" was looking for an answer to a friend who had announced, "I'm from Buffalo. Where do you come from?"

Freud reports that when little boys and girls understand that girls lack a penis, the lack may appear to be the result of castration.[46] This misconception might be less likely to appear if it were made clear to children that boys have penises and girls do not; that girls have vaginas, boys do not. Many little girls of preschool age show directly some form of what Freud termed *penis envy* (which is said to underlie some later feminine envy of masculine prerogatives). The universality and depth of such envy, however, are not fully established. Parents are safe in treating manifestations such as a girl's wanting to urinate standing up matter-of-factly, but reassuring her, if she shows signs of dismay, that she is properly constructed in the way of girls and women. Little boys, too, may express feelings of sexual deprivation. Many little boys resent at times that they can never have babies inside them or that they cannot nurse babies.

A great many questions besides the ones we have specifically mentioned will, of course, arise. There are a number of excellent sources on which parents can depend for guidance in answering these questions. Regardless of professional approaches to sex education, parents have to find the ways that suit them, their values, and their moralities best. In matters of sex education, as in other areas of parent-child relationships, certain broad principles apply: respect both for the child and for one-self, and treating the child and his concerns seriously but not solemnly. In general, given the strong emotion that inheres in sexual matters, and the vagueness of children's ideas about them, parents are usually well advised neither to shroud the facts of life in secrecy nor to overwhelm a child with unwanted and indigestible information. The child's questions can be answered simply and directly and briefly. His curiosity on the verbal plane will ordinarily be quickly appeased, and his tendencies to concrete investigation will probably be affected by parental instruction only in the degree of guilt they arouse. It might be borne in mind that sexual strivings have a large component of curiosity. They come not merely from a desire for sensual pleasure but also from an urge to explore and to know—particularly to know about what is ordinarily veiled. Some of this urge to know can be satisfied through verbal information rather than direct experience, and by satisfying the child's curiosity one can help reduce the intensity of his strivings to manageable proportions.

NOTES   (Starred items are recommended as further readings.)

[1] Personal communication.

[2] Personal communication.

[3] Roberts, K. E., and Schoellkopf, J. A., "Eating, sleeping, and elimination practices of a group of two-and-one-half-year-old children," *American Journal of Diseases of Children,* 1951, 82, 121-152.

[4] Williams, Lucretia, Observation record, Vassar College Nursery School, 11-4-40.

[*5] Murphy, L. B., *Social Behavior and Child Personality,* New York: Columbia University Press, 1937. See also Stone, L. J., "Experiments in group play and in readiness for destruction," in Murphy, L. B., and associates, *Personality in Young Children,* New York: Basic Books, 1956, pp. 201-263.

[6] *Social Behavior and Child Personality,* pp. 173-191.

[7] Dawe, H. C., "An analysis of two hundred quarrels of preschool children," *Child Development,* 1934, 5, 139-157.

[8] Fiedler, Miriam F., Observation record, Antioch College Nursery School. Personal communication.

[*9] Stone, L. J., "He still learns through his play," in *Childcraft,* Chicago: Field Enterprises, 1954, Vol. 13, pp. 156-161. See also Werner, *Comparative Psychology of Mental Development,* pp. 395-402.

[10] Omwake, Eveline, Personal communication.

[11] Stone, L. J., Observation notes, Sarah Lawrence College Nursery School.

[12] Goldsmith, Cornelia, Observation notes, Vassar College Nursery School, 2-4-42.

[13] Call, Dorothy, Observation record, Vassar College Nursery School, 5-12-42.

[14] Call, Dorothy, Observation notes, Vassar College Nursery School, 9-25-41.

[15] *A Long Time to Grow:* Part II. *Four- and Five-Year-Olds in School* (film), Dept. of Child Study, Vassar

College, 1954. (Distributed by New York University Film Library.)

[16] Kidd, Dudley, *Savage Childhood: A Study of Kafir Children,* London: Black, 1906.

[17] Mead, Margaret, *New Lives for Old,* New York: Morrow, 1956, p. 128. See also the discussion of primitive precocity in Werner, *Comparative Psychology of Mental Development.* pp. 27-31.

[18] *A Long Time to Grow:* Part II. *Four- and Five-Year-Olds in School.*

[19] Sully, cited by Werner, *Comparative Psychology of Mental Development,* p. 392.

[20] Williams, Lucretia, Observation record, Vassar College Nursery School, 2-17-41 (age 5:3).

[21] *New Yorker,* April 10, 1954, p. 27.

[22] Ames, L. B., and Learned, J., "Imaginary companions and related phenomena," *Journal of Genetic Psychology,* 1946, 69, 147-167.

[23] Warfield, Frances, *Cotton in My Ears,* New York: Viking, 1948, p. 7.

[24] Warfield, p. 8.

[25] Warfield, p. 9.

[26] Bender, L., and Vogel, F., "Imaginary companions of children," *American Journal of Orthopsychiatry,* 1941, 11, 56-66.

[27] Ames, L. B., "The sense of self of nursery school children as manifested by their verbal behavior," *Journal of Genetic Psychology,* 1952, 81, 193-232.

[28] Williams, Lucretia, Observation notes, Vassar College Nursery School, January, 1940.

[29] *Id.,* Observation notes, 1-26-40.

[30] *Id.,* Observation record, 4-15-40.

[31] *Id.,* Observation notes, 4-18-40.

[32] *Id.,* Observation record, December, 1940.

[33] *Id.,* Observation record, 11-21-39.

[34] Jersild, A. T., and Holmes, F. B., *Children's Fears,* New York: Bureau of Publications, Teachers College, Columbia University, 1935.

[35] Williams, Lucretia, Observation record, Vassar College Nursery School, 2-17-41.

[36] Biber, Barbara, Personal communication.

[37] Horowitz, R. E., "Spatial localization of the self," *Journal of Social Psychology,* 1935, 6, 379-387.

[38] Cited by Horowitz.

[39] Piaget, J., *Judgment and Reasoning in the Child,* New York: Harcourt, Brace, 1928.

[40] Dillon, M. S., "Attitudes of children toward their own bodies and those of other children," *Child Development,* 1935, 5, 165-176; Katcher, Allan, "The discrimination of sex differences by young children," *Journal of Genetic Psychology,* 1955, 87, 131-143.

[41] Rabban, M., "Sex-role identification in young children in two diverse social groups," *Genetic Psychology Monographs,* 1950, 42, 81-158.

[42] Kinsey, A. C., and associates, *Sexual Behavior in the Human Female,* Philadelphia: Saunders, 1953, pp. 104-105.

[43] Freud, *A General Introduction to Psychoanalysis,* pp. 289-296.

[44] Lazarsfeld, P. F., Jahoda, M., and Zeisl, H., *Die Arbeitslosen von Marienthal,* Leipzig: S. Hirzel, 1933; Eisenberg, P., and Lazarsfeld, P. F., "The psychological effects of unemployment," *Psychological Bulletin,* 1938, 35, 358-390.

[45] Stolz, L. M., and collaborators, *Father Relations of War-Born Children,* Stanford: Stanford University Press, 1954, pp. 316-328.

[46] *A General Introduction to Psychoanalysis,* p. 278.

FOR FURTHER READING

Wolff, Werner, *The Personality of the Preschool Child,* New York: Grune & Stratton, 1946. Includes a great many observations of children in action, a number of them from the files of the Vassar College Nursery School.

Isaacs, Susan, *Social Development in Young Children,* London: Routledge, 1933. A rich source of material on social patterns among preschool children.

Griffiths, Ruth, *A Study of Imagination in Early Childhood,* London: Kegan Paul, 1935. The fantasy life of preschool children.

Thompson, Clara (ed.), *An Outline of Psychoanalysis,* New York: The Modern Library, 1955. A selection of writings about psychoanalytic theory and practice; see especially Chapters 12-16, Childhood.

Child Study Association of America, *Facts of Life for Children,* New York: Bobbs-Merrill, 1954 (also available as a paperback from Maco Books). A parents' guide to sex education for children.

Plastic materials

(From *Finger-Painting: Children's Use of Plastic Materials*)

The nursery teacher

(From *A Long Time to Grow: Part 1*)

Making friends in nursery school

Projective play techniques:
Miniature Life Toys.
Balloons.
(See pages 153 and 397 ff.)

CHAPTER 7

The Preschool
Child: 2

The Preschool Child's Thinking and Perceiving

In this section, we shall deal with the preschool child's *cognitive* functioning. The length of the section is not a precise measure of its relative significance in the life of the preschool child. Significant though this aspect of development is, it bulks even larger here because some general formulations are introduced which apply at all developmental periods, and because some of the less familiar ideas introduced might be unclear if presented in too abbreviated a fashion. Under the term "cognitive" are lumped such aspects of behavior as thinking, perceiving, remembering, forming concepts, generalizing, and abstracting, and the sphere of intellectual activity in general. In older, classical psychology, cognition was thought of as an area of functioning distinct from those of emotion (*affection*) and motivation (*conation*). We hope it will be evident in our discussion that these areas are not so easily separable. Even though "cognitive" is an unsatisfactory term in that it represents a wholly artificial partitioning of behavior, it is a very useful term in that it groups together a number of closely related aspects of functioning.

It should also be clear that we are singling out this topic for discussion here in order to help clarify and label accurately many of the phenomena we have been talking about all along. For instance, our account of the development of sex roles can be read as an account of how the child forms *concepts* of "boy" and "girl," of "man" and "woman." Other examples of cognitive development are involved in the treatments in the last chapter of play patterns, reality and fantasy, family and social relationships, etc.

175

While we shall concentrate primarily on the mental processes themselves, they cannot be observed in a vacuum. Hence we can perhaps best view these processes by considering how the child deals with his *physical environment,* where his emotional involvements are less pronounced than in the more human realm. Also, it is in connection with concepts of *number, causality, time,* and the like that Western civilization has developed its highest abstractions. Thus, it is in these fields that we find the best opportunity for observing how the child's concepts, with progressive maturation and cultural tutelage, move step by step toward the adult's. The process of cognitive development is at least partly a process of learning a language. Each language makes its unique distinctions and organizations of reality. Hence language both records and channels modes of thinking. Here, as elsewhere, we shall be concerned primarily with Western, and more specifically American, modes.

Concept Formation

As we have said, perception and conceptual thinking are very closely allied. Both are ways in which the individual recognizes and organizes uniformities and differences in his experience. It will be simplest for our discussion to begin with how the individual deals with objects and their properties, although this is certainly not the infant organism's starting point (see pages 84-91 and note again the examples given there). We have already seen there how perception develops from mass diffuseness to crude blob-like percepts, representing a first rough differentiation of salient meanings from the perceptual mass, and proceeds to a more sharply differentiated awareness of stable and co-ordinated objects. *Concepts* follow a comparable line of development. While there is considerable disagreement about the distinction between percepts and concepts, for our purposes a concept is a percept that has been given a meaningful label: by naming something we see, we implicitly state that it is like other things having the same name and different from things having different names. From this standpoint, concepts can appear only as the child learns language.

Since the child's perception has already become somewhat differentiated by the time he acquires his first words, there is no stage of concept-formation corresponding to the wholly diffuse first stage of perception. Instead, the earliest concepts develop when a special sound —a word—comes to designate a crudely defined area of experience. However, these first global meanings or concepts are so poorly differentiated and vaguely bounded—so comparable to the early blob-like percepts—that we have ventured, by analogy, to call them *"globs"* rather than true concepts. Take, for example, what we can infer of the early glob-meaning of a word like "doggie." When it is first learned, it is likely to be applied not only to the family dog, and not only to other dogs, but to a great variety of things which for the child have some point of similarity to a dog: a stuffed animal, a cat, a squirrel, a picture of an elephant. (The glob stage corresponds to that of beginning speech, possibly late infancy or early toddlerhood.)

As the child acquires a number of words, each standing for a similarly globby, loosely defined notion, he goes on to the next stage, where the glob-meaning becomes a simple *concrete concept* (but not yet a full-blown true concept), characteristic of late toddlerhood and the early preschool years. That is, it is now more narrowly defined, more sharply differentiated and refined, so that "doggie" and "kitty," "baby" and "doll," "daddy" and "man" are different and mutually exclusive concepts. It is important to note that the development of concrete concepts involves two kinds of differentiation. First, there is the differentiation between things having different names. This differentiation in turn depends on another kind, a differentiation of the underlying perceptual characteristics of the things which are distinguished from each other. In order to tell a dog from a cat, there must be some recognition of attributes which are essentially dog-like and others which are essentially cat-like. Although the child can recognize such attributes, he does so on a rather crude perceptual basis. That is, he cannot define them and make explicit comparisons in terms of them. Their attributes (hairiness, patterns of movement, characteristic noises, etc.) make a difference in how the child reacts; but because they remain *embedded* in the objects themselves, we use the qualifying term "concrete." But these are concrete attributes of a particular kind: what appear to the adult to be highly concrete properties of objects—for instance, their size, shape, and color—may be very distant and abstract for the child, who is attuned to their emotional meanings and behavioral possibilities rather than their formal characteristics (see our earlier discussion of action-objects, etc., pages 88-89).

Concrete concepts become *true concepts* when the child can do something with them beyond attaching them to concrete realities, when he can compare them, combine them, describe them—that is, *think and talk about their attributes*. (True concepts are likely to appear first in the later preschool years.) At earlier stages, what was perceived determined what could be named; once conceptual thinking begins, however, the word may determine which things are perceived, which attributes are differentiated and combined. "Doggie" becomes a true concept when the child can deal verbally simultaneously with, say, "doggies" and "kitties": "Doggie bark. Kitty meow." A simple utterance of this sort tells us that the child has abstracted characteristics—the dog's *bark*—generalized them—*all dogs bark*—and compared these characteristics with those of other species—*cats do not bark, they meow*. At this early point, the preschool child can only deal with differences between concepts and not with their similarities. He can generalize (*all dogs*) within a concept but cannot single out the common features of differing concepts. Although he can say how dogs and cats differ, if he is asked in what way they are the same, he will probably struggle to combine them, as in the reply, "The dog fights with the cat."

Only at a somewhat later stage of development, somewhere in the school years, when he can deal simultaneously with likenesses and differences, will the child be able to recombine concepts into higher-order *categories:* dogs and cats, for all their differences, are alike in being *animals*. To return to the glob-concept "doggie," we might have assumed from its diverse applications that the young child was mistakenly using "doggie" as the equivalent of the category "animal." However, an abstract category like "animal" combines differentiated concepts, taking account of both likenesses and differences, while the glob "doggie" was based entirely on gross similarities and failed to take note of significant differences. Although the preschool child probably cannot say what a cat and a dog have in common, foreshadowings of abstract comparisons are seen at this time, as when the four-year-old watching a cow being milked remarks, "It's like a water pistol!"

It is probably not until after the end of the preschool years (children like Stuart apart) that the child can deal with likenesses between concepts and group them into abstract categories. The average age at which some kinds of relationships can be handled is known quite accurately from the standardization of intelligence tests (e.g., "In what way are wood and coal alike?"; age seven on the Stanford-Binet[1]) or from such studies as Kreezer and Dallenbach's[2] (or, more recently, Robinowitz's[3]), which fixes the ability to deal with "oppositeness" at about age six. Needless to say, as we have noted with other norms, there is a broad spread in the ages at which any of these functions may appear. It should likewise be obvious that nobody, child or adult, ever lives completely on one plane of abstractness or concreteness. Faced with brand-new situations, we always have to begin with globs and work toward concepts; when we encounter a new word, we first recognize a diffuse area of meaning and have to work out, in the course of repeated encounters in different contexts, a precise definition.

Concepts in Action

Now that we have surveyed the general trend of concept development, let us look at some examples of the kind of thinking with concepts that is characteristic of preschool children. One consequence of the disparity between concrete and abstract concepts is that—as close examination shows—adults and children often do not understand each other as well as both assume, since they often use the same words with quite different meanings. It often happens that a child uses a word with seeming appropriateness in familiar contexts, only to reveal to us a wholly unexpected meaning when he applies it in a new context. The following quotations from preschool children contain such revelations: "When you want to start a car you must turn on the permission"; "Market set go"; (five-year-old G-man, snatching up toy telephone in doll corner:) "Calling headcutters. Calling headcutters." We also frequently find in the speech of preschool children incorrect but strikingly logical extensions of language usage: "Nokay" as the opposite of "O.K."; (three-year-old asserting her good conduct:) "I am so being hāve." Such usages are not quite the same, of course, as the poetically original inventions we sometimes find in preschool language: "You don't look like you are"; one little girl liked to "secret around in the night"; a little boy riding to school complained, "Look at that old truck busying up the street so we can't get through"; a four-and-a-half-year-old girl produced this joyous combination of words and sounds, in true Lewis Carroll fashion, in the course of telling a story:

> "There's nothing true about that so don't be so glee." "I'm not full of glue, I'm just appearing to." Thumbly, thumbly, glantering damously. Clitter clatter, sing the clitter clatter and the violins some time over. . . . Sing the songs of meener, with the doors of the clitter and the marches too in the dark of the pleasantly opter.[4]

Usually, such constructions represent a somewhat incomplete differentiation of ideas and are unlikely to appear in the more structured language of the adult (whose metaphors are of quite a different stamp), but they are at a more advanced level than the confusions in the first set of examples.

Although the preschool child's concepts are becoming increasingly specific and differentiated, then, it is evident from these examples and others to follow that they often differentiate along lines surprising to the adult. A great number of influences are at work to determine the particular pattern of differentiation followed, many of them irrelevant to the essential nature of concepts. We have mentioned several of these influences before: the child may be more impressed by the concrete externals of a situation than its essential features; he cannot always distinguish between his own feelings and outside events; his is a complete world at any given moment, so that he is not aware of gaps that may be obvious to the adult, any more than any of us is aware of his blind spots. Further influences will be mentioned in later sections. Here we want to stress that the preschool child has not had time to learn a great many things, and that his new experiences tend to be assimilated into the pattern of what he already knows. For the preschool child, of course, family relationships are the prototype of all relationships, and these overshadow the less personally significant abstract relationships that adults often deal in. Thus when the child is given a formal classification test consisting of blocks that offer a number of abstract principles for grouping—color, shape, size—he may ignore all of these and instead base his arrangement on the intimate, concrete scheme of his own existence and group the blocks into families, large ones being the "father" and "mother" and smaller ones the "babies." Here the child relies on the attribute of size, but in a concrete way tied to his emotionally relevant reality. Even the concept "family," however, is still indistinctly articulated for the preschool child. A four-year-old, for instance, meeting his teacher's husband, asks, "Mr. Jones, are you Mrs. Jones' daddy?" and the next moment, to Mrs. Jones, "Are you his mommy?" A mere adult cannot really know, of course, whether the child means these relationships to be taken literally, or whether, lacking the concepts "husband" and "wife," he is trying to ask something like "Are you the daddy in the family in which Mrs. Jones is the mommy?" At the same time, children can certainly live quite comfortably with unnoted inconsistencies and contradictions that adults would find very troubling. The lack of abstractness in preschool children's ideas of family may also be observed in the indignant retort of a five-year-old to the assertion that people in the same family cannot marry: "They can, too! My mommy married my daddy!"

At any age, the fundamental barrier to clear abstract thinking is the weight of emotional significance in some of the terms involved. For instance, in one intelligence test item addressed to much older children, the question is asked, "How are a president and a dictator alike?" The strong emotional loading of the differences between these two heads of state may make it impossible for the child to pick out the common feature. Strong, and sometimes inappropriate, emotions are likewise the basic difficulty in dealing with areas where adults' prejudices are strong, such as the long controversy over the relative intelligence of Negroes and whites, or over the evaluation of studies of extrasensory perception. For the preschool child, the emotional meaning of a term may be primary even where it is wholly incidental to the adult. One child climaxed a torrent of spluttering invective with "You—you—you wrong number!"

As older preschool children wrestle, then, with problems of what goes with what, they show various intermediate forms of true abstraction. Such semi-abstractions are often seen in the block-sorting test referred to above. Some children develop *clusters:* one block may serve as the starting point, the others being arranged around it in terms of some similarity of each, one by one, to the central block, but without regard to any feature common to them all. Thus one block "belongs" because it is the same size as the key block, another because it is the same shape, another because it is the same color. Some children arrange the blocks to form a *chain,* based on shifting relationships, instead of a cluster: block A goes with block B because it is the same color, B with C because it is the same shape, C with D on the basis of size, and so forth.

The concreteness characteristic of children's concepts is often to be found in their descriptions and narratives, which tend to be rambling, loose-jointed, and *circumstantial:* everything is equally important and must be included, so that the listener needs to be nicely attuned to detect the central theme and direction of what the child says. In the same way, young children learn things in wholesale bunches and not in a systematic, organized way. They can memorize yard after yard of fairy tale and nursery rhyme (not to mention singing commercials), but they cannot paraphrase or summarize their learning; they can only recite it. If they are interrupted in the middle of a recitation, they may find it impossible to resume where they left off and be obliged to start again from the beginning.

Up to now, we have been discussing the development of concepts of objects (people and things) from the initial glob stage to the point where the concept included detachable properties or attributes that could be talked about in the abstract. At first, these attributes seem to be *absolute* (attributes like big, fast, red, good) and are embedded in the objects themselves. Later, they become increasingly *relational* (furrier, thinner, softer, smaller), permitting comparisons between objects and classes of objects. So far, we have been concerned chiefly with relationships of likeness and difference based on the abstraction of objects' perceptual attributes. In the sections that follow, we shall talk about other kinds of relationships based on the attributes of situations, attributes which may not have so easily definable a perceptual existence.

Concepts of Relationships

There is a still more abstract kind of abstraction than that based on the immediately observable properties of things. This kind of abstraction is involved in the concepts that constitute relational frameworks of time, causation, space, number, and the like, which can be thought about—once the child is old enough—without reference to particular objects, events, or their properties. It is abstractions of this sort that we shall now be discussing.

We must remember that our particular ways of viewing the passage of time, cause-effect relationships, the distribution of things in space, are likely to seem the obvious and only logical system for ordering the world. However, the anthropologist, or even the historian, knows that people can develop quite different schematizations. The Balinese, for instance, have ". . . a complex cyclical system of days, grouped into concurrent weeks. . . . And of these weeks they have a complete series from a two-day week to a ten-day week. . . ." [5] Unless the Balinese knows where he stands with respect to all these weeks at any given moment, he feels badly disoriented, just as we do when we suddenly discover that today is actually Friday when we have been acting as if it were Thursday. Unlike us, the Balinese have little regard for *elapsed* time. They know precisely when, in terms of their many calendars, a child's birthday falls, but they are not likely to know—or care —how old he is. The Balinese organization of space is also different from ours.[6] The primary directions in Bali, in addition to north, south, east, and west, correspond to seaward and inland. While most of us probably could not point on demand to the north, if the Balinese does not know at all times where his cardinal directions lie, he cannot act at all, for these determine the direction of the temple and the graveyard or, within the home, the kitchen and latrine, or in what direction his head must point when he lies down. Other societies have their own versions of the world differing from ours and from each other's. Moreover, for most non-European cultures, abstract organizing principles are not, as with us, deliberately stripped of all personal and emotional meaning. Thus it is clear that the child, in acquiring the organizing concepts we are about to consider, is not only growing in his thinking ability but is in addition learning some basic lessons of his culture. Equally obviously, although we shall speak of "children" or "the child," we shall be talking specifically about children learning our Western society's conceptual framework.

TIME CONCEPTS   Children's concepts of time are especially interesting, perhaps because time is such a slippery realm for us adults that we can easily feel for the child in his fumbling after these abstractions. We never directly *perceive* time. We are aware of changes and recurrences and rhythms, in the environment and in our own bodies, of waiting for things to happen or of hurrying to get things done. From such experiences, helped along by what we are taught and by such concrete images as Old Father Time and remorselessly flowing rivers, we build our abstract ideas of time. But even though *abstract* time comes to consist for us of fixed measured intervals, we also live in a *personal* time that behaves in peculiar ways: at moments of suspense, a minute may feel like hours; when we are busy or enthralled, hours may seem like minutes; we dream of time machines, fountains of youth, fresh starts, and eternal bliss. For the child whose clearly remembered past can be measured in hours and whose future is a myth he has to accept on the word of adults, time acts even more oddly. We have already discussed, in the last chapter, the beginnings of time sense as shown in the toddler's use of language, where the first divisions of the day are expressed in terms of activities: Time to eat, Time to go out, and so forth. Even when the child has begun to have some notion of himself moving about in time and, later, of formal landmarks and intervals (holidays, minutes, hours, days, etc.), these may not yet have their standard meanings. One four-year-old insists, for instance, "It is not 'today'! My mommy said it was Monday!" An understanding of the relationships between yesterday, today, and tomorrow may be delayed until age ten, although we know of one preschool child who announced to her dumfounded parents, "Today is yesterday's tomorrow." Many preschool children, first becoming aware of the phenomenon of time, are entranced to learn of their own unremembered past and beg their parents to tell about "when I was a baby"; such tales, of course, usually strike the child as fascinating fragments of remote prehistory. It seems usually to be the fourth birthday which brings the first realization that this is one of a series, and also that in some magic way birthdays are a measure of growth. Most children expect to be bigger and somehow transformed after their birthday, like the child who said, "And anyway, after my birthday I won't look the same to you any more because you will have to look at me with a birthday—not just me." A study by Ames gives data on the average age at which a fairly typical sample of American children acquired various time concepts.[7] For instance, three-year-olds tended to know their own age, four-year-olds when their next birthday was due, five-year-olds how old they would be on their next birthday; at four, children began to know what day of the week it was, at five the month and the year.

Initially, of course, these formal time concepts have little to do with the child's fluid, personal time. A statement by a four-year-old suggests that he planned to grow up backwards in time so as to join those who were already mature: "Pretty soon this will be the olden days and I'll be a man." Numerous children, as we have pointed out, plan as it were to catch up and marry their parents. Here, of course, the preschool child, with his great concern about growing up, is inclined to be far more aware of his own potential for change than of other people's. Adults especially are seen as changeless, even though the child may know, but without much conviction, that they once were little and some day will be *very* old. Fortunately, we have a record of the very moment when disillusionment on this score came, at age five, to Stuart —the moment when (as usual, rather precociously) he realized that time is the same for everybody. He says to his teacher:

> It would be funny if I was big and you were little. I wouldn't pay any attention to you and I'd make you do things you didn't like to. [Here, incidentally, we have another glimpse of how adults may appear to the preschool child.] But I guess I won't ever be able to do that to you 'cause I won't ever be able to catch up to you. I won't ever be able to be the same as you at the same time.[8]

For all the rapid development of ideas of past, present, and future, of short and long time intervals, even at the end of the preschool period there is still no overall, consistent framework of time, but a patchwork of unco-ordinated time concepts which in no way restrict the movement of the child's thought.

SPATIAL CONCEPTS   Our concepts of space are fairly easy for most adults to grasp—or were, before Einstein came along to confuse every-body—even though many people have occasional trouble with road maps. Nevertheless, it takes quite a while to master these notions, and we find that children's spatial ideas are often markedly different from ours.

We can recognize five major stages in the development of spatial concepts, although any one person (at any age) may operate on several different levels. First, there is *action space,* consisting of the locations to which the child anchors his movements, and the regions in which he moves. Second, there is *body space,* based on the child's awareness of directions and distances in relation to his own body. Third, there is *object space,* where objects can be located relative to each other in terms of directions and distances transferred from body space, but now without direct reference to the child's body. The fourth and fifth stages of space are not truly "stages," but are mutually interdependent. The fourth stage we shall call *map space,* the elaboration and unification of concrete spatial experiences into more or less extensive "mental maps" dependent on some system of co-ordinates or cardinal directions which may apply to rooms or regions, to towns or nations. Although map space may be concrete in the sense that it relies on visual images, it is abstract both in the sense that it involves principles of organization independent of particular objects and in the sense that a great deal of conceptual understanding is brought to bear in formulating mental maps. A final stage, *abstract space,* involving definite visualization for some people but not for others, comes with the ability to deal with abstract spatial concepts necessary to mapping or navigational problems, geographical or astronomical ideas, or problems of solid geometry, even including, at the most abstract levels, multidimensional space beyond our experienced three dimensions. It is interesting to observe that many people who lack a kinesthetic "sense of direction" or the visual imagery necessary for map space can still function adequately or even brilliantly with regard to abstract space, which depends primarily on symbolic (verbal, mathematical) relationships.

The preschool child has long since developed an elaborate *action space* and moves easily among familiar locations. He quickly explores the possibilities for movement of new terrain and soon makes it his own. In addition, he is beginning to orient himself in terms of *body space:* his space of locomotion has become traversed by a number of spatial relationships dependent on his own body and his perceptions of it. In this way, he knows up and down, sideways, and next to, although he has not yet differentiated left and right; he knows near and far, at first perhaps in terms of arm's reach and of "far, far away"; he knows in front of and behind *himself.* These locations and directions exist in a kind of coalescence and, early in the preschool years, depend strongly on the particular pathways he has followed through the regions he knows. An illustration of how the child's spatial organization is at first rather rigidly bound to action patterns is shown by an incident the Scupins recorded involving their son Bubi, age three:

> While visiting the bear-cages in the zoo we went up one flight of stairs leading to the place and left by another. Today, when we approached the same place by the stairs by which we had left the day before, the child held back, saying angrily, "These are the wrong steps. These are the going-down steps . . . the others are the going-up steps." [9]

The dimensions which at first inhere in the child's own relationships to specific objects soon are applied to *object space,* the relationships that hold between one object and another, apparently by a process of analogy or transposition. An object can be beside another, although it cannot, for most of the preschool period, be *behind* or *in front of* another object. An object can, however, be *on* or *under* or *above* or *below* another, it can be *inside* or *around.* In the latter preschool years, there begins to be an overall co-ordination of familiar spatial regions. The child may be aware of something around the corner; he can take detours to reach a goal, provided these detours are not too complex. Thus when Maier had children walk through an enclosed swastika-shaped maze, it was not in general until the age of six that they were able to grasp it as a unified whole rather than as a number of unrelated routes. [10]

The child of preschool age is scarcely likely to have any dealings with *map space* or with schematized, *abstract space.* Nevertheless, a few children of preschool age may begin to grasp the concept of the world as round, as shown in the following quotation from Stuart, at age four and a half, caught struggling with this notion.

> Miss Williams, what is the end of the world? . . . I don't see how it is a *place,* because my mommy says the world is round, and so there could not be any end where the world stops, or where you could fall off. It goes around, and then when you get to where you start, it goes round again. [11]

In general, however, the preschool child is still largely oriented toward particular objects or habitual routes. He cannot yet go far in conceiving of himself and objects as part of a larger integrated space with multiple possibilities for movement. This may account for the fact that he delights in games of chasing, or even brief hiding, but does not yet play hide-and-seek.

QUANTITATIVE CONCEPTS   Late in toddlerhood or early in the preschool years, the child develops his first notions of quantity. These begin with ideas of one and more than one (usually expressed as "two," regardless of the actual number), of more than and less than, of bigger and smaller, of once and again. These ideas underlie numerical concepts but are still far removed from them. It has been shown experimentally that, during the preschool period, the child increases in his ability to discriminate perceptually between larger and smaller numbers of things, such as groups of marbles.[12] While still of preschool age, he is likely to go beyond this purely perceptual stage to number-names for collections of two, three, or even more objects. This has no connection with the fact that he may be able to "count" to ten or twenty or higher. Although the number-name "two" or "three" cannot yet be manipulated abstractly, it has a real meaning, while repetitions of number sequences are but strings of sounds without content and without any notion that seventeen, for instance, is "one more than" sixteen. By the time a child is five, he may be genuinely able to count objects in small series. He can even take two blocks from here and three blocks from there and count the new total. However, the arithmetic abstraction $2 + 3 = 5$ is beyond his powers. Nor can the numbers he uses to count with be transferred to notions of size, length, or value of money. We might remark in passing that the whole idea of money as a medium of exchange, of currency representing various values, of what goes on in making a purchase and receiving change, remains a total mystery throughout these years. Children play store, passing money back and forth, but this is only an imitation of adult gestures.[13]

Ordinal numbers, indicating successions rather than totals, also develop only in their cruder forms during the preschool period. Initially, they appear in the absolute, highly personal form, "Me first!" It is a long time before "last" appears, and still longer before the child has command of "second," "third," and so forth.

As we have suggested, the non-numerical quantitative concepts (big, little, some, a lot, a little) of the preschool child, being concrete, are very much at the mercy of perceptual qualities. Because a four-year-old child cannot simultaneously take account of different dimensions, he sees a quart of water in a tall, thin jar as more than a quart of water in a short, squat one. This is true even if he watches the same water poured from one jar to the other—as it changes containers, it grows or shrinks for him.[14] In Piaget's terms, that is, objects lack *conservation* for the preschool child.[15] When one attribute changes, they all seem to change. This phenomenon is not essentially different from the lack of *constancy* displayed by the preschool child when he fails to recognize his teacher out of school.

CONCEPTS OF CAUSALITY Perhaps the most interesting aspect of the preschool child's thinking, for purposes of helping us understand his world, is the way he conceives of cause and effect. While modern physicists or philosophers challenge the validity of causal notions, these are an important part of our everyday thinking. But the very young preschool child probably has no idea that events have causes. He is pleased or displeased or indifferent when things happen, but it seldom occurs to him to question what brought them about—they simply *are*. We mentioned earlier the young preschool child's rambling style of narrative; it is worth noting that the elements of such narratives are typically held together by the "conjunction" *'n' then,* while words indicating a causal sequence—*because* (in its true sense), *therefore, and so,* etc.—never appear. When the preschool child first does begin to ask "Why?" he is probably looking for a justification rather than an explanation (when, to be sure, he is not using it for quite different purposes, such as parental harassment). It is important to note that even though the child is surrounded by technical marvels—radios and automobiles, television and clocks, airplanes and air-conditioners—he requires no explanation of them. In fact, it is exactly these familiar things that it is hardest to see and wonder about. The familiar is not always obvious—consider how long people lived with gravity before it occurred to Newton that it was worth thinking about—and we might even make a case for science as being the business of making the obvious evident. Also, as we said earlier, the child's world is so full of delightful and dreadful potentialities that nothing seems too extraordinary. It is usually only late in the preschool years or during the school years, after the child has built up some standards of the possible and the impossible, of the expected and the unexpected, that he is struck by anomalies—how is it that heavy iron ships can float?—and begins to look for general principles.

The child—at least in our society—seems to go from unquestioning acceptance to an assumption that human or human-like agencies are the causes of events. Although we can find out something about the child's concepts of causality by asking him questions, the most satisfactory way of getting at his assumptions is by listening to the questions *he* asks. His causal questions usually begin by asking, in effect, "Who did it?"; "For what reason?"; "Why that way?" Here he is drawing on the familiar human sphere of self and other people as the prototype of all action, just as he does in his concepts in other areas. Thus a child seeing a space blanketed with pine needles, asked, "Why did they put these here?"—making quite clear the assumption of a conscious agency. It is likely that, pressed to investigate further, the child would have looked around and decided, "They fell off the trees" or, even, "The wind blew them down." But spontaneously, children at this age seem to see most events as motivated doings. Even where a specifically human agent is not implied, motivation or purpose still seems to be involved and may be ascribed to things adults conceive of as totally inanimate. Sometimes this purpose resides in the objects themselves and sometimes in external forces. In other words, the young child's perception of the environment is often *animistic,* that is, he endows it with the qualities of life which Western European adults ordinarily reserve to animals and men. This sense of purpose in events underscores the fact that preschool children have little notion of accident or coincidence.

Since the necessary foundation of all the child's relationships with the environment is his relationships with people, it takes him some time to learn that there are impersonal forces at work in the world. The animism of young children is, of course, seldom absolute and may never become explicit. Many familiar inanimate objects tend to lose their vitality, and the spirit world is pushed back toward the horizon, toward the physically or temporally remote, the strange, the ambiguous, toward things on the periphery of awareness. Even so, animistic qualities may cling to toys made in animal images, to emotionally charged objects, to things that move or make characteristic noises. Again, the child may fluctuate—as he does with respect to reality and dreams and fantasy (see page 156)—between a materialistic and an animistic view of the world. His favorite doll may at one moment be an active, animated participant in his play, only to be tossed carelessly aside, lifeless and inert, a minute later. Stuart conveys something of the animistic attitude when he speaks of "discouraged songs" and "tired songs" and "happy houses," when he asks whether it hurts the ground to have holes and what it feels like to be a stick of wood, when he tells how his clock moves in response to changes in his activities. Certain of these ideas are grounded in such perceptual imperatives as the moon or the shadow that follows us, which it may take years to depersonalize.

But just as the child's material world may be shot through with vital forces, so do things which the adult would consider altogether insubstantial, such as one's own feelings, often take on some of the solidity of the material world. A few further quotations from Stuart, with his usual precocious clarity, will illustrate this point:

A voice is a fast thing, isn't it? It's a sound! Are other sounds voices of things? Is the day got a voice, a sound? Where is your voice? It comes out of your mouth. *Does* it, *is* it, *in* your mouth? (Here Stuart begins playing with his idea.) Are all the words stored up some place in your mouth? How can you get food in if all those words are in your mouth? How much space does a word take? Words are thin little things. But some of them make a big noise. A sound—is it bigger than a word? . . .[16]

Did you ever have a red pain in your throat? The pain it was there. I could not see it, but it was there. It is funny—I could not see it. . . . It is funny, it was *my* pain in my throat. Why could I not see it? I could feel it, it was mine, mine pain. . . .[17]

Your insides is like if another person lived inside your skin. . . .[18]

It is apparent that the preschool child is in transition toward the more stable, more compartmentalized, and causally more orderly world of adulthood. It should likewise be apparent that adults never fully grow out of the magical world of childhood. The authors like to think that this is as it should be. Most of our verbal play demands that we be able to straddle the worlds of magic and reality, as the child is beginning to do when he plays with the idea of a man with a peach tree growing out of his head; when he deliberately toys with the idea of growing up in reverse, starting as an adult and becoming a baby; when he imagines what it would be like to live under the sea; and even when he collaborates in the prefabricated fantasies of an animated cartoon. For the adult, music and art and literature and love, and even science and mathematics, have no meaning without magic; without magic, we are cut off from our roots in universal human experience and wander forever homeless.

Thinking

In talking about the structure of the preschool child's concepts, we have also, of course, been talking about his thought processes. It should be evident from what we have said that "thinking" is not necessarily a matter of withdrawing into a corner and brooding about something. Rather, thinking is embodied in our every word, gesture, and action. When the child builds a block tower, caresses a seashell, asks a question, or strikes out at a playmate, he is thinking. That is, he is in the process of formulating a concept of reality, fitting new experiences into the framework of his established reality, rearranging his reality to accommodate new experiences, trying out his notions to see how they work: he is constantly solving problems and learning. It should be emphasized, however, that the child solves problems according to the standards of his developmental level: since his world has magical foundations; since objects can change their character either in response to external shifts or to the child's feelings; since the child thinks less in terms of general principles than of personal emotional significance; since his concepts are relatively rigid and resistive to change; since he can tolerate inconsistencies and contradictions; and since he is subject to few demands for practical, "realistic" achievement, we can expect that he will learn a great deal factually without any basic revision of his conceptual structure.

It is important to see that development from less mature to more mature conceptual structures is to a fairly large extent the product of necessity—the demands of cultural reality and tutelage—and does not come about automatically. Thus we learn the facts and principles that we *have* to know, in the fields that we have to know about, until, as our body of knowledge becomes more tightly knit and more general, our curiosity will not be satisfied before we have worked an issue through to its ultimate essentials. But it is because we develop most fully only in those areas having personal relevance for us that even as adults we have blank spaces, blind spots, and inconsistencies in our intellectual make-up. In areas where we are ignorant, adult thinking can be as magical or as primitive as that of any child. Consider, for instance, the non-mechanical adult dealing with an automobile. For such an individual, the engine is a somewhat frightening Thing under the hood. It might as well be a glob. If he—or she—peers at the machinery when the hood is raised, certain crude attributes may be differentiated: it is greasy and noisy, there is a big round thing on top, some wires, a confusion of pipes and protuberances, and a faint suggestion of a malevolent will of its own. Oddly enough, nothing much is moving.

At this point, the person can recognize it as an engine, and we would say that he has a concrete concept of it, rather than a glob-concept. If he is then exposed to, and is willing to absorb, some automotive mechanics, he will be able to make some sharper discriminations and to point out and name various attributes: spark plugs, air cleaner, carburetor, and ignition harness—which he can trace from coil to plug. He might even get to an understanding of some of the unseen parts: cylinders, valves, crankshaft, and so forth. Along the way, there may be childish fumblings and errors as the individual forms hypotheses on the basis of past experience. Because the fan and fan belt are the most conspicuously active parts, they may be seen as making the car go. Such a possibility seems no more far-fetched to an adult faced with so mysterious an entity than does the magician's legerdemain to the child. Eventually, the once-naïve adult will be able to organize the various parts of the engine into a functioning totality composed of many differentiated and interrelated sub-systems. He may even go on to a more abstract level where he is aware of how general principles apply in the functioning of an engine, where he will know about the similarities and differences between gasoline engines and diesel or steam engines. Once his concept of engine has begun to differentiate, it can never again be a glob. In fact, his whole concept of an automobile will have been changed: the hood is now only a shell, the controls now play some tangible part in the operation of the car and no longer act by magic.

The essential thing to understand is that adults, in a novel situation, dealing with a new kind of problem or subject matter they know nothing about, can only recapitulate the same steps that the child goes through in his conceptual development. The adult's original concept, "engine," may be as blurred as the toddler's concept, "doggie." This recapitulation may not be as visible, first of all because the adult, unlike the young child, thinks silently and hence keeps his fumblings to himself, and second because he can often progress much faster than the child, helped along by the skills acquired through long practice and by principles transferred—if sometimes erroneously—from other areas. A further point is that once adults have worked through concepts in many areas, and co-ordinated many areas in terms of increasingly general and abstract principles, they reach a point of no return. They live in a different world and can recapture the world of childhood only by an intellectual act—which is why people write and read books about child psychology.

A School for the Preschool Child

It is only because the term is convenient and has become firmly lodged in the literature of child development that we continue to speak of the "preschool child." All ages are equally pre- and post-something else. We could, if we wished, speak of adult maturity as the pre-senescent years. At the same time, each age is complete in itself as well as a way station. Insofar as the term preschool implies incompleteness or inferiority, it is misleading. As with the child, so with the school. A preschool—that is, a *nursery school* or a *kindergarten*—must be thought of as a real school, providing opportunities for genuine learning. One cannot identify a good preschool by its name. A neighborhood play group can at times serve some of the functions of a sound preschool. A number of day-care centers are in effect preschools. On the other hand, some nursery schools and kindergartens may in fact be nothing more than custodial establishments that attend to children's routine needs and keep them safe, busy, and out of mischief while parents pursue their own affairs; they may be highly regimented in the interests of administrative efficiency rather than of children's growth. Such inadequate provisions for the care of young children echo the concept of *pre*school that we want to avoid: a time of waiting, of sitting still or marking time in anticipation of things to come, rather than a period of exploration and experiment. The notion of the preschool as a mere prelude is seen likewise in the stress on conformity in many establishments' entrance requirements—"good" eating and toilet habits, for instance—rather than on the child's need for, and ability to profit by, the school's offerings.

We must, however, signal certain differences between a preschool and a grade school. The preschool child's life is still centered in his family, and the preschool is accordingly designed on a family pattern with teachers fulfilling a complicated role that includes many quasi-parental functions. The preschool's subject matter is for the most part left embedded in its natural, living context, with far less emphasis on abstractions and classifications. It is nonetheless a real school with a bona fide curriculum. The preschool offers the child opportunities to learn but does not make demands for achievement. The preschool's program makes provisions for the child's brief attention span and consequently greater mobility. Its furnishings are scaled to the child's proportions, so that adults visiting a nursery school for the first time may have the sensation of entering a Lilliputian universe where everything, including washbasins and toilets, is built to the child's own specifications. It should be noted, however, that these differences between preschool and the early grades are in the process of obliteration as—in keeping with modern views of childhood—some of the arbitrary formalities of the grade school are relaxed.

The Raw Materials of a Preschool

The main aims of a preschool, then, can be stated in terms of meeting needs and providing scope for growth. The materials it works with in fulfilling these functions can be grouped under several heads. First and foremost come space and time—free space and free time to move about in freely, and articulated space and time to challenge the child's adaptability and to provide a stable yet variegated framework. Second come the human qualities provided by teachers and age-mates as the child takes his first steps outside the family circle into society at large. Third come learning materials: play equipment, blocks, plastic materials (paint, water, clay, lumber, and so forth), books, musical equipment ranging from percussion blocks to a phonograph, pet animals, and—this is very important—community resources: farms, stores, firehouses, railroad stations, docks, woods, brooks, and lakes. Needless to say, these materials are not used singly but are woven into a curriculum. But before we go on to discuss their organized patterning, let us look at their individual importance.

In its use of free space and time, the preschool attempts in some respects to give our now predominantly urban children the kinds of experience a majority of children once found on farms. Needless to say, the freedom of space in a preschool is always free *within limits:* the yard is securely fenced; there are things to climb, but they are not sky-high. Too free a space, in addition to exposing children to physical dangers, leaves them disoriented and insecure. Nevertheless, young children need room and time to wander and explore, to follow their own thoughts through, sometimes in conversation and sometimes alone, to be aware of changing vistas and the changing lights of days and seasons, to watch events unfold and to trace them from origin to conclusion. By structuring space as well as leaving it free, the preschool gives children darkened corners to retire to and feel snugly alone. It sets up its shelves and materials in spatial organizations which to the children may seem like fascinating mazes whose mysteries they can unravel and wonder at. By providing systematic and stable arrangements of space, it invites them to discover for themselves how space is polarized into up and down, sideways and forward and back, into inside and outside and contiguous with and separate from, into on and over and under and of and against. By structuring time into schedules and routines it provides a sense of recurrences and order and stability and predictability. We can see, then, that the preschool tries to treat space and time as the city does its parks, leaving some areas wild and virgin, trimming and civilizing others, and paving some parts over so that they can serve specified purposes. There is one fault to be found with our analogy. When one paves over a playground, it is lost to nature. When a preschool sets up a schedule, it can do so provisionally and revocably.

A good preschool program can let its schedule suddenly revert to the primeval state, it can shift it to capitalize on a snowstorm or other event, it can leave room for surprises and improvisation and spontaneity.

The human resources of the preschool, as we have said, are of two kinds, the teachers and the other children. A good preschool supplies teachers in great abundance, for it is to them that the child must first shift some of his attachment to his family before undertaking affiliations with his peers. The teacher, however, is not a mother, nor is she simply a warder. Dealing with children so young, she must be prepared to ladle out affection freely, but without infantilizing the child or intruding on him. She will be alert to the child's vacillation between babyishness and assertive maturity, and will be able to respond accordingly. She will have to perform such maternal functions as helping the child with his clothes, with feeding, with toileting, and with naps. She will protect him: from aggression by other children, from impersonal dangers, and, when necessary, from his own impulses. She will give him the discipline, the guidelines to behavior that he cannot yet find for himself. Here, as always, there is an attempt to maintain a balance between leaving the child free to find his own structure and giving him one to use. The preschooler's passions, as we said earlier, can become violent, so violent indeed that he may frighten even himself; when this is in danger of happening, the teacher has to intervene and help him understand and control the raging forces within him.

The other children of his own age give the preschooler his first experience in socialization. We must emphasize "of his own age." We do not mean that the preschool child should be shut off from children of other ages. A preschool works best, however, when children of like age are grouped together and so do not have to be inhibited from exercising their superior strength on younger children or protected from pushing around by older ones. With children of similar competence, the preschool child can safely fight out minor battles and try out his feelings and ideas on people to whom his formulations are likely to make good sense. Among his peers, he can learn to co-operate and to share—not only possessions, but sympathies, feelings, and thoughts—as well as to assert himself.

The learning materials of the preschool can be infinitely varied. Storybooks provide the children with ideas, experience with the possibilities of language, factual information about the world at large, and a chance to exercise creative imagination. Read aloud to a group, they provide a fine opportunity for shared feelings, for getting to know each other as well as what is in the story. Opportunities to listen to music, to make music, and, especially, to move to music are an essential part of preschool life. Creative materials such as paints and clay and dough —and sticks and stones and dirt and snow—are important from two points of view. First, the child likes to explore them for their sensory qualities alone, without any thought of making anything out of them. Later, he will learn to shape and manipulate them to give solid external expression to his thoughts and feelings. The doll corner, with its toy appliances and its grab bag of adult clothes, provides the settings and the materials for the enactment of the ever-recurring domestic themes that dominate dramatic play. As a parallel to domestic play, many nursery schools now have occasional projects of cooking. The youngest children can shell peas and squeeze orange juice with a fair amount of adult supervision. Slightly older children can make fruit gelatine. Older children can undertake cookies and even birthday cakes. Later in the preschool years, when such themes as steamship, road building, railroad, and doctor begin to emerge more strongly, dramatic play increasingly incorporates creative materials like blocks and boxes, and formal toys such as trucks and dolls and bulldozers. These toys, however, are of a kind that require involvement on the part of the children, and are not merely windup affairs calling for spectatorship. While the preschool is usually equipped with a variety of structured toys, the emphasis is on materials which can be used in diverse ways, giving full rein to the child's imagination. Out-of-doors, of course, preschool children want lots of big-muscle toys and equipment: wagons and tricycles, hollow blocks, boards, large packing boxes, slides and tunnels and jungle gyms, trees and rocks and slopes—spaces to traverse and vehicles in which to traverse them.

The natural resources at the nursery school's command provide more than places to run and hide and look, however. The leaves that fall from the trees in autumn, the squirrels busily gathering acorns, the rabbits and woodchucks and pheasants that leave tracks in the snow (as well as the ducks and white rats resident at the school), the sap rising in the trees and the tadpoles in the ponds in the spring—all supply the raw material for the child's first delvings into natural science. In spring, the children can even plant their own seeds and watch them grow. If these wonders are not available in the school's neighborhood or in nearby parks, of course, field trips are in order. But what urban schools may lack in raw nature can be compensated for by the rich materials available for social sciences. If the country child can see food being grown and harvested, the city child can see it being marketed. He can also visit the shoemaker down the street, the museums, the garbage trucks, the corner policeman, even the dynamos humming in the local power station.

We have not pretended to catalogue the school's resources for learning and growing—and for just being what one is—or to exhaust their multiple potentialities. We simply want to suggest the kinds of experience available in a well-planned and well-operated nursery school, and the values a child can derive from them.

Curriculum in the Preschool

We have already outlined the content of the preschool curriculum in discussing the school's resources. But these resources are not merely made available to the child for him to use at odd moments, as he sees fit, nor are they flung wholesale at the child with the expectation that he take full and grateful advantage of the benefits offered him. They are planned and scheduled and measured out in keeping with the child's capacity for absorption. We should remember that the child may be gluttonous for information one moment and ready for repose the next. He may be bursting with physical energy now, and with ideas a minute hence. He may be highly sociable for a time, only to feel the need for solitude thereafter. The preschool tries to balance listening with talking, action with contemplation, application with relaxation, regulation with freedom, boisterous with quiet play.

The key to the preschool's curriculum lies in its routines, the stable sequences that punctuate the daily cycle: clay time, outdoor time, juice time, music time, bathroom time, story time, lunch time, bathroom time, nap time, block time. Except for such critical interludes as juice, bathroom, lunch, and nap, these "times" need not be the same from day to day. Sometimes, dividing the group may be in order. Small groups of children can go off for special purposes: a walk, a visit to the school kitchen, a tour of the boiler room. Seldom, of course, is everybody doing the same thing at the same time. While the majority have a workout with the percussion instruments, a stalwart minority may continue with a block-building project, or ask one of the teachers for a story, or sit on the sidelines, thumb in mouth. Obviously, if non-participation seems to be too much the rule for any given child, because he lacks interest in his fellows, is afraid of them, or is an outcast, teachers look for means of drawing him into contact with the others.

This, too, is part of the curriculum. The devices for reattaching a child to his fellows are many. Perhaps the most basic one is for a teacher to institute a sub-group of two or three children, with him as a member, and undertake special activities—walks, field trips, party arrangements, etc.—with the idea that shared pursuits, proving enjoyable, will become a permanent part of the pattern of his life. At the same time, a child who is scorned by his peers may, when they are exposed to him on an individual rather than a mass basis, become more acceptable to them.

As we said earlier, of course, no element of the daily schedule should be altogether rigid and unyielding. Holidays, birthdays, or merely an unusually festive spirit may be the occasion for special projects. At the beginning of the preschool years, a minimum of planning and anticipation is possible. By age five, however, children can tackle long-range projects entailing preparations that may for a while supersede the regular schedule. The Christmas party, a puppet show, a play are among the possible enterprises. Sometimes a group of older children may initiate a sustained play program such as the building of a railroad terminal or, outdoors, a playhouse or irrigation canal. A well-conceived preschool will be ready to let the children pursue their own inventions to a logical conclusion, even when this means the encumbrance of semi-permanent block structures in the classroom or of gaping ditches in the playground.

Possibly the most usual departure from routines will come with the field trip. Field trips can be of two kinds. One can be suggested by adults—it occurs to the teachers that the children would enjoy and benefit from a visit to a milk-processing plant. The second kind arises spontaneously from developments in the normal routines—the preschool teacher must always be alert to the cues for special explorations. A story about trains, or a child's account of a trip by railroad, offers the opportunity for a visit to the local freight yards to see the switch engines at work and the freight trains arriving and departing. Such trips are likely to be especially profitable in terms of giving substance to the things the children know only through language, and by suggesting questions for further discussion and, perhaps, further field trips.

For all this flexibility, however, the basic framework of routines has to be retained. It is both educational and reassuring to preschool children, who need stabilizing landmarks to which they can orient themselves. The variety of the curriculum, too, should be seen as an introductory survey of the universe, and not as a collection of nuggets of learning that the child is supposed to retain. It is the delight of knowing

—if only for a minute—that such things exist; it is the raising of questions that the child can ask his teacher, his parents, and himself; it is the basic orientation to learning as a great spiritual adventure that the preschool tries to instill. Premature attempts to demand that specific learnings be retained, however, are likely to operate in the contrary direction. This does not mean that one never reminds a preschooler of things he has known and forgotten, or never encourages him to apply past learning to the solution of present problems; it does mean that the demands of the preschool for accomplishment are appropriate to the children they serve, and must take account of the fact that the child is entitled to his seemingly static periods of digestion, recapitulation, and just plain enjoyment.

A Teacher for the Preschool Child

What we have said so far implies that the preschool teacher has to have rather extraordinary qualifications, has to be, indeed, something of a Renaissance Woman—there is no basic reason, of course, why a Renaissance Man wouldn't do as well, but preschool teaching has become something of a feminine prerogative. It is now time to make certain of these qualifications explicit. It is, however, almost impossible to weigh the virtues of a good preschool teacher, and the order in which we discuss them does not necessarily mean an order of priority.

It is certainly important that a teacher—at whatever level—like children. As a human being, she will not like all children equally, but she will not make the children too aware of the fact. As in any occupation, one does best when one's job is a pleasure, and the surest way to enjoy teaching is to enjoy seeing children in action. But enjoyment and effectiveness in teaching, as in parenthood, are vastly enhanced when liking for children is coupled with a thorough knowledge and understanding of them. Again, as in the case of parents, though, understanding does not mean a relinquishing of adulthood to become once more a child. It is important to be able to feel the child's wonder and confusion and grief, but from a secure standpoint in adulthood where one can help the child straighten out his feelings.

A preschool teacher has to know about a great deal besides children. If she is going to deal with the cosmic questions her pupils ask—about God, Santa Claus, Jesus, death, and life—she is going to have to be prepared in advance. Apart from metaphysics, she will have to cope clearly and honestly with such issues as what happens when you flush the toilet; why did Mommy go and is she coming back; tell me about when I was a baby; can I look under your dress; and a variegated host of questions impossible to predict but essential to anticipate. She can convey by her answers that learning is exciting, or that grownups are stupid, or that the world is full of fascinating mysteries, or that curiosity is dangerous and the child had better learn to keep his ideas and questions to himself.

It is evident that the teacher's qualifications are more than intellectual. She will do well to have an abundance of physical stamina. Keeping pace with a pack of preschool children can be a strenuous business, especially at those moments when they all decide to go their separate ways at full speed. She must be prepared to suppress her fears or revulsions when the children present her with pet mice, frogs, snakes, and other fauna (or pieces of them) she might otherwise find unattractive. She must be more or less shockproof, but this does not imply a lack of emotion. She will have occasion to become angry, but in an adult fashion. She will inevitably be moved to occasional laughter, but a sympathetic laughter in which children can share, and not a laughter that makes them feel ridiculous. She will have her irritable days and her depressed days, but without imposing her moods on the children or expecting that they be overly sympathetic and considerate. *Unlike a mother,* the preschool teacher keeps the children's needs in the foreground, for the most part subordinating her own interest to theirs. Even while a preschool is helping its pupils to grow, it remains more child-centered than any home could healthily be. It would seem, in effect, that the central qualification of the preschool teacher is maturity, but a special form of maturity responsive to childhood and its magic. The nursery school teacher is a person who can respond appropriately to both sides of the ambivalence expressed in Stuart's dictum on growing up:

> Being big is the best, best thing, isn't it? . . . [But] sometimes I wish I didn't have to grow big. *NOW!* That's why you must take care of me and we will pretend I'm a little baby and have a long time to wait till I grow big.[19]

NOTES

[1] Terman, L. M., and Merrill, M. A., *Directions for Administering Forms L and M Revision of the Stanford-Binet Tests of Intelligence,* Boston: Houghton Mifflin, 1937, p. 25.

[2] Kreezer, G., and Dallenbach, K. M., "Learning the relation of opposition," *American Journal of Psychology,* 1929, 41, 432-441.

[3] Robinowitz, Ralph, "Learning the relation of opposition as related to scores on the Wechsler Intelligence Scale for Children," *Journal of Genetic Psychology,* 1956, **88,** 25-30.

[4] Call, Dorothy, Observation record, Vassar College Nursery School, 5-4-42. (We are indebted for the immediately preceding quotations to Eveline Omwake and Beatrice B. Stone.)

[5] Bateson, Gregory, and Mead, M., *Balinese Character,* New York: New York Academy of Sciences, 1942, p. 5.

[6] Bateson and Mead, p. 6.

[7] Ames, L. B., "The development of the sense of time in the young child," *Journal of Genetic Psychology,* 1946, **68,** 97-125. See also Bradley, N. C., "The growth of the knowledge of time in children of school-age," *British Journal of Psychology,* 1947, **38,** 67-78; Springer, Doris, "Development in young children of an understanding of time and the clock," *Journal of Genetic Psychology,* 1952, **80,** 83-96.

[8] Williams, Lucretia, Observation record, Vassar College Nursery School, 1-15-41.

[9] Scupin, E. and G., *Bubis erste Kindheit,* Leipzig: Grieben, 1907. Cited by Werner, *Comparative Psychology of Mental Development,* p. 173.

[10] Maier, N. R. F., "Reasoning in children," *Journal of Comparative Psychology,* 1936, **21,** 357-366.

[11] Williams, Lucretia, Observation record, Vassar College Nursery School, 5-7-40.

[12] Long, L., and Welch, L., "The development of the ability to discriminate and match numbers," *Journal of Genetic Psychology,* 1941, **59,** 377-387.

[13] Strauss, A. L., "The development of conceptions of rules in children," *Child Development,* 1954, **25,** 193-208.

[14] Bassett, L. B., *A Study of Some Concepts of Physical Relationship Found in Preschool Children,* Senior Thesis, Vassar College, 1956.

[15] Piaget, J., "How children form mathematical concepts," *Scientific American,* November, 1953, 74-79.

[16] Williams, Lucretia, Observation record, Vassar College Nursery School, 2-26-41 (age 5:3).

[17] *Id.,* Observation record, December, 1939 (age 4:1).

[18] *Id.,* Observation record, December, 1940 (age 5:1).

[19] *Id.,* Observation record, 1-15-41 (age 5:2).

FOR FURTHER READING

Hartley, R. E., Frank, L. K., and Goldenson, Robert M., *Understanding Children's Play,* New York: Columbia University Press, 1952. The psychology of preschool children as revealed in their play patterns. How parents and teachers can foster sound development through play.

Isaacs, Susan, *Intellectual Growth in Young Children,* London: Routledge, 1930. An excellent source of observational and experimental data on the cognitive functioning of preschool children.

Read, Katherine, *The Nursery School,* Philadelphia: Saunders, 1950. The qualifications of an effective preschool program.

CHAPTER 8

The Middle Years
of Childhood: 1

Introduction

The "middle years" of childhood can be roughly defined as ages six to twelve. Their starting point is usually marked formally by entrance into the first grade and physically by the loss of the first baby teeth; the end point is marked by a number of events, of which the most conspicuous may be the physiological event of the pre-pubertal growth spurt, the beginning of the end of childhood proper. Various labels have been attached to this period—the *school age,* the *gang age,* the *latency period* —all pointing to important characteristics of development at this time. While it is obvious that these years are referred to as the "school age" because the child is in school, we might stress that this is in fact a good time for learning the things that school has to teach. Indeed, learning what things are and the right way to do things is one of the imperative needs of this period. The label "gang age" points to the fact that during this period affiliation with one's age mates—the gang—becomes of cardinal importance. The term "latency" has been applied because to the psychoanalyst this is a time of sexual quiescence between the infantile sexuality of the preschool years and the mature sexuality that comes with adolescence. For others, this is above all a period notable for its ritualism and its literalism about what it knows and thinks; for still others it is a period of slow physical growth between two spurts.

The middle years are perhaps the age adults know least about. One reason for this is that during the school years children turn their backs on adults and actively shut them out from much of the world of childhood. Beyond the family-centered, home-based life of earlier years,

202

children join a separate, neighborhood- and school-based society of their peers, forming groups along lines of age and sex. At this time, the values of one's peers become considerably more important than anything one's parents can possibly say. Moreover, young school-age children are learning to keep their thoughts to themselves; they not only stop thinking out loud, but are likely to do so abruptly and with a vengeance. To bolster their often resistant, bland, masked taciturnity toward adults, as well as their peer-group solidarity, they form secret societies; although a given society may last no more than a few weeks, it may be protected by mortal oaths, binding for life and countersigned in blood (or some convenient substitute such as red ink). Another factor in adult ignorance about the school years is that adults take this age for granted, as though it had no secrets. Most research dealing with school-age children, for instance, is concerned with how to do things *to* children—educate them, civilize them—rather than with what they are like.

Yet, when we stop to think about it, the lack of real adult knowledge about the school years is somewhat surprising. It is during the school years that people begin to have organized, continuous memories rather than the piecemeal, episodic ones of the preschool years, so that in later years there is a link to this era. Actually, the school years lie just over the horizon for most adults and can readily be brought back when the proper cues are given: recalling the feel of a loose tooth which one works about with one's tongue; recalling how the now-fallen tooth was put under one's pillow at night so that the fairy could replace it with a coin; the pungent smell of chalk dust and ink and oak in a school classroom; the flavor of a banal childhood joke such as the Little Moron stories; or, in the case of a Marcel Proust, the flavor of biscuit dipped in camomile tea. While parents look back fondly on their children's *preschool* years, it is their own *school* years about which they wax nostalgic.

The middle-aged child spends as much of his time as possible in the society of his peers (contemporaries), where he learns first-hand about formal social structures, whether democratic or authoritarian, about being a leader and a follower, about justice and injustice, about loyalties and heroes and ideals, and about countless less elevated topics. As Biber—whose formulations have considerably influenced the authors' thinking about this entire developmental period—has suggested, the preschool child becomes a member of the human race, while the school child becomes a member of his society.[1] In fact, he is becoming a member of two rather different societies. On the one hand, teachers and parents are indoctrinating him in the ways of society at large with its adult-made rules. Among his friends, on the other hand, he lives in a special childhood culture marked by its own traditional games, rhymes, riddles, taunts, and so forth, transmitted virtually intact from one childhood generation to the next, sometimes over a period of centuries, with no help from adults and sometimes in spite of them.

As with other age periods, we have to make our customary reservation in talking about the school years as though they formed a single

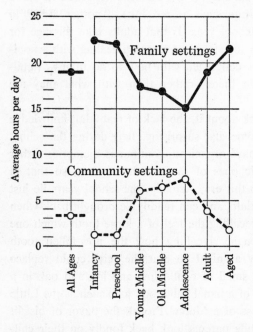

Average hours per day spent in family settings and community settings by residents of "Midwest" of different ages. (From Wright, H. F., "Psychological development in Midwest," Child Development, 1956, 27, 265-286, p. 269.)

step-like unit. Although there are no fixed stages within this period, we have chosen to distinguish three subdivisions of the middle years: early, middle, and late; these correspond approximately to the American school divisions of primary (grades 1-3), elementary (grades 4-6), and junior high school (grades 7-9). The six-year-old retains many babyish characteristics, including a taste for silliness and a willingness to be cuddled. He is likely to be but a fringe member of the gang, imitating its ways with literal dead seriousness and doing the bidding of the older children. By the time he is nine, he is sparing with his affections (particularly if he is a *he* and not a *she*), an active member of the gang, and skilled in its ways. By age twelve (with exceptions and variations), he has developed a cocksure air, is controlled and competent, scorns all things he considers childish, and is fiercely independent. Girls, by age twelve, have outgrown the long-legged, knobby gawkiness of the early school years and often merit the description of "womanly"— although they may be about to enter still another awkward age. Our scheme does not, however, fit boys and girls equally well. Girls move much faster than boys during this period and, by the time they are in junior high school, are more likely to have crossed the frontier into early adolescence.

The middle years are a period when children's rate of growth slows down. We should not assume, however, that physical changes come to a standstill, but only that the rapid tempo and abruptness of the earlier years have given way, temporarily, to a more gradual pattern of change. The average six-year-old first grader is slightly over three and a half feet tall; by the time he begins his preadolescent growth spurt (average age eleven [sixth grade] for girls, thirteen [eighth grade] for boys), he is crowding the five-foot mark. During the same period, his weight will double, going from forty to eighty pounds. Most boys double in muscular strength between the ages of six and eleven, while girls lag somewhat in this regard.

Perhaps the most evident changes come in the child's physiognomy, the cast of his facial features. From birth to adolescence, the brain case takes the lead in growth over the face, so that during these years children have a small face crowned by a domed forehead. In the neonatal period, facial features are indistinct and more typically neonatal than clearly individual. During babyhood, the child's face is round-cheeked and full, thanks to the fat pads that fill it out. The fat pads dwindle during toddlerhood, and, by the later preschool years, the child's face has a leaner look. It is the successive losses of baby teeth and the eruption of permanent ones that distinguish the face—or faces—of the middle years. The baby teeth go approximately in the order in which they came, beginning with the front teeth and moving symmetrically back. The six-to-seven-year-old is noted for his gap-toothed grin. When permanent teeth come in to fill the gaps, they may loom disproportionately large so that the eight-year-old is distinguished by his outsize, "tombstone" front teeth; it is only in adolescence, the age of the nose and the chin, that the face fully catches up to the teeth in size. Later losses of baby teeth during the school years are not so conspicuous, since they occur further back, but the shedding of old teeth and the acquisition of new ones goes on until age eleven or twelve. In addition to the more easily perceived and gradual physical changes such as those we have described, many less obvious ones are taking place during the middle years: changes of proportion, of bone composition, of tissue distribution, and so forth.

Not only do boys and girls mature at different rates, as we have noted, but questions of masculinity and femininity become prominent during the school years—indeed, the authors toyed briefly with the idea of writing two chapters here, one on boys and one on girls. During this period, boys associate more and more ostentatiously with boys, and girls with girls, each group pursuing separate interests and identities until communication is cut to a trickle. In adolescence, of course, the sexes will suddenly find new reasons to come together again, as before the school years, but this time as the separate types they will have since become.

The Society of Children

The school child is quite a different creature from what he was as a preschooler and from what he will be as an adolescent. Both the preschool child and the adolescent strive, each in his own fashion, to grow up, to be like the adults around them. The preschool child was focused on family relationships; his games tried out the roles and activities of the grownups who represented all virtue, freedom, and power. The adolescent too will be oriented toward the grown-up world of which he will soon be a part, sometimes grasping at, and sometimes fleeing from, adult responsibilities and privileges. But the school-age child, although he lives within society at large, seems to pick his way through it, preoccupied with the concerns of childhood. It is almost as if he is now, for the first time, ready to be a child. One of the most striking characteristics of this age in our own and many other societies is that it forms a special, separate sub-culture with traditions, games, values, loyalties, rules, and memberships of its own. This children's sub-culture shares many of the attributes of primitive cultures. It is handed down by word of mouth, it includes many rituals whose original meaning has been lost, it is hidebound and resistant to alien—in this case, adult— influences.

In one sense, the peer-group affiliation of the middle years, the immersion in being a child, looks like a detour on the road to maturity. From another standpoint, however, it appears as a necessary and valuable stage in the process of finding one's own identity. During the preschool years, the child has acquired a first identity from his parents, an identity that is in effect an identification. Now, with this much of a foundation, he is ready to begin the quest for an independent existence. As he has grown in stature, he has been able to see his parents more realistically, he knows their frailties and imperfections, and realizes—although still dimly—that he has to find stability in himself. This "detour," then, is an essential moving away from the parents in which a genuine and separate identity can be formed. But the new identity toward which the school child is moving differs from that of the preschool child in more than the matter of independence. Most significantly, he is becoming less egocentric, more detached from his own viewpoint. He is more aware of himself in objective terms, according to the labels that society attaches to him: male or female, age six to twelve, white or colored, poor or rich, and so forth. The gang, too, has its set of labels by which it knows the child and he knows himself. The gang is quick to seize on any idiosyncrasy of appearance, manner, skill, or whatever, and thereafter to treat the child in terms of this trait. The stereotype by which the gang identifies the child is often expressed in his nickname: "Skinny," "Fatso," "Four-eyes," "Dopey," "Professor," "Limpy"—the total frankness, especially of boys, often startles adults. Most children wear their nicknames, even opprobrious ones, proudly, as a badge of their belonging. Any recognition, even if only contempt, is better than being ignored. Even the outcast or scapegoat would rather have the gang persecute him than ignore him, and even the label "Stinky" means that he has an identity in the eyes of others. Now, the child's view of himself comes not only out of a feeling that he is loved and accepted by his family, but also from a sense of adequacy and competence, that he can do the things that are demanded of him, and that he has a role to play. All this further implies that he is becoming capable of criticizing himself, of viewing himself and his achievements through the eyes and according to the standards of others.

Child society is a proving ground where the child learns to live with people outside the family, but it has dangers as well. The child's declaration of independence is not a simple withdrawal from adults, but in some part a turning against them. Because children sense that it is a risky thing to question or oppose adults, the "independence" which children share may turn into a new slavery, demanding a complete subservience to the group as a source of reassurance against the risks of such defiance. The developmental danger of the gang age lies in the failure, then, to go on to relative independence of the group and group

standards. Some children who meet persistent rejection by the group
may feel isolated and unworthy, and, failing to find group acceptance
and group support, return to an identification with adults. It is worth
noting that the "good boy" or the "good girl," who may appear to
adults as a model for childhood, may be missing out on an important
part of experience and headed for trouble. Indeed, such a child's
estrangement from his mates may be made worse by adult acceptance,
as he gets to be known as a "goody-goody," "Mama's boy," or "teacher's pet." Other children, still less visibly to the casual eye, run the risk
of so complete an identification with or absorption in the group that
they acquire little ability to think for themselves without recourse to
group opinion. They feel threatened and disoriented if obliged to take
a stand without knowing the "right" way of thinking. It is, of course,
perfectly normal to experience some discomfort and anxiety when one
is ignorant of or in conflict with the standards of the group,[2] but a mature identity permits us to know what our own opinions are and to
stand by them confidently even in opposition to the group.

Needless to say, the child does not dwell wholly within his childhood
culture. At home and in school, no matter how he may resist, he is
exposed to and assimilates adult culture. The very parental precepts
that he argues against one day, he may be heard passing along as his
own convictions to the other children the next. One nine-year-old girl
listened—or, rather, seemed not to listen—with great impatience to her
parents' protests about the rough reception being given a new child in
her class, and expressed some disgust with adult lack of understanding.
Yet, a few days later, she was overheard earnestly telling a visiting
classmate the exact essence of her parents' views. At this age, a child
must make an idea his own before he accepts it, and will not take it in
merely on adult say-so. As most adults realize, they often sound fatu-
ous to the school-age children they try to influence. But they ought not
on that account to abandon their notions of conduct and morals. For
the child, after all, continues to identify with the important adults in
his life even as he resists them. We might also make the contrary point
that little pitchers have big ears. Just as the child may seem deliberately
deaf to parental lectures, he may seem casually deaf to conversations
directed over his head. Even when he is not really attending, he is
hearing and learning a variety of facts and opinions and attitudes which
parents might prefer to keep to themselves. Nevertheless, the child has
to practice a certain duality—and even duplicity—and will behave in
quite different ways according to whether he is in the company of his

peers or adults. Later on, we shall talk more about children's contacts with adult society, how they resist it, take it in, and conflict with it. For the present, we want to look at middle childhood where it is purest, in the peer group: kids moving in packs and doing things in packs.

Childhood Tradition

As an introduction to childhood society, we shall look at its culture, perhaps best seen in the ancient tribal rituals. We do not use the term "ancient" lightly. While historical research is handicapped by the gulf between adult and child, and by the fact that childhood culture is primarily a spoken rather than a written one, it has been possible to trace many still-common children's games and chants back to the Middle Ages and beyond to Roman and Druid, and perhaps Sanskrit, sources.[3] This culture has been handed down from generation to generation, but from generations of almost-adolescent children to the generations of younger brothers and sisters whom they initiate. Adults, looking back, will realize that this is a world which closed behind them and which they do nothing to communicate to their children. Grownups may teach children baseball, but children teach children one o'cat. In fact, to recall the games and chants and rituals of the middle years is, like the evocative loose tooth, another effective passport to our own childhoods. And when, comparing recollections, one of us encounters a minor variation in the wording of a rhyme, he feels strong indignation at this intolerable unorthodoxy. Such indignation is a further clue to the relative fixity of this culture. To add one more accent to the feat of transmitting a culture virtually intact down through the ages, we might point out that while it takes only three or four adult generations to span a century, there are perhaps fifteen childhood generations per century. This remarkable durability depends in large part on children's love of ritual for its own sake and on their (mostly unspoken) sense of magical power in the literal repetition of forms which share the character of rites and incantations. Moreover, any violation of the strict formula is felt to nullify its potency, or carries with it a sense of tempting fate.

GAMES AND CHANTS A painting called "Children's Games" by the sixteenth-century Flemish painter Brueghel shows children at pastimes already venerable in his time yet most of them precisely like those one can see on any contemporary American playground, centuries, languages, and nations away. Among the more durable of children's games are hopscotch, marbles, crack-the-whip, hide-and-seek, duck on the rock, blindman's buff (often rendered "bluff"), Red Rover, dodge-ball, keep-away, jacks, London Bridge—the reader is invited to supply his own favorites. London Bridge is believed to date back to the medieval custom of entombing someone alive in the foundations of a bridge to propitiate the river spirits. In fact, many children's traditions preserve early forms of adult culture. The metal forms used in jacks are derived from the knuckle-bones used for a similar game in Roman times. There are countless chants, many of them equally antique, such as the accompaniments to London Bridge and ring-around-a-rosy, to skipping rope, and to ball-bouncing. Closely allied are the counting-out rhymes: "Eeny, meeny, miney, mo"; "One-potato"; etc. There are the rhymed guessing games: "Buck, buck, you lousy muck, How many fists have I got up, One, two, or none?" This particular specimen has been traced back to Nero's day: *Bucca, bucca, quot sunt hic?* [4] Some sayings are commentaries reserved for special occasions: "Ladybird, ladybird, fly away home"; "Last one in is a rotten egg"; "I scream, you scream, we all scream for ice cream"; "It's raining, it's pouring, The old man is snoring"; "No more spelling, no more books, No more teacher's dirty looks." Some are magical incantations: "Rain, rain, go away." Others are taunts: "Susie's mad, and I'm glad, And I know what will please her"; "Roses are red, Violets are blue, If I had your mug, I'd join the zoo."

Despite the fact that all these sayings have their fixed occasions and significances, the words of many of them are empty of literal meaning for the child. Yet the charm of saying them—and the need to say them precisely—is there. Much of this charm seems to stem from the sense of participation, the feeling that one is in the know, that one has the key. The sense of a fraternity-like membership is well demonstrated when two children, catching themselves saying the same thing at the same time, instantly fall into the ritual of locking their little fingers together, making a silent wish, and then exchanging the prescribed phrases before they break the hold with a ceremonial flourish and remain mute until a third person speaks to one of them and breaks the spell—if they speak without this release, the wish is lost. All the other children are aware of their relation to the rite and of their power to enforce silence until they choose to free the chief participants. The point of our example is not simply the religious adherence to a communal ritual, but its dependence on the appropriate interaction among members of the group. If the other speaker or one of the surrounding children does not properly play his role—for the game is spoiled if the principals are too quickly liberated—this is sensed as a gratuitous and offensive destruction of a magical moment and will be greeted by the indignant and almost equally ritual cry of "No fair!"

Young school children play their games, just as they recite their sayings and perform their rituals, according to ironclad formulas that permit of no variation. Later in the school years, this initial absolutism mellows somewhat in favor of a degree of relativism. Piaget, in his investigation of children's concepts of rules and morals, found definite changes with age in the way rules are conceived.[5] Early in the school years, they are accepted as *given:* timeless, immutable, and inherent in the game itself. If it is pointed out that children in the next county, say, follow slightly different rules, this departure from The Right Way may be viewed as pitiably ignorant or verging on the sacrilegious. When a child enters a new community, he is often made to feel somewhat ashamed of the incorrect rules he used to follow. When, in the middle of the middle years, the child begins to realize that the rules come from somewhere, he may conceive of them as the work of some obscure Rule-maker who fixed them for all time. Still later, minor changes in the rules are permitted, provided everyone agrees—there arise what adults would call local ground rules. Finally, late in the school years, children can grasp the fact that rules are arrived at by consensus and serve merely to define the conduct and purpose of the game in an orderly way. It should be noted that this development in the conception of rules runs parallel to a change in the kind of games children play. Increasingly, during the middle years, children engage in competitive games, games which do not simply run their course, like London Bridge and Farmer in the Dell, but have an outcome, a score. Nevertheless, ritual predominates for most of the school years, in the compelling nature of rules, in the self-contained quality of games, in the inflexibility of sayings, in the conservatism of children's attitudes.

OTHER CHILDHOOD RITES   In addition to communal rituals, there are many others which though solitary still are defined by the child culture and carry strong group sanction. Among these are the superstitious observances (not walking under a ladder, holding your breath while crossing a bridge); obsessive counting (including counting by fives or by tens or backwards) and humming; avoiding or stepping on sidewalk cracks, touching every lamp post, and so forth. Many children invent private rituals as well. One adult recalls how he had to be in bed and under the covers before the door swung shut or else the (imaginary) mice under the bed would bite his toes. A woman recalls how she had to get upstairs before the basement toilet stopped flushing lest she be captured by some nameless bogey; it is interesting to note that this ritual was taken over, in modified form, by each of her two younger siblings in turn. We might point out that these two examples, in common with most private rituals—including those of adult compulsive neurotics (to be discussed later)—serve to ward off some specific or nameless threat.

There are still other forms of behavior in the middle years, which, although less ritualistic than those we have described, are still closely bound up with the traditional childhood culture. There are the ever-recurring childhood *jokes and riddles,* which seem wholly threadbare to adults but which come as revelations to each new wave of children and are for them the essence of sophisticated wit: "Why does the chicken cross the road?"; "Why do firemen wear red suspenders?" There are the *stunts,* the tricks one learns to do with one's own body, control of which now becomes so important and which has so many peculiar and unsuspected potentialities. School-age children learn to make themselves cross-eyed, to see double, to contort their faces into horrendous shapes, to rub their stomachs while patting their heads, to perform exercises in double-jointedness, to cross their arms and clasp their hands and be perplexed as to which finger is which—late in this period, a fortunate, gifted few will even be able to wiggle their ears. A verbal equivalent of such stunts is the competitive mastery of *tongue twisters.* The learning of body tricks goes along, of course, with the learning of *physical skills.* It is during the middle years that children learn to use their bodies effectively: from hopping on one foot and turning somersaults to jumping, vaulting, swimming, diving, skating, playing ball, and the rest. The development of these capacities is, of course, closely related to the child's new sense of identity in terms of his specific competences.

Yet another characteristically ritualized way of dealing with the world that appears at this time is the making of *collections.* At least in the early school years, collections should more properly be called aggregations: pocketfuls or drawerfuls of the incredible and often somewhat unspeakable miscellany that every mother of a school-age child has had to cope with. Later in the school years, collections tend to become more homogeneous and orderly: stamps ranged neatly on the pages of an album, dolls propped neatly on a shelf. But no matter how disorderly or even repulsive the child's accumulations appear to adults, to the child every length of twine, every broken piece of cheap jewelry, every faded sea shell deserves the designation of "very valuable." Often, in fact, the objects the child collects, in keeping with the general tenor of his ways, take on highly charged magical or talismanic qualities.

Early in the school years, the child gains a sense of shared secrets and control of mystery through simple participation in ritual. Later in the school years, similar feelings are expressed in a flowering of *coded talk and writing*. We might note in passing the communicative nature of this phenomenon, pointing again to the group orientation of the middle years. Apart from the sense of shared activity, we can see in the child's taste for cryptology the pleasure of having a secret *from* those who are excluded—probably other children, certainly the adults—and a touch of the magic found in the special priestly language of many societies. As in so many other aspects of school-age behavior, form is considerably more important than content. Children are often hard put to find anything to talk secretly about, but even the most commonplace message takes on a mystical tinge when phrased in Pig Latin or Op, or painfully transcribed into one of the many letter-, number-, or diagram-substitution ciphers.

THE MEANING OF RITUAL   The traditional childhood culture serves many developmental functions and needs, which we wish here only to survey briefly, reserving some of our discussion for later contexts. The school child, as we have suggested, has reached a point in his development where he can be aware of his essential human aloneness in a vast, powerful, and largely unpredictable world. He has to deal with this awareness in two ways. First, as an individual he must master and control reality. Second, he must find emotional strength in the company of his peers. His childhood culture meets both these needs exactly on the level of his capacities. His rituals, his skills, his collections provide a magical domination over reality. His rituals are for him a pure distillate of know-how and to some extent a substitute for practical accomplishment, his skills give him reassurance as to his own strength, his collections can be seen as the world reduced to a scale where he can possess and manage and order it. At the same time, by taking on the childhood culture, by conforming to it in minutest detail, the child demonstrates both to his peers and to himself that he belongs, that he is one of them, and is entitled to the security of their loyalty and support. In short, growth—especially growth toward independence—is always to some degree disturbing and disruptive, and the school-age child resorts to the devices of his culture to hold his world together. He surrenders wholeheartedly to the absolutism of peer-group authority in place of the absolutism of parental authority. However, the very fact of this shift implies both a new flexibility, which the child must capitalize on, and a new instability, which he must counteract.

The Peer Group

Until now, we have talked largely of the highly formalized traditions in the culture of childhood society. Now it is time to look more closely at the actual society, at children functioning in groups, at how these groups are organized, what they do, and what their activities tell us about children in this age range. Children ordinarily refer to the pack of kids they run with as "the gang," and we shall adopt their terminology, emphasizing that in our usage it by no means necessarily connotes delinquent behavior. The gang may have many varying degrees of organization, from a loose cluster of children playing in the school yard or street, to clubs for the sake of having clubs, to special-purpose clubs such as ball teams or delinquent gangs organized as fighting forces.

A WORLD APART   Let us stress the separation between the society of the gang of kids and the adult world. It is fascinating to walk down a city block and observe the child and adult societies carrying on their activities in and around each other but mutually oblivious except when they interfere with each other. Children step aside for cars without breaking the rhythm of their game. Adults are unaware that they walk through a game of stickball at a crucial moment, while the children barely pause to let the intruders pass. The conversations of the adults and the chants and jeers of the children mingle in the observer's ear but do not interpenetrate each other. And along the shifting boundaries between these worlds are strung the younger children, on whom the older brothers and sisters are keeping a bored but remarkably efficient eye or who are just making the transition to the gang. For the roles of children in the gang, and their attitudes toward it, vary with age. The six-year-old, as we have said, is still largely home-based and parent-oriented. At this age, and often for another year or two, children are just beginning to gravitate to the gang, hanging around on the outskirts, watching, listening, taking in, imitating doggedly, and participating when they are allowed to. For children of these early middle years, older children are invested with enormous authority and prestige. In many ways, they seem to appear more grown-up and knowing than adults. By age eight or nine, a marked change appears in children's patterns of affiliation and loyalty. Parents are often distressed to find that their erstwhile loving child seems, during his third or fourth year of school, to have lost his affectionate and confiding nature and become a stranger to his family. He may adopt odd mannerisms and startling turns of speech; he may become sloppy in dress and highly resistant to bathing (girls remain neater than boys but nevertheless often go through a bathless period); he may become as reticent as he formerly was talkative, and seem to live only for the moment when he can tear from the house and join the other kids, leaving, whenever possible, chores and lessons undone. He may display an insolence wholly at odds with his former good nature and give the impression of laboring under a heavy secret. Parents, seeing their child drawing away from them, may be inclined to become more demonstrative or possessive, to quiz the child about what is ailing him, or to storm at him for his lack of filial devotion. (We shall have more to say shortly about parental dealings with the school-age child.) At this point the child is taking one more stride on the road to maturity, he is filing his own individual Declaration of Independence. As we have seen, the child's independence is of a strictly limited kind, being subject to the control of the gang, but valuable insofar as it is the start of emancipation from the parents.

CHILD VERSUS ADULT   It is not his parents alone but adult authority in general from which the child declares his independence. On the lips of a school-age child, "the grownups" is a term of derogation. The pattern of defiance of adults combined with intense group affiliation may often be observed most clearly in school situations. In the more strictly regulated schools, group indignation toward adults may appear only in *sotto voce* mutterings or playground gripe sessions, perhaps centering around a teacher's invitation to "let me know who is throwing those spitballs," a drastic infringement of the children's code on snitching. In schools where the children are free to express resistance to authority more openly, even though the occasions for conflict may be few, the teacher expects an occasional wave of protest or defiance, often around the familiar rallying cry of "It's not fair!" and sometimes over issues which the children seem to have invented as an excuse to plague the adults—or, more properly, to try their strength against the adults' from the safety of group cohesion. In such cases, of course, some of the children may half-humorously half-recognize that they are inflating a trivial issue out of all proportion. The gang exists not only as an end in itself but also as a fortress, making it safe to test out resistance to adult authority. Indeed, the gang often becomes an alternate authority to be pitted against that of parents: "Gee, Ma, all the other kids . . ." (are going swimming, or staying up later, or not wearing rubbers, or watching a forbidden television show). Sometimes gangs, particularly of boys, behave in ways that seem expressly designed to arouse adult authority just so that they can then outrun or outwit it. Thus, for instance, it is no fun to steal apples from an orchard or a pushcart unless you are seen and chased. Adults who view such behavior either disapprovingly or indulgently may be missing the psychological point: I can stand up to adults and survive.

The child, inherently something of an extremist, almost inevitably overdoes his declaration of independence. Every child in the middle years is more or less in the position of what Mead has called "the immigrant personality." [6] The child of immigrant parents in the United States typically finds himself ashamed of his parents' foreign, "old-fashioned" ways and strives feverishly to be as unlike them and as like the host culture as possible. So it is with the school-age child. In his case, of course, the host culture is the sub-culture of childhood. And his parents, no matter how solidly American, are no longer the source of all wisdom and power. Indeed, they may appear all too contemptibly weak and mundane and merely human. This is the age at which some children first become prone to "foundling fantasies," daydreams, often reaching the point of profound conviction, that the child is of exalted birth and has by some dreadful mischance fallen into the hands of lesser foster-parents. As a matter of fact, in our society the attitudes of both immigrant and native-born parents abet this reaction in their children. In the case of immigrant parents, no matter how firmly they cling to the old-country customs and values, they themselves are likely to feel ashamed of their ignorance and differentness and to take pride in their children's successful Americanization. Even native American parents have a marked tendency to assume, as do their children, that the younger generation will outstrip the older in attainment. As Mead has pointed out, parents are aware that the world their child is growing up in is literally not the one they knew as children. The children know this, too, and feel that their parents come from a different world, just as though they were immigrants. Children have always retorted that "times have changed" when parents launch upon a lecture with the phrase, "When I was a boy (or girl)," but now both parties are well aware that times have indeed changed. Unfortunately, this realization has tended to weaken parents' confidence in their own authority. How can they hope to prescribe for life in a world transformed beyond recognition by political, economic, moral, social, technological, and philosophical revolutions? As we shall see later, parents must somehow continue to find the strength to be parents, but meanwhile let us return to the child and his gang.

SOCIAL ORGANIZATION   We have already pointed out that the middle years are not all of a piece, and that the characteristics of social organization change within this era of development. Younger children, as we have noted, lurk around the fringes of established neighborhood groups, drinking in the wisdom and manner of the older children, avidly learning and practicing the rituals we have described, and occasionally merging with the group. Probably the first real coalition of younger school children consists in the sharing of a secret. Genuine affiliation and membership, and the climax of love for the secret society, are found in the middle of this age range. By the time the later middle years are reached, groups and gangs are less likely to exist exclusively for the sake of belongingness or for the formal rites they practice, and are more likely to be organized around particular kinds of activities and functions. The older school child is likely to be involved in and handle easily multiple memberships and affiliations. The fact that he is moving closer to adult society and its cleavages is also evident in the composition of the groups and cliques to which he belongs. In the patterning of social organization during the middle years, as in other aspects of development, we can see at work the general principles of increasing differentiation followed by functional subordination. For instance, the gang spirit at first appears as something valuable in its own right, so that just being with the gang is satisfaction enough; later, the value lies in the things the gang does.

In neighborhoods where families tend to stay put and where there are many children, the neighborhood play group with its unannounced but regular meetings before and after supper is likely to include a variety of ages, with occasional divisions into "big kids" and "little kids." In some areas, there is direct continuity between early childhood and adolescent street corner society, or even adult-sponsored delinquent gangs, some of which preserve their organizational frameworks and names intact while successive generations of children pass through them.

Left to themselves, children are likely to define their affiliations on a geographical base: the home block (except in rural areas). Outside "our block," one has a strong sense of being in alien or even hostile territory. It is worth noting that in many American communities geographical divisions correspond closely to racial and ethnic divisions, a fact which may help perpetuate in children's society the same segregations and prejudices that exist in adult society. In fact, recent research, which played a part in the Supreme Court's decision on school segregation, indicates that segregation is as much a cause as an effect of prejudice.[7] (Needless to say, specific indoctrination in prejudice also plays its part.[8]) Children's groupings along geographical lines are, however, counteracted by other influences: schools that draw on a wide geographic base, adult-fostered visiting relationships, friendships formed at summer camp, and the telephone, although this last has not become the potent factor in the life of the school child that it will be in the adolescent's.

THE SEX CLEAVAGE   In addition to groupings in terms of age and geography, there is also the matter of grouping along sex lines to be considered. (We shall deal more systematically in a later section with the differences, as opposed to the separation, between boys and girls in the school years, although certain of these differences inevitably come in for mention here.) In the early middle years, the cleavage of the sexes is a casual, almost accidental affair. Boys and girls are learning to like different kinds of activities, and in pursuing these they follow separate paths. Girls continue to play house and begin to like hopscotch and jacks, while boys roam farther, play rougher, wrestle, and learn baseball. But by the middle of this period, the sex cleavage becomes conscious and institutionalized. At least when in the presence of their gangs, boys and girls elaborately shun each other and speak with ringing contempt of the opposite sex. Here, as in asserting independence of adults, one must go to extremes to establish the purity of one's boy-ness or girl-ness. At this time, virtually all boys go through a period when they reject all females, with the possible exception of their mothers, loudly announcing vows of total, permanent celibacy. They are particularly puzzled and outraged when they see their just-older heroes, who until now have shared and perhaps even taught them their misogyny, suddenly beginning to tolerate and indeed seek out the company of girls. Girls, on the other hand, although they often express the same disdain for boys, are more likely to carry along, partly from their early domestic play, a romantic vision of domesticity in which they picture themselves as brides and even as mothers, but mated to a misty figure bearing no resemblance to the horrible boys they know. In the same vein, girls may continue throughout this time to enjoy "love" movies, while boys are volubly disgusted by them. Sometimes the hostility toward the opposite sex is deeply felt, but at other times and for other children, of course, it merely means going along with the mores of the gang in order to preserve one's status. In the neighborhood play group, there may even be some occasional mingling of the sexes in foot races or games of tag. The neighborhood group may also be the setting for the breaking down of the barriers between the sexes that comes in the latter middle years, shown in the first clumsy reaching out for each other in the guise of teasing, "kidding," and scuffling. In the case of girls, however, there is a tendency with the approach of puberty to move toward older boys rather than to become reconciled with their male contemporaries.

A few years back, *Life* magazine, in an article entitled "The Pigtail Set," gave a vivid portrayal of girls at the height of the school years. Here is what *Life* had to say:

> [The pigtail set's] busy, ten-year-old members comprise the happiest and best-adjusted group of citizens in the country.
>
> In a tight little world dominated by the radio [now TV] serial, the skinned knee, and the chocolate marshmallow walnut tutti-frutti sundae, the pigtail set lives a wonderful life. It is wonderful chiefly because its members are old enough to enjoy a certain amount of freedom without yet being bothered by the perplexing problems of adolescence.
>
> The typical pigtailer is around ten years old and, according to statistics, there are more than 1,000,000 [now more] of them in the U. S. About a third of them actually wear pigtails. Unlike her teen-age brothers and sisters, whose lives have been profoundly altered by the jalopy and juke box, the pigtailer's habits are the changeless habits of generations of American [and other] children. She still spends hours dressing up in her mother's clothes [preferring, *Life* says elsewhere, ". . . filmy dresses, long gloves, floppy hats, parasols and plenty of costume jewelry"]. She skips rope, climbs trees and plays hopscotch at a pace calculated to exhaust an Olympic decathlon champion. She loves to play house or nurse. She is fond of pets. And although she feels a little old for dolls, she plays with them a good deal on the sly.
>
> . . . [They walk or bicycle to school] in large, noisy groups. They love school, they love their teachers, they love art, arithmetic and geography. They also love the Girl Scouts. Best of all they love to eat, which they do incessantly and recklessly.[9]

Among the pigtailer activities described by *Life* are playing beauty parlor; reading comic strips (Orphan Annie, Blondie, Tarzan, Mandrake the Magician, Bringing Up Father, Li'l Abner, Popeye); making faces; learning to dance; going to the movies and sitting "in large, vociferous gangs in the balcony, where their enthusiasm often requires an usher's restraint. Their favorites are animal pictures and musicals"; and eating.

Boys do many of the same things, of course, even if separately from girls. For the boy, however, the gang is more likely also to be the place he learns quantities of sex lore (which is still poorly differentiated from the facts of elimination), where certain of this lore is put to practical test, where he first samples tobacco, where he may get caught in a round of dares leading to spectacular and sometimes disastrous feats of physical prowess, where he gets his eye blackened and his nose bloodied and his clothes torn, where the pack spirit ranges in search of pranks that may overflow into vandalism, where cops and robbers or cowboys and Indians or other games may be enacted with hair-raising fidelity to the models provided by television and comic books. Unlike the ten-year-old girl, the ten-year-old boy will not be heard proclaiming his love of school. He either violently dislikes school or feels that he should. Moreover, no ten-year-old boy would be caught dead saying that he "loved" anything—there are distinct differences from girls in the vocabulary boys prefer or tolerate. Boys, except for their devotion to cowboy or spaceman costumes in the early school years, and, later, sanctioned occasions like Hallowe'en or plays, have no use for activities such as dressing up. In boys' gangs, as compared to girls', there is more emphasis on emulation, on being able to do what the toughest can do, on competition, on physical skill, and on bravery. Not all boy gangs, of course, are preoccupied with physical action. Some groups of boys, perhaps the more bookish ones, like to relive the Robin Hood or King Arthur legends, or invent private countries or planets or historic events which they can draw or write about or stage in makeshift but no less heroic dramatizations. As we suggested earlier, direct defiance of adults is more common in boy than in girl gangs. Indeed, girls generally remain on terms of much greater intimacy with their parents during this time than do boys.

Although most of the gang-centered activities of the school years are simply the extravagant assertion of a new-found independence and group feeling, they sometimes have an ominous cast and do proceed directly into delinquency. We should point out, however, that the structure and appeal of delinquent gangs are in many respects the same as those of non-delinquent ones. The delinquent gang, like any other, provides a basis for one's feeling of worth and competence, for one's exhilarating sense of emancipation from adult restraints; the fact of delinquent behavior is almost incidental, a function largely of neighborhood traditions and ways of gaining prestige.

MEANINGS OF GANG MEMBERSHIP   Toward the middle of the school years, group life is often marked by a change from the loose, shifting organization of the gang or neighborhood group to short-lived but tightly and elaborately organized clubs, usually with an overabundance of officers, codified rules, ceremonies, oaths, and vague but portentous secrets. When they band together into clubs, children enunciate ambitious if ill-defined purposes and goals, but the underlying, unspoken motivation seems to be to further formalize and solidify the children's sense of belonging. As we have already indicated, the ritual of these clubs brings its own pleasures. Something of the flavor of a school-age club, apart from the ceremonial aspects, is well conveyed in the following quotation from the *New Yorker:*

> The rules of a secret society of nine- and ten-year-old girls in a certain community on Long Island that shall here be nameless are as follows:
>
> 1. Do not tell a white lie unless necessary.
> 2. Do not hurt anyone in any way.
> 3. Do not hit anyone except Ronny.
> 4. Do not tell a black lie.
> 5. Do not use words worse than "brat."
> 6. Do not curse at all.
> 7. Do not make faces except at Ronny.
> 8. Do not be selfish.
> 9. Do not make a hog or a pig of yourself.
> 10. Do not tattle except on Ronny.
> 11. Do not steal except from Ronny.
> 12. Do not destroy other people's property, except Ronny's.
> 13. Do not be a sneak.
> 14. Do not be grumpy except to Ronny.
> 15. Do not answer back except to Ronny.*[10]

The tendency to absolutism and legalistic morality of this age is clearly implied here. But what of Ronny? Aside from being a boy and presumably scarcely human to these girls, he may serve as a reminder that the feeling of inclusion seems to necessitate someone's exclusion. Just as six-year-olds need to have a secret *from* somebody, the ten-year-old's club can induce a feeling of "we"-ness only by leaving out "them." Usually, a number of children are left out and they in turn form an equally exclusive club of their own. Sometimes, however, the exclusions are aimed at a particular individual, a Ronny, a scapegoat. In general, children engage in this kind of activity largely to reinforce their in-group feeling, but it need not be pernicious. Patterns of friendship and ascendancy change quite rapidly among school-age children, and today's pariah may be tomorrow's favorite. However, while friendships and enmities last, they are felt intensely. Rejection by the entire group points to the despotic nature of majority rule: the excluded child experiences a strong, if perhaps temporary, inner conviction that the group must be right and that there must be something wrong with him. Herein lies the tragedy for the permanently or repeatedly excluded individual, whether the exclusion is on personal or ethnic grounds. Every child who comes into a new neighborhood or a new school is at first a minority group member as he faces the bristling outside of the in-group feeling.

HOME AND FAMILY   Now that we, like the child, have exaggerated his independence of his family, it is time to bring them back together again. To begin with, not all group life is lived outside the home. Singly or in small groups, children visit each other's house, becoming involved in kite- or model-building projects, often of grandiose scope and limited duration, or sharing enormous marathon feasts in front of the television screen, sprawled in the remarkable postures whose restfulness baffles adults. But the child has siblings as well as friends, and we should take a moment to look at his relationships with his brothers and sisters. Granted that every family and every relationship is unique, we should still like to risk some generalizations. If siblings are fairly close in age, and are all within the age-band of the school years, their contacts at home are likely to be marked by bantering, bickering, battling, and bedlam, interspersed with some joint activities, some comparing of notes on people, school, and so forth, and, lest we overlook it, some more or less harmonious sharing in whole-family enterprises and chores. When sibs fall in different developmental stages, when a school-ager has a preschool or adolescent brother or sister, the gulf is likely to appear unbridgeable. The post-pubertal elder is inclined to be particularly critical of the grubby, noisy, ill-mannered, sassy youngster. He sometimes expresses this in open rage, sometimes in elaborately haughty doubts as to their common parentage. The school-ager, in turn, shrewdly hacks away at the adolescent's new and precarious dignity. He tends to see his preschool brother or sister as underfoot or tagging along, disturbing his property, and receiving favors and indulgences from the parents such as he was certainly never granted in the long bygone days. The elder child is highly jealous of the hard-won prerogatives of his age, while the younger resents them as preferential. If the younger child is much younger, and so not in competition with the school-ager, he is likely to be treated indulgently and affectionately—if sometimes as a nuisance. Parents, all too aware of the war-torn aspects of sibling relationships, are often genuinely startled to learn how the children close ranks in family solidarity outside the home when one of them is threatened or abused. The terms "kid brother" and "big sister" may be used disparagingly, but they also carry considerable affection, even though this is supposed to be veiled from the gang. It should further be pointed out that lower-class children of school age, rather more often than middle-class ones, are likely to be put in charge of their younger sibs, who play on the edges of the group while the games go forward. It should be noted, too, that the responsibility for younger children in the lower classes tends to be coupled with real authority over them. It is possible that wielding such authority is satisfying in itself, fits in well with the drive of this age for independent status, and facilitates identification with the parents.

What is more, for all their insistence on freedom and privacy from adults, for all the fault they find with their elders and their elders' ways of thinking, children do not suddenly stop loving their parents. Indeed, as in the case of sibling solidarity, the same children who criticize their parents freely will not tolerate the slightest slur on them from outside the family. Parents can no longer remain high on a pedestal, but if they can bring themselves to climb down gracefully, they will find that there are other bases on which to be parents. And let us stress that there is no sight more pathetic than a father or mother trying to be a "pal" to son or daughter (not that there is any lack of things they can enjoy doing together). But there are plenty of peers around to serve as pals, and the child needs his parents as parents—which means as adults and not as pseudo-children. He needs them as refuges when he finds himself cut off from the gang in one of its periodic realignments, when he is sick or at other vulnerable moments, and simply at times when he wants to be a member of his family, trading news and jokes and confidences, asking for information and advice and help with his homework. At bedtime, he may even welcome a small amount of cuddling—here again we should signal a sex difference, pointing out that girls remain rather consistently demonstrative during this time. And the child continues to boast of his parents' achievements to the gang, partly because this may give him prestige but also because he is identifying with his parents. This identification, as we have said, is usually by a process of unconscious or perhaps grudging absorption. The child's conscious models are the gang and the gang's heroes: cowboys, nurses, athletes, aviators, and so forth. When, however, one's father happens to be in an interesting occupation—for the six- or seven-year-old, say, plumbing, fishing, garbage collection—and works where his child can watch him, there is likely to be a direct and conscious identification. The case, of course, is more difficult for mothers, whose domestic occupations form the accustomed background of the child's experience and are all but invisible. Even if she has a career, it is unlikely that she follows one with the twin specifications of glamor and visibility.

Whatever the manner of the child's identification, he continues to need regulation at home. For one thing, he may need parental backing to enable him to maintain his own values in the face of group pressure —we have already seen how he can assimilate parental ideas and pass them along to the gang as his own. Just as he expects privileges—later bedtime, an allowance—in keeping with increasing maturity, so he is able to accept increasing responsibilities in the form of chores appropriate to his age. When the child shares in family prosperity or hard times, when he contributes by picking up his room at age six or shoveling the driveway at age twelve, when he has a part, suited to his age, in decisions affecting the whole family—whether to buy a pet, where to spend a vacation—he is becoming aware of the bonds of reciprocity that tie together a family, and, eventually, the world. It is worth noting that the democratic privileges accorded to children are still limited and subject to adult authority. Children in the school years are usually not ready for full democratic self-determination.

We must likewise bear in mind that adult authority cannot be as absolute as in the earlier years of development. Parents must adapt to the fact that school-age children are committed to the mores of the peer group. Without the group, the child's growth toward individuality and a sense of self-reliance are endangered. He may overidentify with adult values. He may seek his friendships among, and to some extent identify with, children of the opposite sex. He may strive excessively to meet the standard masculine or feminine qualifications. He may resort to a more or less constructive withdrawal from social pursuits, taking refuge in fantasy, becoming overconcerned with scholastic achievements, or becoming exaggeratedly individualistic—often with the secret hope that his behavior will call him to the attention of his fellows. It is evident that the peer group is a mixed blessing, but also that it plays an important and perhaps indispensable part in growing up.

Sex Roles and Sex Differences

We have already alluded to the fact that during the middle years boys and girls begin to pursue separate interests and diverging lines of development. We have explained in earlier chapters why it is futile to argue about the extent to which sex differences are biologically fixed and the extent to which they are culturally determined. However, we can point to some of the factors operating in our culture to produce our versions of boy-ness and girl-ness, bearing in mind that the social climate in which children grow up has as substantial an effect upon their development as the food they eat and the air they breathe. We must also remember that there is something of a snowball effect in development, that children, having assumed certain attitudes that go with masculinity, are then more open to the incorporation of other aspects of their sex roles, so that masculinity breeds further masculinity, and femininity femininity.

In the paragraphs below, where we shall detail some of the ways in which boys and girls in our society differ, we can see several interrelated influences at work. To begin with, there is the fact, by now so commonplace that we are liable to overlook it, that child rearing, at home and at school, is very largely in the hands of women. For girls, this seems to simplify the identification process. They slip easily and quickly into the ways provided for them—in Benedict's term, there is considerable *continuity* between their childhood and adult roles.[11] In one respect, however, we feel that there is some disadvantage for girls as well as for boys in having so much of their upbringing taken care of by women: just as boys may lack male models to identify with firsthand, so may girls lack males to relate to. We have spoken earlier and shall speak again of what we regard as a somewhat unfortunate trend toward a feminization of our society. For boys, the situation is somewhat more difficult. Mothers and teachers are less likely to sympathize with the ways of boys. Or, rather, they have mixed feelings about them, feelings which are reflected in the inconsistent standards boys are required to meet.[12] On the one hand, boys are pressed to meet the standards of decorum laid down by female preceptors. On the other hand, if boys fail to exhibit a certain amount of spirit, of aggressiveness, of roughness, adults—women as well as men—become somewhat perturbed and feel that "something is missing." The boy is taught obedience, generosity, and kindness, but if he does not stand up for his rights he is scorned as a sissy. He is expected to be both Tom Sawyer and Little Lord Fauntleroy. But the boy does not have to meet conflicting demands only from adults; he is faced with a further disparity between adult standards and peer-group standards. Girl peer-group mores, on the other hand, as we can see from the list of rules of the Anti-Ronny Club, cited earlier, closely parallel adult mores. Again, apart from con-

flicting standards, boys more than girls are expected, perhaps in anticipation of their later responsibilities, to be ambitious and to strive for
tangible achievement, thus increasing the risk of failure. All this is not
to say that boys have greater problems than girls, but that their problems are of a different kind.

Sex Differences

In this summary of sex differences, we shall draw heavily on Terman
and Tyler's excellent review of research in this field.[13]

Most obviously, there are *physical differences* between the sexes.
Apart from differences in genital structure, which exist from before
birth, there are sex differences as regards size, proportion, strength,
chemical balance, and so forth. We should not, however, make the mis-
take of assuming that these are primary and immutable. We do not
really know which is the chicken and which is the egg: whether, that
is, boys and girls develop psychologically as they do because of their
physical constitutions, or whether certain aspects—strength, vigor, metabolism, etc.—of their physical constitutions develop in accordance
with the activity patterns they learn. Boys and girls do not differ markedly in size until puberty although, up to age eleven, boys are consistently taller and heavier. Beginning at age six, however, boys show an
increasing superiority in "vital capacity"—sustained energy output—
and muscular strength. These differences correspond to—that is, may
either influence or partly depend on—boys' continuing preference for
active play as opposed to girls' growing preference for quieter pursuits.
Homeostatic mechanisms (for the regulation of physiological equilibrium) are more stable in boys than in girls; note, for instance, how
much more common blushing is in girls. Needless to say, hormonal patterns likewise differ between the sexes.

One often hears arguments about *differences in intelligence* between
males and females. In terms of intelligence test scores, the answer is
unequivocal: neither is more intelligent. There is, however, evidence
that, beginning in the school years, boys and girls manifest different
types of intelligence. An intelligence test score may be thought of as
an average of tests in special areas of functioning—language usage,
memory, spatial sense, etc.—and even though boys and girls are equal
in terms of overall averages, they show distinct patternings of special
abilities. Girls, for instance, do better in the verbal sphere, particularly
with respect to language fluency, boys in the realm of quantitative and

spatial relationships. In general, too, girls do better school work than boys, but boys excel in science and mathematics. Boys, it would seem, are more at home with abstract materials, girls with the personal and immediate and emotionally toned. Indeed, the venerable folk notion that men are more rational and analytic and women more emotional and impressionistic or even intuitive, which scientific psychology was about ready to discard, has now been given a fresh lease on life by recent experimental findings.[14] Here again, of course, we are not prepared to say with any certainty whether these differences are biologically or socially determined.

As we might expect, boys and girls display considerable disparity in *tastes and interests*. Terman, on the basis of a survey of children's interests, has devised a scale of objects and activities ranging from most masculine to most feminine, with a region of shared activities in the middle.[15] Among the things that appeal most strongly to boys are tools, guns, kites, bicycles, marbles, wrestling, boxing, football, machinery, fishing, and so forth. Girls like dolls, dressing up, hopscotch, cooking, playing house, sewing, dancing, parlor games, etc. Boys and girls both enjoy such things as Red Rover, follow-the-leader, croquet, volleyball, dominoes, parcheesi, tiddlywinks, card games, coasting, hiking, tag, jackstraws, and, to suggest that their mutual contempt is something less than total, post office. Terman's study was made in 1925, and there seem to have been some changes in the ensuing interval. Nowadays, for example, we can see a trend toward greater participation by girls in strenuous games and sports, but such participation still drops off sharply at puberty. And, of course, we still cannot say what is cause and what is effect, the extent to which such preferences arise spontaneously out of being a boy or a girl or the extent to which the child accepts them as appropriate to his or her sex. It is likely that children might often enjoy activities assigned to the opposite sex but are restrained by a sense that to do so—or even visibly to want to do so—would be a betrayal of their sex role. In middle-class children, for whom sex roles are not always sharply defined, there is some evidence that these clear-cut preferences emerge at increasingly later ages, especially in boys.

The latency period, as we have said, is a time when boys and girls are often impelled to possess and dominate the world by putting it on a shelf in the form of *collections*. There are characteristic differences between the collections made by boys and by girls. Typically, boys collect

T A B L E 4 Composite Distribution of "Referral Problems" in Four Metropolitan Child Guidance Centers*

(N = 2,500 Children; average 1.9 complaints per child)

REFERRAL PROBLEMS	UNDER 6		6 TO 10		10 TO 14		14 TO 18		ALL AGES			TOT. AS % OF N
	M	F	M	F	M	F	M	F	M	F	TOT.	
Academic Difficulties	3	0	358	126	322	117	146	54	829	297	1,126	45
Mental Retardation	16	9	166	94	180	123	50	35	412	261	673	27
Aggressive and Anti-Social Behavior	45	12	242	65	192	39	115	45	594	161	755	30
Passive, Withdrawn, Asocial Behavior	38	15	174	74	110	50	60	25	382	164	546	22
Emotional Instability and Anxiety Symptoms	45	16	205	86	108	46	49	25	407	173	580	23
Hyperactivity and Motor Symptoms	24	12	139	59	69	24	20	5	252	100	352	14
Sexual Behavior Problems	6	1	12	10	13	6	6	6	37	23	60	2½
Toilet Training	27	7	50	25	36	14	0	2	113	48	161	6½
Speech Defects	25	9	62	19	26	9	10	1	123	38	161	6½
Miscellaneous	14	17	90	38	71	51	34	29	209	135	344	14

* Reference: Gilbert, G. M. "A Survey of Referral Problems in Metropolitan Child Guidance Centers," *J. Clin. Psychol.*, 1957, 13, 37-42.

stamps or fragments of machinery or archeological and geological specimens, girls collect dolls or odd bits of cloth, and both collect pennants
and souvenirs from far places.

As soon as children become able to read on their own, the *reading
tastes* of the two sexes diverge. Boys like tales of heroism and high adventure, girls like stories about home and school, and, quite early,
romantic (but hardly erotic) love: here again we can see the continuity
of girlhood and womanhood contrasting with the discontinuity between
boyhood and manhood. Of course, it is possible that the very adults
who write the books and stories, and the editors, librarians, and book-
sellers who disseminate them, do a great deal to define which books
with what sorts of content will be directed to boys or to girls, and peer-
group pressures reinforce such definitions. In any case, boys quickly
develop a taste for factual, informational literature, while girls prefer
fiction. Boys become interested in world events, while girls remain interested primarily in home and community. Girls sometimes read books
addressed to boys, but boys almost never read those meant for girls.
Analogous differences are seen in comparisons of children's tastes in
radio, television, and motion pictures. It is notable that boys like hu-
morous movies, girls do not. Girls, on the other hand, enjoy "love"
movies, while boys do not. The comic book has succeeded somewhat
in breaching the barrier between the sexes, boys and girls both liking
many—but by no means all—of the same publications.

It is in overall emotional and personality differences that description
becomes most difficult. There do, however, seem to be decided sex differences in the nature of personality disturbances. Boys are consistently
more prone than girls to minor and major emotional, scholastic, and
behavior problems. (See Table 4.) Boys are more likely to stutter, to
have reading disabilities, to wet the bed, to develop tics, to be undis-
ciplined, and to get into trouble with the law. The most central male
difficulty seems to be control of aggression. It is in this area that cultural demands are most equivocal, with conflicting and subtle pressures
to act out one's feelings in some circumstances and to restrain them in
others. But the incidence of misbehavior is not simply a matter of what
children do; it is also a product of how adults judge what children do.
It has been shown that girls' behavior is judged more leniently than
boys', indicating that the greater frequency of misdeeds in boys is partly
a function of greater adult sensitivity to it. A similar tendency would
seem to be at work in the fact that although girls get better grades in
school, boys score higher on academic aptitude and achievement tests.

To some extent, boys' misbehavior is judged more stringently than girls' because boys make more noise in the course of misbehaving—boys have more available physical energy than girls. Another factor, mentioned earlier, in school problems may be the preponderance of women teachers, whose expectations and standards may be inappropriate for boys.

We must further consider that boys in our society are oriented toward active mastery and control of the environment, whereas girls take on a more passive, accepting orientation. This activity-passivity distinction may help us understand observed sex differences that might otherwise appear contradictory to those just set forth. Girls, for instance, score higher than boys on neuroticism scales and measures of fearfulness. It is not easy to assess such elusive qualities as neuroticism and emotionality, but the consensus of research is that at all ages females are more emotional (except in the matter of physical aggression) than boys. Prior to puberty, at least, girls are more subject than boys to "nervous habits": nail-biting, thumb-sucking, etc., with a large exception made for stuttering. Girls are considerably more social-minded than boys, showing greater sensitivity to social relationships, greater co-operativeness, and greater generosity. On the other hand, there is evidence that they are more likely, when they feel safe from detection, to cheat and lie than are boys. It is possible that the traditional passivity of girls—in our society—renders them immune to the stresses entailed in active mastery, but at the same time, by placing them at the mercy of the environment rather than of their own resources, breeds social conformity and timidity.

It appears from what we have said that even today, when women have been largely emancipated, have access to the same education as men and, increasingly, to careers at a high economic and prestige level, and when we are more aware than ever before of the social pressures working to produce sex typing, certain obvious differences persist between the outlook and functioning of males and females. Although we should like to be able to go even further toward understanding and explaining sex differences, it is not necessarily with the aim of reducing them: almost everyone will agree that such differences have decided virtues. An understanding of sex differences will contribute, however, to our more general knowledge of how people develop and of how we can further development. Meanwhile, it appears that the ancient jingle still has some truth:

> Snips and snails and puppy-dog tails,
> That's what little boys are made of.
> Sugar and spice and everything nice,
> That's what little girls are made of.

Latency

At the beginning of the chapter we defined Freud's concept of latency as a hiatus in sexual activity between the infantile (phallic) stage of the preschool years and the adult (genital) stage beginning at puberty.[16] Freud saw latency as the logical outcome of the Oedipus complex. In his view, the Oedipal situation ends with the complete *repression* (driving out of consciousness) of sexual strivings, which then lie latent until the physiological events of puberty bring them boiling once more to the surface. In these terms, the deliberate cleavage occurring between boys and girls in the middle portion of the middle years, accompanied by a lavish show of indifference and even animosity toward the other sex, would indicate a going to the opposite extreme—in psychoanalytic language, a *reaction formation*—in order to keep sexual impulses under control. The upsurge of intellectual curiosity we find in school-age children would represent, in this view, a redirection of the repressed sexual energies, a *sublimation*. Likewise, the school child's rituals, chants, and rigid adherence to strict rules and formulas can be seen as magical devices for controlling repressed strivings, including the anxieties and hostility that are presumably aroused by the resolution of the Oedipal drama. For instance, children's elaborate avoidance of sidewalk cracks, accompanied by the rhyme "Step on a crack, Break your mother's back," can be seen as a magical denial or warding off of hostility toward the mother.

In point of fact, the collective and individual rituals of school-age children that we described earlier do bear a marked resemblance to the behavior of adults afflicted with what psychiatrists call a *compulsion neurosis*. Adult compulsions take many forms: an insatiable need to wash one's hands; an incessant taking stock or tallying of everything countable, such as passing freight cars; arranging everything neatly and repeatedly before beginning work; apparently meaningless but obligatory rituals that precede every action and sometimes become so protracted that the action itself is never begun. There seem to be two major types of such compulsions, both relevant to the behavior of children in the middle years. The first reflects insecurity and uncertainty, a need to make sure that everything is in order so that one may safely act, or may even be a device for postponing a secretly undesired action indefinitely. Correspondingly, we can see how the child, at least partly adrift from the emotional moorings of home and dependent on the somewhat capricious support of his peers, might therefore find the reassurance of order in rituals and formulas. The second type is a disguised, symbolic representation of an impulse or past event that was too strong to be repressed but too threatening to be admitted to awareness or acted on. Thus, compulsive handwashing might be interpreted as a response to a feeling of uncleanliness generated by one's own unacknowledged "dirty" cravings. Analogously, the child's rituals may serve to keep his repressed Oedipal strivings under control.

The original Freudian notion of latency, however, has had to be modified in the light of current findings. Certainly sexual interest and play are not snuffed out during the latency period. It is worth noting that while Freud had to combat the popular conception that there was no infantile sexuality to become latent, the post-Freudians are obliged to combat Freud's idea that a gap exists in the chain of overt psychosexual development. A possible reconciliation, not inconsistent with psychoanalytic theory, is that it is only the Oedipal aspect of sexuality —that is, attraction to the parent of the opposite sex—that is repressed during latency, making possible attention to other sexual objects. Children, regardless of any theory, are eager to acquire forbidden information from friends and to pass it on to other friends. When the gang is not looking—or, more rarely, under its aegis—boys and girls do meet and compare anatomy and even make awkward, largely ineffectual sexual experiments. By the middle school years, there is a steady traffic among children in smutty stories, which may be poorly comprehended but which are sure to elicit giggles. Children likewise giggle together over the dictionary in which they look up words referring to sexual and excretory matters, or over the Bible in which they seek out references to fornication. The doctor's child is guaranteed a period of popularity by allowing his friends to consult the plates in medical texts. It should also be remembered that much of the teasing and tussling that goes on between boys and girls is a form of crude amorous play. Most sexual activity in this period, though, consists in the exploration of one's own body. Indeed, the curiosity that children show about the functioning of their bodies at this age, including the stunts and tricks to which they are addicted, probably has some sexual component. It is not always easy to tell, of course, the extent to which apparently sexual behavior is motivated by sexual cravings and to what extent by simple curiosity, particularly curiosity about the unknown and forbidden. But whatever the basis, children are aware that genital curiosity and masturbation, and inquiry into "dirty" things, bring them face to face with very explicit threats from adults, or, at the very least, with a strained reserve and vague but strong taboos. As a result, most children experience some anxiety and guilt in connection with their sexual investigations.

Adults, of course, are by no means consistent in their taboos. They themselves, as children are aware, violate the taboos. Also, parents in speaking of sex communicate directly to children our culture's ambivalent view of sex as a mixture of beauty, shame, and vulgarity. Boys especially may be allowed to listen while men—usually outside their families—talk of sexual matters and exchange dirty jokes. Then, too, certain adults may instruct children in direct sexual experience. This holds true for boys more than for girls, and most often takes the form of homosexual experience. A great many boys, and a lesser percentage of girls, have at least one actual homosexual experience during the school years. They are usually initiated by an adult or adolescent, or a child who has been so initiated may in turn initiate his gangmates. Although the exchange of sex information among peers may help prepare them for such behavior, the idea of homosexuality seems to occur spontaneously to very few children. Overt homosexuality in the gang usually takes the form of group masturbation or mutual masturbation, however, and seldom includes the practices engaged in by adult homosexuals. In spite of recent findings on heterosexual and homosexual activity during the school years, however, we still do not know a great deal about individual variations in this respect. It should be added, however, that homosexual explorations are usually outgrown, and often forgotten, during or after adolescence. It should further be stressed that the "crushes" which children late in latency often develop for adults of the same or opposite sex do not necessarily have an explicitly erotic meaning.

Sex Education

Parents, as we said in the last chapter, have a responsibility for providing their children with honest information about sexual matters. With all the excellent printed material available on this subject, such as the manual published by the Child Study Association of America, parents themselves need not lack for information and guidance. The authors' notions about the basic attitudes and approaches to this topic have already been suggested. Here we would like to mention only a few essential principles applicable to the school years.

First, there is timing. The school-age child, with his greater wariness about expressing his feelings, and sensing the taboos of adult society, is less likely than the preschool child to cue his parents with specific questions. All the same, the chances are that he is picking up information and misinformation—and attitudes as well—from his contemporaries, and if the parents wish to give their views priority, they would do well to impart information sooner rather than later. As with the preschool child, this is never done once and for all; it must be taught and retaught at increasingly complex and specific levels. Certainly in dealing with children in the latter middle years, there is no reason why a girl should be left to experience her first menstruation as a shocking surprise, as so many girls still do, or why boys, for that matter, should not have some factual knowledge of the menstrual cycle instead of deep ignorance or a dim awareness, whether drawn from Biblical or other sources, of some great female secret. The principle of timing applies not only to anticipating events or rival sources of information, but is important also in terms of giving information while it is still primarily of informational interest, and while the child is not yet swamped by current emotional problems.

Second, parents of school-age children, even those parents who are reasonably unembarrassed in discussing sex, will appreciate the sense of an observation by a ten-year-old to her teacher: "My parents are very understanding and all that, but there are some things it's easier to talk about with other people." Perhaps because of Oedipal repressions, or perhaps merely from a recognition of culturally imposed restraints, the school-age child may wish to avoid the implications of his own parents' sexuality and find it easier to assume the necessary distance and objectivity with someone else. The "someone else" may even be a book, designed for young readers, of which there are several admirable ones, or it may be an uncle or aunt, a physician, a clergyman, a recreation group leader, or a teacher, although none of these positions necessarily guarantees that an individual possesses the requisite skill and wisdom for the task. The teacher who sets out to impart sex information must feel secure herself, must have already won the confidence of her charges, must be free from the threat of parental indignation, and must deal with small enough groups of children so that she is not lecturing but discussing, maintaining a one-to-one relationship with each child. The tittering bystander changes the whole tone of the situation. Under such optimal conditions, the teacher can deal with mixed groups of boys and girls. However, if she makes tactful opportunities for it, she is more likely to be approached by individuals or by small same-sex groups in search of information.

Third, even the most sexually honest and informed adults, who would like to spare children some of the threats and falsehoods about masturbation that other generations have known, will hardly wish to advocate masturbation. They may, however, be able to let the child know that they are aware that such a thing exists, that they know that the genitalia yield pleasurable sensations, and perhaps even allude to the fact that "in the past" masturbation had erroneously been thought to carry with it the danger of disease, insanity, feeble-mindedness, debility, or extreme degradation. This may arm the child against some of his own almost inevitable anxieties and against the ominous tales he will surely hear from other children or from well-meaning but misinformed adults. If parents do this, they should do it briefly, indirectly, and unintrusively, without threatening the child's privacy and making him feel cross-examined or spied on. Again, this need not be done by word of mouth. The better sex literature designed for children usually includes a reasonable discussion of masturbation, which should help reduce the child's anxieties.

Finally, parents would do well to keep in mind that sex is not merely a matter of where babies come from. Nor, in talking to children, is it enough to say that sex is beautiful or that it occurs in a context of love. Parents will have done only part of the job of sex education if they have not incidentally conveyed, particularly before the upheavals of adolescence, some idea of the urgency of sex drives, of the pleasure of genital experience, and, more subtly, of the place of sex in superficial as well as in more profound and lasting relationships between men and women. The parent who has been frank in these respects will find it easier to convey the role of sex in mature love, and the desirability, in terms of such later relationships and of one's own feelings of integrity, of accepting restraints on and postponements of gratification. In the last analysis, it is not parental admonitions but the lessons of strong family ties, of solid affection, and of discrimination which the child unconsciously learns at home that will determine his own judgment and good taste in sexual as well as other areas of behavior.

Growth Latency

While the notion of a strict latency of sexual drives depends on an acceptance of the Freudian view of development and is partially contradicted by the facts, there is another sense in which the concept of "latency" is quite applicable to the middle years. This notion, which we have chosen to call *growth latency,* refers to a relative quiescence in physical development during this period. The middle-aged child is on a plateau of growth between the first growth spurt of infancy and the one that precedes puberty. Certainly, as we have said, physical growth and reorganization do go on during latency, but at a slower pace, without the abrupt emergences of earlier and later phases. In speaking of physical development, we have previously mentioned (Chapter 2) the principle of *asynchronous growth,* referring to the fact that not all parts and systems of the organism develop at the same rate. A number of workers, including Todd, Krogman, Olson, Flory, and Sontag, have developed the notion of "growth ages," providing separate measures for various aspects of growth.[17] Thus, in addition to a child's chronological age, we can speak of his Mental Age, Reading Age, Height Age, Weight Age, Dental Age, Grip Age (based on strength of grip, in kilograms), Carpal Age (bone ossification as determined by X-rays of the hand and wrist), plus whatever other variables we may want to trace through time. Each growth "age" represents the average of development in a given respect at a given age. Although all a child's growth ages are necessarily correlated with each other to some degree, since it is not usual for him to develop sideways or backwards in any area, he may stand at widely disparate points of maturity on different measures. During the middle years, as another aspect of growth latency, there seems to be less asynchrony in growth than at any other stage of childhood. At the same time, children in this period are following what Bayley has called definite "paths," which correspond to various rates and patterns of development and allow fairly accurate predictions to be made of eventual growth status.[18] Such predictions can be important, since social status during the school years is closely correlated, particularly for boys, with growth status, and the big, fast-growing boy may reach his ceiling early and be forced to considerable re-evaluation of his social standing as the erstwhile shrimps shoot past and overshadow him.

Latency in growth, a characteristic peculiar to human beings and certain of the great apes, may be the physiological counterpart of the psychological phenomenon of middle childhood as a period apart from all the rest. Both physically and psychologically, the school years are a relatively quiet interlude between two periods of turbulence. They are the "halcyon days of childhood," the era to which so many adults look back with a nostalgic, and perhaps misdirected, sense of longing.

NOTES   (Starred items are recommended as further readings.)

[1] Biber, Barbara, Personal communication.

[2] *Cf.* Asch, Solomon, "Studies in the principles of judgments and attitudes: II. Determination of judgments by group and ego standards," *Journal of Social Psychology,* 1940, 12, 433-465. Asch's classic experiments on the influence of group opinion on individual judgments have given rise to a spate of research, much of it on personality differences between those who can and those who cannot resist group pressures.

[3] Mills, Dorothy, and Bishop, M., "Onward and upward with the arts: Songs of innocence," *New Yorker,* November 13, 1937, pp. 32-42. Several sources not available to the authors are cited in Leopold, W. F., *Bibliography of Child Language,* Evanston: Northwestern University Press, Northwestern University Studies in the Humanities, 1952, 28. Among these are: Bolton, H. C., *The Counting-Out Rhymes of Children. Their Antiquity, Origin, and Wide Distribution,* New York-London, 1888; Böhme, F. M., *Deutsches Kinderlied und Kinderspiel,* 1897; Redlich, F. A., Kinderspiel und Schülersprache usw, *Auslandsdeutsche Volksforschung,* 1937, 305 ff.

[4] Mills and Bishop.

*[5] Piaget, J., *The Moral Judgment of the Child,* New York: Harcourt, Brace, 1932. (A section of this book, entitled "The rules of the game," appears in Hartley, E. L.,

Birch, H. G., and Hartley, R. E., *Outside Readings in Psychology,* New York: Crowell, 1950, pp. 648-653.)

[6] Mead, M., *And Keep Your Powder Dry,* New York: Morrow, 1942.

[7] See, for instance, Radke, Marian, Trager, H. G., and Davis, H., "Social perceptions and attitudes of children," *Genetic Psychology Monographs,* 1949, 40, 327-447. (A condensed version is included in Kuhlen and Thompson, *Psychological Studies of Human Development,* pp. 304-311); Trager, H. G., and Radke, M. Y., *They Learn What They Live,* New York: Harper, 1952.

[8] *Ibid.,* See also Lasker, Bruno, *Race Attitudes in Children,* New York: Holt, 1929.

[9] *Life,* June 17, 1946.

[10] *New Yorker,* September 18, 1954.

[11] Benedict, Ruth, "Continuities and discontinuities in cultural conditioning," *Psychiatry,* 1938, 1, 161-167.

[12] *Cf.* Mead, M., "When do Americans fight?" *Nation,* October 17, 1942, pp. 368-371.

*[13] Terman, L. M., and Tyler, L. E., "Psychological sex differences," in Carmichael, *Manual of Child Psychology,* pp. 1064-1114.

[14] Shevrin, Howard, Unpublished Ph.D. dissertation, Cornell University, 1954.

[15] Terman, L. M., et al., *Genetic Studies of Genius,* Stanford: Stanford University Press, 1925, Vol. I.

[16] Freud, *A General Introduction to Psychoanalysis,* pp. 286 and 289.

[17] Todd, T. W., "The roentgenographic appraisement of skeletal differentiation," *Child Development,* 1930, 1, 298-310; Krogman, W. M., "Trend in the study of physical growth in children," *Child Development,* 1940, 11, 279-284; Olson, W. C., and Hughes, B. O., "The concept of organismic age," *Journal of Educational Research,* 1942, 36, 525-527; Flory,

C. D., "Osseous development in the hand as an index of skeletal development," *Monographs of the Society for Research in Child Development,* 1936, 1; Sontag, L. W., and Reynolds, E. L., "The Fels composite sheet: I. A practical method for analyzing growth progress," *Journal of Pediatrics,* 1945, 26, 327-335.

[18] Bayley, Nancy, "Individual patterns of development," *Child Development,* 1956, 27, 45-74. See also Nicolson, A. B., and Hanley, Charles, "Indices of physiological maturity: derivation and interrelationships," *Child Development,* 1953, 24, 3-38.

FOR FURTHER READING

Withers, Carl, *A Rocket in My Pocket,* New York: Holt, 1948. A charming collection of rhymes and chants, including many variant renderings.

U. S. Children's Bureau, *Your Child from Six to Twelve,* Washington 25: U. S. Government Printing Office. Periodically revised.

Valentine, C. W., *The Normal Child: And Some of His Abnormalities,* Baltimore: Penguin, 1956. An English psychologist speaks his mind on the phenomena of childhood and the theories used to account for them.

MacCracken, H. N., *The Family on Gramercy Park,* New York: Scribner's, 1949. Fascinating and lively reminiscences of a New York boyhood.

Cary, Joyce, *A House of Children,* New York: Harper, 1956. Semi-autobiographical account of boyhood summers on the Irish coast; an excellent evocation of childhood experience.

Hughes, Richard, *A High Wind in Jamaica,* New York: The Modern Library, 1929. A wholly fictional, but psychologically penetrating, account of the world of children.

The changing face of childhood
(See pages 144 and 205.)

The gang

Boys take pride in
mechanical skills.

The school-age child seems to
turn his back on his parents.

(From *Meeting Emotional Needs in Childhood*)

The tricks and skills of childhood

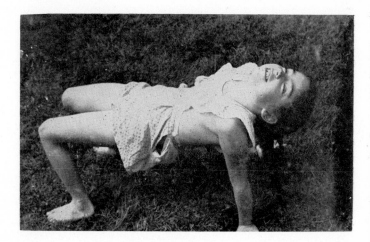

DISCOVERY
Discovery is something that exists already and you find it.
INVENTION
Invention is something that does not exist It is something that you make.
Jane K.

The "liberal" school

(From *Meeting Emotional Needs in Childhood* and *Learning Is Searching: A Third Grade Studies Man's Early Tools*) (See pages 255 ff.)

CHAPTER 9

The Middle Years of Childhood: 2

Cognitive Functioning in the School Child

In speaking of the school years, we have referred only incidentally to the fact that the school-age child goes to school. In developmental terms, going to school is a singularly appropriate thing for him to be doing—however much a small boy might feel called upon to deny it. Actually, the small boy's protests probably reflect adult misteaching or the peer-group mores rather than his own feelings about learning. When left to their own devices or placed in schools which encourage instead of deaden curiosity, children of this age are gluttonous learners. Somewhere around the beginning of the school years, a major shift in cognitive development seems to take place, eventuating in various general and specific learning readinesses—reading readiness, number readiness, and so forth. Over and above the maturational factors in readiness, discussed earlier, the basis for this seems to be that the child, having established a basic security in his family relationships (and, in Freudian terms, having turned away from emotional involvements with his family), now in the early school years characteristically turns his attention outwards, away from himself and toward the world at large. He concentrates now on objective outer reality, including not only what is immediately present and personally relevant, but, increasingly, notions of things distant in time and space. He wants to know what things are, how they work, what they are for, how they are made, and where they come from. Make-believe is no longer blended hit-or-miss with his reality. He has not dropped make-believe, but it is more private than before, and he uses it in a spirit of deliberate "pretend." From all of this it follows that he avidly wants to *know*.

But his desire for learning takes two forms. He wants not only knowledge but know-how: he wants to catch on to the skills and tricks and competences and procedures that are the mark of the initiate. Many kindergarteners seem to have a half-formulated belief that mere enrollment in school will somehow magically confer this. Even at a slightly higher level of sophistication, abilities like reading seem to the child to depend on knowing the "trick" of getting things out of books. Thus the same forces that make him embrace the rituals of the child culture partly govern his approach to more formal learning and give to this some of the other's ritual flavor.

Symbols

Although, as we shall see in a moment, the learning of the child in the early middle years continues to be largely concrete and action-oriented, one of the fundamental distinctions between his learning and that of the preschool child is in the use of symbols. For the preschool child, symbols have not yet been differentiated from the things they stand for, and exist on the same level of reality and magical potency as the physical world. The school-age child, by contrast, has begun to understand symbols as representations of reality, although they continue to have a reality of their own apart from the world of things. This differentiation of two layers of reality shows up in the delight that school children take in playing with symbols and meanings. They become fascinated by rhymes, anagrams, codes and ciphers, foreign words, onomatopoeia, and puns. They like to play with negatives, as in the poem about "The Little Man Who Wasn't There." That symbols have not, however, been completely differentiated from practical reality is shown in children's literalism: their unquestioning acceptance of the words of rituals without wondering what they refer to, and the fact that it is only in the middle or late school years that a child can grasp the notion of sarcasm or irony, where one often says the opposite of what one means. It is evident also in the way children use words even before they have literal meaning, in the way they pick up big and impressive words and use them indiscriminately. Indeed, for many young school children, language may not yet have become differentiated into single words, but is still understood and used globally;[1] this may be one factor in beginning reading difficulties. In general, however, children of this age are becoming very much aware of language as something to be dominated and exploited, and, as at any point of near-mastery, practice their skills indefatigably. Those schools which, in order to avoid a premature experience of failure, postpone reading instruction until the end of the first year or later often face the resentment of their pupils, who are clamoring for this particular skill in symbols both for its own sake and as a mark of achievement. For as Plant, among others, has pointed out, the school child is no longer primarily concerned with the security provided by his family, but wants to be recognized for his competence, for what he can do, and to this end wants to be able to do things.[2]

General Information

As the child develops an objective orientation, he begins to wonder both about himself as an object and about the cosmos in which he must locate himself. During this period, he becomes more interested in and able to absorb general principles, forerunners of possible future interests in philosophy, psychology, and the biological and physical sciences. He becomes aware of his own place in time and acknowledges, despite its unreality, that the world existed before he appeared on it. He speculates on what it means to be ten or twelve or twenty, about when he will be grown-up (perhaps at age twelve or fourteen), he understands birthdays as punctuation marks and not as turning points in growth, and he ponders the mysteries of life and death. He becomes aware of the processes of his own body, of his senses, of the hiatus of sleep. He learns about germs and disease, and may have fits of hypochondria. In the same way, if he is a city child, when he first learns where meat comes from, this may be quite disturbing, producing a phase of righteous vegetarianism. He thinks about cause and effect and is likely, because of his tendency to accept what is given, to be quite fatalistic in his outlook. He not only observes but sometimes pauses to note what he is observing: he sees the flash of a distant axe and realizes that the sound arrives after the vision. The concept of gravity comes to him with the force of revelation. He becomes interested in how the family car operates, and, as most breakfast food advertisers have discovered, he is a pushover for realistic fantasies about space travel, speaking with great authority about rocket propulsion and the structure of the solar system. He is fascinated to hear about distant peoples, especially those who, like the American Indian, have been highly romanticized and who are of personal concern to him. Not only do they appear to him to limit their activities to such sensible pursuits as hunting, fishing, sitting around campfires, and waging war, but their seeming disdain for such civilized trappings as clothes, baths, and bedtimes is likewise intriguing.

As the child grows older, he becomes less concerned with separate nuggets of information and increasingly with abstractions and generalizations. He wants to learn about attitudes, opinions, and points of view. This does not mean that he is learning to be impartial: as we have seen, each new thing involves him totally and passionately, and his early formulations on democracy, justice (more often, injustice), nationalism, slavery, or the propriety of war are likely to be pure and intense and absolutistic. Even the older middle-years child has little patience with political compromise or with the idea of hewing to the middle of the road. Nevertheless, he has moved a long way from the egocentricity of babyhood and the preschool years.

Needless to say, this shift in orientation does not come about all at once. The child's concerns in the early middle years with the objective world are still on a concrete, action-process level. He still needs to experience things first-hand. From direct experience, he goes on, toward the middle of this period, to a delight in vicarious experience, using the ability to share other people's feelings about things which are not present. From this he moves on, in the later school years, to true abstraction, where he can consciously contemplate the world in its objective timelessness. But in order for his knowledge and thinking to become conscious, he first has to be able to question reality, he has to become skeptical. This means that he has to break away from his early acceptance of everything as real and everything as possible, he has to question his own perceptions and ideas, he has to interpose a certain distance between himself and the environment, between, as it were, himself and himself. A by-product of this new detachment is that, compared with preschool days, the tables are turned: previously he was a transparent object of appraisal for adults; now at the same time that the young school-age child becomes aware of himself as an object and keeps more of himself to himself, he can return the gaze of adults and do his own appraising, a gift that they may find somewhat unsettling. His detachment also means that he sets standards for himself, that he can be critical of his own performance ("Isn't this a stinky drawing?"). His new awareness of the objectivity of the world means that he uses language socially; as Biber has put it, he no longer merely radiates his feelings, he tries to communicate them.[3]

Concept Formation

In the next section, we shall discuss how schools may use—or misuse and destroy—the child's eagerness to learn. Here we shall try to describe how, under favorable conditions, the child understands, organizes, and thinks with the things he learns. As usual, we shall emphasize the contrasts rather than the similarities between the child's thinking and the adult's, adding the customary caution that everybody at every age operates on a mixture of levels of maturity, and seldom on one level at a time.

In speaking of the preschool child, we described how his concepts develop from a glob-like stage into true concepts, but are not likely to attain the status of categories: grouping together classes of objects and taking account of both similarities and differences (a dog and a cat are both *animals*). Beginning early in the school years, however, the child is able, subject to certain limitations, to deal with true categories. Both his abilities and his limitations in this respect perhaps show up most clearly in his response to the concept-formation items that are a part of standard intelligence tests, of the type "How are a cat and a dog alike?" Abstract similarities may still be obscured by patterns of concrete action for the school child, as when he says that a cat and a dog are alike "because they fight together." Comparisons may be made in terms of concrete, ego-related attributes instead of abstract ones: a plum and a peach "are both juicy," or "you eat them both," rather than *fruit*. A child may focus on specific details rather than more general points of similarity: a cat and a dog both "have eyes, and ears, and fur, and legs, and a tail. . . ." His comparisons may be somewhat vague: a pair of scissors and a copper pan are "both made out of the same thing," rather than of *metal*. The child may have special difficulty dealing with the similarity between opposites, such as *first* and *last;* it requires a fairly advanced stage of conceptual development to realize that in order to be opposite, things must belong to a common domain. By the end of latency, children's "mental structures" are essentially the same as those of adults. A child's concepts may still differ from the adult's, however, in terms of the amount of knowledge he has at his disposal, in the extent to which his concepts have been worked into a uniform, integrated system, in the depth of his self-knowledge, and in the emotional valuations he places on various facets of experience.

Magical Thinking

An important component of the preschool child's cognition was the liberal strain of magic that permeated his reality and appeared most clearly in his animistic thinking. As we have already seen in this chapter, the school-age child has his share of magic, too. Now, however, the child's magic is more separated and formalized, as in superstitions and rituals; objectified, as in ghosts, witches, and so forth; and internalized in his own wishes, aspirations, and fears. The supernatural is a separate realm for the school-age child, and on that very account more credible. The central process in the child's magical thinking seems to be a growing self-awareness, particularly awareness of his feelings as his own. But at the same time that he internalizes his feelings, he objectifies them. When he becomes aware that he is frightened, for instance, he has to find something to be frightened of; just as he seeks a scapegoat for his animosities, he seeks a feargoat, so to speak, for his fears. In general, children of this age come to attach their fears to real objects—animals, kidnapers, etc.—but fears of imaginary agencies persist throughout the school years.[4] The feargoating (and lovegoating—as in "crushes"—etc.) nature of the child's feelings is revealed not only in the fact that he may fear nonexistent things, but also that he fears real things out of all proportion to their actual menace. In short, he finds or invents objects around which to crystallize his diffuse and nonspecific feelings, as we saw earlier in the case of private, compulsive rituals.

Moralism

In addition to the factual and emotional dimensions of the child's thinking, we must now take account of the extra dimension of morality. Preschool children, as theologians are inclined to agree, are (once the stigma of original sin has been removed) amoral. The school-age child, by contrast, is moralistic. Even though the child may be oblivious to factual inconsistencies, he is acutely sensitive to moral inconsistencies, particularly those that affect him. Having been told that he lives in a free country, he cannot reconcile this with his not being allowed always to do as he wishes. One of the battle cries of this age is, "It's not fair!" —indicating that the child has detected an inconsistency. Even accidental misfortunes are often judged as unfair, as when it rains on the day of an outing, and someone, even if it be the Almighty, must be brought to book. Perhaps in keeping with his superego development and his need to control his own impulses and to direct his own achievements, the school-age child is inclined to pass excessively rigorous judgments. Children judge each other much more harshly than would adults. The child, for instance, with his still limited notion of the internal mainsprings of behavior, judges by the externals of an act, with little regard for motives and extenuating circumstances (which indeed are comparatively recent additions to our civilization's concepts of legal justice). Thus he will see as more reprehensible a child who, in trying to help his mother, accidentally breaks several plates than one who, in a fit of spite, deliberately breaks a single one.[5] Again, perhaps because he himself has grown capable of dissimulating and telling lies, the child now views lying as a major crime. In general, it would seem that the child's new independence obliges him to put the world into rigid compartments—as usual, he overdoes things—and the inconsistency of either injustice or untruth is a threat to reality itself. It may appear to adults that school-age children are willing to flout every established moral tenet; but when we examine children's value systems, we find that they are bound by codes (especially those they impose on each other in the gang) far more stringent than most adults could tolerate. On the other hand, along with a sense of morality, children also develop devices for avoiding guilt when they do violate their codes. Like adults, school-age children become masters of rationalization, denial, and self-justification. When the preschool child wants to undo a misdeed, he simply abolishes it from existence. The school-age child, for whom facts are far more stubborn, must somehow utilize the magic of words to transform his deeds or to make them fit in with his general concepts of what is right and wrong. This process is facilitated, of course, by the child's literal-mindedness: he is often more concerned with the letter than with the spirit of a rule. He will argue legalistically and litigiously for the narrowest possible interpretation, so that what he has done falls outside the letter of the law: "You said not to run. I was galloping." Later in the school years, of course, children relinquish much of their moral absolutism in favor of tolerance, relativity, and flexibility, just as they learn to be more dispassionate about the standards of the gang and the eternal fixity of rules for playing games. Adults, too, find themselves coming in for censure: a casual expletive, such as the child himself would delight in using in the gang, on the lips of an adult may provoke real moral indignation.

In normal learning situations, the child's thinking proceeds in a fairly orderly fashion. However, because his ideas are still somewhat diffuse and not too well-organized, he may find it hard to follow through on a discussion of a single topic. One thing reminds him of another, and a class discussion in the early grades may range in a matter of minutes from nutrition to spacemen to politics to playthings and back again. This is not without its value. Such rambling, tangential interchanges enable a teacher to lead his group over the whole field of human learning and to place particular problems in their living contexts. When discussion leads to debate, however, young children become unduly aroused and egocentric, hurling assertions back and forth with no notion of either persuading or being persuaded, and often backing these assertions by references to authority: "My mommy said . . ." A good teacher can sometimes capitalize on such arguments to introduce the notion of "let's find out." Children's reasoning may likewise be impeded by moral considerations: what is bad is also untrue and therefore beyond discussion. Jersild reports how even a fifth grade refused to debate the question of whether war could be avoided by ceding territory to Hitler; the practical issue was completely submerged in its moral implications.[6]

Eidetic Imagery

One aspect of cognitive behavior in the early school years deserving mention is the phenomenon of *eidetic imagery,* which, although it is rather common in school-age children, has not been extensively studied. Eidetic imagery is something like what is popularly referred to as a "photographic memory"; children so endowed can examine a picture briefly and then reproduce it in great detail from a mental image. Eidetic imagery is not mere memorization: the eidetic child can spell out from a street sign pictured in his head long foreign words which he cannot even pronounce; given a table of numbers of, say, five columns by five rows to look at for a minute or so, he can turn his back and "read off" the numbers in any direction from his image, and not simply in the usual left-to-right, top-to-bottom order; furthermore, such images are visualized concretely in space—so concretely, indeed, that they may block out real objects in the room. Eidetic imagery seems to be independent of intelligence: it occurs in mental defectives and geniuses alike. There are wide individual differences in eidetic capacity, although, as we have said, we do not really know how extensive it is. Since it becomes less frequent with increasing age, we might, by reasoning backwards, assume that it is almost universal in preschool children, but the difficulties in studying it at this age are formidable. In spite of this decline with age, some adults still retain their eidetic skill. Although eidetic memories are more vivid and detailed than highly abstract ones, they are a somewhat cumbersome form of knowledge: with increasing maturity, there is a greater tendency to remember the abstract gist, the verbal and symbolic essentials of experience rather than the concrete totality. In general, the decline in eidetic imagery corresponds with the child's shift from a concrete to an abstract orientation.

Word Meanings

The preschool child, learning words, apprehends and uses them in ways peculiar to his maturity level and his own personal feelings, without any notion that words have established dictionary meanings which he is supposed to observe. Indeed, for the preschool child a word is not a symbol of some reality, it is itself a living reality. The school-age child, by contrast, has some notion of words as symbols with relatively fixed meanings. He is very much concerned with processes of communication and the public meanings of words. Nevertheless, the school child does not learn word meanings from a dictionary, but from the way they are used in day-to-day situations. For this reason they tend to be assimilated to the structure of his own experience (at the same time that they are reshaping his experience according to the adult culture), and the way the child understands language gives us further insight into the nature of his thinking. One effective device for studying children's understanding of language is to ask them to define common proverbs. A nine-year-old, for instance, defines *Absence makes the heart grow fonder* as "It makes your heart grow weaker, I guess." On further examination, it develops that the primary misunderstanding is not of the word "fonder," but of "absence": "absence," to this child, as to many others, meant "sick," by a process of you're-absent-from-school-because-you're-sick. But it is not only the meaning of single words which the child interprets in his own way. A proverb may be taken less as a general statement than as a description of a particular event or person; a ten-year-old, for instance, defines *Out of sight, out of mind* as "Well, maybe it means someone that is sort of dumb." The general meaning of proverbs is sometimes subordinated to a personal reference to the child himself, as in this nine-year-old's interpretation of *A stitch in time saves nine:* "Like if you had a broken hand, you stitch it, like if someone got hurt, say, like a nine-year-old, he needed stitches. . . ." The metaphorical phrasing of some proverbs may throw children off: *The wheel that squeaks gets the grease* is usually taken quite literally by nine-year-olds; children ten and older may see that the words are used metaphorically, but have difficulty taking "grease" as something desirable and so are likely to render the proverb, "People that get out of line [or *squeal*] get in trouble." Here as elsewhere, morality may play a part: in defining *Revenge is sweet,* many children are frankly baffled, some deny the truth of the statement without attempting to define it, and some are obliged to change the meaning of the proverb, even to the extent of forcing the words out of shape, so that it becomes, "You don't revenge too hard," or even, "It means the same thing as forgive."

The school child's increasing familiarity with language processes enables him to attempt new forms of humor. The preschool child plays with word sounds—pooh-pooh, etc.—the school child with word meanings. Puns, where the same word is used simultaneously in two different senses, are a particular favorite at this age, but particularly in the later middle years. Indeed, punning lies at the base of many childhood riddles, such as, "What has four legs and flies?" Children also learn to use humor to control their feelings, by making jokes about sensitive topics, and as a weapon, by making wisecracks. The school child may learn to act "the good sport" about jokes of which he is the butt, but throughout this age he takes himself much too seriously to want to make jokes about himself.

Perhaps we should stress again that our description of thinking processes applies for the most part to younger school-age children. By eleven or twelve, when the child has collected a sizable body of facts and skills, when he has been taken in and humiliated by the hoaxes of older children and adults, when he has had time to think through a number of problems and to discard some of his earlier illusions, most of these childish tendencies will have disappeared. As we said earlier, many of the dimensions of adult experience may still not have become meaningful to him, but his basic conceptual processes are already in good working order.

A School for the School Child

In this section, we want to discuss those formal institutions, other than the family, that our society provides for the indoctrination of its school-age young. Foremost among these, of course, is school, but the child is likewise subject to adult supervision in the scout troop, the recreation center, and similar agencies which perform school-like functions, and most of what we have to say applies to these as well. In our discussion, we want to take account of what these institutions are, what they do, the problems they face, and how they can best supply what we consider to be the conditions for optimal development in terms both of satisfying the child's needs and of shaping him to the adult culture.

While the school child's spirit may be in the gang, his body is in school. Indeed, from the ages of five or six, the child for years spends a half to two-thirds of his waking hours, on any school day, involved in school work; no other single activity, except sleeping, consumes so much of his time. It is in school that the child is confronted most directly with the adult culture he is to assimilate, that he resists it, struggles to master it, sidesteps it, and drinks it in. The child entering school may feel some trepidation about his ability to cope with this new and somewhat formidable challenge, but this trepidation is usually outweighed by the fact that going to school—or, if he has already been to preschool, going to a "real" school—is a mark of maturity and a source of pride. In addition, it offers him a chance to find out all the marvelous things known to older children and adults. Yet, all too often, the child who enters first, or even second, grade bursting with curiosity and enthusiasm leaves it much dampened by what he has encountered there. He may have found that the teacher, sharing the traditional belief that children hate school, treats the work as though she expected it to be resisted. He may have found that the topics proposed for his edification bear little relationship to the immediate curiosities he arrived with. He may have faced rather empty and bewildering drills whose relevance to his present or future needs is clear to the authorities but invisible to him. He may have been confronted with inadequately prepared teachers who cannot answer his far-ranging questions or who suppress all question-asking as a digression or as sheer impertinence. Some children undoubtedly keep their own direction and their interest in knowledge despite such reverses, but for too many the first year or two of school effectively if wantonly demolishes their intellectual curiosity. This is a decidedly paradoxical state of affairs. All the necessary ingredients of intellectual growth are present: supply, in the form of accumulated knowledge and wisdom, and of teachers to dispense it; demand, in the form of the child's curiosity and his ability to assimilate learning; and timing, in the sense that supply and demand meet head on. And yet, with frightening frequency, the process falls flat on its face. Since schools are one of the most important institutions we have and one intimately involved in child development—which is, after all, the concern of this book—we need to examine this paradoxical failure in more detail. If we look in turn at the place of education in our culture, at the history of schools and teaching in the United States, and at educational philosophies, it may be possible to cast some light on the murky atmosphere of mingled hopes and disappointments that surrounds our schools.

To begin with, then, we must make clear some of the attitudes, including contradictory ones, toward education that exist in our society. We Americans, it seems, have never been able to make up our minds whether we like education or not. On the one hand, our massive public school system stands as a monument to our devotion to learning, and every commencement exercise resounds with tributes to the schools as the training ground of democracy. At tax hearings, however, when the subject of overcrowded buildings and underpaid teachers comes up, the school is stripped of its rhetorical glamor and is painted as a collection of needless frills. Again, the same teacher who on commencement day is extolled as the guardian angel of our young is portrayed in our folk humor and cartoons as an embittered and iron-handed spinster who takes out her frustrations on the hapless children given into her custody. At best, she is regarded as a relatively ineffective participant (or non-participant) in the world of practical affairs, and receives none of the respect granted the learned in most European and Asiatic societies. Our ambivalence extends to learning itself. On the one hand, we see universal education as a great blessing; we need educated people to man our technological civilization; it is learning that sets us apart from the beasts in the field. On the other hand, we cast opprobrium upon the "egg-head"; we scoff at "book learning"; we often express the feeling that the schools teach dangerous nonsense that threatens the settled order of things. In spite of our ambivalences, we still feel, apparently, that the education of our young is one of the central concerns of our society. Curiously, as individuals, each citizen is convinced that education is a subject that he knows well, and that, given a free hand, he could straighten out the mess in Academe in no time at all. Some of our negative feelings about education are early communicated to our children, making it difficult for them to approach school with the enthusiasm that is developmentally so timely. Quite early, adults (especially men) convey to children (especially boys) that school is to be spoken of disparagingly, that it is something of a penal institution, that it is less an opportunity than a forced drudgery, and that real life ends at the schoolhouse door.

Growth and Change in the Schools

Historically, universal free schooling in this country is still fairly new. Its origin is usually placed in 1836, when the Massachusetts State Board of Education was established, or at about 1850, by which time the principle of free public schools had gained a firm foothold in the northern states.[7] In recent decades, the principle has been applied to increasingly higher levels of education, until now, in many places, it is thought appropriate to provide free education straight through the university graduate school. Despite the apparent triumph of this principle, there remain many unresolved educational issues and problems. Still inherent in many of the conflicts we see today is the issue of education for everybody versus education for an elite, and many comparisons of the functioning of our schools with those in other places and at other times fail to take account of our broadened base of education. By and large, American schools and American society have made their decision to broaden the base of education. This by itself leads to the problem of keeping more children in school for longer periods until they have acquired the basic education deemed necessary to life in our society. The expansion of education in the last half-century can readily be seen in the average educational level attained by different age groups in our population. As of 1950, only 56 percent of people in the sixty-five to sixty-nine age range had an eighth-grade education, as compared to 86 percent in the twenty-five to twenty-nine range. For high school education, the proportions in the same categories are 18 percent and 53 percent; college, 4 percent and 8 percent.[8] Broadening the base of education has further meant adding on new kinds of education, particularly in the late elementary and the secondary years, to provide vocational training and training in the practicalities of life for those to whom the older academic subjects seemed unsuited. Many of the current problems in our schools come down to the one problem of sheer quantity: too many children per room, too few buildings, too few teachers, too little money. This problem has been made well-nigh desperate by the advancing wave of children that has already inundated the grade schools and is threatening to engulf the high schools and colleges. The rising tide of children reflects the tremendous rise in birth rate which began during World War II and, to the confusion of the population experts, has continued ever since. To cope with the quantities of children, schools have been forced to a number of expedients such as double shifts and emergency certification of partly trained teachers, while harried school boards try to keep costs near the levels the traffic used to bear. Under these circumstances, it may seem fantastic to talk about ideals for education, but this the authors, with their heads firmly in the clouds, intend to do.

Most American education takes place in the public schools. In addition to these, we have parochial schools, which are essentially like public schools with religious education added; we have private, independent schools ranging from those modeled on the English "public" schools, citadels of traditional, academically-oriented college preparation, to private, experimental, "progressive" schools with an influence on educational theory and controversy far out of proportion to the number of children they deal with. These several types of school do not correspond precisely with types of educational philosophy, but their diversity suggests the variety of approaches and aims that exists today.

The spread of universal free education is only one of the changes that have taken place in the past century. Another important trend has been the feminization of teaching. Most teachers used to be men. But since teaching was one of the first respectable occupations opened to women, they have entered it in large numbers, and, at least at the preschool and early elementary level, teaching has come to be thought of largely as women's work. We have already mentioned that we see some disadvantages, particularly for boys but also for girls, in the predominance of women teachers. We might also remind the reader of what we said earlier about the augmented role of women in American life generally, with father being pushed into a secondary position, and the drawbacks this may have.

Still other changes in our educational system reflect our changing social structure. As a people, we have a unique degree of social and geographical mobility, so that the child who begins school in California as the son or daughter of a factory worker may finish school in Connecticut as the child of an account executive, or in Georgia as the child of a sharecropper. In one respect, at least, American mobility is in one direction: we are becoming an increasingly urban nation, a trend slightly complicated in recent years by drainage to the dormitory suburbs. In 1836 some 10 percent of our people lived in cities; today, the figure is roughly two-thirds.[9] This has had marked effects on the pattern of education. It has meant a change from the one-room little red schoolhouse to the factory-type school of the city. Even in rural areas there has been a shift to consolidated school districts, with factory-schools rising in half-empty stretches of countryside. (A by-product of such centralization may be that children spend from one to three hours daily commuting on the school bus.) The one-room schoolhouse was, by all accounts, a fairly wretched affair, especially prior to the reforms between 1836 and 1865. It was uncomfortable, ill-equipped, and often presided over by a poorly educated and perhaps tyrannical teacher. (Although even in 1954-55, 38 percent of public elementary school teachers were not college graduates.[10]) Nevertheless, it had certain virtues which may have been lost as it yielded to the modern, well-equipped, professionally-staffed, centralized school. First and foremost, it was small. This meant that the teacher knew all his children personally, and that the children knew each other. In class, the children were grouped according to ability levels, while on the playground they were free to mingle and separate on the basis of age and interests. Because the children were all in one room, there was a leakage of the varied subject matter across grade boundaries, if only because the children could not help overhearing. This meant, in part, that the younger children could be alerted to what was coming, that they could be stimulated, intrigued, and sparked. Our large present-day schools, while housed in a far better physical plant, with bigger libraries, gymnasiums, and other special facilities, and perhaps with better salaries for teachers, have at the same time become administratively unwieldy and may be plagued by bureaucracy. In some cases the chief purposes of school have become lost in administrative red tape: the many levels of supervision over the teacher, the elaborate forms for report-making and bookkeeping, the fixed curriculum handed down from above. It has been found that elementary school teachers spend between 21 percent and 69 percent of the school day on "housekeeping, clerical, and other activities requiring little or no professional competence." [11]

As we can see, something has happened to the teacher as well as to the school. It should not be necessary to point out that teaching carries with it less prestige than other professions in American society, even though teachers are required to meet ever more rigorous formal standards of preparation. We have already mentioned the folklore, often expressed in sardonic cartoons and jokes; we might also point to the very concrete expression of our feelings about teachers in the salaries we give them, which, except in a few localities, often look like the leavings on the community plate. Equally serious, however, is the decline of the teacher's status within the school itself. Her classroom conduct is regulated and supervised down to the minutest detail, her initiative has been restricted, she is judged as much by the quality of her book-keeping as by the quality of her relations with her pupils; in short, she has all too frequently been made into a clerk who follows the procedures laid down for her, rather than a professional charged with the intelligent, sensitive, and imaginative performance of one of society's most vital responsibilities. The school, of course, does not exist for the teachers, but for the pupils. But the de-professionalization of the teacher has immediate consequences for the kind of education pupils receive. Possibly the greatest consequence, and certainly the most dismal one, is the dullness that pervades our educational system. It is hardly surprising that our children have little enthusiasm for books and learning, that they arrive at college only half prepared; or that so many children, even well-endowed ones, leave school in discouragement long before their time, seeking a breath of the fresh air of meaningful activity outside the musty confines of the centralized syllabus.

It is the usual practice of observers of the difficulties and shortcomings of our educational system to look for devils. We have implied that the devils are neither the teachers nor the children. We may have implied that they are the local or central educational authorities: superintendents, school boards, state departments of education. Actually, it should be obvious that our educational system is an immense, widely ramified institution whose policies are less the result of specific planning from logical premises than of social forces and climates. For all their standardization and uniformity, our schools are not part of a centralized "system." In fact, this is one of the fundamental ways in which our country differs from most European ones, where, typically, a national ministry defines the policies and directs the operation of the country's schools. Nor are American schools governed by forty-eight sovereignties, for the state education departments, while going far to set the framework of education in their own states, do not really control the scores of thousands of relatively autonomous school districts, each of which usually has its own elected school board, its own budget to raise, and its own policies to devise. The nation-wide uniformities come about by virtue of the similar training received by school superintendents and other professional administrators, from the standards set for eligibility for state financial aid, and from the mass production of textbooks, teaching aids, and other school materials. The actual policies are determined by professional and elected officials in response to the pressures constantly and vociferously operating on them, plus such attention to the voice of professional conscience as they can manage. By the very nature of these pressures, however, the policy makers are likely to be least aware of the children in the classroom and most cognizant of demands for new schools, echoed by the anguished cry of the taxpayer. Parents' and citizens' groups frequently arise, claiming to speak with the voice of the people, and the administrator moves warily between demands that he cut down on frills and that he add some new service espoused by a band of embattled crusaders. In the face of conflicting pressures, the administrator may choose to remain paralyzed at the point where the pressures cancel out, in preference to being buffeted about like a soccer ball. We should also note, however, that not all citizens' groups are concerned with this or that specific pet project. Certain more enlightened groups, well-exemplified by the Connecticut Fact-Finding Commission on Education, are more concerned with assessing the total picture than with proposing panaceas.[12]

The administrator is caught primarily among the practical demands of pupil surplus, teacher shortage and dissatisfaction, the performance of specific educational functions, and the necessity of balancing his budget, so that problems of educational philosophy and teaching methods may receive summary treatment. Nevertheless, there is considerable pressure on policy makers at all levels from the protagonists of what appear to be diametrically opposed views of educational philosophy and methods. For the sake of simplicity, let us refer to these two camps as the "traditional" and the "progressive." Here, too, the pressures seem to have averaged out, resulting in what the authors choose to call a "compromise" education, a pallid, washed-out, uninspired, and uninspiring program that offers a little something for everybody and not much for anybody. Most of our discussion of educational philosophy will start with the traditional-progressive polarity and the compromise between them, but only with a view to suggesting that there may be a fresh and useful approach, lying along a quite different dimension, on which people of good will can agree.

The Liberal School

Critics of education are far more likely to say what they are against than what they are for, and find it easier to find fault than to advocate. The exchanges between traditionalists and progressivists are usually couched in vituperative negatives, and every flaw in our society is willingly laid at the door of the opposite persuasion. As a matter of fact, both sides seem to be beating horses that have been dead—or at least half-dead—for some years past. Perhaps in the era from 1910 to 1920, when the progressive movement began, it practiced doctrines as extreme as its critics say, while the traditions against which it was protesting may well have been as hidebound and obsolete as it claimed. Nowadays, compromise in various shades rules the roost, but by a process of selective perception and description it can still be made to appear as rigidly traditional or as arrantly progressive as one wishes. During World War II, for instance, the then Army Surgeon-General, shocked by the high rate of rejection of potential draftees on neuropsychiatric grounds, "explained," with all the weight of his high position, that this was the result of coddling by progressive educators. He apparently was unaware that progressive education in anything like pure form had never existed in more than a tiny percentage of our schools, and in even fewer at the time when the potential soldiers he was concerned about were children. It thus appears that although traditionalism and progressivism have largely disappeared from the scene, they still are scare words capable of arousing fierce loyalties and antagonisms. And apart from their importance as rallying points, they continue to define the dimension in which much American education, and thinking about American education, takes place. We prefer to start afresh, defining as we go our concept of the "liberal school"—a name we have chosen to set it apart from the traditional-compromise-progressive groove and also to suggest a downward extension of the liberal arts that are the nucleus of the college curriculum. And if some of our premises sound as though they have been taken from the traditionalist or progressivist book, we hope that this will not bias our case. As far as we know, the term "liberal school" has not been used before, but enough schools have already realized or closely approached such an educational pattern to demonstrate that this is not merely an idealistic goal. Much of what follows, although it may sound like theorizing, is actually a description of what takes place in some schools we know well.

In stating as we have that children in the middle years are alive with curiosity about every conceivable subject (unless, in the case of boys, it be romantic love), we are ranging ourselves with those who feel that education can be meaningful and interesting and need not, in general, be forced. By the same token, we are not substituting carrots for sticks, singing piously of praise versus reproof, advocating gold stars, irrelevant rewards, or sugar-coating. We favor, rather, keeping the acquisition of skills and knowledge intrinsically rewarding, sometimes on an immediate and sometimes on a long-range basis. In short, we believe that the child himself should be enlisted as much as possible in the learning process; that he should not be seen as a receptacle at the far end of a pipeline through which the teacher pours her accumulated wisdom; that the teacher should stand beside or behind the child, guiding him toward a knowledge that exists independent of them both; and that the emphasis should be on learning and acquiring skills for finding knowledge as well as on teaching. As we have said, the child learns in different ways as he grows older. The young child learns concretely: he counts on his fingers, he wants pictures of what he is learning about, he thrives on trips to dairies and fire stations—things without a personal reference tend to elude him. But the concrete props that are necessary for a child in the primary grades are superfluous for older children, who indeed become impatient with and even scornful of them when a teacher fails to recognize the intellectual growth that comes in the middle and upper grades. Good teaching does not depend on the use of particular approaches, but on those that are relevant. Older children can and want to learn abstractly.

A teacher who operates within this sort of framework must be given plenty of scope for imagination and ingenuity, so that she can fit her teaching to the particular children she is working with. This means that she must have reasonably small groups to work with so that she can know her children individually and take time to help each one over his rough spots. Even more, it means on a social level that we have to recruit, select, prepare, pay, and keep first-rate teachers: teachers with a thorough education themselves; teachers who understand child development and like children; and teachers who are equipped with a repertory of techniques which they can draw on as they see fit according to the circumstances, who have a basic commitment to teaching as a rewarding humanitarian profession, and who have the gifts of personal maturity, stability, and flexibility.

There have developed two quite distinct approaches to the education of teachers. On the one hand, there is special professional education for teachers—teacher-*training*—in which major stress has been placed on techniques of teaching. This approach has received (and has recently been trying to act on) some well-deserved criticism to the effect that teachers with such preparation often do not know enough to provide stimulation or adequate intellectual nourishment for children, and that such training may be technical rather than truly professional. On the other hand, some colleges and universities, in their impatience with this trend, have held in effect that any well-educated person who chooses to do so can teach. Here again the authors do not accept either extreme, nor are they content with a compromise which merely adds together training and "content" courses. Instead, they favor a first-rate liberal education, in which is embedded a thorough study of child development, as already in effect in a few colleges. In this view, a well-educated person who chooses to teach can do so provided she thoroughly understands the person who is being taught, and is in basic sympathy with him. Within this framework the necessary methodology and technology of teaching can find their place without overshadowing these fundamentals. Techniques of teaching which grow out of real understanding of who and what are to be taught will not be static prescriptions but will vary from class to class and from teacher to teacher.

But just as a good teacher cannot be the slave of her techniques, so she cannot be the slave of her teaching materials. A good teacher cannot be expected to confine herself to standardized, glossy textbooks pitched to a scientifically calculated average; the more a textbook is made to fit experimentally predetermined criteria of readability, interest, and so forth, the less genuinely interesting, it seems, it becomes. (The same holds true for teachers themselves, of course.) A good teacher cannot be bound by a prefabricated syllabus designed to cover a specified number of well-specified learning units in a specific time—which has been known to leave a teacher of a fast class with several weeks at the end of the semester "with nothing to do"—or aimed at passing mass-produced, machine-graded achievement tests, valuable as these may be when used as reference points rather than goals. The teacher, to teach effectively, must be able to modify her program to meet the individual capacities and needs of her pupils, to relate it to current issues and community problems, and to take advantage of special learning opportunities, permanent or transient, in the community.

Very often, we find that published curricula or publicly espoused teaching programs are couched in terms of the so-called "child-centered" school, and yet, although teachers and administrators may honestly subscribe to such a view, these programs—perhaps because their users have never seen the real thing in operation—often are reduced to pseudo-progressive verbalisms. For instance, the teacher of a course in methods for use with school-age children informed his audience that there was a trend toward classroom participation by the children: "For example, you might say to your class, 'All work and no play makes Jack a dull—' " and dramatically cupped his hand to his ear, waiting for the indicated participation.[13] Other earnest if literal-minded seekers after advanced techniques hear that it is a good idea not to restrict a class to a single textbook; but instead of providing a variety of interesting literature, they add one or two or even three more readers of the same kind, diversifying the child's experience by introducing him to Tom and Joan as well as Dick and Jane. The schools need teachers who are imaginative and creative rather than literal-minded; they need principals who can tolerate creativity and individuality in teaching, including departures from the standardized framework, and the extra noise that goes with excitement about learning; and they need administrators who recognize that a paste-up of traditional and progressive approaches is doomed to sterility. It must also be recognized that teachers teach best in terms of the methods they know and understand and feel comfortable with, and that mere directives to adopt a new "method" will be quickly undermined.

Discipline and Authority

One of the storm centers in the traditionalist-progressivist controversy is the matter of classroom authority and control—in short, of discipline. The traditionalist fumes at or caricatures the teacher who is merely a benevolent spectator in the classroom; at such terms as "exploring" and "self-expression"; he points to the plaint of the cartooned child, "Do we have to do what we want to do again today?" He accuses his opponents of following Freud's lead in never inhibiting the child, apparently unaware that Freud was strongly for inhibitions and would have been horrified at the thought of a child's growing up without them. The progressivist, not to be outdone, trembles with indignation at the domineering teacher who anchors the children, with their hands demurely clasped, to old-fashioned, screwed-down desks; who, unmindful of the vital importance of group feeling to school children, cuts off all communication among them on the grounds that whispering is naughty; who doles out dry-as-dust learning bit by bit. And they weep for the child befuddled by lessons he cannot hope to understand but still is obliged to absorb. In the compromise school, we find progressive practices grafted on to an essentially traditional structure, making for a strange hybrid of rigidly controlled, teacher-determined, book-determined, curriculum-determined authority phrased in the clichés of "activities," "learning by doing," "don't you want to . . . ?" and "shall we . . . ?" In the compromise school, the teacher often seems to feel that she is asked to renounce or mask her authority. There results a kind of anxious, strained, spurious indulgence backed up by impersonal, anonymous "expectations" that, because the teacher is not free to wield her personal authority but is afraid that the children might break "loose," make for an especially rigid framework. In the schools that fit our conception of "liberal," there is genuine involvement and self-direction on the part of the children; at the same time, there is genuine authority and direction from the teacher. There need be no contradiction here unless teacher and children are working at odds with each other, and our assumption is that they are not. Authority—discipline— is not a problem in itself for this kind of teacher. A strong, self-confident person who knows her children, on whose good sense, fairness, affection, and humor the children can rely, and who is free to make a curriculum that will hold the children's interest, can preserve order without invoking the principal, and has no fear that high spirits and conversation spell chaos.

Perhaps our notions about direction and control can be clarified by reference to an experimental study in social psychology. This research was not undertaken with a view to solving educational problems, but it has powerful implications for this field, in terms both of the conclusions and of the formulation and design of the experiment. At a time when the rise of dictatorships posed crucial problems for society and social research to deal with, Kurt Lewin (himself a refugee from Nazi Germany) and his collaborators, Lippitt and White, initiated a series of studies on the effects of authoritarianism.[14] In their first approach to the problem, they saw a simple dichotomy between authoritarian and democratic conditions. As in most dichotomies, the "bad" was easier to define than the "good." In the present authors' view, the crucial turning point in the experimenters' thinking about the problem came when they recognized that there was a *tri*polar relationship to deal with. A contrast could be drawn among three (and conceivably, of course, more) types of leaderships: *authoritarian, democratic,* and *laissez-faire.* The distinction between *laissez-faire* (which, translated into educational terms, seems to correspond to the extreme progressivism that is the target of educational traditionalists) and democratic (our "liberal") was that the democratic leader (or teacher) retained his authority and adult responsibility while the "non-directive," *laissez-faire* leader was essentially a benevolent bystander. Democratic and authoritarian leadership differed in that the democratic leader, while retaining his authority, listened to and worked with the group, whereas the authoritarian leader dominated and directed it from on high. Specifically, in the main experiment, adult leaders worked with three groups of ten-year-old boys formed into clubs to carry on such activities as theatrical mask-making. To eliminate the effects of personality differences among the leaders, each adult assumed in rotation autocratic, democratic, and *laissez-faire* roles carefully worked out in advance. Each group of boys was exposed to all three types of leadership, but no group ever had the same leader playing different roles. Some of the club sessions were filmed, and squads of observers recorded the behavior of the leader and children. Especially important was the recording of the children's behavior with the leader absent, a condition provided for in the design of the experiment.

In the autocratic or authoritarian role, the adult gave specific instructions, one step at a time, to each child. Throughout, he was the only one who knew the dimensions and scope of the project as a whole, thus preventing any co-operative work among the children except as it was mediated through him. He criticized freely and firmly but not abusively, directing his criticisms toward the individual rather than toward the work; answered direct questions; but otherwise remained aloof from the group. The *laissez-faire* leader told the children what the task was, showed them the available materials and equipment, and then left the rest up to them, indicating that he would be present to answer direct questions, but remaining largely uninvolved. In the democratic role, the leader discussed the overall plan with the children, suggesting, and allowing them to suggest, steps to be taken. He permitted the children to have a say in the division of labor and other aspects of organizing the work. He participated actively in the project without dominating it and provided leadership without depriving the children of initiative. It is clear that he had the most difficult but also the most rewarding role.

The experiment yielded a wealth of findings; here we shall be concerned only with those having a bearing on education. Quantitatively, both the autocratic and democratic groups were equally productive, while output in the *laissez-faire* group was low. Qualitatively, however, the work of the democratic group was superior to that of the *laissez-faire* or the autocratic group. In the course of the project, the *laissez-faire* group lost interest, and its activities became desultory, with considerable horseplay. The presence or absence of the leader made little difference. In the authoritarian group, the maintenance of production apparently depended on pressure from the adult leader, for, when he left, work tended to cease. In the democratic group, interest and motivation remained high, and even when the leader was absent, work went on in the established pattern. Even more significantly, members of the authoritarian group either became indifferent and apathetic or developed rather intense aggressiveness. This was evident, for instance, in the persistent finding of scapegoats, which seemed to have become built into the structure of the situation, since, when one victimized child withdrew from the group, a new scapegoat was found. Besides the work stoppages that occurred every time the autocratic leader left the scene, there was a cork-out-of-the-bottle effect: all sorts of feelings, largely hostile, exploded. This behavior may be evidence of the strain generated in children by rigid external controls of this kind, and may be compared to the way children explode out the doors at three o'clock from schools where they are similarly held in check. Significantly, a similar explosion took place when groups changed from authoritarian to democratic leadership. A comparable phenomenon is likely to appear when schools make the change from authoritarian to democratic organization, often leading to the belief that the rigid controls of the old regime were really necessary to maintain discipline. This phenomenon may be especially conspicuous if a single class in an essentially authoritarian school tries to adopt democratic methods.

The Practices of Liberal Schools

In the more seasoned and successful of the liberal schools, private and public, an approach analogous to Lewin's democratic leadership prevails. Such schools assume and build on the eagerness and desire for knowledge we have spoken of; the early need for concrete, inductive experience; and growth toward pleasure in and ability to handle abstractions. Such schools free the child of arbitrary and unnecessary restraints—folded hands, no whispering—and of deadly and deadening routines—thirty-five children in turn reading aloud the same passage from the same book. They do not, however, tolerate the anarchy that sometimes reigned in the early progressive schools. They provide scope for group and individual projects and research, and go as far as possible in the direction of original problem-setting, direct experience with subject matter, and the use of first sources rather than canned, diluted ones.

In the early grades, they know that effective learning can be built on the child's drive toward reality, his need to know what the world is all about, to understand how things are done, how they are put together, where they come from, and his desire to master tricks of the adult trade such as the magic of the written word and using numbers. They give him time and encouragement to figure things out for himself, to see things in action, to formulate and record his ideas; to read not only from textbooks but from charts, from accounts of exciting activities and events he himself has taken part in, and from "real" books; to put his thoughts in words and to communicate them to other people, sometimes by dictating stories and articles before he himself is able to master the mechanics of writing; to experience the satisfaction of achievement, to drill and memorize multiplication tables, spellings, and so forth, as these become needed and their value is apparent to him. By the time he is in the third grade, the child is learning about other, perhaps more distant people, sharing their experience vicariously so that he will have some feeling for them as living people, rather than merely acquiring some notion of their strange and perhaps sub-human differences. At the same time, he is laying the groundwork for his coming interest in viewpoints and attitudes. In later grades, such schools rely more exclusively on the child's developing ability to grasp experience through symbols, without the same need as before for concreteness. At all times, the child is kept informed about the relationship of what he is doing to what he has been doing and is going to be doing.

In teaching the child, such schools, knowing his delight in exercising and working hard at what is his own, make sure he is kept learning at a pace that stretches his thinking apparatus without overwhelming him or making his task look hopeless. They adapt their teaching and demands to the child's ability, urging him on when he falters but recognizing and accepting that everyone does his share of backsliding, that everyone has spells of barrenness and vacancy. At the same time, they do not try to drag a slow child up, or a bright child down, to somebody else's average. They likewise accept children's occasional need to rebel, being able to cope with insurrections without becoming disorganized and without surrendering. They know that children cannot always manage the entire job of self-control and are prepared to clamp down when it is in the child's and the group's best interests. They know that children sometimes are lazy and need some prodding. They know that children are sometimes impatient and would rather reach a goal in one magical leap, by-passing all the intervening steps, and they are prepared to insist on first things first. They know that the child is bound up in the values of his group of childhood society, but that he will outgrow his slavish conformity and that meanwhile, no matter how oblivious he seems, he is absorbing an education. Indeed, they encourage affiliation with and loyalty to the gang as a valuable part of the learning process, intervening only when the children's absolutism and intolerance threaten harm, or when the gang takes on an anti-social aspect. Where the traditional school, in attempting to give children responsibility, alienates the "monitor" from his group by artificially investing him with adult powers, the liberal school allows groups to plan and function together, and, without pitting children against each other, on occasion lets the able speller help the poor one, or the child skilled in arithmetic or baseball coach the less skilled. They know that as children develop, they become more self-critical and work to improve past performances, competing with themselves without any need to compete with their fellows (although they become aware of and respect each other's special skills); and that they make demands on themselves and accept rigorous demands from the teacher, including, in the upper grades, extra assignments and homework. On the other hand, they know that children, like adults, often grade their own achievements unrealistically high (or low) and need a critical, hard-headed evaluation of their efforts. Throughout, the child is kept working not for the sake of grades or "rewards" but for the intrinsic satisfaction of moving step by step in his own understanding, completing tasks, and meeting and mastering new ideas. Children do not explode out of such schools; indeed, the teachers or the custodians may have to evict them when it comes time to lock the building.

The liberal school, unlike the compromise school, does not march forward under the banner of "adjustment." It allows for vigorous, outspoken individuality. It recognizes as its goal for the child not adjustment, with its risks of submissive conformity, but becoming an interested and interesting person. It knows that much important development—even social development—takes place in solitary imaginings rather than in social groups, that one of the chief avenues to good social relationships is developing interests which are not necessarily social but which can be shared, and that a sound social sense is not to be measured by counting the number of social "contacts" a person makes.

The liberal school, needless to say, shares with all schools certain of the problems of our society. The factor of increasing urbanization, which we discussed in connection with the way schools are organized, brings other problems in its wake. For one thing, it means that children have little play space except in the city streets. As a result, the school is often given the responsibility of providing after-hours recreation and hobby facilities for its pupils. Urban living further means, especially for the middle and upper classes, that family friendship patterns, church affiliations, and other community contacts may correspond but poorly to neighborhood distributions, so that the family in times of crisis, major and minor, turns increasingly to the school for help. What with one factor or another, the school is being forced to assume functions—ranging from guarding the child's mental health to making sure he knows how to swim, to giving him an opportunity to roam through a forest, to providing sex education, etc.—that formerly belonged to the family, the neighborhood, and the family's spiritual and medical advisors. Whether or not this trend is inevitable, we regard it as somewhat deplorable. We believe the child's family has the primary responsibility and privilege of raising him, and the more this function is turned over to some outside agency, the more the family's enjoyment and sense of competence is depleted, the more it loses the richness of shared experience, a loss that cannot be compensated by "helping" children with their homework. We further believe that this multiplicity of functions dissipates the school's energies and further contributes to the need for a complex, interlocking bureaucracy. While it is true that the school must educate the whole child—no matter how hard it might try, it could not do anything else—it should not have to undertake the whole education of the whole child on a full-time basis.

Other Programs for School-Age Children

What we have said about the teacher and teaching applies almost *in toto* to other adult-led childhood enterprises such as recreation groups, community centers, scouting, Sunday school, and the reform of delinquent gangs. While different kinds of training may be necessary or sufficient for leaders in these situations, it is still imperative that a leader have a genuine zest for the activity, a thorough understanding of child development, a knowledge of the individual children he will be dealing with and their individual needs, an awareness of the forces governing adult society, and how to make his ideals and purposes relevant to those of the children. In school, one can force the child to attend, at least in body, but outside of school the leader who cannot attune his program to the needs and values of the children soon finds himself without a following. If he is working with delinquents or in a high-delinquency area, he must likewise understand that he is not dealing with children who are simply bad, or who only need to have their time occupied with wholesome pursuits to keep them out of mischief, but with children engaged in winning social prestige through feats of daring and, at least in part, conforming to a well-articulated sub-culture with values and standards that they may find vastly more familiar and meaningful than those of the respectable, alien, "teacher-y" middle class. Even where the case is less urgent, as in ordinary recreation groups, one has to meet the child on his home ground or the program will evaporate in a cloud of boredom or fisticuffs. Too many so-called recreation groups make wholly arbitrary impositions on the child and fail to enlist his active participation. Some national organizations for children, investigating why members quit, have found through research that their leaders are often quite autocratic and that children lose interest in what appear to be time-killing activities that neither capitalize on their enthusiasms and curiosity nor permit them to exercise initiative and direction.[15] In one such study, the largest single cause for drifting away from the organization was friction between child and leader.[16] It is admittedly difficult to find adults, who often must be unpaid volunteers, to undertake the task of leading and supervising children's activities; and it is not surprising that the ranks of both paid and amateur workers are not made up exclusively of gifted, insightful, inspired, or well-trained leaders. We can nevertheless hope that as knowledge about human behavior and development gains greater currency, and as awareness of the importance of education for the welfare of society spreads, we shall have an ever-larger pool of qualified persons in these fields to draw on. And because they are qualified, their work will be more effective, more meaningful, and hence more rewarding to them.

NOTES   (Starred items are recommended as further readings.)

*[1] Werner, H., and Kaplan, Edith, "The acquisition of word meanings: A developmental study," *Monographs of the Society for Research in Child Development,* 1950, **15.**

[2] Plant, J. S., *Personality and the Cultural Pattern,* New York: The Commonwealth Fund, 1937, p. 100.

[3] Personal communication.

[4] Jersild, A. T., Markey, F. V., and Jersild, C. L., *Children's Fears, Dreams, Wishes, Daydreams, Likes, Dislikes, Pleasant and Unpleasant Memories,* New York: Bureau of Publications, Teachers College, Columbia University, 1933; Pintner, Rudolf, and Lev, Joseph, "Worries of school children," *Journal of Genetic Psychology,* 1940, **56,** 67-76.

[5] Piaget, *The Moral Judgment of the Child.* Piaget's findings on the moral development of Swiss children have been supported and extended by investigations in this country. See Lerner, Eugene. "The problem of perspective in moral reasoning," *American Journal of Sociology,* 1937, 43, 249-269; MacRae, Duncan, "A test of Piaget's theories of moral development," *Journal of Abnormal and Social Psychology,* 1954, 49, 14-18.

[6] Jersild, A. T., *Child Psychology,* New York: Prentice-Hall, fourth edition 1954, p. 455.

[7] Moore, E. C., *Fifty Years of American Education,* Boston: Ginn and Co., 1917, pp. 17 and 22.

[8] Teachers for Tomorrow, New York: Fund for the Advancement of Education, Bulletin No. 2, 1955, p. 53.

[9] U. S. Bureau of the Census, *Statistical Abstract of the United States,* Washington 25: U. S. Government Printing Office, 1955.

[10] *Teachers for Tomorrow,* p. 28.

[11] *Teachers for Tomorrow,* p. 41.

[12] Hechinger, F. M., *An Adventure in Education,* New York: Macmillan, 1956.

[13] Stone, Beatrice B., Personal communication.

[14] Lewin, K., Lippitt, R., and White, R., "Patterns of aggressive behavior in experimentally created 'social climates,'" *Journal of Social Psychology,* 1939, 10, 271-299; Lippitt, R., and White, R., "The 'social climate' of children's groups," in Barker, R., Kounin, J. S., and Wright, H. F. (eds.), *Child Behavior and Development,* New York: McGraw-Hill, 1943, pp. 485-508.

[15] Hendry, C. E., Lippitt, R., and Zander, A., *Reality Practice as Educational Method,* New York: Beacon House, Psychodrama Monographs No. 9, 1944.

[16] Hendry, C. E. (director), *Scouting for Facts.* (A series of booklets issued 1944-45 reporting on research into why boys leave the Scout movement.)

FOR FURTHER READING

Piaget, J., *Judgment and Reasoning in the Child,* New York: Harcourt, Brace, 1928. An analysis of thought processes.

Biber, B., Murphy, L. B., Woodcock, L. P., and Black, I. S., *Child Life in School: A Study of a Seven-Year-Old Group,* New York: Dutton, 1942. The characteristics and classroom behavior of boys and girls in the young middle years.

CHAPTER 10

Adolescence: 1

Introduction

By the end of the school years, the child has found a way of life that is essentially satisfactory. And then, with the coming of adolescence, he discovers that he has it all to do over again. He stops being a child (although he does not wholly want to) and is not yet an adult (although he may think that he is). Adolescence, it appears, is a way station in development, neither this nor that, but something of both. As a way station, it is a phase that no one looks forward to, that adolescents themselves deny, and that only a few fading athletes or aging women look back on with regret—and then usually with the reservation that it is their adolescent bodies they want, leaving their adult mentalities as they are. It is a period whose most universal and pervasive feeling is of being out of step. Perhaps the in-between-ness of this age can be conveyed by the plight of a speaker invited to address an audience of high school students. How does he begin? "Teen-agers" is acceptable as a label, but hardly as a salutation. "Ladies and Gentlemen?" He will be met by embarrassed giggles or by scorn at his patronizing tone. "Boys and Girls?" He will promptly feel the hostility of his audience. He will probably have to settle for some such device as "Students" or "Citizens of the Future."

Writers on the subject of adolescence—beginning, as far as formal psychology is concerned, with G. Stanley Hall [1]—have been struck by the adolescent's agonies of self-consciousness, his preoccupation with who he is and where he belongs. They have noted his proneness to religious conversion, to idealism, to a sense of the futility of it all, and to rebellion and iconoclasm. Adolescence has come to be known as a time of inner turmoil, as the period of *Sturm und Drang,* of "storm and stress." Needless to say, this inner turmoil has its external counterparts,

268

which means that the adults who have to deal with the adolescent come in for their share of turmoil, too. There was long a tendency to attribute the turbulence of this age to the physiological upheaval associated with puberty, and, by implication, to the discrepancy between the adolescent's biological maturity and mental immaturity. More recently, it has become evident that this explanation is unsatisfactory. For one thing, as anthropologists have pointed out, there are cultures in which adolescence is not a period of *Sturm und Drang,* suggesting that physical changes—which occur everywhere—are not enough to account for adolescent turmoil. Furthermore, careful observation has shown that the adolescent crisis does not coincide with, but tends to follow by a year or more, the period of most rapid physical change; for some individuals, in fact, there seems to be virtually no correlation between physical changes and typically adolescent behavior. For these reasons, we are obliged to view adolescence as a cultural phenomenon apart from the strictly biological one of puberty that signals its onset.

This makes it necessary to separate the vocabulary of physical manifestations from that of cultural ones. There are three terms which we should immediately make clear: pubescence, puberty, and adolescence. *Pubescence* refers to the period of about two years preceding puberty, and to the physical changes taking place during that period. Its beginning is marked by a spurt in physical growth, and it continues with a change in body proportions, the maturing of primary and secondary sex characteristics, and an assortment of other physical changes. (Some writers refer to the period of pubescence as "pre-adolescence." Psychologically, to be sure, pubescence is in some respects closer to the school years than to adolescence. However, "pre-adolescence" is a confusing term because it is sometimes used to designate the middle years as a whole.) *Puberty* is the point of development at which the biological changes of pubescence reach a climax marked by indicators of sexual maturity: in girls by the *menarche,* the first menses, and in boys by a number of signs, the most reliable probably being the presence of live spermatozoa (detectable under the microscope) in the urine—into which a very small number escape from time to time. We might also note in passing that puberty is sometimes given a legal rather than a biological definition: in England, for instance, all girls, in the eyes of the law, reach puberty at twelve, and all boys at fourteen. *Adolescence,* finally, is the entire period that begins with the pubescent growth spurt and ends—when? For the moment, we shall evade the issue and say that the end of adolescence comes with full social maturity, without stating how such maturity is to be defined. But even the beginning of adolescence is not always as clear-cut as we have implied. The menarche, for instance, occurs at an average age of just under thirteen, but it has been known to appear at ages ranging from three years and seven months to twenty-six, extremes which it would hardly seem reasonable to include in adolescence. Puberty comes quite commonly anywhere from two years before the average until two years after, and the normal range is usually considered to be four years earlier or later than the mean. The average age at puberty in boys—with the same wide range of normal variation as girls—is slightly under fifteen. This means that there is on the average a two-year lag for boys which applies to all areas of development at this time, including social maturity. This lag makes for certain dislocations which we shall discuss later.

Like all the other age periods we have talked about in this book, adolescence is a period of continuing change, and we shall find it necessary to draw distinctions between "early" and "late." Early adolescence, as we shall use the term, extends from the beginning of the pubescent growth spurt until about a year after puberty, when the individual's new biological organization has become fairly well stabilized. Late adolescence, of course, is the remainder of the period up to adulthood.

The central theme of adolescence is the finding of one's self. The adolescent must learn to know a whole new body and its potentials for feeling and behavior, and fit it into his picture of himself. He must come to terms with the new constellation of meanings presented by the environment. He must define the place he will occupy in adult society. This means an intensified self-awareness—largely manifested as *self-consciousness*—and a new push for independence. In early adolescence, the individual continues to seek independence—although with new vigor and in new areas—almost in the way he did in the middle years: he wants more privileges, more freedom from adult supervision and restraint so that he can follow the dictates of the gang (which he now probably calls "the crowd"). For the young adolescent is still primarily concerned about his status with his immediate peers; he strives to be as much like the others as possible, largely as a result of feeling out of step with them. Individual differences are now more clear-cut than at earlier ages, but a uniqueness which is still only half-understood is not completely welcome. The older adolescent shares the younger one's concerns but is, in addition, confronted by the problem of where he stands with respect to the entire adult world of independence, mar-

The adolescent peer group

(TOP and MIDDLE: Courtesy of
H. Armstrong Roberts.
BOTTOM: By Alfred Eisenstaedt.
Courtesy of *Life,* © 1950
Time, Inc.)

The public and private life of the adolescent

(UPPER: By Ralph Crane. Courtesy of Black Star. LOWER: By Grey Villet. Courtesy of *Life,* © 1956 Time, Inc.)

Differences in physical maturity between girls of the same chronological age. Left: post-menarcheal; right: premenarcheal. (See pages 304 ff.)

(From Barker, R. G., Wright, F., Meyerson, Lee, and Gonick, M. R., *Adjustment to Physical Handicap and Illness.* New York: Social Science Research Council, 1953, p. 32)

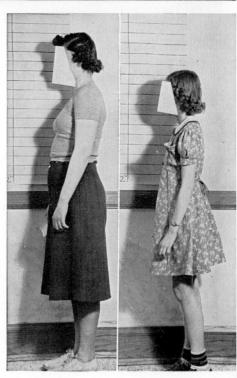

riage, jobs, politics—in short, he must now find an identity as himself rather than as a member of either his family or his gang. We can say that the young adolescent is concerned with who and what he is, and the older adolescent with what to do about it.

In these chapters, then, we shall first consider the peculiarly Western European phenomenon of adolescence as a cultural invention. From this survey we shall go on to consider relations between adolescents and their parents. Then we shall move on to the adolescent's relations with his peers, and the things they do together. Then we shall take up the adolescent himself: the biological transformation he undergoes; how he conceives of his new body and of himself in general; sexuality in adolescence; his new attitudes, interests, and values; then, coming full circle, back to adult society and what it can do to further the adolescent's struggle toward maturity. Finally, we shall have a few words to say about the maturity that lies ahead for the adolescent.

Adolescence as a Cultural Invention

In primitive societies, there is no equivalent for our concept of adolescence. In some primitive societies, the transition from childhood to adulthood is so smooth that it goes unrecognized. More frequently, we find that the young person on the threshold of maturity goes through a ceremonial adolescence. Such ceremonial observances are called *puberty* rites, since they are usually timed to the onset of sexual maturity. They may range in complexity from a simple haircut or a change of clothes to being tattooed or having one's teeth filed, to periods of fasting or isolation or a search for a vision. Such initiation periods seldom last more than a few weeks, and even the longest of them are negligible compared to the five to eight years of adolescence common in our society. At the conclusion of the puberty rite, the young person is granted full adult status and assumes it without any sense of strain or conflict. Not only is he officially grown up, but he knows and other people know that he is actually ready for adult activities, including marriage. Except for the ceremonial punctuation of the puberty rite, childhood status tends to be continuous with adult status. It is tempting to go beyond these generalizations about other societies and to report the diverse ways in which the seal of maturity is bestowed. But this would involve venturing deeper into anthropology than is appropriate. The essential fact that emerges from comparing our own culture with others is that the psychological events of adolescence in our society are not a necessary counterpart of the physical changes of puberty, but a cultural invention —not a deliberate one, of course, but a product of an increased delay in the assumption of adult responsibilities.

It would appear that as societies become more complex there develops an interlude of apprenticeship separating biological maturity and adulthood. Indeed, a long adolescence is a relatively recent phenomenon in our own society. It is worth noting that such ceremonies as the Christian confirmation and the Jewish Bar Mitzvah, both held at about age thirteen, were originally puberty rites signaling the individual's official entry into adulthood. We might also recall that Shakespeare's Juliet was only fourteen, and that in colonial times marriages often took place in the early teens. On the law books of many states today, the marriageable age is still set at twelve for girls and fourteen for boys, although it becomes a matter of nationwide interest when, occasionally, young people assert their legal prerogatives in this regard. Now, in our upper classes, the girl "comes out"—implicitly, into the marriage market—at age eighteen. In our middle and lower classes, she may make her debut somewhat earlier, at a "Sweet Sixteen" birthday party. The important point is that one's attainment of adulthood must be given some external recognition, that in our society there is no single criterion by which the adolescent can know that he has been recognized as an adult, and that the various tokens of adulthood—financial independence from the parents, completing school, marriage—in many cases are being deferred to increasingly greater ages. In sum, adult ambiguity about the adolescent reinforces his own ambiguity about himself.

Part of our society's notion of when the child is ready for adult functions is, as we can see, written into law, while another part exists as part of our traditional beliefs. The law is by no means consistent, of course, either from state to state or from one area of functioning to another. The age of consent for girls may be anywhere from twelve to eighteen. According to the state he lives in, the individual may be allowed to drive an automobile at fourteen or not until he is eighteen. Up to age twenty-five, the individual must pay more for insurance on his car than after age twenty-five. The age at which one may legally be sold alcoholic beverages may be either eighteen or twenty-one. Seventeen-year-olds may enlist in military service, and eighteen-year-olds can be drafted. In most states, however, the voting age is set at twenty-one. And at the same time that eighteen-year-olds are being drafted, with the notion that they may have to fight a war, many authorities are concerned with making the boys' military surroundings more homelike, both to ease

the shock of transition and to provide a wholesome moral climate—
i.e., draftees should still be treated as children. We might also consider
the effect of child labor laws which, while serving the wholly admirable
function of protecting children from exploitation in sweat shops and
migrant labor camps, may also sometimes impede the adolescent from
getting practical experience and a sense of growth, accomplishment,
and independence. The situation is further complicated by the attitude
of industrial insurance companies to the effect that young workers are
accident-prone, hence expensive, and so to be excluded from employment.

Furthermore, our society's views of when the child should stop being a child and become an adult may be very much influenced by transitory conditions. In the depression of the 1930's, there was considerable
pressure to keep young people in school and out of the overcrowded
labor market. "Youth groups" were formed whose members were often
mature people, if not actually middle-aged. In war time, by contrast,
when manpower was badly needed for the armed forces and for defense
factories, the pressures were in exactly the opposite direction. More
recently, in a period of prosperity and technological growth, there have
been cross-pressures: young people were wanted immediately for industry, but, both for the individual's own practical advantage and to
meet the country's need for trained experts, advanced education was
becoming increasingly necessary. Over and above fluctuating standards
as to when adolescence ends, the atmosphere of social instability—generated both by world events and by technological progress—has lately
made the adolescent's lot much harder than in years past. He not only
has to find himself, but he has to find himself in a world that refuses to
stay the same from one week to the next.

In the face of the general prolongation of childhood, we should point
to some recent reversals of this trend. For one thing, the age of marriage is going back down. This has been happening slowly for the past
century, but has become most pronounced since 1940, so that in 1956
the median age of marriage for men was twenty-three and for women
twenty.[2] An appreciable number of marriages nowadays are undertaken prior to full financial independence, and are subsidized by parents. Several states have moved to lower the voting age to eighteen.
Perhaps most striking is the change in dating patterns among adolescents. Although younger boys and girls have always gone to shows and
parties together, the real "date" used to be considered proper only for
later adolescence. Currently, dating at age thirteen or fourteen is not

uncommon and, in spite of some adult resistance, is becoming increasingly widespread. A recent report on one presumably typical suburban community even indicates that dating there begins prior to the teens.[3] Furthermore, thirteen- and fourteen-year-olds may now "go steady"— although this term has lost some of its previous meaning of an informal engagement; it now seems to mean that boy and girl enter into a contract, sometimes for a specified length of time, that they will accompany each other on whatever dating occasions may arise. The same tendency appears in the increasing frequency with which young people work part time, whether at baby-sitting, doing the neighbors' chores, or at regular jobs. There are a number of minor milestones (which may appear anything but minor to the adolescent) which are now passed at ever lower ages: the age at which girls are allowed to wear lipstick, or when they get their first "formal." At some time during the past thirty years, the age at which boys get their first long trousers (formerly quite a ceremonious affair, with the boy feeling embarrassed and pleased) has been pushed down almost to the cradle, and "knickers" have vanished from the streets. Now the pressure is for a dinner jacket at an early age. The age at which the boy gets a razor of his own, of course, is probably too closely tied to biological growth to be lowered greatly. It remains, however, as one of the symbols of progression toward adulthood, symbols which in our society replace the puberty rites of more primitive societies.

This current lowering of the age at which various milestones are passed appears to be in part an upward diffusion of lower-class practices to the middle and upper classes. In general, mature status is granted relatively early in the lower classes, and middle- and upper-class children (particularly boys) have always envied the freedom of their lower-class contemporaries. Parents in the upper classes used to resist their children's clamor for various privileges on the grounds that certain things were "vulgar" or that "there's plenty of time yet for that." Now, with the extensive leveling that has taken place in our society, vulgarity is much less of an issue. As for time, parents now are inclined to share the adolescent's feeling that it is fast running out, and that he might do well to taste life's pleasures while he can. Even though people live longer than ever before, there are now so many demands upon their time that it seems to slip away almost before it has begun.

Although adolescence seems to have arisen almost by accident out of the changing pattern of our society, it has become solidly institutionalized as a period when the individual is no longer a child but is still immature, and it has been bound about with rationalizations. That is, our culture is inclined to say that adolescence is inherent in the adolescent's incomplete maturity. We should like to make the point, anticipating later discussion, that the immaturity of adolescents is largely a product of the way we treat them, that interactions between the adult world and adolescent world too often form a vicious circle, and that some of the conflict between these two worlds could be eliminated to everybody's benefit. While the authors share the belief that the complexities of adult life in our society demand an extended apprenticeship, and that a certain amount of conflict between the generations may be inevitable and perhaps even desirable, there is room to doubt whether the apprenticeship our society provides is the most effective one.

The Adolescent and His Parents

If the adolescent's chief practical problem is to find a secure definition of himself as an adult independent of the authority and support of his family, it follows that he has to break numberless familial ties based on authority, affection, responsibility, respect, intimacy, and possessiveness —not to mention the force of habit. In this section, we shall deal primarily with how the adolescent and his family work toward and at the same time resist making this painful rupture, and the stresses it entails. In developing this picture, we shall lean to the side of exaggeration and even caricature to show the classic view of adolescence.

It should be noted at the outset that parents and their adolescent children spend some part of their time getting along with each other very nicely, sharing discoveries and fresh looks at experience, talking over problems and plans, and simply enjoying each other's company. Nevertheless, the child's development has taken him further and further from home, both in body and in spirit, until home sometimes seems only a rooming house where he eats, sleeps, leaves his clothes to be picked up and laundered, reads the paper, watches television, and makes and receives phone calls. Chores may be executed in the context of an authority-resistance relationship rather than as a shared work experience, which deprives them of much of their value. The adolescent's own room, if he has one, or the privacy of a hotly contested bathroom, serves as a refuge where he can study and register his own growth, where before the mirror he can experiment with, practice, and perfect the masks he wears. Mealtimes are perhaps the only remaining opportunity for real exchanges with his family. And although the dinner table may serve as a forum, it can also serve as an arena. All in all, a substantial portion of the adolescent's time with his family is colored by feelings, on both sides, of frustration, outrage, humiliation, sullenness, resentment, or dramatic despair.

Underlying a great many conflicts between parents and offspring are the twin attitudes of ambiguity—doubt on both sides as to where the child stands developmentally—and ambivalence—contradictory feelings about the desirability of his growing up. In short, the situation is complicated by the fact that not only do parent and adolescent war with each other, but each is at war with himself. We have chosen to name this state of affairs *dual ambivalence*.

As we have seen in previous chapters, ambivalence about growing up is characteristic of all the ages of childhood beginning with toddlerhood. The reader will remember Stuart's theme, proposed during our discussion of the "first adolescence" of the preschool years: "Being big is the best, best thing. . . . But not now. Today *you* must take care of me." This ambivalence becomes particularly acute in adolescence. There are important distinctions here, however, between early and late adolescence. The young adolescent's ambivalence stems largely from the ambiguity resident in his own body, so that he is not sure whether he *should* be acting like a child or an adult. He tends to repudiate his childish self, but hardly with assurance or without regrets. He demands privileges, but views their corresponding responsibilities as onerous. In other words, he wants the privileges both of childhood and adulthood. From the parents' standpoint, of course, responsibilities are as much a mark of mature status as are privileges. To the child, however, because they are imposed by his parents, responsibilities appear as tokens of his subordinate position and so are degrading as well as burdensome. The older adolescent, by contrast, is more likely to see the essential linkage between privileges and responsibilities; and the latter are no longer merely something disagreeable, but something that he has to do and fears he may not be able to do. As a result, every time the adolescent reaches for adulthood, he exposes himself to the possibility of failure. Consciously, of course, the possibility of failure seems unthinkable to the adolescent, but it repeatedly crops up as a chilly, threatening presence.

But it is not only the danger of failure in meeting adult responsibilities that causes the adolescent's ambivalence about growing up. Adult privileges in themselves hold half-sensed terrors. The adolescent is by no means sure that he wants to liberate and indulge the new forces at work inside himself. These forces are not yet really his, and he cannot be sure that he can control them once they are free. Thus, protest and grumble though he may, he sometimes feels a secret relief when his parents add the weight of their authority to his own uncertain controls. Indeed, it is likely that the vehemence of his protests is directed to some extent against the unspoken anxiety his new potentials cause him. An early version of this ambivalence can be seen in a composition by a high school sophomore who says, "The parents should make it their job to see to it that their children do their homework" (which, it is promised, will insure "less juvenile delinquencies"), and in the next breath, "Parents should treat boys of fifteen years of age as grownups and not children. . . ." [4] These statements are representative of the fundamental adolescent attitude toward parents: If the parents intervene in the child's life, they are snoopy and domineering; if they do not, they are unfeeling and neglectful. Since parents are damned if they do and damned if they do not, it appears that they cannot win. This does not mean that what they do is of no importance. As we shall see later, adolescents need something to rebel against, as a way of telling themselves that they are grown-up, and parents have to provide limits as something tangible for the adolescent to fight, as well as for his own security.

Parents, of course, are eager to have their children grow up. Indeed, most parental criticisms of adolescents are couched in terms of childishness. But although a great part of parental urging is toward preparation for adulthood, its actual assumption remains for them in the comfortably remote future. The weight of parental pressure, often unknowingly, is frequently in the direction of retarding growth even where there is no open regret over the loss of "my baby." Parents' reluctance to accord adulthood to their children seems to have various possible roots. For one thing, they know their own children too well and are all too aware of their weaknesses. They fail to see, however, that these weaknesses can only be overcome by coping with actual problems, and that no one is ever fully armed in advance for adult life. As a counterpart to their knowledge of their children's weaknesses, they are also—perhaps too much—aware of the hard realities that await their children, and so want to protect them. More basically, perhaps, to have their children grow up may be threatening to parents. It may, by a process of reverse identification, reawaken their own past adolescent fears and conflicts and yearnings. It may bring home to them with new force how the years have slipped away and that they are now members of an aging generation. It may even breed a species of jealousy over the pleasures that still await the adolescent but are disappearing for his parents with the coming of middle age. It may imply the end of the parents' usefulness, or it may spell a lonely life in quarters that have suddenly become too big. Then, too, parental resistance to the child's growing up may stem from unwillingness to relinquish authority built up over a decade and a half. We should point out that parental resistance is often greatest against the oldest child, who in many areas has to break trail for his younger siblings.

We should also emphasize that parents do not suddenly develop ambivalent feelings about their child's growing up when the child reaches adolescence. The parents' ambivalence dates back just as far as the child's: even as they are applauding his first steps and his first words, they are experiencing pangs of regret at the passing of infancy. Throughout the child's development they may go beyond the care made necessary by the child's immaturity and the dangers he faces, and into the realm of overprotection, producing excessive attachment and dependence. If adolescents are not always as well-prepared as they might be to cope with adult freedoms and responsibilities, it may sometimes be due to an intermittent, if loving and largely unintentional, sabotage of their autonomy by parents.

Against this generalized background of dual ambivalence, conflicts can arise on almost any subject. And much of the passion that goes into these conflicts is probably generated by both parties' need to drown out feelings contrary to those they are expressing. It should be noted that parental ambivalence sometimes takes the form of differences of opinion between the parents, preventing them from offering a united front to the child. Among the favorite topics of dispute between adolescents and their parents are dating, friendships, time schedules, clothes, chores, money, automobiles, school, morals and manners, and access to the telephone—not necessarily in this order of prominence or importance. In all these matters, the adolescent wants to be free and unconfined, but at the same time he is beginning to see himself enmeshed in a network of reciprocity that inevitably restricts his freedom of action. Often, indeed, it is this very inevitability against which the adolescent is fighting, rather than the specific restriction he is made to observe.

It is worth pointing out that the inescapability of mutual responsibilities may add another dimension to the adult's ambivalence. When a parent rages against his child's disregard for the rights and sensibilities of others, his emotion may be in direct proportion to his own occasional wishes that he could repair to a tropical isle, slough off his responsibilities, and live a life of anarchic selfishness. No matter how well adults —particularly males—have adapted themselves to a way of life based on social reciprocity, they cannot restrain a secret twinge of sympathy for those who refuse to yield. The adolescent is often shrewd enough to detect this particular ambivalence and to be outspokenly aware of his parents' own departures from the strictures they lay down. It is quite common to hear adolescents speak of their parents as "hypocrites." While this allegation may have some truth, parents' "hypocrisy" often reflects a desire to communicate to their children some of the lessons they themselves learned too late. And it may be, of course, that these lessons inevitably and in the nature of things must always come too late. The adolescent, faced with the urgency of his wants and feeling that his parents know nothing of his situation, is hardly ready for this kind of instruction.

Now that we have looked at the classic pattern which we have named dual ambivalence, it is time to examine certain departures. For one thing, reservations about the value of growing up are far more common in the middle and upper classes than in the lower class. In the lower strata of society, the pressures are rather more consistently on the side of early maturing and assumption of adult roles. This does not, of course, mean that there is no conflict between the generations. While the lower-class child is more likely, with parental approval and even urging, to leave school and to get a job earlier than his middle- or upper-class counterpart, there is also pressure from the family to have him stay at home and contribute his earnings to the family. Here, too, then, we often find much friction about freedom and money. The situation may be further complicated by the fact that many lower-class families belong to immigrant or other minority groups, with traditions of more explicit and complete parental authority, entailing additional problems in identification for the children and conflicts between mores.

On farms and ranches, where the youngster's life necessarily is centered in the home and home place, and where he participates directly in a relatively self-sufficient family economy, there tends to be less of a gap between the generations. The parents are inclined to welcome and accept the child's growing up, and he finds it easier to demonstrate his competence in the terms by which they measure maturity. It is largely in an economy of specialized services centered outside the home that conflicts arise most easily.

Another departure from the standard pattern of dual ambivalence is to be found in some of the families where there is no outwardly visible conflict. This seemingly idyllic condition is sometimes more ominous, psychologically, than a rather considerable amount of adolescent turmoil. One way this state of external peace comes about is through an extremely authoritarian and repressive attitude on the part of the parents. The effects of an authoritarian upbringing can be seen in a composition written by a fifteen-year-old girl:

> I'm glad my parents are people who know what is best for us to do and know how to go about making us do it. There are many parents today who do not know how to handle their children. As a result of this the children become too independend [sic]. Then the parents wonder why they do not get good marks in school. . . . When [my mother and dad] say no once there is no use asking a second time, because they will not change their minds. Mom says she wants us to grow up and get a good job and be respected by other people, if nothing else. . . . It makes me proud and happy when I think about how my parents have protected me from becoming a junvenile [sic] delinquent.[5]

We can see from this that the writer's parents have done an effective job of indoctrinating her with their values. Needless to say, democratic-minded parents also want to impart values to their children. But they distinguish between basic and superficial values, and between necessary or desirable ways of behaving and those with moral implications. They know that the basic values are learned indirectly, and not in terms of external and rigid rules of behavior. They know that there is room for differing opinions about how values are translated into action, that in real life one is sometimes forced to choose between values, and so do not try to map out in detail a "correct" way of thinking for children.

Sometimes, however, the apparent calm which masks authoritarian submission is obtained by practices which superficially seem at the opposite pole from authoritarian coercion. A pseudo-democratic parent may not browbeat, but instead "explains" his sweet reasonableness. In this way he may convey to the child that by clinging to his own wishes or convictions he is willfully hurting the parent. He may convince him that such wishes fly in the face of what "everybody" knows to be normal. He may convince the child that his still elusive feelings really point in quite another direction. He may stack the cards of logic to make certain consequences obvious. In short, he deviously manipulates the child into reaching the parent's point of view as though it were his own. Such techniques are reminiscent of the spurious marshaling of the facts by advertisers or politicians. An adolescent so indoctrinated is more helpless than the browbeaten one. In his strivings for independence, he is likely not to know what to turn against, and may be filled with a vague uneasiness and guilt.

Such uneasiness may also overtake the child of *laissez-faire* parents, but he is likely to compensate for their passivity by inventing, and imputing to them, demands and issues to struggle against. In adolescence as at earlier ages, the child needs strong guide lines laid down by his parents; he may not want to follow them, but he wants them for reference. Meanwhile, he will reject parental sympathy: how could *he* (or *she*) possibly understand? There is a gulf between the generations, and it is as well to acknowledge that, when the adolescent does join the company of adults and can be reconciled with older people, his parents will be among the last that he accepts, just as they will be the last to accept him. Parents, after all, are inclined to see their offspring as babes in the wood, needful of constant support and succor and protection. This is more overtly shown by mothers, who weep at their children's weddings and graduations, but fathers feel it too. To adolescents, parents' love will seem somewhat possessive and intrusive and constricting, and the parents themselves survivors of the Ice Age. We shall have more to say in a later section on sound adult practice in dealing with adolescents, but for the moment we shall close on the remark of a teen-age girl who, preparing blissfully for her first formal dance, turned to her helpful mother and asked, "Did they have parties like this when you were alive?"

The Adolescent's Activities and Associates

Like the school-age child, the adolescent shuttles back and forth between two cultures, that of adults and that of his peers. Now, however, the situation has changed radically. For the peer group no longer views itself as a childhood society, but as a new kind of adult society, the kind that will rule the future. To this end, there is an implicit conspiracy of silence among adolescents about their own and each other's pasts; the very thought of their recent immaturities is too agonizing to bear. This emphasis on being grown up—"sophisticated"—does not, of course, lessen frictions between the two worlds. The beginning of adolescence, in fact, is often a high point in the rejection of adults (although an occasional one who represents an ideal, or one who, like the athletic coach, flatters the adolescent by treating him bluntly and without reserve, may become the object of fierce admiration). Nevertheless, the problems that concern adolescents have to do with how to be adults, and especially with how to get to adulthood as fast as possible. In adolescence, the crowd is still primarily a same-sex group, but as youngsters of both sexes grow toward adulthood they feel free to mingle and to pair off. But in early adolescence, and to some extent throughout this period, they feel safer doing things in groups, including the exchange of overtures between the sexes. With increasing age, the crowd is less likely to be a neighborhood group, although the neighborhood (and neighborhood hangout) and school still provide the nucleus.

TABLE 5   Percentage of Adolescents Engaging in Certain Favored Leisure-Time Activities

(Adapted from Bell, H. M. *Youth Tell Their Story*. Washington: American Council on Education, 1938.)

	BOYS (N = 6872)		GIRLS (N = 6635)	
ACTIVITY	%	RANK	%	RANK
Individual Sports	21.6	1	11.1	5
Reading	16.7	2	35.0	1
Team Games	15.7	3	1.1	8
Loafing	13.1	4	5.4	6
Dating and Dancing	10.9	5	13.7	2
Moving Pictures	9.4	6	12.0	4
Hobbies	5.5	7	13.4*	3*
Radio	1.8	8	2.2	7

* Includes Handicrafts.

The adolescent has far greater mobility—he may even have a car—than the school-age child and can maintain friendships over a wide geographical radius. He is now likely to form friendships along lines more like those followed by adults, including the social discriminations adults practice.

Let us emphasize that the description we shall give of the adolescent among his peers does not apply to all adolescents. Also, much of what we have to say applies only to outward behavior, and does not do justice to adolescents' inner feelings. In later sections, we shall see how these inner feelings may be quite at variance with what outward behavior might lead us to believe. There is almost as great diversity among

TABLE 6   Percentage of Adolescents Reporting a Marked Increase or Intensification in Certain Attitudes or Activities

(Adapted from Valentine, C. W. Adolescence and some problems of youth training. *British Journal of Educational Psychology,* 1943, 13, 57-68.)

ATTITUDE OR ACTIVITY	BOYS		GIRLS	
	%	RANK	%	RANK
Reading	90	1	79	1
Interest in other sex	84	2	61	11
Religion	78	3	74	3
Group games	73	4	70	6
Music appreciation	69	5	71	5
Great ambition	66	6	57	12.5
Depressed mood	61	8	76	2
Appreciation of nature	61	8	66	7.5
Gregariousness	61	8	64	9
Writing poetry	56	10	57	12.5
Playing music	54	12	66	7.5
Art appreciation	54	12	62	10
Father's influence less	54	12	39	19
Same-sex attachment	50	14.5	72	4
Writing stories	50	14.5	48	16
Drawing and painting	45	16.5	57	12.5
Father's influence greater	45	16.5	27	23
Mother's influence less	44	18	35	20
Aversion to other sex	43	19	45	17
Mother's influence greater	40	20.5	42	18
Idea of running away	40	20.5	33	21
Thoughts of suicide	38	22	29	22
Teacher idealized	37	23	57	12.5

adolescents as among adults, and they cannot be characterized as a group. Therefore, we are beginning with the most visible manifestations of the adolescent peer group at the peak of adolescence—the sophomore and junior years, say, of high school. Later, we shall point out certain age differences and individual variations.

One of the chief keys to the nature of adolescence, of course, is given by looking at the people adolescents go around with and how they spend their time—and we should remember that adolescents sleep less than younger children and so have more time to spend. The tables on pages 282 and 283 give a general picture of what adolescents like to do, with some indications of differences between younger and older ones, and between girls and boys. We should note, however, that the research on which these tables are based was done some time ago, under different social conditions (economic depression, wartime) and even, in one case, a different country. And though they tell us about preferences, they do not tell us how much time youngsters spend on various activities.

As we have seen, the adolescent spends less and less time at home, and the warmth and intimacy of home seem to mean less to him than its conveniences as a base of operations. A major portion of his time, at least until the legal school-leaving age and probably well beyond, is spent in school, and a varying but often sizable block of time goes into homework. For a goodly number of adolescents, the academic side of school appears as wasted time. The adolescent in many schools and neighborhoods lives in a climate of anti-intellectualism, and even those who find school work attractive may feel that it is socially fatal to be known as a grind. Indeed, just as the school-age child learned to hide his true feelings from adults, the adolescent is learning to keep them from his peers (other than close friends). However, even if the education that school offers him is a burden, school is still important as the source of friendships, and even as the site of certain shared activities— dances, athletic contests, plays, clubs. The primary social life of the school appears as wasted time. The adolescent in many schools and the teacher's authority lapses. The commotion is enormous, partly as an explosion of pent-up exuberance and partly for display—it is important for both sexes that they be noticed. The boys show themselves at their most masculine, deep-voiced and swashbuckling. The girls are at their most feminine, extravagantly vivacious and alluring. And no matter how interested the clusters of boys or of girls seem to be in their own groups, they are really proclaiming how interesting they are—it makes a large difference in their behavior whether anyone worth-while is watching. There is some pairing off of steadies and best friends. A few boys may sneak into the boiler room for a cigarette—less because they want it than because it is the sophisticated thing to do. There is a constant exchange of greetings, much making of plans and dates, comparing of notes and trading of gossip. The school's big wheels may be busy politicking, but so is everybody else. All the students are, in a sense, running for office, for a recognition by others that will tell them where they stand.

While it is true that the adolescent wants to be widely liked—to be popular—and while he tends to court important figures and shun lesser ones, he is becoming selective on a variety of other counts. He is obliged to select his friends from the people he is thrown among at school, of course. But the high school population breaks down into sets. We are using the term "set" to describe the major blocs into which adolescents distribute themselves. Actual friendship groups— "cliques" or "crowds"—usually form within the boundaries of a set, and only rarely across such boundaries. Certain personality types form sets: the politicians, the brains, the wolves. Basic orientations toward the future determine who will be friends: those who plan on college and are therefore committed to academic achievement, or at least to high marks, will tend to stand apart from those who are living only for the day they can quit school and get a job. A set's members may have in common only the fact that they feel rejected by everyone and so draw together into a company of lepers. The serious students (as opposed to those who merely work for grades), the intellectual types, may seek each other out. Those who share an interest—in radio, in auto mechanics, in writing, in chess—are drawn together. And cutting across divisions based on common goals, common tastes, and common interests are other powerful divisions based on socio-economic classes, of which we shall say more later. Where the school-age child's peer group was peopled with friends, best friends, and faceless strangers, the adolescent has a wide circle of casual acquaintances as well. One of the adult social skills he is acquiring is the ability to exchange flip, breezy greetings with people he knows only slightly, and the number of such exchanges is to some extent a measure for himself and others of how near he is to his goal of popularity.

Thus the actual pattern of teen-age associations is very intricate, based as it is on personal likes and dislikes, arbitrary class lines, and keen attention to the overall hierarchy of popularity within the school. In considering joining a club, the adolescent may be far less concerned with the club's program than with who its members are and where he stands in relation to them—or where he wants to stand. Status in the hierarchy determines dating patterns, whom you hang around with in and outside school, whom you emulate and whom you despise, and the adolescent is constantly checking up on how he is doing by noting other people's responses to him. In many high schools the hierarchy is even more sharply formalized in fraternities and sororities. Candidates for membership are screened through a cold-blooded selection process and are subjected to crude, uninhibited, searching, and often brutal personality analyses. A successful candidacy produces a feeling of total triumph; rejection one of total, abysmal loss. Because adolescents are so often uncertain about themselves, they go to great lengths to shun the unpopular and cultivate the popular, knowing that they will be judged by the company they keep. What most adolescents fail to realize, of course, is that they are all in the same boat, that they are taken in by other people's masks just as other people are taken in by theirs. Adolescents are much too self-involved to be able to see deep into other people's feelings.

Now that we have seen how high-school society is organized, let us turn back for a moment and look at the development of social relationships during adolescence. The junior high school years, particularly in grades eight and nine, are marked by a spectacular developmental mismatching of boys and girls. The average junior high school is populated by young ladies and male children. This makes little difference to the boys, who are still woman-haters, but entails some hardships for the girls, who are ready for masculine companionship. Their male contemporaries are uninterested and uninteresting, and they find it difficult to penetrate the social life of the high school. They are usually forced to make do with the materials at hand, and a school dance is likely to be characterized by the young ladies towering over and dragging around grudging and grubby escorts who would rather be playing baseball. Although it is of less immediate concern to the children, the running of a junior high school is complicated by the fact that teachers have to deal simultaneously with two distinct levels of maturity and hence patterns of interest—over and above increasing individual variety—in every class. It is possible that this developmental disparity in the junior high school years is responsible for the fact that girls thereafter seek boy friends who are older than they.

Around the sophomore year, boys begin to catch up to girls in maturity, and the interests of the two sexes, while not identical, now better complement each other. The boys give up their bicycles and, for the most part, the neighborhood games, and become more oriented to social pursuits, physical activity taking second place. Soon they move into the social structure we described above, where the central concern of both sexes is dating, a concern closely intertwined with problems of prestige and status, where the football game itself becomes less important than whom you go with and how you behave while you are there.

Although friendships are formed, displayed, and checked up on in school, activities spread out from the school into the community. One of the fixtures of teen-age society is the *hangout*. It is permissible to go to the hangout alone, but preferably one goes with a few people of one's own sex, hoping and expecting to meet and mingle with a bunch of the other sex, without the formalities or financial responsibilities of a date. Some community centers try to serve as hangouts, replacing less savory commercial establishments. Those that succeed best are the ones that best succeed in reproducing the atmosphere of the neighborhood hangouts and make the youngsters feel comfortable in their clumsy amorousness. Most often, however, the deliciously dangerous (but outwardly blasé) encounters between the sexes take place on the premises of those drug stores, candy stores, diners, and so forth, whose proprietors are willing to sacrifice the magazine display and, usually, their adult patronage in order to become a juvenile social center. Adolescent social life goes on around as well as within the hangout. Boys cluster near the entrance, appraising and commenting on the clusters of girls who stroll casually by and back again, ostensibly bound on some errand or absorbed in shop windows—the frankness of the mating calls and the amount of wolf-whistling and skirt-twitching are governed by class differences, but the basic phenomena remain the same, the behavior of the school corridor transplanted to the street.

As a change from the hangout, adolescents may go to the movies, sometimes on dates (often, to reinforce each other's courage, on double or triple dates), and often in same-sex herds which there mingle with other opposite-sex herds. The same group roams about in jalopies—or, in recent prosperous times, in good cars. When two or three boys in a car can gather in a like number of girls, they may go to a drive-in movie, which often becomes a petting arena (the 1956 slang for the drive-in was "passion pit"). They sometimes go to big dances, although, before late adolescence, dances are really "big" only for girls: rather often, girls arrive at dances in their most elegant formals, accompanied by boys wearing their studiously casual daytime attire—here again we can observe the relative continuity of girlhood and womanhood, versus the discontinuity between boyhood and manhood. The girl, of course, is lost without a date, so that a steady is a real asset. Perhaps the most important part of herd life, however, takes place when the herd is dispersed to its various homes and the telephone is brought into play. On

the phone, friends can have intense, confidential discussions, impossible
in the public eye of the herd itself, about their and other people's doings. It is worth noting that the protracted phone calls that drive parents
to frenzy are usually between members of the same sex. The opposite
sex is still pretty much of an enigma to the adolescent, and each side,
uncertain of itself and the other, hesitates to let down its guard. At least
until later adolescence, when a boy phones a girl, the conversation is
likely to be brief and to the point—almost, indeed, curt and abrupt.

Our description of adolescent herds may sound like a caricature, but
it is essentially true. However, as we have said, it is not true equally for
all adolescents. Some youngsters participate very little in herd life,
sometimes because they have overriding interests, sometimes because
they are outcasts. Needless to say, interests apart from herd activity
may sometimes be cultivated in response to rejection, rather than as
an expression of genuine preference. Ordinarily, however, the alternative to herd life is not strict solitude but a preference for more individualized relationships. The teen-ager who does his homework conscien-
tiously finds that he has very little time for the crowd. Some youngsters
alternate periods of study with periods of group life, some choose one
or the other, but very few are able to combine them. Adolescents in the
upper socio-economic strata may also lead a herd existence, but more
of it is likely to be led in their homes. Some youngsters fanatically pursue their hobbies to the exclusion of group interests. Some like to read
a good deal. Some are the children of parents who strictly limit group
participation. For some, the money necessary for an occasional soda
with the crowd is simply not to be had. Finally, nowadays, a lot of adolescents are busy at jobs, whether baby-sitting or doing odd jobs around
the neighborhood or tending counter in the hangout.

Conformity and Popularity

The dependence of the adolescent on peer-group values and judgments is, if anything, even more slavish than that of the middle-years
child. The problem is still one of belonging, but now of belonging to
an adult society. Since the grownups will not admit the adolescent to
their world, he and his fellows must build a new and better kind of
adult world. But since this is the only way he can realize and demonstrate his adulthood, he must seize upon and display all the trademarks
of his kind, so that nobody can possibly miss them. Rigid conformity
is the rule, extending to questions of dress, adornment, how to wear
one's hair (as important for boys as for girls) and even what color to

wear one's hair (there are occasional epidemics of peroxide blondness or dyed streaks among boys, too), posture, vocabulary, and intonation. The individual and his crowd are ever eager for innovations, but innovations within the framework already provided. When an adolescent wishes to assert his individuality, he tends to do so by carrying whatever fad is prevalent one more step toward its ultimate utterness. Partly because the individual wants to stand out, and partly to reassure himself of the solidity of his new culture, he is always striving for vividness and extremes. He seizes, for instance, upon the latest slang—these examples, of course, will be outdated by the time this appears in print: "cancer stick" for "cigarette," "cubic" for "worse than square," "bird-dog" for "attempt to take over someone else's date." "Cool" has already filtered out of teen-age and into school-age culture. Fads and crazes propagate rapidly among teen-agers, so that we have the fascinating spectacle of very fast change within an essentially conservative setting. To some extent, the adolescent culture has been put on a commercial basis. Many fads, for instance, now originate in the fertile brains of adults—magazine and newspaper columnists, composers and publishers of music, clothing manufacturers—who, skillfully gauging the temper of the adolescent times, plant or pass along ideas for new fashions in dress and decoration, for new kinds of parties, new slang, new wisecracks, a new kind of music such as rock 'n' roll. To the adult, such fads may appear as hopeless juvenilia, but to adolescents they are a part of the new adulthood that will displace the drab one of the oldsters. And since so much of the time the adolescent does not have a great deal that he wants to do, cannot have the things he does want, and isn't sure that he wants them anyway, he uses such passing fancies to fill up the vacancy of waiting.

The change from the middle years in the characteristics that win esteem from one's peers has been the subject of various experimental studies. Research by Tryon and by Kuhlen and Lee, for instance, shows marked shifts from before puberty in the traits that are important for social prestige.[6] Prepubescent boys are admired if they are aggressive, sloppy, boisterous, talkative, good-natured, and group-minded; provided they have a sufficient number of these "masculine" characteristics, they may also have a few "feminine" ones such as gentleness. After puberty, they are expected, while preserving many of the same traits, to look to their grooming (which may not mean the same thing as in adult terms) and to develop social savoir-faire and initiative. Physical skill, although estimable, becomes less decisive than before. Prepubescent girls are expected to be ladylike: friendly, pretty, docile, tidy, quiet, gracious, and enthusiastic (but, we gather, not *too*). After puberty, they are expected to become more buoyant, outgoing, and dominant. They may also make the choice of becoming "sophisticated"; if they do, they gain favor with boys but lose it with the other girls. The total effect of this shift in desirable traits, according to Tryon, is that almost everyone experiences a change of status in passing from prepubescent to postpubescent society. Of her two hundred children, followed from the fifth grade to the twelfth, not a single individual held "top status" throughout, and some of the changes were very marked indeed. Here is one more adjustment for the young adolescent to make, and one more factor contributing to his feeling that the ground is shifting under his feet.

These studies were done by a combination of techniques often used in research on children's social relationships and attitudes. The first of these is the *sociometric* method, whereby individuals are asked to name the people they like best. (The actual questions can be varied to suit the circumstances: "Whom would you like to sit next to?"; "Whom would you like to have visit you?"; "Whom would you like to go camping with?" From such expressions of choice—and sometimes of rejection—a map or chart of relationships within a group may be drawn, revealing at a glance the frequently selected "stars" or leaders, the rejected or ignored isolates, friendship clusters, and reciprocated or unreciprocated preferences.) Each individual in a group can be assigned a popularity score based on the number of times he is chosen. The second method is the *Guess Who* technique: a descriptive statement is given—e.g., "This person fights a lot"—and the child is asked to "guess" whom in his class it refers to. By matching the traits contained in the Guess Who statements with the popularity rankings obtained sociometrically, one can determine which traits children value most and least. In one study, teachers were asked to predict which children would be chosen by their peers. It is an interesting sidelight on the growing gulf between the generations and their standards that kindergarten and first-grade teachers were able to predict popularity with 65 percent accuracy, while seventh-grade teachers were only 25 percent accurate.

As we shall see again later, when we discuss the adolescent's self-picture, he is highly dependent on his fellows to tell him who he is. Excommunication at this age has more drastic, although probably less permanent, effects than during latency. It should be noted that members of adolescent fighting gangs (male and female) will bleed and sometimes die to establish their loyalty to the group. As an extreme example of the lengths to which adolescents will go to preserve the esteem of the group, we have the "chicken race," in which the individual is required to ride in a fast-moving car to the edge of a precipice without losing his nerve. In an even more lethal form, two adolescents will drive their cars from opposite directions, at high speed, each with his left-hand wheels on the center line of the road; whoever swerves first is "chicken."

In fact, the dependence of the adolescent on his peers is in general so severe that it has been labeled the "popularity neurosis," to which American adults are not always immune. The adolescent does not try to measure himself against some eternal standard of virtue, but against what he thinks will make people like him. His concern about his "personality" is often less a search for inner security than for the tricks that will gain him outer acceptance—being a football hero, playing the piano, developing a sense of humor, augmenting his vocabulary, being "interesting." The devices are legion, and again the adult commercializers have moved in with stories and articles on how to be popular: what to say on a date, how to obey one's parents without losing face; or, in the case of girls, how to be popular without committing oneself. And for those who cannot buy popularity at any price, there is a great deal of literature providing fulfillment in fantasy.

The need for popularity stems partly from the lessons parents teach their children: it is important to get along with people, to have people like you, to be well-adjusted, to harken to the voice of public opinion. But it becomes especially acute in terms of the adolescent situation. Lacking a strong and stable self, the adolescent cannot be satisfied with what he is; he needs someone out there to tell him he is all right. Nor can he judge his own worth in terms of what he produces—jokes, conversation, the product of a special talent, his appearance—unless it meets with general acclaim. And the louder the acclaim, the better. The adolescent is not one for subtleties (except his own, which he treasures), and unless his audience is loudly appreciative, he may doubt its sincerity. He may not realize, of course, that their appreciation is in turn a seeking for his approval. As we have said, the adolescent in his self-consciousness cannot see that the youngsters to whom he is looking for support are looking just as hard to him, that at this age everyone feels out of step. Ironically, the occasional adolescent who is not concerned with popularity and goes his own way may find that his peers flock round him as a tower of strength. Although parents are very probably sympathetic with the adolescent's quest for popularity, conflicts still arise on this subject. This is because his parents are blind to the standards by which he chooses those people it is important to be in with and those it is better to keep at a distance. To parents, almost every adolescent other than one's own child looks like a potentially bad influence; parents want the adolescent to be popular, but they are hard put to say with whom.

Class Differences

We have already pointed out that the pattern of adolescence among lower-class youngsters may be quite different from that in the middle classes. For one thing, they are largely shut out from participation in the middle-class society. This exclusion is of two kinds. First, there is straightforward discrimination against lower-class youngsters. Hollingshead has painted a grim picture of how lower-class children in many American communities may be treated as second-class citizens by teachers, employers, public agencies, and by their middle-class contemporaries.[7] Second, although closely related to the first, there is psychological exclusion. Even those areas of participation which are open to lower-class youngsters—school, school-sponsored clubs and activities, etc.—are cast so strongly in terms of middle-class interests and values that lower-class children find little that is attractive in them. Here we find a vicious-circle effect: like any out-group member, the lower-class adolescent may accept the valuation of himself imposed by the in-group and conform all the more closely to a middle-class stereotype of the lower classes. In so doing, he both "justifies" middle-class rejection of him and finds middle-class ways of thinking increasingly alien. Because of such practical and psychological barriers, only those lower-class adolescents who are remarkable in some way—as scholars or athletes, in personal charm, in strength of ambition—can move with any ease into the middle classes. It is possible that Hollingshead placed a more pessimistic interpretation on his findings than the data require. Similar studies in other parts of the country, especially in smaller towns, have shown less class discrimination than in Hollingshead's Elmtown. Still other authorities feel that our society is becoming more rigidly stratified than ever. It is possible that one's views of the social class structure in the United States depend partly on which phenomena one looks at. From one angle, there is a marked leveling trend visible: in terms of money, of both local and national mobility, of sharing in the mass-produced goods and culture of our society, distinctions between classes are gradually being obliterated. In terms of who one's friends are, however, it appears that ever-sharper distinctions are being drawn. We must also consider the age at which people form fixed class identifications; this varies not only with family background but with the particular community in which one happens to live. In general, however, we have to recognize class distinctions even though we do not countenance them.

As we mentioned earlier, the lower-class adolescent is spared certain stresses of middle-class adolescence. His parents are more willing to accept him as an adult, and he is freer to quit school and get a job. As a result, he may, paradoxically, have more money to spend and more freedom to spend it than his more prosperous contemporaries. Indeed, although middle-class youngsters may speak disdainfully of and hold aloof from those who live across the tracks, their disdain and aloofness are often tinged with envy. Middle-class children may wish, for instance, that they had the sexual freedom they attribute (with some justice, according to Kinsey's findings[8]) to the lower classes. Middle-class boys may date a lower-class girl in hopes of finding her sexually compliant, or they may join a crowd of lower-class boys in order to share in their sexual enterprises. In fact, envy may produce a fair degree of emulation, so that, contrary to what we conceive of as the usual pattern, there is a steady spread of culture upwards from the lower classes, much of it by way of adolescents. Because of their freedom, lower-class youngsters may take on a certain glamor for those in the middle class. But what middle-class adolescents tend to imitate is the style rather than the content of lower-class behavior. They may adopt the fashions in clothing and adornments of the lower classes. They may decide that rock 'n' roll music is the thing. Particularly interesting is the way middle-class youngsters take over lower-class slang, often innocently unmindful of the rich and sometimes obscene metaphors it may entail, responding instead to its quality of toughness, vividness, and daring. But in spite of adult prejudices, there is a flow of people and ideas back and forth across class boundaries. It is interesting to note that members of racial or ethnic minorities, particularly in low-tension areas, are often accepted on their own merits by their adolescent contemporaries—as long as they are in school. Outside school, where the in-group members feel themselves exposed to adult eyes, they are likely to become cool and distant. We should note that all the impediments to assimilation of ethnic and lower-class out-groups do not come from the middle-class white North

European Protestants. Out-group members themselves form strong group identifications—many adolescent fighting gangs are organized according to ethnic groupings, with the Poles pitted against the Irish, and the Italians against the Negroes, and all of them against the Gas House Gang—and resist surrendering this identity.

New Trends in Adolescence

All that we have said so far about adolescence is consonant both with research findings and with literary insights. It fits the adolescence the authors' generation knew; it doubtless fits the experience of much of the present adolescent population. Yet there are reasons to think that in recent years certain new tendencies have been appearing, evident particularly in the patterns of upper-class and upper middle-class adolescence. We point to these new phenomena tentatively and with caution, because there is as yet little research evidence to support the impression of the authors and some of their colleagues that, at least for these population segments, much of the inner *Sturm und Drang* and outer turbulence have been drained from adolescence.

If our diagnosis is correct, it may become necessary in the future to describe an adolescence in which relationships with parents no longer revolve about the themes of dual ambivalence, which is no longer marked by the adolescent's overheated rejection or denial of his own immaturity, or characterized by eternal frictions and misunderstandings between the generations. Many present-day adolescents seem less uncomfortable and out of step, less fearful about growing up and assuming adult functions, than those we have described. This new type of adolescence may be more common among girls, for whom problems of authority are not so strenuous, than among boys. The change seems to be based on a fundamental shift in authority patterns and in parent relationships both during and before adolescence. If parents wield less authority and impose fewer absolutes, there is less to fight against. Many of today's adolescents manifest little resentment or rejection of their parents of the sort psychologists have long thought inevitable. If the reality of this trend is confirmed by research, and if it proves to be a stable one, a crucial new issue arises: Do these adolescents move smoothly and without stress into a true maturity, with a strength of identity equivalent to that forged in the overassertiveness of "adolescent rebellion," or do they become docile, less differentiated, incomplete adults of the kind produced by pseudo-democratic parents (page 280)?

In any case, it may be well to bear in mind, in reviewing the classic picture which we have given of the adolescent, his parents, and his friends, that this new, less troubled breed seems to be emerging. The phenomenon of a smooth adolescence will also modify the suggestions at the beginning of Chapter 12 for the adult's dealing with adolescents, suggestions stemming from the classic view of adolescence as a turbulent period.

NOTES (Starred items are recommended as further readings.)

[1] Hall, G. S., *Adolescence; Its Psychology and Its Relations to Physiology, Anthropology, Sociology, Sex, Crime, Religion, and Education,* 2 vols. New York: Appleton, 1904.

[2] Data compiled by the Metropolitan Life Insurance Co.

[3] Seeley, J. R., Sim, R. A., and Loosley, E. W., *Crestwood Heights.* New York: Basic Books, 1956, p. 70.

[4] From the files of the Department of Child Study, Vassar College.

[5] Department of Child Study, Vassar College.

*[6] Tryon, C. M., "The adolescent peer culture," in the *Forty-Third Yearbook of the National Society for the Study of Education,* Part I Adolescence, 1944, pp. 217-239; Kuhlen, R. G., and Lee, B. J., "Personality characteristics and social acceptability in adolescence," *Journal of Educational Psychology,* 1943, 34, 321-340 (an abridged version is contained in Kuhlen and Thompson, *Psychological Studies of Human Development,* pp. 344-351). As parallels to Tryon's and Kuhlen and Lee's studies, see Stone, C. P., and Barker, R. G. "The attitudes and interests of pre-menarcheal and post-menarcheal girls," *Journal of Genetic Psychology,* 1939, 54, 27-71 (abridged in Kuhlen and Thompson, pp. 257-266); Sollenberger, R. T., "Some relationships between the urinary excretion of male hormone by maturing boys and their expressed interests and attitudes," *Journal of Psychology,* 1940, 9, 179-189 (in Kuhlen and Thompson, pp. 34-40); Jones, M. C. and Bayley, N., "Physical maturing among boys as related to behavior," *Journal of Educational Psychology,* 1950, 41, 129-148 (in Kuhlen and Thompson, pp. 40-49).

*[7] Hollingshead, A. B., *Elmtown's Youth,* New York: Wiley, 1949.

[8] Kinsey, A. C., and associates, *Sexual Behavior in the Human Male,* Philadelphia: Saunders, 1948; *Sexual Behavior in the Human Female,* 1953.

FOR FURTHER READING

Mead, M., *From the South Seas,* New York: Morrow, 1939. (See especially *Coming of Age in Samoa,* also published separately.) The transition from childhood to adulthood in three primitive societies.

Levy, John, and Munroe, Ruth, *The Happy Family*, New York: Knopf, 1938. Parent-child relationships during adolescence are treated in the first chapter.

Horrocks, J. E., "The adolescent," in Carmichael, *Manual of Child Psychology*, pp. 697-734. A survey of thinking and research on adolescence. For a more extended treatment, see the same author's *The Psychology of Adolescence*, Boston: Houghton Mifflin, 1951.

CHAPTER 11

Adolescence: 2

Pubescence, Puberty, and Physical Development

As we have noted, the latency period ends with the growth spurt that signals the approach of puberty. It is now time to look in more detail at the physical changes that take place during adolescence, with puberty as the climax. The child's growth first begins to show an upturn from the plateau of early latency about four or five years prior to puberty, that is, at about age eight in girls and ten in boys; but it is roughly in the two years before puberty that children really shoot up. Growth is most rapid about a year before puberty, and the time of most rapid growth is known as the *Maximum Growth Age* (MGA) or *apex*.[1] Following the apex, growth levels off until age seventeen, on the average, in girls, and nineteen, on the average, in boys, by which time physical growth is virtually complete. During this nine-year span of growth, the child increases in height by about 25 percent and doubles in weight. From an average yearly gain in height of two or two and a half inches before pubescence, there is an increase up to three and a half inches yearly in girls and four or five inches yearly in boys. From an average annual weight gain of about four and a half pounds in girls and five pounds in boys, there is an increase up to more than eleven pounds annually in girls and twelve to fourteen pounds in boys. These figures do not apply equally to early-maturing and late-maturing children. It may be, of course, that the need to provide raw materials for this increase, and fuels to maintain it, accounts for the voracious appetites we observe in teen-agers. Early growers, in general, not only start sooner but grow faster than late growers; but they also stop more quickly, so that their total growth is compressed into a shorter time interval. Since girls mature earlier than boys, they are larger than boys between the ages of eleven and fourteen, a reversal of the usual relationship.

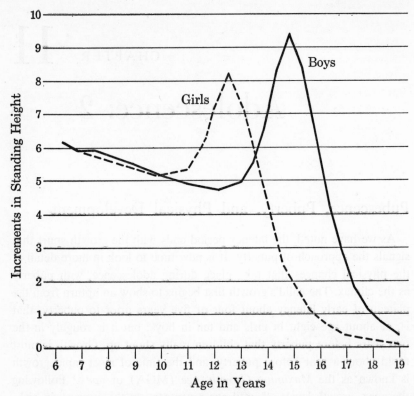

Increases in height of boys and girls ages 6-19, adjusted for individual variations in timing. (Adapted by Kuhlen, R. G. [The Psychology of Adolescent Development, New York: Harper, 1952, p. 33] from Shuttleworth, F. K., "The physical and mental growth of girls and boys age six to nineteen in relation to age at maximum growth," Monographs of the Society for Research in Child Development, 1939, 4, no. 3.)

Like all growth, that which takes place during adolescence is not merely a matter of increase in size but also of differentiation and functional subordination. The differentiation process goes on at both the anatomical and the physiological level, deep in the body and on its surface, resulting in changed organic structures, changed proportions, and changed ways of functioning. The key to all these changes—although obviously not their ultimate cause—lies in the *pituitary gland,* an endocrine gland recessed in the base of the brain. At the time of pubescence, there is an increase in activity in the pituitary, sometimes known as the "master gland" because its secretions influence growth and activity in all the other endocrines, notably the thyroid, the adrenals, and the gonads (sex glands: the testes in males and the ovaries in females), and through them, physical growth in general. Secretions from certain of these glands in turn inhibit the pituitary, making for a balanced pattern of endocrine activity.

Now let us look at some of the specific differentiations that take place during pubescence, beginning with changes in overall proportion, then treating some outstanding part changes, and ending with those changes most closely related to sexual maturation.[2]

In both sexes, growth during pubescence is centered in the extremities—neck, arms, legs—rather than the trunk. This accounts for the long-legged, gawky or coltish look so characteristic of the age. In boys, there is a marked broadening of the shoulders. In girls, the hips broaden as the bony pelvic basin enlarges. Changes of proportion can likewise be seen in the face. Now the lower portion of the head begins to grow in earnest, with the nose and the chin taking the lead, and the forehead appearing small by contrast. Certain changes of proportion are related to changes in tissue distribution. Especially in girls, a layer of subcutaneous fat develops, rounding and softening the contours of face and body. Boys, too, go through cycles of subcutaneous fat development, but this is generally less pronounced than in girls and is subordinated to the development of muscle and bone, so that boys have a leaner, more angular look than girls.

A number of changes appear on the surface of the body. The most conspicuous of these is perhaps the growth of body hair: pubic and axillary (armpit) hair in both boys and girls, and, in boys, facial and chest hair. (Of course, a sprinkling of facial and chest hairs is quite common in girls, too, and in no way contradicts their femininity.) The pubic hair appears first—indeed, the literal meaning of "pubescence" is the development of pubic hair. It begins, at about the time of the growth spurt, as a fine down centered just above the genitals, whence, during the remainder of adolescence, it spreads horizontally and then vertically until it surrounds the genital area. As it spreads in area, it becomes longer, coarser, darker, and kinkier in character. In boys, facial hair appears before axillary hair, first as a darkish shadow on the upper lip. Chest hair in boys does not appear until late in adolescence and continues growing through young manhood—one of the sources of the feeling of being out of step is boys' concern about whether they will ever have hair on their chests, the ultimate mark of virility. In both boys and girls, the skin undergoes changes: it becomes coarser, with larger pores, and the sebaceous glands become more active, producing an oily secretion; as a result, young people at this time become more subject to blackheads and acne. The composition of sweat is altered, becoming much stronger in odor. Much adolescent self-consciousness is caused by awareness of the odors of sweat and menstruation. Adolescents are a special target for the manufacturers of all kinds of deodorants and skin ointments.

The shift in physical organization is further reflected in blood pressure, in basal metabolic rate (BMR: the rate at which the body in a resting—*basal*—state consumes oxygen), and in pulse rate, all of which show a rise at about the time of puberty. Pulse rate and BMR (relative to body size) thereafter decline, with girls continuing to have a consistently higher pulse rate and a lower BMR than boys. Prior to puberty, blood pressure is higher in girls than in boys, but after puberty the reverse is true.

The critical changes of this period, of course, are those directly expressive of sexual maturity. Puberty, as we have said, is the climax of sexual development, marked by the menarche in girls and the production of live sperm in boys. Puberty does not, however, mean full sexual maturity. In girls, for instance, the year or so after puberty is marked by menstrual irregularity and apparently remains a period of infertility. Indeed, in some primitive communities, notably Samoa, this time is set aside as one of sexual license and experimental promiscuity for girls.[3] Less is known at present about when actual fertility begins for boys. Visible changes in the primary sex characters—the genitalia—of girls are limited to a slight enlargement, although the fact of menstruation is evidence of internal changes. We have already described a number of changes in secondary sex traits in girls, such as the appearance of body hair, the widening of the pelvis, and deposits of subcutaneous fat. Certainly the most important of the girl's secondary sex characteristics is the breasts. Beginning early in pubescence, the areolas (the areas surrounding the nipples) become elevated and conical in form, larger in diameter, and more deeply pigmented, while the breasts themselves become increasingly mounded. Some boys, too, undergo slight and temporary enlargement of one or both breasts during pubescence.

In boys, the development of the external genitalia is more marked and more obvious than in girls. To begin with, there is considerable increase in size. One of the first signs of pubescence in boys is an enlargement of the testes. The testes and the scrotum, as they grow larger, become pendulous. In keeping with the need of sperm cells for a fairly constant temperature (cooler than ordinary body temperature) in order to survive, an effective heat-regulating device is built into the testicular structures: when the outside temperature decreases, the testes are drawn closer to the groin as a source of body heat, and vice versa. Meanwhile, the shaft of the penis becomes greater in length and circumference, the glans (the head of the penis) grows until, in some cases, it emerges from the foreskin, and the penis as a whole becomes pendulous. Although the penis has been capable of erection since birth, erection hitherto was most likely to be in response to local stimulation or irritation and carried with it little sense of sexual urgency. Toward puberty, the penis becomes erect very readily, either in response to sexually provocative sights, sounds, smells, or other sensations, or spontaneously, as a function of the individual's new biological capacities. Now erection of the penis is accompanied by strong, unequivocal feelings of sexual desire— or, more precisely, a desire for sexual release. Indeed, beginning shortly after puberty, boys may have spontaneous ejaculations of semen during sleep (*nocturnal emissions*), sometimes together with erotic dreams. Perhaps the most publicly noticeable secondary sex trait in boys is the "change of voice," due to enlargement of the larynx, or Adam's apple. Most boys go through a period when their voices fluctuate treacherously and instantaneously between a resonant baritone and a squealing falsetto. Girls likewise have a change of voice, but to a smaller and less noticeable degree. Their voices become slightly deeper and considerably fuller.

One of the characteristic features of pubescent physical development is *asynchrony,* which we defined earlier as the tendency of the body's various organs and sub-systems to grow at separate rates. Asynchrony (sometimes called "split growth") is especially evident during pubescence, when arms, legs, noses, chins, and so forth, may suddenly sprout individually, with no regard for overall proportions and harmony. In fact, the two sides of the body may grow at different rates, although at puberty they generally end up in approximate balance. Needless to say, people at all ages display varying amounts of asymmetry between the left and right halves of their bodies.

We have already remarked on the wide individual variations in rate of maturing, and pointed out how deviations from the average may contribute to the adolescent's feeling out of step. Although the average age at menarche is just under thirteen, it is quite common for the menarche to come at any time between eleven and fifteen, and the normal range extends from nine to seventeen. Boys show similar variations in age at puberty, with, of course, the scale displaced two years upwards. It is likely that many adolescents could find reassurance about the changes—or lack of changes—taking place in themselves from recent findings which permit quite accurate predictions of when an individual will reach mature physical status, and how big he will be. By taking into account the individual's age, body build, skeletal development, and sexual development, it is possible to classify him as belonging to one of several typical growth patterns each of which follows a relatively fixed curve. In fact, eventual adult stature can be predicted within approximate limits as early as age two in girls and two and a half in boys.[4]

Now that we have seen the changes that take place in the adolescent's body, it is time to discuss the way these fit into his changing views of himself.

The Adolescent Self

From all that we have said in this book, it should be clear that a person's view of and feelings about himself cannot be wholly separated from his view of and feelings about the rest of the world. Nevertheless, in this section we shall focus primarily on the adolescent's adjustment to his rapidly changing body, and on his concept of himself in relation to society at large. We have necessarily anticipated this topic in preceding sections and shall return to it in those that follow. But the pursuit of selfhood is the chief—and sometimes morbid—preoccupation of the adolescent and so deserves a separate discussion in its own right here. The key to the adolescent's self-awareness is the dominant feeling of being out of step: with one's peers, with the adult world, with one's ideals, and, to a large extent, with one's own body.

From an adult perspective, the physical changes of pubescence seem to go on at a rapid clip, and we might judge that the main problem of this period is learning to live with a body that always seems to stay one jump ahead of its owner. This is only partly true. Certainly the young adolescent often seems not to know what to do with his gangling arms and legs, new internal stirrings seem to take him unawares, and boys are somewhat at a loss to cope with the vagaries of their voices. It is not for nothing that this has been called "the awkward age." Nevertheless, body changes can also seem excruciatingly slow to the adolescent. The boy may daily fondle the fuzz on his lip or cheek, wondering when he should begin to shave it off, or he may watch anxiously the slow growth of a hair on his chest. The girl may measure her height once a week, anticipating the time she will reach some magical standard, or she may hopefully lay in a supply of bras.

But whether body changes come too fast or too slowly, too soon or too late, they can be a source of agonized self-consciousness. First of all, the awareness of new and only imperfectly identified potentialities for feeling, acting, and being acted upon can be unsettling. Equally important, however, is the way physical changes and their psychological counterparts are reflected back to the child from the environment. This mirroring occurs at all levels: the child's awareness that his clothes are too tight for him; the realization, nowadays especially in girls, of how inappropriate a former style of dress has become; the way adults tease boys about change of voice and wanting to have girl friends—an imputation the pubescent boy is at some pains to reject; a girl's becoming aware of the appraising way men stare at her—or sometimes even approach her; the realization that one has outgrown one's playmates, or that they have outgrown one, not only physically but in terms of interests; and the emergence of new significances in what people say and do, or simply in the way things look.

This is a time of painful sensitivity. Girls may find that they cannot bear to be looked at; they may adopt a hunched or cringing posture to minimize their height or their breasts; they may adopt voluminous and somewhat bizarre clothing to conceal their bodies; they may be prone to fits of apparently unprovoked weeping. Girls may react to menstruation with quiet, warm satisfaction, with feelings of uncleanliness, or with a sense of panic. Boys are traditionally less modest than girls about their bodies, but at this time they may find all manner of excuses not to expose themselves in the school locker room or swimming pool, for fear their development differs grossly from that of their fellows. Obviously, these body awarenesses are closely tied to sexual feelings, which we shall treat separately in the next section. Here we wish to stress the out-of-step-ness, the feelings of gaucheness, incompetence, and vulnerability that go with the essential ambiguity of the pubescent years. This ambiguity is beautifully expressed in a poem by Phyllis McGinley, "Portrait of Girl with Comic Book":

> Thirteen's no age at all. Thirteen is nothing.
> It is not wit, or powder on the face,
> Or Wednesday matinées, or misses' clothing,
> Or intellect, or grace.

Twelve has its tribal customs. But thirteen
Is neither boys in battered cars nor dolls,
Not *Sara Crewe,* or movie magazine,
Or pennants on the walls.

Thirteen keeps diaries and tropical fish
(A month, at most); scorns jumpropes in the spring;
Could not, would fortune grant it, name its wish;
Wants nothing, everything;
Has secrets from itself, friends it despises;
Admits none to the terrors that it feels;
Owns half a hundred masks but no disguises;
And walks upon its heels.

Thirteen's anomalous—not that, not this:
Not folded bud, or wave that laps a shore,
Or moth proverbial from the chrysalis.
Is the one age defeats the metaphor.
Is not a town, like childhood, strongly walled
But easily surrounded; is no city.
Nor, quitted once, can it be quite recalled—
Not even with pity.[5]

Even the adolescent whose maturation keeps pace with that of his contemporaries is likely to feel badly out of step with them. Still more difficult is the case of the person who is growing according to a deviant —but still normal—"growth path." At all ages, physical maturity is an important determinant of how one stands with one's peers; and how one stands with one's peers helps determine, especially in adolescence, how one stands with oneself. There are two types of deviant growth patterns which are especially likely temporarily to enhance the adolescent's feelings of dislocation: unusually early maturing in girls, and unusually late maturing in boys. (Girls who are slow to mature and boys who mature early are at least in step with their contemporaries of the opposite sex, and so have a chance to find companionship, although they, too, are obliged to come to terms with a new self-image.)

The early-maturing girl suddenly finds herself towering over her contemporaries, her clothes no longer fit, and she finds herself still engaging in activities for which she doesn't seem to have quite the right body. She feels pretty much as she did before, but not quite, and her childish interests strike her as slightly off key—although what else she should be doing she does not quite know. The other children cannot really treat her as one of themselves, either the ones who are the same chronological age or those who are the same developmental age. Teachers and other adults besides her parents now treat her differently, too: they somehow seem to expect too much of her, as though they assumed she knew a lot of things she has not yet had a chance to learn. Her parents are not quite sure how to treat her—what demands to make, what privileges to accord her—because they are forced to choose between two disparate sets of cues: her known chronological age and recent behavior, and her suddenly mature appearance. Even they often forget that she is emotionally and intellectually still in the school years. In addition, they may be slightly alarmed at the way she is growing and wonder if she will ever stop—a feeling she herself has known more than once. Fortunately, her predicament ordinarily ends before she has had time to become permanently dislocated: her growth slows down, and her contemporaries sprout up around her—many of them, in fact, surpass her.

The plight of the late-maturing boy is somewhat different. He is the one who has been left behind, who in the middle of high school may still be barely over five feet tall and speak in a soprano voice. Both boys and girls of his age have moved on to other interests and other ways of life, and he has nothing in common with them except chronological age and school grade. Or if he tries to share their interests, his body build is so little in keeping with the masculine ideal that they find it hard to accept him as one of themselves. Nor has he anything in common with the much younger kids whose maturational age matches his. He is truly in a social no-man's-land. In his relationships with his age-mates, who used to be his peers, he has not merely stood still but has regressed seriously. When, however, he does suddenly reach puberty, he will probably find it easy to catch up, covering in a few months the ground it has taken them two or three years to traverse. He will, of course, have to do a great deal of reorganizing of his self-concept to take account of his new status.

It is obvious that a person's notions about himself are deeply embedded in his experience of his own body. Nevertheless, growing stronger through the years, there is a sense of oneself as a person more or less distinct from one's body, a personally experienced version of the concept of "psyche" or "soul." Overlapping and extending beyond the need of early adolescence to become habituated to a new body, then, there is a further need to define oneself as a personality. This differentiation of self-as-person from self-as-body may help to account for the adolescent's basic ambivalence, in that his body is not truly his to control and is full of disturbing uncertainties, secrets, and impulses that may be his undoing as a person. This same split in the self-image may also enable an adolescent more or less simultaneously to feel vulnerable, incompetent, and even unworthy, and yet to assert arrogantly his readiness for full adult privileges. No matter what happens, he can project blame outwards: onto the environment which does not understand his real, interior self, or onto the body which behaves apart from his own volition and even, at times, contrary thereto. Nevertheless, his body cannot be disowned. Apart from the demands it makes on him and the gratifications it offers, it is the façade he shows to the world. As such, it becomes enormously important to him that his body be presentable. The younger adolescent spends hours before the mirror trying desperately to read off from his own features the secret of who he is, and, incidentally, of what he looks like to other people—which for him, at the moment, is more or less the same thing. The older adolescent spends hours before the mirror trying on hair arrangements and facial expressions and postures, worrying a pimple on his chin, trying to gauge how best to achieve maximum effect—that is, to reveal his True Self. It should be noted that the perpetual solitary self-appraisal of the adolescent is more emotional than objective. He (or she) is able to see himself only through the haze of an ideal image. An unhappy adolescent will focus on the ways in which he fails to meet this ideal, and appear to be quite unaware of his assets. Another adolescent, less prone to self-disparagement, will equally unrealistically blot out of consciousness any unsightly features (as opposed to blemishes), lingering intently over any that seem promising.

The adolescent's search for himself appears, then, to be more than merely an attempt to find something that is already there. More basically, it is also an active attempt to create a personality. As he tries on various roles and manners, his interior experience crystallizes and becomes his own, to feel, to think about, to change, to conceptualize, and to act upon. Particularly in early adolescence, the child may feel that he is capable of being or doing anything—if only he knew what he wanted to be or do. Like the preschool child, he more or less systematically sets about trying on the ready-made roles provided by the culture, in search of the one that fits him. Some of these roles are modeled after particular personalities—movie stars and parts, heroes of the day, and so forth. Some are based on culturally defined "types": the sweet young thing; the strong, silent man; the moll; the square-shooter; the sophisticate; the esthete; the zany; the bohemian. More and more, with increasing age, as youngsters become concerned about the choice of a career, roles are based on occupational types: the doctor, the lawyer, the reporter, the nurse—in general, the more dramatic-seeming the field, the better. And throughout, of course, the adolescent is seeking to model himself according to the ideals of his peer culture. We might note here that the adolescent search for an identity is peculiar to cultures in which there is a fair amount of social mobility. In cultures where the adolescent has only to fit himself into a predetermined niche in a rigidly defined hierarchy, the problems are completely different.

It can be seen that the adolescent, like the preschool child, is still inclined to seize on the externals of a role rather than on its essence. This concern with outward appearances sometimes verges on the magical, as when an adolescent chooses a new name to be known by. This choice is made with earnest care, and only after much weighing of alternatives, since it must express in pure form the very innermost self. A similar force seems to lie behind the new and ornate handwritings many adolescents adopt. The adolescent is seeking to capture the style of his models, a style expressive of a certain approach to life which he can sense but not put into words. He is discovering not only what various styles of existence feel like to him but also what sort of reactions they elicit from others. These reactions have to come mainly from peers: in early adolescence, from peers of the same sex; in later adolescence, increasingly from peers of the opposite sex. Parents make an unsatisfactory audience. When, in the course of quick-changing roles, the adolescent girl decides to wear her hair in ringlets or to speak in a lazy, insolent drawl, or when the boy decides to wear his shirt casually unbuttoned to the navel or to greet what people say with a cynical, sneering grunt, parents are very likely to react by asking, "Who are you being today?" The adolescent is always taken aback when adults fail to recognize the true self now on display. He fails to see any inconsistency, however, in the fact that he not only discards his old roles but repudiates them wholly and contemptuously: "But, Mother! That was ages ago! I was only a baby then!" Indeed, he may be guarding himself against the knowledge that his present self is as ephemeral as past ones, and so cannot tolerate any reminders of what he once was. To have his baby pictures shown—above all to his peers—brings him to the depths of mortification. In short, every new personality is assumed totally and cannot be questioned—this week—and every old one is remorselessly buried. Yet even here there is a hint of ambivalence. The adolescent, adrift as he is, may have a private urge to anchor himself in his past and may secretly welcome reminders (in private) of his forgotten babyhood.

It is apparent from what we have said that the adolescent is still very much dependent on other people to tell him what he is and where he stands. He cannot really feel the parts he plays unless he gets some sort of reaction from his surroundings. The more other people take him for granted, the less he can take himself for granted. The implicit feelings of other people contained in their normal dealings with him are often too elusive and ambiguous to suit him: he wants to be told directly. It is by no means unusual to hear an adolescent ask a contemporary, or even a trusted adult, to tell him how his clothes look, whether his voice has a pleasing tone, and even whether or not he is attractive. Ordinarily, of course, the adolescent prefers to be reassured and even flattered, but he would rather hear an unpleasant truth than be left in doubt. Indeed, adolescents—especially those at the beginning of this period—have arrived at formalized devices for learning other people's opinions of them. One of these is the round table, a gathering dedicated to airing each other's faults and failings. Another, which generations of school administrators and parents have tried in vain to abolish, is the slam book. This is usually a school notebook with each page headed with the name of a particular individual. In it, people are invited to set down, with absolute frankness, their opinions about the person whose name is at the top of the page. The adolescent may flinch at every blow he receives via the round table or slam book, but he actively seeks the reflection of himself they give. These blows are hammering into shape an image of himself that he can carry around with him, that he can contemplate critically and even try to reshape, but that in any case is his own. With such an image, he can better judge what people are reacting to in him and so is able to move on to more subtle methods of self-evaluation. By late adolescence, he may, with luck, be able to reintegrate the various selves he now knows—his body, his public personality, and the private core of feeling that is the "real me"—into a single functioning scheme that he can take for granted without endless embarrassment and introspection.

Adolescent Sexuality

A major part of the self-image that emerges in adolescence has to do with the further sexual awakening that comes with biological maturation. In Freudian terms, pubescence spells the end of latency and the beginning of adult genitality. The task of this age, according to the psychoanalysts, is to master (i.e., to inhibit, control, and direct) sexuality in the service of mature love and to transform surplus sexual energies —that is, to *sublimate* them—into productive work. As Freud has pointed out, sexuality affects and is affected by one's behavior in every sphere. Even if one does not accept Freud's notion of sex drive as the basis for all positive (that is, non-destructive) motivations, it is still necessary to acknowledge its pervasiveness and importance, particularly in adolescent behavior. It is for this reason that we have chosen to devote a separate section to adolescent sexuality, beginning with how it appears to the adolescent; going on to our society's often ambivalent ideas about it; to what the facts of sexual activity seem to be; and, finally, to the adolescent's task of reconciling his feelings with his own values, imposed restraints, the evidence of widespread violation of these restraints, and the secondary feelings of guilt, anxiety, and tension that are likely to be concomitants of sex in our society.

The first point to be made is that the experience of the sexual capacities that come with puberty is not the same for boys and girls. In boys, sexual desire is highly specific and is clearly centered in the genitals. It can easily be aroused by a variety of external stimuli—words, pictures, etc.—or by random thoughts, or it may be deliberately sought. Sexual desire in boys is urgent and aims toward rapid discharge of tension in orgasm. Among girls, there are wide normal individual differences. Some girls experience desire in much the way that boys do. Others may not experience direct sexual urges until later in life. For most adolescent girls, however, it appears that "desire" is not the correct word to use, and we do better to speak of "sexual stirrings." These, unlike masculine desire, are diffuse and not as clearly differentiated from other feelings: romantic yearnings, maternal cravings, mild intoxication, enthusiasm, pity, malaise, sensual pleasures such as having one's back rubbed or one's hair combed, or even such emotions as anger and fear. Many girls find, in fact, that sexual arousal comes about only when they are experiencing a generalized heightening of tension or excitement. Ordinarily, in girls, specifically sexual arousal must be brought about by direct stimulation of the body, particularly of the erogenous zones. In girls, sexual arousal, once attained, seems to be less climax-oriented than in boys—that is, it is felt more as a state to be maintained than as the prelude to orgasm (although there is every reason to believe that most girls are capable of orgasm). The lower intensity and specificity of sexual feelings in girls than in boys may be related to several factors. It may stem from the greater and more consistent repressive attitudes toward female sexuality in our society. It may correspond to the lesser degree of anatomical differentiation of the female genitalia. Even the fact that the girl's genitals are less visible to her than are the boy's to him may reduce the clarity of genital sensations. In addition to differences between boys and girls in the nature and strength of sexual feelings, there are important differences in timing. For boys, the peak of sexuality—measured by the frequency with which orgasm is sought—comes a year or two after puberty, at sixteen or seventeen, following which there is a slow but steady decline.[6] In girls, the peak comes much later, often not until age thirty or beyond—the actual timing seems to depend a great deal on the amount of sexual experience.[7]

Simply because sexual desire appears early in boys in a sharply differentiated form easily distinguished from other body states, we should not assume that it is uncomplicated by other feelings. It becomes involved, first of all, with the universal adolescent feeling of embarrassment. The boy may be afraid that he will let slip at the wrong moment some indication of the thoughts that are so often with him. He may be afraid that an erection of his penis will be visible to other people. Because of the many conflicting ideas about sex that he has picked up, he may be confused about how he should act. A special source of confusion is his ignorance of how girls feel about such matters—the folklore, after all, paints them as both saints and Jezebels. He may have doubts about his own sexual adequacy. He may have "learned" that sexual indulgence weakens people. Sex may appear dangerous merely because it entails such violent feelings. He may have been frightened with descriptions of venereal diseases. And he may, of course, believe that this new area of sensation is sinful or unclean.

For boys, sexual cravings are initially quite separate from notions of love. Although a boy, when aroused, would prefer a female sexual partner, he may not be too discriminating and may be willing to settle for release through masturbation or homosexual activity. When, however, a girl does invite a boy's favors, even though she yields herself only within sharply defined limits, he finds it very easy to fall in love with her. But this love is quite different from the one he feels in later years as a husband and father. It is more an extended form of the affection he feels for his male friends, and seems to be compounded of shared intimacy, the ability to let down one's guard, and the glow that comes from being liked, all in the atmosphere of excitement generated by sexual desire. Needless to say, the qualities which the girl has for him are largely a projection of his own needs onto a convenient object, and may have little to do with her actual characteristics. In maturity, he will become capable of reintegrating his various kinds of feelings about people, based on rather more objective judgments, into new patterns of love.

For girls, love takes priority over sexuality. Young girls strive mightily to fall in love, partly because it is the thing to do and partly because it seems the answer to some inner need. But the adolescent girl's visions of romance are as diffuse as her sexual stirrings. As we mentioned in the last chapter, girls in our culture are taught or easily assume an attitude of passive acceptance. This passivity makes for greater role continuity from girlhood to womanhood, but it also makes for greater insecurity as an individual. That is, girls, more than boys, may tend to form an unstable identity that cannot stand on its own and must be nourished on a stronger identity—usually that of the male with whom a girl falls in love. The male is expected to be the dominant figure, as shown in our social convention that the boy pays the check. In the adolescent girl, love is often expressed in a desire to surrender to someone stronger. This may mean, both to the girl and her partner, sexual surrender, but its more basic origin may be a need to merge her identity with a stronger one. Perhaps this is one reason why so many young girls are attracted to physically powerful males (much to the despair of sensitive, tender-minded boys). It may also help to account for girls' vacillation about surrender: implicit in the idea of surrender is the danger of being completely taken over by the other person. It is likely that both true sexuality and mature affection—including such elements as respect, understanding, appreciation, and tenderness—can emerge only after the girl has found security in belonging to (which in practice may mean possessing) someone else. We can see how, in girls, romantic feelings centering about a possessive surrender point straight to domesticity. For the adolescent girl, relations with the opposite sex seem to be directed quite consciously toward finding love, specifically connubial love. Although boys are not always aware of it, she is usually finding a husband—or practicing finding one. Going out with boys, of course, may also have a meaning in the competition with other females, as a kind of self-validation and as evidence of desirability. The boy, on the other hand, is concerned first with sexual stimulation and gratification, second with companionship, third with love, and only remotely, some time in the dim future, with marriage. We might note in passing that girls are strongly encouraged and abetted in their pursuit of domesticity by their mothers; quite early in their daughters' adolescence, mothers may begin a painstaking cultivation of the mothers of eligible boys. In sum, when adolescent girls become "boy crazy," it is apparent that for many of them sexual cravings play only an indirect part in this manifestation.

It should not be supposed that the factor of intellectual curiosity, which played so large a part in sexual explorations at younger ages, is totally submerged by more urgent considerations during adolescence. On the contrary, curiosity is greatly intensified at this time. Boys and girls alike are voracious for factual information and obtain it from whatever sources they can. Part of the frustrations of this age come from not even having a vocabulary with which to talk about things which are of such vital importance to them. Curiosity now, of course, goes beyond simple anatomical and physiological information and extends to "What do you do?"; "What is it like?"; and "What happens when?" One of the difficulties of this period comes with the idea that there must be something more that one does not know about; even adolescents with a fair amount of sexual experience often feel vaguely cheated or baffled. Their experience somehow never measures up to the erotic episodes they read about in books or find in motion pictures. Many adolescent discussions of sex, and much reading of erotic literature, have as their unspoken theme the search for the "something else" that lies beyond immediate human experience. Young people's craving for knowledge is not, of course, merely a desire to find out what sex does or should feel like to them, but equally what it is like for the opposite sex. In the folklore, in literature (written largely by men), in scientific publications, there is an amazing ignorance of female sexuality. Boys are inclined either to project their own sexuality onto girls or to see girls as indifferent or hostile to sex; in any case, they are uncertain what to believe. Girls have a better notion of what boys are seeking, but are not particularly understanding about or sympathetic with goals so different from their own; as regards their own sexuality, they often do not know what to think.

Among the social upheavals of our time, we must count a drastic revolution in sexual morals, if not so much in what people do, at least in a recognition of what they do. The stringency of our legal codes, which often reflect now obsolete views, can be seen in Kinsey's estimate that 85 percent of male adolescents at one time or another have been, legally, sex offenders.[8] It is obvious that official morality is widely at variance with actual practice, while psychological principles and personal morals drift uncertainly in between. Although Kinsey's data must be treated with some skepticism, because of sampling deficiencies—Kinsey's respondents tend to be drawn from that portion of the population which is most willing to talk freely about sex and which has had the greatest amount of sexual experience—and because of dependence on recollections (which can easily and involuntarily be distorted), they do offer us insights into the phenomenal extent of sexual activity in adolescence. They also contain a great deal of information concerning social class (as measured by education) and sex differences in this area. We find, for instance, according to Kinsey, that boys first experience orgasm at an average age of slightly under fourteen.[9] (This is younger than the age of fifteen usually accepted as marking puberty in males. This discrepancy may reflect a sampling error in Kinsey's study, or it may be better evidence of when boys actually reach puberty.) By late adolescence, on the other hand, 47 percent of girls have not yet experienced orgasm.[10] Following the first ejaculation, 99 percent of boys find some regular sexual outlet.[11] During adolescence, 92 percent of boys practice masturbation,[12] whereas, by age twenty, only about 40 percent of girls have masturbated.[13] Some 37 percent of boys have one or more homosexual experiences during adolescence,[14] as compared to 10 percent of girls.[15] While 73 percent of boys have sexual intercourse at least once during adolescence,[16] only about 20 percent of girls do.[17] By age twenty, some 77 percent of boys have had erotic dreams culminating in orgasm,[18] as compared to 9 percent of girls.[19] By age twenty, 45 percent of boys have visited a prostitute.[20] Lower-class boys are less likely than upper-class ones to practice masturbation, are more likely to engage in homosexual practices, and have easier access to sexual intercourse.[21]

In this sphere, as in others, we find that the standards for boys are more ambiguous than for girls. While boys are expected manfully to restrain their baser urgings, or are encouraged to work them off in athletics, or to wash them away with a cold shower; and while they are threatened with various unpleasant consequences of sexual indulgence, it is nevertheless taken for granted that they will sow some wild oats, and they are to some extent encouraged in this by fathers and other adult males. As a result some boys are ashamed of their virginity, while others cling to it. (It should be noted that we are discussing here American, and not Western European, values. In parts of Europe, an explicit double standard prevails, and there are various provisions made for sexual outlets for adolescent boys.) There is little doubt, from Kinsey's data, how boys tend to resolve this ambiguity. What Kinsey's figures do not tell us, however, is the amount of guilt and anxiety that this resolution costs, or even how much satisfaction it provides. For girls, the formal standards remain univocal, reinforced by fears of unmarried pregnancy, the desirability of being a virgin at marriage, and the lesser acuteness of sex drives. Ambivalence does enter, however, in two ways. First, there is the matter of maintaining popularity with the peer group, and more particularly with the boys who are potential husbands, which may require promiscuity or near-promiscuity. Second, there is the effect of the moral revolution, which has produced a psychiatrically backed mythology attributing to girls a sexuality identical with that of boys. Particularly in the educated classes, this has had the result of making many girls feel that to be normal they must want sexual experience, that they should attain a sexual climax readily, that they should engage freely in sex. It is probable that this view has left a fair number of girls and young women feeling guilty and inadequate because their own feelings fail to correspond to what they have been told about them. It is also likely that some girls have become actively promiscuous in search of what they are told to believe is normal experience, and have ended up feeling cheated, blaming either their own "frigidity" or the inadequacies of their partners. In short, works such as Kinsey's have been treated not only as descriptions of what does go on, but have also been taken as prescriptions for what should go on.

To complicate the picture further, we should point out that girls early learn—or develop—an elaborate provocativeness in manner and dress that may have little to do with feelings of sexuality. This is in keeping with what Mead describes as the demands our culture makes on women: they must be both seductive and virginal, they must play the game of love but not to the end.[22] In very young—preschool or latency —girls, provocative behavior often seems almost like the ritual mating pattern of lower species, instinctual movements that appear of their own accord under the right circumstances and betoken little about the organism's feelings. In adolescent girls, provocation becomes more highly mannered and deliberate, and it is hard to judge the extent to which it expresses their still inarticulate sexual stirrings. It is sometimes simply a part of role-playing behavior and quite devoid of real sexual significance. It is sometimes an exploitation of the body to gain attention and popularity. In later adolescence, it often becomes a device for ensnaring a desired marital partner. To a large extent, behavior of this kind is merely what the culture dictates as normal, and not to engage in it would be abnormal. To be "desirable," for instance, girls in our culture may feel that they must be buxom and, what is more, must make a prominent display of their buxomness. To this end, they resort to intricate props, paddings, and dress styles designed to show bosoms to their best, if highly artificial, advantage. Boys, too, have become convinced that the breasts are the badge of seductiveness, which may point to an infantile strain in our culture's version of masculine sexuality.

We shall have more to say in the next chapter about what we consider appropriate standards of sexual morality.

Adolescent Idealism

The adolescent, like the preschool child, is full of contradictions. These contradictions, however, are likely to be diverse expressions of a common theme, the search for oneself and one's place in the world. Since much of what the adolescent does may strike adults as offensive or bizarre, it may be hard for them to see that, beneath the superficial "values" of dress, wisecracks, and poses, a thread of idealism runs through much of his behavior. In this section, we want to emphasize the side of the adolescent that we do not see when he is with groups of his peers, and which he may conceal from all but his closest friends. Indeed, when he complains that his parents do not understand him, he is saying that they fail to see this side of him. The adolescent is busy losing old illusions and building new ones to take their place. Or, at times, he becomes convinced of the hopelessness of all illusions, old or new, and lapses into cynicism or despair, no less genuine for the melodramatic display he makes of them. The air of bored sophistication he sometimes affects is meant to convey that he has seen through the flimsy pretenses of the world around him and feels above its pettinesses. But even though his disillusionment is often grist to his histrionic mill, it more often means that he is really searching for an ideal and decent world for his ideal and decent self to respond to. And when he lashes out at adults, it is often in protest against the world they have bequeathed him and in punishment for its corrupt lack of idealism. Needless to add, his idealism is often at war with his own humanity, the sordid cravings and weaknesses that threaten to undermine his purity from below. Adolescent boys, especially, may be quite conscious of and troubled by a sense of dual personality, one carnal and one spiritual. And through it all, of course, the adolescent tends to enjoy his suffering for the romantic picture it gives him of himself and for the emotional workout it affords.

A great part of the adolescent's idealism probably stems from his resistance to growing up. Particularly in early adolescence, he wants to enjoy his new powers in total freedom uncontaminated by the practical demands of life. Furthermore, very little that he sees around him matches the glory he senses in his new powers. By comparison, the world of everyday adult activities, the world of political machinations that he reads about in the papers, looks tainted and shopworn. The young adolescent, viewing himself largely from the inside, experiences himself (when he is not embarrassed, despondent, or self-accusing) as pure spirit, and the only worthy external counterparts of this experience are to be found in the majesties and austerities of religion, in the beauties of nature, in certain idealized public or fictional personalities, in poetry or music, in political abstractions—in short, in reality seen from a great distance. He may form violent crushes on adults who seem to measure up to his ideal, and it may be a long time before he realizes that even the most exalted human beings have feet of clay. In point of fact, the objects onto which he projects his idealism, as when he falls in love, may reach him at quite a different level, but they nevertheless become invested with the "significance" he feels in himself. As reality, including self-knowledge, closes in on him with the passage of time, he fights all the harder to escape it and preserve his dream of paradise or Utopia.

In this setting, there are a number of more or less typical ways in which adolescent idealism may be manifested. One of these is the quest for sincerity, for honesty between people. Adolescents often proclaim their intention of speaking with utter frankness about all things to all people, on the grounds that any other course is craven and dishonest; perhaps fortunately, very few actually carry out such a program (unless in slam book entries). The search for sincerity is the theme of two fine novels about adolescents, Mark Twain's *The Adventures of Huckleberry Finn*[23] and J. D. Salinger's *The Catcher in the Rye.*[24] It should be stressed, of course, that the adolescent's search for the genuine—by which he means the ideal—in the outer world is also an attempt to assure it in himself. We can see this in Holden Caulfield's repeated insistence, in *The Catcher in the Rye,* "I mean it. I really do," which serves both to reinforce his own belief that he has now grasped an essential point and as an invitation to see through his mask into the real self he is now revealing. In spite of his disillusionment, the adolescent clings to his conviction that there must be a hidden core of sincerity somewhere among the world's hypocrisies, just as there is a core of beauty, hidden from the world's eyes, in the real self.

As long as the adolescent can hold to the conviction that there are external counterparts to his ideal self, he can keep going, often on a plane of high elation. But when, perhaps after being refused permission to use the family car or having been stood up on a date, he feels that he stands alone in a chilly, unresponsive world, he is prone to depressions of the sort that the Germans have aptly named *Weltschmerz*—world pain. It was this phenomenon of adolescence that most impressed early European writers on the subject, and that we find memorialized in the writings of Goethe[25] and Mann.[26] It is in a state of *Weltschmerz* that the adolescent likes to take long, solitary, nocturnal walks, or write long, melancholy poems, or toy with the idea of suicide—a special kind of suicide following which the adolescent can stand by disembodied and contemplate the remorse that other people will feel "after I'm gone." It is in times of *Weltschmerz,* too, that the adolescent may become deeply attuned to the plight of the world's downtrodden and oppressed, a concern that may be a new stage of genuine sympathy with humanity at large. (As we might expect, the adolescent insists that the world's wrongs, once he has become cognizant of them, be put right *immediately.*) Usually, the adolescent's fits of *Weltschmerz,* especially in our unromantic day and in our pragmatic American society, do not last long and can be dispelled by a phone call to or from a friend.

On the same basis, many adolescents are highly susceptible to the appeals of religion. Different religions may appeal to the adolescent in different ways. He may be enthralled by the colorful pageantry of one, by the austere stringency of another, by the militantness of another, or by the castigations of another. In any event, his religion entails a projection of himself beyond mundane reality and into the absolute. His concern with religion is, of course, part and parcel of his concern with the nature of the world into which he is moving; and the nature and existence of God, and the need for and the possibility of faith, are among the topics endlessly debated in adolescent bull sessions—which, incidentally, provide adolescents with one of their best opportunities to find out how other people feel and to try out their own opinions.

One of the features of adolescent idealism, and one that is at a low point on the current scene, is the tradition of adolescent rebellion. This is something more than rebelling against one's parents. In the *Sturm und Drang* notion, the adolescent is expected to challenge all existing values, and not merely the authority of his parents. Indeed, there is reason to believe that such rebellion against general values may be a disguised and unconscious rebellion against the authority of a father whom one dares not challenge directly. In our society, rebellion is directed more straightforwardly against the parents, instead of being displaced toward social institutions. Another factor seems to be at work in the decline of adolescent rebellion in the traditional sense. This is the fact that the adolescent has been largely deprived of things to rebel *for* as well as against. A generation ago, the adolescent might become a communist or socialist, an atheist, a bohemian, or an advocate of free love. Nowadays, with all the adults jostling each other to get into the middle of the road, there seems to be a dearth of ready-made doctrines which the adolescent can espouse and offer as alternatives to the corruption and mediocrity he wants to escape from. His familiar reality may still strike him as base and vile, but the only current Utopia that his idealism can stomach is the one fabricated by the genius of advertising men, which is in effect an idealized version of his everyday life. Even the religion he turns to has probably arrived at a well-adjusted working arrangement with reality, and may merely clothe the workaday world with the external trappings of religion. In short, the adolescent may rebel against what he knows, but he has little to offer except more of the same, and he finds himself adjusted to the very things he feels maladjusted to.

It is the authors' view that this is not a sound situation. First of all, we do not feel that one can live comfortably with a system of values until one has tried out a variety of other ones, no matter how irrational, until one has wrestled with values and convinced himself that these are really the best. Second, the Utopian notions past generations of adolescents have subscribed to have never been entirely discarded even when the rebel returned to the fold. Thus, the residue of lost visions has been blended into the established values and has worked for orderly social change. Third, and perhaps most immediately serious, is the fact that dissatisfaction unsupported by alternative ideas and ideals may produce a purely negative, destructive form of rebellion. Children who are merely against something are, to change the original meaning of Lindner's term, rebels without a cause.[27] It is the authors' suspicion that many of the seemingly senseless anti-social acts of adolescents—vandalism, rape, sadistic attacks—express a blind rebellion of this sort. The idealistic rebellion of adolescence is a good thing when it is harnessed to idealistic schemes, no matter how unworkable in practice, since it gives body and depth to the values the adolescent emerges with. But left blind and formless, rebellion can sour into pervasive cynicism or explode into violence.

A few youngsters carry their idealism beyond adolescence and settle down to careers which give it some practical expression—the arts, a religious vocation, teaching, scientific research, political or other kinds of crusading, and so forth (although it should not be assumed that everyone working in these fields is necessarily an idealist). Most youngsters, however, by late adolescence have pretty well come to terms with things as they are. They have given up the idea of working any radical changes in the social or political structure, in the culture's value system, or in economic thinking, and are trying to find their own realistic place in society as it is given. This is the time when they have to weigh the advantages of further education or training against the appeal of getting directly to work, when they have to balance their own capacities against their often grandiose ambitions, and when they have to balance their preparation and ambitions against the employment situation. This is often stressful for the adolescent on two counts. First, in our diversified civilization, the variety of possible occupations is truly bewildering and defies classification. Indeed, despite the almost total vocational and geographical mobility open to the adolescent, the choice of a career is largely settled by accident: whom you know, what you hear about, what is available locally. Second, the thought of having to measure up, on his own, to the rigorous standards of commercial competition will probably provoke a final upsurge of ambivalence. All his life the adolescent has been hearing the question, "What are you going to *be* when you grow up?" Now the question has suddenly and alarmingly become, "What are you going to *do* when you finish school?" The sense of panic that this question arouses may be enough to send his ideals and ambitions toppling, so that he heads for a safe and not too elevated niche in a government agency or a large corporation with many fringe benefits, and gives up his idea of prospecting for diamonds or uranium, of escaping to a South Seas paradise, or of regenerating the world.[28]

NOTES   (Starred items are recommended as further readings.)

[1] The concept of MGA is defined in Shuttleworth, F. K., "The physical and mental growth of girls and boys age six to nineteen in relation to age at maximum growth," *Monographs of the Society for Research in Child Development,* 1938, 3. The term "apex" is used by Stolz; see Stolz,

H. R. and L. M., *Somatic Development of Adolescent Boys*, New York: Macmillan, 1951.

[2] Among the numerous sources we have drawn on in this section, particular mention is due to Shuttleworth, F. K., "The adolescent period: A graphic atlas," *Monographs of the Society for Research in Child Development*, 1949, 14, 1; and * "The adolescent period: A pictorial atlas," *Monographs of the Society for Research in Child Development*, 1949, 14, 2.

[3] Montagu, M. F. A., "Adolescent sterility," *Quarterly Review of Biology*, 1939, 14, 13-34 and 192-219. Mead (*Male and Female*, New York: Morrow, 1949, p. 202) takes issue with this interpretation.

[4] Nicolson, A. B., and Hanley, C., "Indices of physiological maturity: Derivation and interrelationships," *Child Development*, 1953, 24, 3-38.

[5] From *The Love Letters of Phyllis McGinley*, New York: The Viking Press, 1954, p. 11. Originally published in the *New Yorker*.

[6] Kinsey et al., *Sexual Behavior in the Human Male*, p. 219.

[7] *Id., Sexual Behavior in the Human Female*, p. 353.

[8] *Sexual Behavior in the Human Male*, p. 224.

[9] *Ibid.*, p. 187.

[10] *Sexual Behavior in the Human Female*, p. 513.

[11] *Sexual Behavior in the Human Male*, p. 192.

[12] *Ibid.*, p. 500.

[13] *Sexual Behavior in the Human Female*, p. 141.

[14] *Sexual Behavior in the Human Male*, p. 624.

[15] *Sexual Behavior in the Human Female*, p. 452.

[16] *Sexual Behavior in the Human Male*, p. 550.

[17] *Sexual Behavior in the Human Female*, p. 286.

[18] *Sexual Behavior in the Human Male*, p. 520.

[19] *Sexual Behavior in the Human Female*, p. 197.

[20] *Sexual Behavior in the Human Male*, p. 598.

[21] *Ibid.*, pp. 335-363.

[22] Mead, *Male and Female*, p. 291 and passim.

*[23] Clemens, Samuel L. (Mark Twain), *The Adventures of Huckleberry Finn*, 1884.

*[24] Salinger, J. D., *The Catcher in the Rye*, Boston: Little, Brown, 1951.

[25] Goethe, J. W. v., *Leiden des jungen Werthers*, 1795.

[26] See, for instance, "Tonio Kröger" (1903), in Mann, Thomas, *Stories of Three Decades*, New York: Knopf, 1936, pp. 85-132.

[27] Lindner, R. M., *Rebel Without a Cause*, New York: Grune & Stratton, 1944.

[28] Our impression of the conservatism of present-day adolescents and the modesty of their ambitions seems to be confirmed by the findings of an opinion research organization specializing in adolescence. See "Bobby-soxers' Gallup," *Time*, August 13, 1956, pp. 72-73. The existence of this organization points to the commercial institutionalization of the adolescent character.

FOR FURTHER READING

Zachry, Caroline, *Emotion and Conduct in Adolescence,* New York: Appleton-Century, 1940. Survey of adolescent development, with special emphasis on educational problems.

A number of articles on specialized topics in adolescent development have been collected in Seidman, J. M. (ed.), *The Adolescent: A Book of Readings,* New York: Dryden, 1953.

CHAPTER 12

Becoming Mature

Helping the Adolescent into Adulthood

In the last two chapters we have spoken of how, during the past few centuries, young people have had to serve an ever-longer apprenticeship before being admitted to adulthood. We have indicated that there is something to be said for an extended childhood, in terms of how much the simplest citizen is nowadays required to know, the complexities of the problems that people have to deal with, and the longer life span they have in which to reap the fruits of maturity. But we also have questioned whether the particular apprenticeship present-day adolescents serve is the best one for them and for society as a whole.

We have so far left open, just as our society does, the answer to the critical question in dealing with these issues: When does adolescence end? As has become clear, the very fact that this question has no simple, clear-cut answer is a major source of the discomfort that the adolescent and those around him feel. The individual is grown up when his society tells him he is. If our culture, unlike simpler ones, provides no single ritual to convey this information, then the best we can say is that adolescence ends when adults begin more or less consistently to treat the individual as one of themselves. We have to add a proviso: adults other than the individual's own parents. This was expressed by General Hershey, Director of Selective Service, when he said that a boy becomes a man ". . . three years before his parents think he does—and about two years after he thinks he does." [1]

It is in the behavior of teachers, parental friends, uncles and aunts, employers, and others, especially strangers such as waiters and policemen, that the youngster can read his own maturity. And these people, less biased than his parents, will be reacting to something in his appearance and manner that betokens adulthood. As we suggested earlier, there is a good deal of circular reinforcement in this process. The sooner people begin to take his adulthood for granted, the sooner he falls into the part. Early in the process, there may be some irony on the part of adults, and some self-consciousness on his part (it is usually a long time before the adolescent can without awkwardness refer to himself or herself as Mister or Miss), but even as a formal game, recognized as such by both sides, it serves the adolescent as a way of feeling part of adult society. The interesting thing is that the adolescent, for all his straining, usually passes into adulthood without being aware of it. At some point, he realizes that he no longer half expects people to challenge his adulthood, and, looking back, sees that he has already passed the frontier which he was still half anticipating.

The basic theme of this section is that adults can best help the adolescent by treating him as much as possible, at least in public, like an adult, without, however, throwing him so wholly on his own that he is overcome by anxiety. In elaborating this theme, we shall have to remain on a level of some generality, to allow for all the divergences possible among families and individuals. In the things we have to say to parents, the same underlying principles of parent-child relationships that we have outlined throughout this book still apply, with the changes of emphasis made necessary by the adolescent character described in the two preceding chapters.

Parents

The parents of an adolescent soon learn that they cannot persuade him that they think he is grown up simply by telling him so. For one thing, he hears this only on Mondays, Wednesdays, and Fridays, alternating with impassioned doubts that he will ever make the grade. And when he does hear it, it is usually coupled with a reproach, a demand, or a stricture: *"Since* you are grown up, I expect . . ." or "I'm surprised that." Adolescents, for all their individual differences, unanimously bristle at such an approach, which amounts to offering them adulthood with one hand and taking it away with the other. It is perhaps for this reason that parents can seldom directly communicate to their offspring any of the principles they would like them to follow, or save them the pain of learning for themselves things that the parents already know. Any lessons which parents want to teach the adolescent about himself must be left implicit, for him to dig out. These lessons must also be contained in the adults' manner rather than in the content of behavior: the adult manner must convey respect for the adolescent, for his somewhat volatile dignity, for his need to feel approved so that he can esteem himself. If this respect is sometimes tinged with amusement, the amusement ought not be allowed to show, although it often helps if the adolescent can laugh at himself. The basic point is always that one is helping the adolescent toward adulthood, and the sooner he learns what it feels like to be treated as an adult, the sooner he will be able to act like one.

The first lesson for parents to learn is how to let go and how not to let go. If they only begin to learn this when the child reaches adolescence, however, it may be too late. We have indicated in earlier chapters that both parents and child must all along practice letting go of each other—like other kinds of weaning, this one is better done gradually. Prior to late adolescence, however, the child has needed the assurance that he was not letting go for good. Adolescence, by contrast, is an exercise in letting go for good and a preparation for a new kind of relationship between parent and child, based on mutual respect between older and younger adults. Parents generally feel, and sometimes announce, that they would gladly sacrifice themselves for their child. Come adolescence, they have to follow through; but they may be dismayed to find that their sacrifice means not giving themselves up but giving up their child. And, remembering the adolescent's own ambivalence, they must likewise help him give them up.

Parents must be at least as committed to the adolescent's need for independence from them as he is. But this does not mean that they abruptly throw him on his own resources—resources which are still quite meager. Adolescence is a preparation for independence, not a time when it is imposed all at once. Indeed, a few parents are so eager to make their children independent that they drive them into a panic of clinging attachment—as we have seen, of course, this can also happen at earlier stages of development. The adolescent's demands for self-determination are in part a demand for reassurance that he is capable of it, and that his parents will stand by him while he tries his wings. Always to give the adolescent literally what he insistently claims he wants (drowning out his own doubts), may force him to renounce it permanently, and it may further appear to him as a betrayal by his parents. Parents, as the adults in the picture, must be able to distinguish between real issues and sham issues, and must have the breadth and humor not to take all conflicts with equal seriousness. The adolescent, in his ambivalence, will often fight the most vociferously for something he is afraid to have. But parents must be aware of their own ambivalences as well as of the adolescent's. They must be basically and firmly on the side of the adolescent's freedom. If they are, they can set forth consistent, unequivocal growing standards for the adolescent to meet.

But they must really be on the side of freedom. They must not be disappointed or condemning if the child shows by sporadic regressions that he is still in the process of growing. It is particularly damaging to rescind a privilege the first time the adolescent abuses it, intentionally or mistakenly. If the adolescent's privileges are not made contingent on immediate and complete success in managing them, he may be willing to discuss the way he handles his affairs.

Parents must also resist taking literally the adolescent's rages, defiance, and belittlings of them. In the heat of altercation, he may mean them whole-heartedly and want them to hurt. But they spring less from a sweeping rejection of his parents than from his need to assert himself as somebody different and independent. In some ways, they resemble the toddler's negativism or the preschool child's "Stinky Mommy!" Neither the four-year-old nor the fourteen-year-old expects his parents to take such outbursts as a final statement of how he feels. Also, in the language of adolescent ambivalence, "I hate you" sometimes means "I'm afraid I love you too much." In fact, as some writers have suggested, battles between the adolescent and his parents may be not only inescapable but positively essential to the growing-up process.[2] If this is so, the adolescent's attacks do not call for retaliation, nor should they elicit lectures about the ingratitude of today's children. If an adolescent wants to be independent of his parents, it is because they have not tied him down with silver cords, and is therefore an implicit tribute to them. The conscious gratitude will come later, when he achieves a certain amount of perspective, when he finds out how successful his preparation has been, and when he is raising children of his own.

As we have suggested earlier, the adolescent who has no conflicts at all with his parents may be in a bad way. He (or she) may have evolved elaborate techniques for lulling his parents' concern, while outside the home he does exactly what suits him. Or, more usually, he has been cowed or manipulated into inert acceptance. If our goal is to raise our children to be people who can think and act for themselves, then we must be ready to let them try on and oppose all kinds of ideas and doctrines. It is only when we doubt the worth of our own convictions that we are unwilling to risk their survival in the market place of ideas. This does not mean that parents ought not to object to their child's more wild-eyed notions—even though the odds are very much against his ever trying to apply them practically. But parents must object on the plane of tough-minded reason, treating the child's discoveries as something worth discussing seriously and respectfully; ideas can be demolished logically in such a way that the adolescent's fragile and touchy self-esteem is not demolished with them. Parental flexibility need not, of course, interfere with definiteness in matters of discipline. And while standing firm on matters of essential principle, the parent can tolerate some questioning and even flouting of lesser regulations. In fact, in occasional minor matters, parents might sometimes even do well to overdo their strictness with the idea of provoking a certain amount of rebellion. If the parent can keep his own self-esteem out of it and then yield on a few issues to which he has no deep moral commitment, he gives the adolescent a needed opportunity to win some of his battles. Just as important, he gives him a chance to oppose something tangible and to propose tangible alternatives, which is the way constructive rebellions occur.

But while, in general, it is desirable that adolescents stand up to their parents, we can sometimes see cases where the stress and hostility are carried to extremes. This may be a sign that the parents are pressing too hard. More often, however, it means that earlier, unsolved developmental issues have been reactivated by the adolescent crisis. When this happens, outside intervention may be necessary: by a psychiatrist, a psychologist, a family counselor, or perhaps simply by a neutral party who can help both sides see the issues more clearly. Adolescence is peculiarly a time when stresses from earlier stages of development are laid bare (and it may also bring out latent conflicts between parents). When a youngster becomes overly suspicious of other people's attitudes and intentions, when he becomes unduly guarded, or negativistic, or excessively violent, there is reason to suspect that his difficulties date back before adolescence. Circumstances may have flawed his basic trust, he may have failed to develop an adequate degree of autonomy, he may have developed excessive early guilt about his body and its functions, he may have met social rejection, he may have become embroiled in parental discord. Often even these complicated difficulties work themselves out in the course of life. In general, what was done when the child was two or five or ten cannot be undone when he is fourteen or seventeen or twenty: it must be dealt with in terms of the new person he has become. Short of the near-redoing of intensive psychotherapy, his problems can only be solved at their new levels and in their new forms. To recognize their early sources, however, is to understand them more fully and to avoid the trap of taking immediate issues —whatever they may be—too literally.

In the matter of sex education, as in other areas, parents must build on earlier foundations. Factual education about sexual matters should be virtually complete before puberty. During adolescence, sex education must be addressed to the meaning of sexuality, to the meaning of the youngster's own body experiences, to answering his doubts and allaying his anxieties. In spite of all their knowledge, many children feel that they are sexually abnormal in some respect, and the only way of reassuring them about this is to let them know what people in general are like. In dealing with the adolescent, it is especially important to recognize that it is possible to be frank and realistic about sexuality without abandoning all moral standards. There can be no doubt that much of the old morality is unnecessarily rigid and, what is worse, blind to the facts that it is meant to govern. For one thing, there has long been a firm conviction that to inform children about sex was to "put ideas into their heads," and was equivalent to corrupting them. The ideas and urges, obviously, are already there, and the problem is to clarify them. It has now been amply demonstrated that having knowledge—and understanding—about sex enables a child to live more easily with his own sexuality. Understanding it, he is better able to manage it and is not forced by his need for knowledge into frantic and sometimes disastrous experiments. At adolescence, and even before, it becomes particularly important to understand the make-up and the feelings of the opposite sex, so that one can react more appropriately to them. Against a background of enlightened understanding, it is possible to put sexual morals on a more rational footing, giving sex its proper place in the integrated fabric of existence, and making of it neither the beginning and end of life nor something to be locked up in the dungeons of the mind. But this functional subordination of sexuality to a total scheme of life can be on either a sound or an unsound basis. For some individuals, sex becomes an instrument to be exploited, a means of manipulating other people. Used in this way, it is incompatible with true maturity.

The particular moral codes that parents try to impart to their children will vary in detail from family to family, from religion to religion, from one ethnic background to another, and according to social milieu, but all of these codes can find arguments on psychological grounds for sexual restraint prior to mature love relationships. As we have said, psychologists do not consider all "inhibitions" bad; it is not restraint but excessive and irrational guilt and anxiety that work havoc with people. True sexual morality is not to be instilled with threats and warnings. It is learned in day-to-day living with one's family. And a family in which the adolescent learns that the opposite sex is to be regarded as prey or as a natural enemy is not going to teach morality. Hence, as in other areas, morality arises from a sense of self-respect and respect for other people, and it is this that parents can impart to their adolescent children.

In later adolescence, the crucial issue is not sex, but love. Love is what the adolescent thinks he is in, or has just been in, or wants to be in, and which the parent views as premature. Most adolescent attachments are only provisionally permanent and are a necessary part of learning and growing. They are a preparation for mature love and the capacity for generously giving and receiving affection. Many parents are apprehensive lest young adolescents fall in love, and regard dating and going steady as an invitation to danger. Later on, of course, they become apprehensive if a youngster does not show signs of falling in love. Even when parents do not object in principle to their children's falling in love, it almost always seems to be with the wrong person. This is partly because, as we have suggested, the adolescent falls in love primarily with himself, projecting his idealistic side onto almost anyone who offers him the slightest encouragement. Needless to say, parental apprehensions about love between adolescents are based on a fear of sexual involvements. It should be made clear that love and sex are usually quite separate things up to late adolescence. For the boy, love is idealized, and his sexuality is felt as almost antagonistic to it. For the girl, her still diffuse sexuality is decidedly secondary to love.

Parents, unless they are dealing with an overly docile child, will find that they can make little headway in cultivating or suppressing or criticizing a particular relationship. They can try to expose their child to what they consider suitable love objects, and they can speak frankly about what they consider unsuitable ones. But if they can think back to their own adolescent pasts, they will recognize and sympathize with and respect the child's feelings, whatever they may think of the objects to which these feelings become attached. Interludes between attachments are the time to talk them over, and especially to try to make clear the differences between the ways the two sexes fall in love.

It is perhaps as well to state honestly that there are very real limits to what parents can do to influence the adolescent's development. Their work has to be done earlier, in infancy, in toddlerhood, in the preschool years, in the school years. Now they can serve as bulwarks and as good examples, or as sparring partners, or they can make the adolescent's life miserable, but his fate is now decided largely outside the home. For this reason, it may be appropriate to examine briefly the provisions society does and can make to help the adolescent across the threshold, beginning with schools.

School and Society

Many of the ways in which schools, neighborhood agencies, and society at large help the adolescent to maturity have been implied or explicitly stated in earlier sections. We should like here to make some additional recommendations, which should be understood as supplements to what we have said previously.

The shortcomings in our educational system are nowhere more glaring than in the secondary schools, and the prevailing attitude of adolescents toward school is a hostile acceptance of a necessary evil. In 1900, only 11.4 percent of people in the fourteen-seventeen age group were in school, compared with 80 percent in the mid-1950's.[3] The relatively tiny fraction of the population that used to go to high school was also a relatively homogeneous one, consisting largely of the most intelligent children and of those committed to a strictly academic curriculum in preparation for college. With the vast increase in enrollments (more than tenfold since 1900, from under 700,000 to over 7,000,000 [4]), the schools have recognized that this curriculum will not do for everybody. Many attempts have been made to introduce special programs for children of different intellectual abilities and vocational aims: trade schools, non-academic courses, non-college diplomas. And in recognition of the fact that this will be society's last formal opportunity to shape many of its future citizens and parents, courses such as Life Education, Education for Family Living, Citizenship Education, etc., have been added on. In general, the high school curriculum is an ill-assorted congeries with no overall plan. Each program is compartmentalized from all the others, with no agreement on what *all* the students need. The various programs are scaled to the students' several levels of vocational outlook, and have little to do with enriching their experience and helping them lead enjoyable, productive lives. There is a high degree of premature and preposterous specialization. The student in a primarily vocational program may miss out on the arts and sciences, and the student in an academic program may miss out on anything having to do with real people. Much of what is taught has been stripped of its true meaning. A course in mechanical skills may be focused specifically on providing operators needed for a particular kind of machine by an influential local industry; academic courses are usually oriented toward examinations and grades and the sharpening competition to get into college. Class work is sharply segregated from adolescent social life, and the latter consequently balloons out of all proportion; some high schools, indeed, seem to exist only for the sake of athletics and other extracurricular activities. It should be noted that the sense of pointlessness is not confined to students; all too many teachers do not really know why they want their students to learn what they are teaching—it is merely the teacher's job to make the students learn it. Most high schools are, in effect, involuntary hotbeds of anti-intellectualism because of the children's hostility and their tendency to see all learning as equivalent to the force-feeding they experience. Finally, the high schools are in the middle of a problem of infinite regress: colleges have to repair the deficiencies of high school preparation, high schools have to remedy the defects of grade school preparation, and the grade schools, presumably, have to make up for all the things the parents failed to do.

A number of recommendations are implicit in the foregoing criticisms. There are two additional points which we consider important. First of all, we should follow through on our assumption of the feasibility of universal education, and not undercut it from the start by the contrary assumption that only a small minority can take an academic education—in the best sense of *liberal* and *liberating* (see pages 255-265)—as a meaningful preparation for real life, and not merely as a collection of learned references. It is, after all, in literature, with its power of enlisting strong identifications, that we learn the profoundest lessons about human relationships and the nature of social institutions. The scientist and the philosopher have been grappling for years with exactly the cosmic problems that intrigue and frighten the adolescent. It is not selling the wisdom of the ages short to take time to give it some relevance for the adolescent and his concerns. But it does take good teaching. If only the student's long-lost interest and enthusiasm can be reawakened, probably remedial teaching at each level will become much less of a burden. The second major point we should like to make is that the school should harness the adolescent social spirit to the job of teaching and learning. Students can be allowed to talk to and teach each other in the classroom, and not only in the debating club—indeed, if it were possible for teachers to sit in on adolescent bull sessions, they might accomplish several times as much as they do in school. Needless to say, the intellectual spread among adolescents is very wide, and not all of them are up to all the high-powered education we advocate. But we believe that more of them could benefit by it than we are usually inclined to credit, provided their antipathies could be dispelled.

School, of course, is not the only service society provides for the adolescent, but the other resources are all too few. In addition to school, he needs responsible, non-family sources he can turn to for information and advice. To provide some of these sources is now the responsibility of the already overburdened school, and it might be more effective to center them—or some of them—in community youth agencies. If, on the other hand, such functions are left in the school, they should be understood as extra functions different from the primary one of education, and specific organizational and budgetary provisions should be made for them. For one thing, there is a need for guidance at the junior high school level. The young adolescent often needs someone he can turn to who can tell him what is happening to him in terms of physical, emotional, and social growth, what course it will follow, what is expected of him, and what he can do about it. He may want someone to advise him on family problems, someone who might also be available to local parents who need help in dealing with their adolescent children. In later adolescence, he needs vocational guidance. This should not be of the limited sort now provided in all too many high schools, where the individual takes a battery of aptitude and interest and group intelligence tests, and the examiner puts them into a machine, turns a crank, and produces a prescription for an occupational specialty. The adolescent needs a counselor who can give him an idea of the variety and scope of existing occupations—including areas the adolescent may never have heard of—and the preliminary steps required, and who can help him plan both imaginatively and realistically for the future. Girls, too, need help in breaking out of the clerk-stenographer-nurse-housewife choice they often seem confined to. Good counseling can, if a girl so desires, help her find ways to divide herself between parenthood and further education or between parenthood and a career, planning her timing so that she can be with her children at the points where they need her most.

The neighborhood, whether through school activities, after-school activities, community centers, grange halls, or whatever, must help fill the vacuum of the adolescent years. And it must, moreover, fill it in

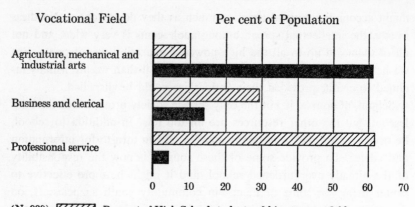

Vocational Field   Per cent of Population

A comparison of high school students' vocational aspirations with employment opportunities in the United States. (Adapted by Horrocks, J. E. [The Psychology of Adolescence, Boston: Houghton Mifflin, 1951, p. 506] from Bradley, W. A., "Correlates of vocational preferences," Genetic Psychology Monographs, 1943, 28, 99-169.)

ways meaningful to adolescents. If, as the facts indicate, the adolescent is not a full-time worker, if he cannot yet raise a family, if he must turn away from his parents and escape from his home, if he must find friends of both sexes, then society has no grounds for complaint—when things go wrong—because it has given him little alternative other than delinquency or boredom, or, for a few, full-time attention to school work. If society does not make provisions for his leisure, he will have to improvise his own recreation, which he does not always do wisely, or have it provided for him by people intent on exploiting him. As we have said, adolescence is a cultural invention, and, like most aspects of culture, it was not deliberately planned or achieved. Real social invention is needed, however, to provide for the needs and energies created by the prolongation of childhood status and the denial of adult status. In spite of good beginnings in a few communities, society has so far done little about this situation except to cry death to the dope peddlers, deplore the state of the younger generation, and threaten to punish parents. It should be evident from all that we have said in this chapter that adolescence is not a problem for parents alone, even though they may bear the brunt of it.

We have already implied that, beyond the limits of what each neighborhood and community can do, there needs to be a general revision of thinking about adolescence. Perhaps it is within our province to offer a few tentative suggestions in this direction. Although legislators and social planners may sometimes see that problems of narcotics addiction, delinquency, reckless driving, high school sex clubs, and so forth, are all related to adolescence, their piecemeal attack on such problems indicates that they have failed to grasp their psychological interconnectedness. It is possible that a certain amount of overall planning based on and leading to a clearer definition of adolescence would be profitable. One thing that could be done is to work for greater consistency in our legal and social definitions of when adolescence ends and adulthood begins. After what we have said, it hardly seems necessary to labor the point that some convergence among the various symbols of maturity would help both the adolescent and the people around him feel less ambiguous about where he stands at any given time, and would give the adolescent less to rail at in the inconsistencies of the adult world.

A second and perhaps more novel possible step might be to acknowledge that adolescence is here to stay, and instead of trying to minimize it, to go further in the opposite direction, formalizing, recognizing, and giving status—if need be, legal status—to it as a period of intermediate maturity. Such a step would give force to our feeling that adolescence is a necessary period of apprenticeship during which the individual has certain clearly defined privileges and responsibilities. The authors believe, on the basis of their observations of adolescent behavior, that many adolescents reach hard for adult status simply because the only alternative is child status, and that they would gladly settle for something in between. A fair example of how this intermediate status could work is shown in the practice in some states of awarding a junior driving license. Another relevant example, which needs further thinking through, is making provision for limited employment during a certain period in the teens. Some states have already done this to some extent, but our child labor laws need to be re-examined, taking into account not only the need to protect the child from exploitation but also the adolescent's legitimate need to find a sense of achievement and status through work. Our school-leaving regulations may also deserve a re-examination. It seems to us by no means obvious that a fixed, arbitrary age tells us whether or not a youngster should be in school. We have already seen the beginnings of an attitude of allowing the adolescent the maturity he can grasp (without adult insistence that it be all or none) in the growing number of marriages of older adolescents and young adults, many of whom, because of a need for extended education, remain dependent on their parents. Parents are now less inclined than formerly to exact the right to control their married sons and daughters in return for financial support. Married college students, who were once firmly excluded from the campus, are now a common sight. In sum, many conflicts between the aspirations of adolescents and the restrictions of adults might be removed if society at large were to recognize and dignify adolescence as a special intermediate period. We are not suggesting that we take all the *Sturm und Drang* out of adolescence, but only that we give it a chance to be the creative ferment of growth which it could be.

A Definition of Maturity

Development does not stop in adulthood. There are, however, two senses in which adults continue to develop. The first of these has to do with the routine, inevitable changes that come with age even after adolescence. In terms of physical development, full maturity is not reached until the early twenties, after which adulthood up to the time of senescence is something of a plateau. In some respects, such as acuity of hearing, a slow decline sets in even in adolescence. From the twenties on, most physical changes can be thought of as aging rather than as maturation. Gradually, but beginning rather early, reaction times become slower, physical vigor and stamina are reduced, there is a drop in sensory acuity, the male's sexual potency is lessened, recuperative powers are lower, the waistline bulges, and hair turns gray. There is a shift in family roles as the individual becomes in turn spouse, parent, grandparent, and oldster. The individual may be moving slowly or rapidly up the ladder of success. His position keeps changing relative to his fellow workers, organizations in which he takes part, and the community at large. This holds true even if his life appears to be at a standstill, since the people around him are changing, too. Sooner or later, everybody retires, and this calls for further adjustments. With age, friendship patterns change, recreational tastes shift, and the world changes complexion.

In this section, however, we are concerned primarily with the other sense in which development may go on, growth toward *true maturity*. Indeed, we have throughout this book been talking about development not only in terms of increasing size and a widening range of capacities, but also in terms of such aspects of maturing as increasing self-integration and more effective functioning as a person. Perhaps the distinction as it applies to adulthood can best be expressed by the difference between the person who feels that his present existence is only a prelude to something yet to come (or an epilogue to something past), and the person who, while looking forward to what the future will bring, is not *waiting* for it; by the difference between the person who panics at the thought of retirement and the one who can hardly wait for the freedom it will give him (or even the person to whom his work is so rewarding that he is going to carry it on regardless of retirement regulations); by the difference between the person who spends his old age as a fossil and the one who spends it as a sage. This second kind of maturing means that the individual keeps on finding new things to be curious and enthusiastic about, that he goes on learning, that he will continue to find something fresh and new in the world every time he looks at it. Maturity in this sense does not come to everybody, and we know no way of guaranteeing that it will, but we propose at least to try to describe the kind of person who keeps on growing psychologically after he reaches adulthood and even long after his tissues have begun to fail him.

Many such models or goals for maturity have been offered. The present authors are not happy about most of them, and have some feeling that to define maturity of this special kind is a hopeless undertaking. Nevertheless, they are inclined to try, in full recognition of the risks. The first of these is the danger of their sharing the "psychologist's error": most psychologists have a strongly human-centered, individual-centered orientation and place great stress on verbal skills, social skills, social consciousness, intellectual attainment, and scientific or artistic creativity. They are inclined to overlook other styles and areas of achievement— they may praise the mechanic's craftsmanship, the clerk's conscientiousness, the businessman's acumen, the athlete's agility, but when they think of accomplishment, the parade of ghostly figures that passes before their eyes is made up of the likes of Socrates, Galileo, Leonardo da Vinci, Voltaire, Jefferson, Goethe, Justice Holmes, Schweitzer, and Einstein. Second, too many of the models for maturity which have been offered seem to be in large part reflections of their authors' own personalities, saying, in effect, "See how wonderful I am," or else, "This is how I wish I could be." Third, criteria for maturity often consist of sets of pious preachments which clothe in toplofty sentiments moralistic imperatives addressed to lesser men. Finally, standards for maturity are all too likely to seem to force everybody into a single, narrow mold, doing violence to the diversity of personality that we have been talking about and extolling throughout this book.

The authors will try to avoid these pitfalls and offer a description of maturity that takes into account man's frailties and imperfections and the variety of individual tastes and traits and endowments. Our procedure has been, first, to think of and to generalize about persons, historical and contemporary, who, in our view, have gone furthest toward effective functioning in all spheres of life—at work and at play, in relations with the world at large, with neighbors, co-workers, superiors, subordinates, with friends and families, and with themselves. (While some of these individuals might agree that we did well to select them, we have not consulted them and we feel sure that those still living would prefer to remain anonymous.) Second, we have borrowed selectively from those authors who have dealt with the nature of maturity, relying especially on the work of Maslow.[5] The result inevitably will reflect the authors' personal tastes and philosophies. In point of fact, however, there seems to be a good deal of agreement on this subject among various writers, whether theologians, psychologists, healers, or philosophers.

If an individual is going to grow toward the kind of maturity we are talking about, he will find it helpful to have secure developmental, preadult underpinnings—he should not have to deflect his energies into refighting childhood battles or nursing old hurts. Maturity can only be built on sound foundations. Unless the child has been able to establish basic trust, his world is quicksand. Without basic trust, he cannot establish autonomy, the trust in himself that enables him, by successive stages, to separate his identity from his parents and then from his contemporaries and stand on his own two feet as an integrated—both internally and to society—individual. The starting point of maturity is reached when, without rupturing his basic emotional ties to the environment, the individual is nevertheless free to move about within the framework they provide, when he no longer has at every moment to question his own identity, his own wishes and aspirations, when his freedom is no longer something to strive for but something to count on and to use responsibly. It is necessary to point out, however, that many people do survive and recover from developmental setbacks along the way, sometimes with therapeutic help and sometimes on their own. But they must somehow get beyond their childhood conflicts. While the task of

wl
si
in
of
wl
an
ab
to
ac
ci
in
int
us
an
to
for
inf
me
ex
ev
suf
of
val
ne
aw
see
suc

l
unl
wit
he
wel
ges
is h
imp
give
alte
and
spo
his

maturity is made harder for such people, they occasionally do especially good, if delayed, jobs of growing up. Adversity, although hardly
to be recommended, does sometimes seem to have a strengthening
effect. We should make clear that growing out of childhood does not
mean abolishing one's past. Apart from the pleasure that childhood
recollections can bring, or the relief one feels in looking back at a
closed chapter of turmoil, having sound foundations means that one can
carry into adulthood those childhood qualities of freshness, enthusiasm,
and emotional involvement that stand a person in good stead throughout life.

When a person can live with his past without being bogged down in
it, he remains adaptable, *capable of continued change*. It is important
to specify, however, what kinds of further change are and are not possible in adulthood. At birth, the individual, subject to constitutional
limitations, is capable of following a great many developmental paths.
Psychologically, at least, he could equally well become a Kaffir, an
Eskimo, a Japanese, or a proper Bostonian. By the end of infancy,
however, he is already irrevocably committed to a particular line (still,
however, with many possible branchings) of development. If he has
started off as an American, he can never go completely back and get a
fresh start as a Samoan. While he might successfully live in Samoa,
he could never think and act exactly as a Samoan does. Similarly, as
the effects and acquisitions of each stage of development are consolidated during childhood, certain doors are closed behind the individual,
and new vistas open up ahead. The only way the individual can "go
back" is via a pathological regression, and this does not mean a return
to early plasticity. By the time he has reached adulthood, the individual's choices are strictly limited by where he has been and what he is
intrinsically capable of becoming, but they are nevertheless incredibly
rich in terms of the new varieties of experience that will become available to him. It is important to note, too, that as the individual matures
he has an increasingly greater say in what further lines of development
he chooses to follow. His early development depended on an accident
of birth and the play of circumstances, but as he moves toward personality integration he develops a species of *self-determination* (it is no
longer fashionable to speak of free will) and becomes able to accept or
refuse the choices offered to him, and, what is more, to invent new lines
of development independent of immediate circumstances. He becomes,
within certain obvious limits, the master of his own destiny.

Another characteristic of becoming mature is the development of

them—he knows where they are and what they are doing—and can act freely without being afraid that some hidden force will take possession of him. The person who tries to avoid or deny his own feelings must, by contrast, perpetually keep watch lest they spring out unexpectedly. This vigilance not only restricts his freedom to act but, what is more, is often in vain. While he is patrolling his defenses in one area, the caged enemy is liable to erupt as an uncontrolled impulse some place else. The integrated person can without dismay entertain notions which, if translated into action, would land him in prison or a mental hospital. Such eventualities might serve to restrain him from acting on his fantasies, but the really important deterrent lies in his knowledge that to carry out his more primitive impulses would probably bring harm to somebody else. Because he is human, it costs him something to keep his thoughts to himself, but far less than the person who has to fight with unknown forces. Being used to his own feelings, the individual is better able to recognize and formulate creative insights when they occur. Most important, a knowledge of his own feelings gives him insight into the feelings of others, and is in addition the surest guarantee we know of against projecting his own feelings onto the environment. It should be made clear that the person headed for maturity is not immune to guilt and anxiety. But he can keep them within bounds, accept them as part of his human nature, and even utilize their motive power instead of harboring them as free-floating energies.

It follows that the mature individual has to be able to live comfortably with his own body, whether it be strong or weak, handsome or ugly, healthy or failing. This does not mean that he fails to groom it or to tend to its ills, but that he can be at ease about it, not wasting his time in futile laments or hypochondria. He can use it as his means of contact with the world, as the vehicle of his feeling and sensation. And just as the individual can never wholly separate himself from his concrete standpoint in time and space and society, so he is always to some extent the captive of his own body. This means that he experiences it both from the inside and the outside, that it is both his and an organism with an existence of its own, that his self-knowledge can never be absolute but contains the same ambiguities as his experience of outer reality. The individual who would become mature has to learn to tolerate ambiguity in himself as well as in the outside world, not in a spirit of futility but in one of plowing ahead regardless.

If the individual's growth toward maturity is rooted in the positive emotional bonds of early infancy, *human relationships* are going to have a high priority for him. In his own life, he may be concerned either with the people closest to him or with people en masse, or even with the fate of unborn generations, but he cannot help having a sense of affiliation with humanity at large. He feels this way in full recognition of human stupidity, perverseness, weakness, and evil. Indeed, knowing his own nature as he does, he is likely to know that human beings are a mixed lot but, all in all, worth bothering about. Needless to say, he will not esteem all people equally, and recognizes gradations of affiliation, from profound involvement with those closest to him through less acute fellow-feeling for those at a distance to real hostility for those who threaten humane principles. But whether his existence is centered in family life or not, he needs and seeks close human attachments. He will be able to give and receive affection freely, without embarrassment or fear for his own integrity. He learns to adapt to various kinds of human relationships and roles: of lover to lover, of spouse to spouse, of parent to child, of man to woman or woman to man, of friend to friend, of student or of teacher. He will find out that close personal involvements cost something in emotional wear and tear, in responsibility for those he is involved with, in loss of freedom, but he gladly pays the price. Most important, in his relationships with people he will become better able to react to the people themselves, not to some image of them formed out of his own needs and character. Similarly, he will want to be close to them for the sake of what they are, and not merely for the sake of the way they reflect him back to himself. When he can truly perceive people and be aware of their awarenesses, he will learn a respect for their integrity—or a compassion for their lack of it—that will forever restrain him from frivolous or selfish meddling with other people's lives. He will not have to go looking for affection. Because he is at ease with himself, because he is open to experience, because he has opinions and enthusiasms, people will want to be with him, to share in his excitement of life. Because he respects himself and other people, other people will respect him.

The person equipped with the human sensitivities that make for maturity will usually have a powerful *concern with social problems* and ways of alleviating them. This does not, however, necessarily imply that he engages directly in working for a new order on either a collective or individual scale. There are other approaches to advancing human welfare than working in the field of social reform or education or mental health, or than performing the functions of a "good citizen," such as voting, or joining the P.T.A., if his temperament inclines him away from these particular activities. One of the most effective forms of good citizenship is to be a sound person, part of a sound family, a good neighbor, and an influence for human charity on the level of personal dealings. An honest businessman—or an effective craftsman—can often accomplish as much, simply by being what he is, as a host of petition-circulators. Or he may function both ways.

For all his social-mindedness, for all his savoring of human relationships, the maturing individual is not dependent on always having company. Typically, he not only is able to tolerate but requires a certain amount of *solitude* in which to think his own thoughts and enjoy his own company. Furthermore, he likes to devote a certain amount of time to unsocial activities: reading, listening to music, gardening— whatever his tastes dictate. This capacity for entertaining himself, for drawing on his own resources, in fact contributes to his social life. It means that he has something to offer people. His wit, his freedom from pretense, even his occasional idiosyncratic crankiness, all the qualities that make him good company are the reflections of the qualities that enable him to be self-sufficient.

The kind of person we are talking about, with his sensitivity to other people's feelings and his respect for other people's integrity, is almost inevitably committed to a *democratic code of ethics*. But he is democratic in a deeply personal sense, and not merely ideologically. He has a sense of humility balanced by self-esteem, and he knows that there are satisfactions to be gained and things to be learned from almost everybody. One of the things that make him interesting to other people is the fact that he is himself interested in what others have to say. And these other people are not only the accepted authorities and pundits. The person headed for maturity is not going to be impressed by high estate or repelled by a low one. Neither, however, will he automatically and perversely disdain the high and espouse the low. Just as the small child judges people less by their station in life than by their emotional warmth, so our subject judges people by their vitality, their strength, their flexibility, their emotional richness, and their honesty—in short, by the virtues he himself strives for—rather than by their objective attainments and social position. Indeed, his own social position may be rather humble—enough admirable people have lived in slums and slave cabins to demonstrate that maturity is not a prerogative of the privileged few.

It is apparent that the person who is becoming mature *does not accept values ready-made*. He is likely to be quite unconventional in his opinions, or to hold them for unconventional reasons or in unconventional combinations. He is looking for a rational, consistent, humane, and realistic system of values, and is not likely to be happy with codes that represent the accretion of habits, traditions, superstitions, or prejudices, of outworn assumptions about human nature and the structure of reality. To look for a set of values of his own means, in effect, to try to extricate himself from his own culture. This can be done only to a limited extent, of course. If the mature individual finds fault with American values, beliefs, and practices, he does it in an American sort of way. He may become an internationalist, but he can never wholly become psychologically an Englishman or a Swiss. Even people who live abroad and come to feel completely at home in their new surroundings present to the natives no problem in recognition as outlanders. Nevertheless, the mature individual may be able to bring a fresh view to standards and assumptions that other people take for granted, and in any case he will be willing to challenge the obvious. And a liberation of this sort is an important part of mature flexibility, creativeness, and the sense of humor that make life worth living.

On the other hand, his original ideas about values are likely to bring the individual into conflict with his society. Most mature individuals want to live within society, even when its goals conflict with theirs. They do not feel it necessary to advertise their emancipated views by going barefoot in the city streets or by refusing to pay their taxes. The individual has to learn when to conform and when not to conform, when to speak out and when to remain silent. His values must be so structured and scaled that he can distinguish between what is central and inviolable and what is peripheral and expendable—or at least postponable. He has to balance his beliefs against his natural wish to lead a quiet, comfortable life, doing his work and enjoying his family and friends. Mostly, of course, among one's friends one can freely express opinions which, stated in print, might look dangerous and subversive. This is because friends see the individual's opinions in the context of their own awareness of his sincerity, decency, humor, balance, and humaneness. Nevertheless, there is always the possibility that the person who tries to think for himself will run seriously afoul of public opinion and be forced to choose between recanting or suffering the consequences of his folly. Since the individualistic individual finds life pleasant, he will not enter upon martyrdom lightly. Nevertheless, he will by definition be committed to certain principles—religious, political, intellectual, ethical, or whatever—that take precedence over his own existence. Obviously, if he can live and struggle for his principles, he would rather do so, but if there is no choice but to abandon them or perish, he may well be willing to die for them. Mature people, in their everyday affairs, are probably brave and timid in about the same proportion as everybody else, but they generally have in common a streak of stubborn moral courage that appears when the chips are down.

To live realistically (which by no means forbids the conscious exploitation and enjoyment of fantasy) means to live in *consciousness of one's own mortality*. If this becomes a morbid preoccupation, it is no better than pretending that one will live forever. But held in perspective, the ability to face the certain expectation of death, of a final limit to one's period of achievement, lends a valuable urgency and importance to what one does, and helps keep one's values in focus and proportion. In general, the mature person has a healthy respect for danger, without being panicked into fleeing from commitments.

Obviously, we have not been painting a design for happiness, or at least happiness in the sense of surcease from turmoil and travail. There are built-in pains and penalties in becoming mature, a few of which we have already mentioned. The individual knows that certain things lie beyond his power of decision or influence, and that he simply has to tolerate them. But as an active person, he would prefer to make decisions wherever he can, instead of merely letting things happen. Because he wants to weigh the evidence and the outcomes, he may find some decisions hard to make—which can be trying for other people as well as for himself. Nevertheless, he knows that he has to go on choosing between alternatives, that each alternative costs him something, and there are things he will never be able to do and experience. He also knows that there are things he will never be able to do again, that he can never recapture his youth or relive his first encounters with certain experiences. He knows that his integrity is continually threatened by practical demands, by temptations, by concessions and compromises, by conflicting values, and can only be preserved at the cost of some psychic strain. If his ideas are too much out of joint with the temper of the times, he may feel lonely and cut off from companionship.

In spite of these drawbacks, he knows that the only real rewards of life come with continued growth, and that there is no room in the one material life he has for major regrets. As Solon pointed out, one can only judge whether a man is happy when he dies. Too many people come to the end of the line with a sense of "Wait! Not yet! I was just going to begin!" The individual who has approached maturity can feel that he has loved and been loved, has done his work, has made his mark on people, and, although he wishes there were more time, that he has made the most of what there was.

In sum, the adult with a capacity for true maturity is one who has grown out of childhood without losing childhood's best traits. He has retained the basic emotional strengths of infancy, the stubborn autonomy of toddlerhood, the capacity for wonder and pleasure and playfulness of the preschool years, the capacity for affiliation and the intellectual curiosity of the school years, and the idealism and passion of adolescence. He has incorporated these into a new pattern of development dominated by adult stability, wisdom, knowledge, sensitivity to other people, responsibility, strength, and purposiveness.

NOTES (Starred item is recommended for further reading.)

[1] *New York Times,* March 5, 1951.

[2] Levy and Munroe, *The Happy Family,* p. 12 and passim.

[3] Fund for the Advancement of Education, *Teachers for Tomorrow,* p. 52.

[4] *Ibid.,* p. 50.

*[5] Maslow, A. H., "Self-actualizing people: A study of psychological health," *Personality Symposia,* 1950, 1, 11-34. The concept of "self-actualization" is also found in Goldstein, K., *The Organism,* New York: American Book Co., 1939.

FOR FURTHER READING

U. S. Children's Bureau, *The Adolescent in Your Family,* Washington 25: U. S. Government Printing Office. A sensitive, sympathetic discussion of the practical problems of adolescence.

Farnham, M. F., *The Adolescent,* New York: Harper, 1951. A psychoanalytically oriented guide for parents.

Allport, Gordon, *Becoming,* New Haven: Yale University Press, 1955. A concise, graphic statement of a humanistic philosophy of personality development.

CHAPTER 13

Disturbances in Development

Introduction

In this chapter, we shall describe briefly certain deviant forms that development may take and some of the disturbances of normal functioning which may arise during childhood. We are concerned here primarily with minor and major *psychopathology*—psychological abnormalities—although we shall necessarily have to discuss those physical abnormalities which have psychological consequences, as well as some of the physical consequences of psychological disturbances. It is not always easy to draw a distinction between "normal" and "abnormal," but, as a rule of thumb, we are here concerned with those children who will need special help in order to get along in the world or who may never be able to lead independent lives. All such troubled or inadequate children will display aberrant functioning most prominently in some one particular area, although closer examination usually shows that behavior in other areas is also involved. Because psychopathology is a pervasive matter, neither diagnosis nor treatment can properly be focused on a single symptom—although parents' (and other adults') worries about how a child is developing are often phrased in terms of what to do about thumb-sucking, about bed-wetting, about stealing, or "about" other specific problems.

As we have seen in previous chapters, at every stage of development there are some ways of behaving which by adult standards may seem odd or disturbing but which are wholly appropriate to the age, and we shall not elaborate further on these in this chapter. Here we shall deal with those manifestations which parents and teachers may become aware of and which they should be troubled about. But since such manifestations can be confused with what is developmentally normal, this chapter should be read against the background provided by the account of development given in earlier chapters.

In the discussion that follows, we shall try to say something about *causes* as well as try to describe certain conditions. In general, a given case of psychopathology can be traced to one or more sets of determinants: faulty hereditary endowment; damage of the nervous system before or after birth; physical disabilities which make the child vulnerable to emotional disturbance; or to situational factors, such as a particular disturbing event, a lack of one or more important ingredients in a child's upbringing, or the general emotional climate in which the child lives—a set of circumstances which make it impossible for him to be at peace with the world. (In a later section, we shall have something to say about particular kinds of environmental situations conducive to abnormal development.) But it is well to admit frankly that we often cannot account for disturbances of behavior and development. Even where physical causes can be clearly demonstrated, these often become so compounded by their psychological and situational consequences that it is impossible to disentangle the part each plays in the child's behavior. In some cases, there seems to be no sufficient cause whatever, no matter how exhaustively we look into the child's history.

We cannot hope, within the compass of a short chapter, to discuss the entire field of psychopathology. Instead, we have chosen to point out a few of the more common, more striking, and more intensively studied kinds of abnormality that arise during childhood and adolescence. We shall take each stage of development in turn and describe the phenomena likely to be seen first or most frequently at that stage— although the physical and psychological origins of some may lie much further back. Although the temptation is strong to include information about treatment and about home and educational management of such children, we shall in general do so only in the most summary fashion.

Infancy

Most of the psychological problems that appear during infancy are of physical origin. Certain of these are hereditary in nature, such as various forms of mental deficiency due to malformations of the brain or to abnormal metabolic patterns. These are often accompanied by visible physical malformations. It might be noted, however, that not all hereditary defects appear at birth; some (such as Huntington's chorea) may not be manifested until middle age. Nor are all psychological disorders of the neonate or infant hereditary; some are the product of intra-uterine influences. We have already mentioned how certain viruses, Rh antibodies, and toxins can be communicated to and injure the unborn baby. In some children, an injury or oxygen deprivation during the birth process is responsible for physical and psychological defects. It is possible that cases of all these kinds are becoming more frequent, not because they occur any more often than in past years but because improved medical care has increased their chances of survival.

Severe mental deficiency often becomes evident early in infancy. Mental inadequacy is of many sorts and degrees. The traditional classification, which is unsatisfactory but which can serve as a convenient reference, categorizes the intellectually handicapped, in order of increasing defectiveness, as dull normal, borderline, moron, imbecile, and idiot. These categories are strictly quantitative and make little allowance for qualitative differences between groups or individuals. They are linked to intelligence test scores (intelligence quotients—IQ's—or mental ages —MA's), which do not tell us about how an individual's functioning is patterned, which have limited reliability, especially in the early years, and which reflect a great many factors other than intellectual capacity, such as willingness to co-operate in testing, emotional upsets, learning opportunities, and cultural differences. The dividing line between moderate and severe mental defectiveness is set at IQ 50 (average equals 100), with imbecility and idiocy falling below this arbitrary cutting point and all the other classes above. In any event, the more subtle determinations of mental capacity cannot be made until long after infancy. The severely retarded infant usually has poor muscle tone, is inactive and emotionally unresponsive, and develops very slowly, so that he may still be lying helpless while his contemporaries are scuttling about on all fours or even toddling. Although it is not at all hard to detect marked retardation, at least by late infancy, intermediate and slight degrees of mental deficiency are very hard to detect in this period, when rate of motor development is the chief measure available. As a further caution, we should recall that there is a wide *normal* range in the rate of development during infancy, and many normal and even superior children develop very slowly during their first six or twelve months but, in their own good time, catch up. In general, if a baby is reasonably active and alert, shows good emotional responses to people and situations, and if his pediatrician is satisfied with his progress, he is probably normal. Even in the rare cases where an apparently sound baby is not normal, there is no way of knowing it this early, and he will have lost nothing by being treated in a normal way—retarded children, too, need tender, loving care.

The parents of a visibly defective infant will early have to face the problem of whether to keep him at home or place him in an institution. This is by no means an easy decision. Although many parents have found it possible to have their mentally deficient children live at home and attend special day schools (which are becoming more common), this may sometimes be done only at great psychological cost. Parents may become overly concerned with the welfare of the defective child, to the neglect of their own interests or of those of other siblings. They may experience resentment of the defective child, and guilt over their resentment. They may feel ashamed in the eyes of the neighbors, although people are nowadays more accepting and understanding of abnormality than previously. Finally, as defective children grow older, their irresponsibility may lead them into trouble. Nevertheless, their main hope of a satisfactory life lies in the kind of emotional warmth and acceptance that they can only find at home.

Among the many forms of mental defect, one of the more common is what Sarason calls the "garden variety," which, because the child is outwardly normal physically, can be detected only in late infancy or beyond, as developmental failures accumulate.[1] Other, specific forms, however, have clear-cut physical stigmata which enable them to be identified very early. A specific type of mental defect which is fairly common and which can usually be diagnosed early in infancy is called *mongolism.* This name comes from one of the identifying stigmata of the condition, an extra fold of skin over the eyelid, similar to that seen in Asian peoples. (It should not be necessary to add that the presence of the mongolian fold in Asians says nothing whatever about their mental capacities.) Mongolism, because its symptoms appear so early, was once thought to be hereditary. Now its origins, along with those of many other forms of mental inadequacy formerly thought to be inherited, are believed to lie at least partially in prenatal, intra-uterine influences. Some authorities, in fact, have pointed to the eighth week of pregnancy as the critical period in which the intra-uterine disturbance responsible for mongolism has its effect.[2] Mongolism is an affliction of the total organism, and some of its other physical signs, including some that do not appear until after infancy, are short stature and slight build; a skull flattened in back; late-appearing, irregularly spaced teeth; a thick, protruding, stubby, fissured tongue; general motor retardation; and various physiological defects including sexual immaturity. In rare cases, mongoloids attain the moron level of intelligence (IQ 50-70), but more are considerably lower. Classically, mongoloids are described as placid, cheerful, and easy to manage, although irresponsible. In point of fact, however, they are sometimes mischievous and irritable; they are often inveterate show-offs. Until recently, the average age of death in mongoloids was fourteen, often of structural weakness in the heart or of the respiratory infections to which they are highly susceptible. Medical progress, however, has worked to their advantage as well as everyone else's, and the average life expectancy of mongoloids is now twenty years. At the same time, new techniques for educating them are being tried with some degree of success.

Another condition found in infancy is *cerebral palsy,* the most frequent form of which is called *spastic paralysis.* Cerebral palsy is associated with injury to the motor centers of the brain at or before birth. Characteristically, the victim's muscles are innervated in conflicting and unco-ordinated patterns, so that he has great difficulty in walking, speaking, eating, and fine manipulations. His body is often racked into twisted postures by muscle tensions, he may involuntarily grimace a great deal, and he shows considerable superfluous movements, sometimes in fixed, repetitive patterns. Because of their unusual appearance, which to the ignorant often connoted insanity or feeble-mindedness, cerebral palsied children used to be hidden away from public view. Cerebral palsy often has secondary effects in addition to motor difficulties: disturbances of perception, epileptic seizures, mental handicap, and so forth. However, these secondary effects are by no means inevitable. Far from being mentally deficient, some cerebral palsy victims become brilliant scholars. Because of the cerebral palsied child's poor motor control, it is often difficult to assess his mental capacity, although special tests for this purpose have been and are being devised.[3] Furthermore, the physical and intellectual problems of cerebral palsy are often complicated by emotional ones. Both the child and his parents may be subject to considerable embarrassment and frustration, and it is not always easy to sort out the contributions of intellectual deficiencies, physical helplessness, and personality difficulties to the victim's functioning. Like other forms of brain damage, cerebral palsy, when it does lead to impaired intellectual as well as motor functioning, may be manifested in either a generalized mental deficit or a specialized one such as inability to learn language. It sometimes happens, in the case of brain injuries this early in life, especially when they are relatively restricted, that undamaged portions of the brain can take over the function of damaged ones, permitting some degree of recovery. However, some effects of severe congenital accidents probably persist throughout life. Nevertheless, the cerebral palsied are no longer automatically relegated to the scrap heap, and new ways of educating them and training them are being tried. They have benefited especially from the physical rehabilitation techniques that have been elaborated and perfected in response to the impetus provided by the need to help wounded war veterans and poliomyelitis victims. Special training for the cerebral palsied often enables them to achieve some competence in speaking, walking, and various manipulatory skills, and many victims can go on to an independent life, including a job, marriage, and parenthood.

Marked *sensory defects,* notably deafness and blindness (there are also rare ones such as reduced sensitivity to smell, touch, or pain), can usually be identified in infancy. Deafness and blindness are not absolutes, but occur in various gradations of severity and in selective losses of sensitivity. In infancy, however, only the more severe impairments are likely to become evident. We should also make explicit that such terms as "deaf-and-dumb" and "deaf-mute" are misnomers. The deaf are perfectly capable of speaking, but because they cannot imitate sounds they do not hear, they need special speech instruction. If, by the age of a few months, a child shows no reaction (usually a startle-response or crying) to loud sounds, does not turn his head or stop crying at the sound of the parent's voice or footsteps, or if he begins babbling and then discontinues it, there is reason to suspect deafness. Assuming that it has been established in a particular case of deafness that the deafness itself cannot be remedied, there is still treatment that can begin in infancy—and the earlier, the better—to help the *child* rather than the *deafness.*[4] Recent studies have shown that even a babe in arms can wear and benefit by a hearing aid.[5] It may bring him sounds—or at least gross noises and speech rhythms—and prepare him to use his residual hearing (usually present even in the so-called totally deaf) to the best advantage possible. Furthermore, the parents by talking to him while caring for him, by immersing him in speech sounds, can help develop a notion of speech, stimulate him to use his own voice, and even foster a kind of natural lip reading. Needless to say, if this procedure becomes forced or strained or insistent, or if the parent's voice is loud enough for the child to hear only when raised in anger or rebuke, its value will be diminished. Any such program, of course, has to be carried out in ways congenial to the parents' own temperaments. Blindness may be accompanied by anomalies in the appearance of the eyes that make it more readily detectable than hearing loss. Even when these are lacking, however, blindness will show up early in the behavior of the infant. If, by the age of a few months, a child's eyes continue not to be co-ordinated with each other (eyes that cross or that move independently of each other are quite normal in early infancy), if he does not turn toward lights or try to follow moving objects with his eyes, or reach out for things in front of him, or try to focus on things that are brought close, if he does not shut his eyes against overbright lights or respond to people's gestures, then blindness can be suspected. Blind children are often slow in walking and talking, but this does not ordinarily represent any basic or pervasive deficiency. Like deaf children, blind children can profit by early help. Most important in the case of the blind child is the emotional warmth and acceptance that makes him secure enough to want to move around and explore the tactual-kinesthetic-auditory-gustatory-olfactory environment he is going to live in. Parents should not forget the senses that the child *does* have; in fact, it is not unusual to find that the parents of a blind child have a tendency to shout at him, as though he could not hear, either.

Blindness and deafness, it should be evident, have psychological repercussions far beyond the deprivation of a single sense modality. We should point out, however, that the child born deaf or blind does not have the experience of loss and frustration that comes to those who lose their sight or hearing later in life. The deaf person will have difficulty with that most human of skills, spoken language, and the blind person will be restricted in physical mobility, participation in active pursuits, and in access to written language. We should also point out that the very complexion of a person's experience is changed by blindness and deafness. The world is given to normal people through their senses working in combination, and it is difficult to imagine—but easy to demonstrate experimentally—how much our visual experience depends on hearing, and vice versa. We have only to consider how much spoken language depends for its full meaning on gesture and facial expression to see the handicap of the blind person. We have only to consider how much we depend on sound qualities to orient us to space to understand the plight of the deaf. In spite of such obstacles, the blind and the deaf, given normal emotional support, opportunity and encouragement to learn, plus special training to help them minimize their disability, can grow up to lead essentially normal lives.

We should point out that one particular form of blindness, *retrolental fibroplasia* (RLF), recently quite prevalent, is almost unique in medical history for having been a serious problem for only a limited period. It was first noted around 1940, since 1954 or 1955 has been declining in incidence, and is now well on its way to extinction. Its emergence was especially disheartening, since, beginning in the middle 1930's, there had been a rapid decline in congenital blindness, previously due for the most part to venereal disease. RLF was an affliction of markedly premature babies (many of whom, in an earlier medical era, might not have survived at all) and consisted of changes, occurring within a few weeks or months after birth, in the internal structure of the eye. Once physicians had become aware of the rising incidence of RLF and had initiated research, oxygen was singled out as the enemy. At first there was some confusion, with one school of thought holding that an oxygen surplus was responsible, and another that it was oxygen deficiency. It now seems to have been definitely established that RLF was due to overgenerous use of oxygen with premature babies. With pure oxygen now used very sparingly, it appears possible to assure the survival of premature babies about as well as before, and at the same time avoid most risk of RLF.

There are, of course, many other physical disabilities that are apparent at birth or during infancy—heart malformations, crippling, deformities, harelip, cleft palate,[6] epilepsy, and so forth. Apart from the issues of their prevention and cure, the management and understanding of these phenomena, as of the sensory defects, belong to the new and growing field of somatopsychology (not to be confused with psychosomatics, which we shall discuss later), calling for a combined medical and psychological approach both to the physical problem and to its psychological repercussions.[7] One of the main problems of somatopsychology is persuading normal children and adults to understand and accept the exceptional child realistically. A great part of the physically handicapped child's difficulty comes from the way other people react to him, and from the image of himself he forms on the basis of their reactions. In terms of the present discussion, consideration of such primarily somatic problems would take us too far afield. It is important to point out, nevertheless, that the normal needs of infancy are not changed by physical illness but may be greatly augmented.

Turning now to less somatically anchored difficulties, we note that infants only a few months old may show the first signs of profound, *chronic, diffuse emotional disturbance*.[8] All these signs may, of course, occur in perfectly normal babies. It is only when they are frequent, persistent, and all-absorbing that they become ominous. Among these signs are prolonged and hypnotic head-rocking, body-rocking, and crib-rocking; steady head-banging; continuous and injurious picking at or rubbing of some part of the body in the absence of irritation; severe disturbance of eating, sleeping, and digestion; indifference to human company; emotional unresponsiveness; and unusual apathy. When eating of feces, or smearing or playing with them, goes beyond the stage of simple curiosity and experiment and becomes an habitual pattern, it also can be a danger sign. We do not know with any assurance the causes behind such early and grave emotional disturbances. They seem, however, to lie in an often subtle but no less profound rupture of the child's relationships with those around him. It should be noted that we do *not* include among these symptoms the loud, frequent, and agonized crying usually charged off to "colic." Whatever its actual cause, it does not appear to do the babies harm in the long run. As long as a baby is emotionally reactive, whether he cries or laughs, he is usually all right. (We assume, of course, that parents do not stop reacting to the baby's distress, or leave him to "cry it out," just because they know that his crying is not a sign of anything serious. Colicky babies benefit by soothing.)

We should perhaps reiterate that our discussion in this chapter is concerned with the less usual and more severe sorts of problems, and that there are certain normal "problems" encountered at every stage of development. Such issues as thumb-sucking, feeding problems, masturbation, and even "oral character" traits, all of which were discussed in Chapter 3, are not in themselves symptomatic of anything much besides babyhood, although there are more and less effective ways for parents to deal with them—or to leave them alone.

Toddlerhood and the Preschool Years

As children leave infancy, most of the possible hereditary or congenital physical defects are likely already to have become evident. Now, more strictly psychological problems sometimes appear. Among the various problems that may arise during these years, there are the less drastic, but still marked, degrees of mental inadequacy—which of course may have a known or unknown physical basis. As the child matures and has to cope with an increasingly complex environment, any intellectual impairment is more likely to become evident. However, we shall restrict our discussion of mental defect in this chapter to the severe manifestations already discussed in the section on infancy and to the milder ones that become important later on when the child has to grapple with school work, to be discussed in connection with developmental problems of the middle years.

During toddlerhood and the preschool years, as in infancy, some children live in a state of *chronic, diffuse emotional strain* which, even though not so disruptive as earlier diffuse disturbances, hampers children's functioning and may be the forerunner of more serious disturbances. There are a number of signs which tell parents and teachers when a child is suffering in this way. These are not signs for which adults need go looking, but to which they can be sensitive and can recognize when they do occur. They are not signs of psychopathology as such, but of distress that needs to be relieved. Let us point out again that no *single* manifestation is cause for alarm, but that combinations of them often signal a need for action. First, one of the most sensitive barometers of a child's emotional state is the quality of his voice. A child whose voice is too consistently shrill, or harsh, or muffled, or flat and toneless may—barring specific hearing defects—be feeling emotions too strong for him to handle, he may be bottling up his feelings, or his emotions may have been deadened. Chronic emotional distress often shows up, too, on a child's skin, in the form of rapid and seemingly unprovoked changes of color, or is even thought capable of provoking an eczematous rash. It can sometimes be seen in the qualities of body movement, either in tense jerkiness or flaccid sluggishness. It may appear in sleep disturbances—including frequent nightmares and strong bedtime fears —in very frequent daytime urination, or in vomiting. When bowel control is not yet in effect by age four, or when nighttime bladder control is delayed past age five, emotional upset may be a factor. The child who spends *long* periods doing nothing, the one who *constantly* plays with his genitals, or the child with *chronic* nervous tics and twitches, may be having emotional difficulties. In overall behavior, chronic disturbance may be expressed in either agitated restlessness or dull listlessness. We should note that emotional upset in children in this age range is usually quite concretely tied to body functioning, whether vegetative or motor. This foreshadows the hysterical and psychosomatic manifestations we shall talk about later.

The distress signaled by symptoms of these kinds can often be relieved quite simply, by giving the child a little more overt affection or a little more freedom, by setting limits more definitely or by scaling down the standards he has to meet, or, if it can be done tactfully and sympathetically, by helping him talk about his feelings and reassuring him about them. Sometimes, however, either the remedy is not so obvious to those close to the child, or the child's feelings have become too strongly embedded to yield to such everyday measures. In such cases, it may be necessary to seek professional help in getting at the causes and perhaps in treating them by psychotherapy.

Profound psychopathology may appear during this period in the form of *childhood schizophrenia*. It used to be thought that schizophrenia (which we shall discuss again in connection with adolescence) could not appear in early childhood. However, in addition to the fairly classical, adult-like form of schizophrenia found in some children—but very seldom in the preschool years—a particular form of schizophrenia (which some authorities consider a separate entity) has been recognized and described within the past two decades. Kanner has labeled this disorder *early infantile autism*.[9] We have elected to discuss autism in some detail because it is a distinct and easily recognizable entity and because it appears to be on the increase (partly because of improved diagnosis which distinguishes it from mental defect), even though it is not a common hazard of development. It will be apparent that many features of autism are merely exaggerations of normal childhood behavior, but exaggerations so gross and so fixed that they become qualitatively different from the normal.

Autism may appear gradually, beginning in early infancy, or abruptly, subsequent to an apparently normal course of development, between the ages of two and three. When it appears in infancy, parents generally report that the child does not call forth the usual parental sentiments, perhaps because he himself does not seem responsive to people. He may be described as "a very good baby," content to lie isolated in his crib. He may not smile, or smiles at things rather than people, he may withdraw from cuddling or seem indifferent to it, he may never hold out his arms as though asking to be picked up. Some, but not all, autistic children show hyperactivity and hypermotility. In addition, they may show remarkable mechanical ingenuity, learning to operate latches, knobs, locks, and light switches long before their time. Their early roamings may take them onto fire escapes, out into the street, or to the top of precarious stacks of furniture. They seem to have little sense of physical danger, and may receive severe injuries without losing their drive to keep going. Some psychiatrists believe that indifference to pain is one of the outstanding symptoms of autism.

When autism appears in the third year of life, the first symptom that parents may become aware of is the failure of normal language development. Quite frequently, the autistic child comes into professional hands initially as a case of suspected deafness. However, autistic children usually do learn to talk, sometimes very well, but their speech fails to follow the normal pattern. Often prominent in their speech is a compulsive parroting of what they hear, called *echolalia* (see page 119). They may pick up a phrase, a name, a snatch of song, or even a long verse, and repeat it endlessly. The most central symptom, running through all their behavior, is the lack of human contact, the emotional flattening, and the preoccupation with inanimate—but preferably mechanical or physically manipulable—things. The autistic child is fascinated by rhythmic, repetitive patterns. Not only does he memorize and repeat songs and verses, but he can spend protracted periods switching lights on and off, flushing a toilet, watching a phonograph turntable spin, lighting matches, or operating a mechanical toy. He himself may like to spin or twirl or roll, or he may adopt ritualized, perseverative gestures or mannerisms. He may also show intense dislike of enclosed places, heading for the wide open spaces every time the adult's back is turned. It will be seen that the autistic child's functioning is unusually concrete and action-centered, and is rigid and perseverative. However, unlike older schizophrenics, he is not likely to have highly elaborated, bizarre, and delusional ideas.

Autistic boys outnumber autistic girls four to one; in the authors' experience, the autistic child is usually the firstborn of his family; and all reports agree that he is usually the child of intelligent but rigid and undemonstrative parents who either intrude on his development with excessive demands or abandon him too soon to his own immature resources. Although it might appear from the autistic child's unresponsiveness that he is emotionally invulnerable, close observation sometimes suggests the interpretation that his unresponsiveness is a withdrawal designed to protect him from hurt. It may be that the apparent increase in autism is partly a function of the times we live in. That is, autism may be a condition peculiar to technological civilization and its premium on rigid and exact performance in many areas. Autistic behavior often resembles an attempt to escape from painful emotions which have become associated with human beings, and to find refuge, order, control, meaning, and feeling in relationships with things—or with human beings reduced to the thing level. It is possible that the child finds satisfaction in sensory patterns instead of human communication, and maintains rigid and repetitive patterns both in the interest of preserving a sort of integrity and of filling up his inner vacancy. This, however, is only one view of autism. Other writers feel that, because of its early appearance, it must depend partly if not wholly on an inherited vulnerability or even an inherited personality pattern. As we said earlier, autism is sometimes confused with mental defect. Autistic children do test low on intelligence measures, but their good basic endowment is shown in their mastery of mechanical problems and, in those who recover, their academic attainments. About a third of autistic children grow up to attain some sort of adult adjustment in the community. According to Eisenberg and Kanner, the best predictive indicator of the possibility of a relative recovery is the acquisition of language by age five; the single most important factor in helping the child recover is acceptance by an understanding teacher at school—an acceptance made difficult by the child's obvious abnormality and his often disruptive behavior.[10] The usual therapies seem to be of little avail, and even those individuals who make the best recoveries still tend to be emotionally somewhat barren.

Returning to more common types of disturbances, we saw in Chapter 6 that the self-awareness of the preschool years often brings with it a number of *fears*—of death and bogymen, of bodily mutilation, of terrors hidden in the darkness, of being orphaned, and so forth. Sometimes these are expressed openly, sometimes they are denied; sometimes a child forms a fear of some specifically threatening object, and sometimes he projects a nameless or unacknowledged dread upon some invented menace (such a projection is called a *phobia*). If the child's phantoms are pooh-poohed, or if they fail to take explicit shape, his fears may be more diffusely expressed, in a generalized shrinking timidity, in somatic symptoms, or in nightmares. When the child is basically secure, specific fears, especially if they can be formulated and dealt with sympathetically and realistically, come and go and do not constitute a major problem. It is only when the child becomes obsessed with some particular threat, amounting to a phobia, or when he is too pervasively and inexplicably anxious about everything, when his nightmares come too often and too terrifyingly, that his fears become symptomatic of real personality disturbance.

Late infancy, toddlerhood, and the preschool years are an especially unfavorable time for *hospitalization and surgery*. This is the period when children can least tolerate prolonged separation from their parents, and when body integrity, the focus of many fears, becomes a major issue. The best opinion seems to indicate that elective surgery should be deferred, wherever it is medically possible, at least until age three and preferably to age five or later.[11] The important factor is being able to talk to the child about what is going to happen and prepare him for what might otherwise be a seriously disorienting experience. No matter at what age the child goes to the hospital, he should be told the truth; hospitalization is doubly traumatic if the child has been led to believe he was going to the circus, or to visit friends. Obviously, conditions arise which make it imperative to operate on or hospitalize young children. When this happens, special measures are needed to prevent secondary effects. In the matter of surgery, for instance, many doctors, recognizing the importance of emotional as well as surgical considerations, have learned to establish a relationship with the child, to let him cooperate in preliminary procedures, to avoid forcible handling, and to let him know as clearly and unthreateningly as possible what to expect. They have learned to give the child sedation in his own room before he is taken to the operating room. Preferably, a parent should be with the child both when he is put to sleep and when he comes out of the anesthetic. As for hospitalization itself, especially if it is prolonged, the main secondary effect to be feared is lassitude and apathy or sustained and generalized anxiety. One countermeasure is the hospital play program, where professionals and volunteers work to give pediatric patients the individual affection and stimulation so necessary to mental health, and for which overworked doctors and nurses may not have time. A perhaps more radical measure, adopted by a few far-seeing hospitals, is to allow mothers to stay with their sick children, or to visit them at any hour or for as long as they wish.[12] Not only does this work to the psychological benefit of young patients, but mothers can assume many routine nursing duties—trained nurses being in short supply—and lighten the hospital's administrative load.

In the preschool years, when language is being elaborated and consolidated, *speech defects* may be noted. Certain of these may have their origins in defects of the speech apparatus, making articulation difficult. The great majority of defects of articulation are due simply to immaturity, and the child straightens out his own pronunciation as he grows, although sometimes these defects linger beyond their appointed time. When the child continues using baby talk long after his contemporaries have left it behind, it may be a sign that his parents are encouraging it by talking baby talk to him, or by overmothering and overprotecting him, or by making babyhood too attractive. When the child first begins to talk, of course, parental baby talk is almost inevitable. Once the child is well launched in speaking, however, it is time for the parents to resume using English. If the child reverts to baby talk after abandoning it, it may be a sign of regression due to some transient or permanent emotional strain—the birth of a younger sibling often has this effect. In such cases, baby talk is not something to be attacked directly. Indeed, non-organic speech defects in general are cured not by direct attack but by providing the child with good speech models.

Probably the most frequent form of speech disorder in young children is *stuttering* (speech specialists today make no distinction between stuttering and stammering). Various theories to account for and various therapies to help stuttering have been advanced. Most theories, whether psychological (in terms of stuttering as a symptom of emotional disturbance) or physiological (in terms of short circuits in the brain), have not been able to withstand the facts, or else have been so abstract as to be untestable. A promising recent approach has placed stuttering partly under experimental control.[13] It is possible that in "natural" stuttering, as well as in stuttering artificially induced in the laboratory, the critical factor is a disturbance of the automatic "feed-back" mechanism. Studies indicate that a smooth flow of speech is dependent on the speaker's listening to and monitoring, without any particular awareness of the process, his own speech output. Normally, the lag between speaking and hearing oneself speak is infinitesimal. Stuttering can be induced experimentally in anyone simply by producing a time lag of about one quarter of a second between the time a person speaks and the time his voice comes back to him. This is accomplished by having the person speak into a tape recorder which after the predetermined interval plays his voice back to him through headphones.

Most therapies, it appears, at best can help the severe stutterer live more comfortably with his stuttering; few cures are claimed by responsible therapists. At worst, for reasons that will become clear in a moment, therapy—particularly if begun too early—may even exacerbate stuttering and make its removal more unlikely. For, along with Johnson,[14] the authors feel that the bulk of stuttering is created by adults who, reacting to normal speech hesitations and gropings, force the child to pay attention to his speech, generating a crippling self-consciousness about it, like that of the centipede who had gotten along perfectly well until an admiring ant asked him which leg he moved first, thereby rendering him unable to move. All young children stumble and hesitate and make errors in speaking, but this only becomes a fixed pattern when parents hear the child's fumblings as stuttering and try to correct them. As with pronunciation, the child, left to himself, corrects his speech production and, with increasing practice, becomes more fluent. Once the child hears his own speech as stuttering, he becomes bound up in trying to control it, and then begins to stutter in earnest, exploding his words and writhing with the effort to keep his voice under control. Whatever other emotional or neurological factors may lie behind stuttering, there is ample evidence that it can be created; hence, it is inadvisable to tell a preschool child that he can talk better, that he should try to speak more slowly, or that he should repeat himself and "this time say it nicely."

Again in this section, let us emphasize that toddlerhood and the preschool years, too, have their normal "problems" calling for no special treatment whatever. Tantrums, negativism, destructiveness, toilet-training problems, thumb-sucking, masturbation, "selfishness," "cruelty," and so forth, at this age are not marks of psychopathology.

The Middle Years of Childhood

The most prominent difficulties of the middle years revolve around schooling and the child's ability to learn. *Learning difficulties* arise from many sources. First, there is *mental retardation,* intellectual disability not so severe as to incapacitate the child, but enough to interfere with school work. A number of children have intellectual endowments equal to their daily childhood pursuits—and even, later on, to simple jobs and having a family—but insufficient to master all the tasks demanded by school. The limitations of such a child's intelligence may not be evident until he goes to school and is asked to deal with abstract symbols. Once his limitations have been detected and verified by careful individual testing and evaluation, two courses of management are possible. The child can be written off as a lost cause and left to suffer out the years he is legally required to spend in school—there is special help available for almost all severely handicapped children, but the merely dull child may not be eligible for it. When such a course is followed, as it all too often is, the child can easily develop a sense of failure and worthlessness. Even his classmates are likely to take over the school's opinion of him and treat him as an outcast. He can react to his sense of inadequacy passively, sharing the world's contempt, or he can deny it and rebel against it in truancy or delinquency. In any case, he is not likely to derive much benefit from his incarceration in school. The second course is to make allowances for his limitations, to find out what things he can do well, to encourage him to pursue such talents as he may have, and, patiently and sympathetically, to give him as much formal education as possible. If this second course is followed, he can have the sense of worth that everybody is entitled to, he can accept his limitations realistically because he also knows his capabilities, and he stands a good chance of enjoying life and of making his own valuable, if modest, contribution to society.

Not all learning difficulties, however, are due to limited intelligence. A large variety of factors, including malnutrition and low socio-economic status, can interfere with learning. A number of children of apparently poor endowment, for instance, have turned out to be suffering from some degree of *hearing loss,* short of deafness, or *impaired vision,* short of blindness. With these disabilities brought to light and corrected as much as possible, children can be put into classes (if necessary, with special facilities) where they can go on to normal achievements—always provided that they have not already been damaged by the experience of failure. For another common source of learning difficulty, which sometimes appears as a secondary effect of physical handicaps, is emotional interference.

Emotional interferences with learning are generally referred to as *learning blocks.* They most often appear in a context of parental overambition and pressure, which turn the child away from the learning process and make of it something extrinsic to his own wishes. Some children try hard to measure up to their parents' expectations, but the very effort that goes into trying produces anxiety that interferes with learning, each failure becomes more frustrating, generating new anxiety and confusion and making the next failure all the more probable. For other children, non-achievement becomes a weapon in an unconscious revolt against parental pressures. The child goes through all the motions of studying hard, applying all the learning devices he has been urged to use, but still, somehow, nothing seems to stay with him. He is consciously blameless, but he can still manage a sort of secret satisfaction at the distress his parents feel at his failure. At the same time, he neutralizes his parents, since he is already apparently doing everything possible, so that they cannot blame him either.

In addition to generalized impediments to learning, there are the *special disabilities* centered about particular kinds of skills or materials, such as reading, spelling, or arithmetic. Special disabilities can be quite independent of intelligence. Possibly the most conspicuous one, because it involves the most basic skill, is *reading disability.* At the moment, theories as to the nature, causes, prevention, and cure of reading disability form an intricate tangle. There seem to be three major viewpoints which only become incompatible when applied wholesale, without regard to where the emphasis should lie in individual cases. All these theories agree that reading disability involves both perceptual and emotional difficulties, but they differ as to which comes first and where the remedy lies.[15]

The first group of theories is based on a neurological concept of reading disability. Due to some impediment, such as mixed dominance in the brain (so that, for instance, a person is right-handed but left-eyed, or vice versa), the child finds it difficult to perceive or analyze the written page in normal ways. As a consequence, he does not learn to read when his peers do, and, because reading is so important, he develops feelings of inadequacy leading to emotional complications. Indeed, Papanek and others have suggested that some proportion of delinquency serves to compensate for feelings of inadequacy due to reading failure, and that many delinquent children, once they have learned to read, no longer feel it necessary to be delinquent.[16]

The second group of theories assigns precedence to emotional factors. In these terms, reading disability is a form of protest against adult authority, an unconscious strike against what "they" want. This view, of course, would make of reading disability a special case of the emotional blocks to learning discussed above.

The third group of theories resembles the first, but views the initial reading failure as due not to structural or functional abnormalities in the brain but to any one of various psychological causes: perceptual immaturity—that is, lack of reading readiness in terms of maturation; a lack of emotional readiness in terms of wanting to learn to read, or of grasping the idea of reading; a lack of correspondence between the teaching techniques used and the ways in which the child is equipped to learn; or (a common event in large classes) failure by the teacher to detect a child's early difficulties and to take whatever measures—including the postponement of reading instruction—seem called for. Consequent to early failure, the child enters the familiar pattern of feelings of inadequacy, which can produce a crippling anxiety or which he can handle by denying the importance of reading, by unconscious revolt, or even by such compensatory mechanisms as minor or major delinquency.

Whatever the sources of reading disabilities, all forms of reading therapy have had some success. What they all have in common is the basis of all good therapy; the sustained, sympathetic attention of one person to the child's difficulties. Once the reading block has been broken, a snowball effect in learning often ensues, accompanied by a general relaxation of emotional tensions, and even, as we have suggested, by a decline in deviant behavior. Sometimes the remedy for reading difficulties lies in a direct attack upon the reading problem, sometimes the immediate problem is better by-passed in favor of dealing with the child's total emotional situation. The decision as to which approach is needed should rest with a well-qualified clinical psychologist, which, ideally, the school psychologist should be.

The correction of reading disability, however, is a difficult and expensive process, and is not available to all children who need it. Furthermore, the problem does not consist only of outright inability to learn to read, but also of poor reading that may handicap a child even into college and beyond. For these reasons, the prevention of reading problems has a certain priority over their cure. The best prevention lies in the proper teaching of beginning reading. Good teaching calls for an individual approach that takes account of the wide spread in reading readiness and in motivation to learn, and so avoids too early pressures. It does not label a child as a reading failure during the first three grades, realizing that if the child is not yet ready to learn to read, he may still be ready to learn a great many other things instead. It makes reading attractive, and not an imposed task. It adapts teaching techniques to individual needs. No one technique for teaching reading has been proven to be best for all children. Many teachers nowadays prefer to begin with the *sight method* (teaching the child to recognize whole words and word combinations), introducing *phonics* (letter sounds) as they go along. Some children need greater emphasis on phonics from the beginning, others pick up the tricks of word analysis largely on their own. Other supplementary techniques such as the *kinesthetic* (word-tracing, designed to reinforce the visual image with a motor pattern) can be added as necessary, although these are usually needed only for remedial teaching.

While we are on the subject of schooling, we should say a brief word about education for exceptional children in general, including the mentally retarded, the physically and sensorially handicapped, the emotionally disturbed, and so forth. (The term "exceptional" usually includes the gifted, whom we are not considering here.) Our basic assumption is contained in what we said about slow learners and, in our discussion of disorders in infancy, about institutionalization. Depending on the nature and severity of the disability, exceptional children need a greater or lesser amount of special education. However, the special education facilities—particularly residential ones—provided for exceptional children have dangers and disadvantages of their own. For this reason, whenever possible, we favor bringing the special services to the child rather than the child to them. The most severely disturbed or severely retarded may have to be placed in residential institutions. But living away from home deprives the child of emotional support from his family, of contact with his normal peers, of a sense of participation in the world's doings, and is not to be recommended except in extreme cases. Sometimes, for administrative convenience, special day school facilities for exceptional children are grouped in one central location. This, too, often works incidental disadvantages to the children, who either spend their day in the company of other exceptional children, or have to commute long distances, or shuttle back and forth between regular and special classes. Wherever possible, exceptional children should be allowed to attend school with their normal fellows, with special teachers or facilities available to meet the special needs. Normal children can benefit by having a chance to know and understand and accept people who are "different," and their acceptance in turn can help the exceptional child make the best possible adjustment to his surroundings. The more closely the regular school can approach the ideal of good teachers, small classes, and individualized instruction, the less need there will be for "special" education (although some need will always remain, especially for severe handicaps) that sets the child apart from everybody else and, in consequence, from himself.

As at earlier ages, children in the middle years may continue to be prone to *generalized emotional disturbances.* These have, again, a number of indicators. Most striking is the persistence of behavior which earlier was quite normal but now becomes infantile: e.g., speech difficulties, tantrums, thumb-sucking, and enuresis. We have already spoken of how even school-age children separated from their mothers during the evacuation of London at the time of the air raids early in World War II began wetting their beds in great numbers.[17] Enuresis may have several causes. It may reflect earlier toilet-training practices. It may be brought on by some present difficulty. In a few cases, it appears that enuresis is an exclusively physiological problem, with no particular psychodynamic implications. Persistent enuresis sometimes yields to psychotherapy, which helps the child stabilize emotionally. It may be corrected by conditioning techniques, although we have previously expressed our reservations about these. What is certainly of no use is negative techniques of shaming and scolding, which, by upsetting the child, may act contrary to control. Other signs of emotional disturbance in the school years are withdrawal from social participation and overcomformity to adult standards of goodness.

A possible factor in many difficulties encountered during the school years is *brain damage,* due to injury or disease. The nature, effects, and diagnosis of brain damage constitute a field of study by itself, and we cannot try to do justice to its intricacies here. It is enough to point out that brain damage can simulate a great many other conditions, including mental deficiency, emotional disturbance, and character defects. It may be so completely interwoven with emotional factors that it is all but impossible to detect and isolate, and only a competent diagnostic team headed by a neurologist can in such cases undertake a diagnosis.

As we pointed out in Chapter 7, *delinquency* often has its beginnings in the school years, although its most serious manifestations usually occur in adolescence. It is simple enough to define delinquent acts —stealing, vandalism, physical aggression, etc.—in terms of social acceptability, but all these acts may have quite different sources in the individual. Therefore, we are forced to draw a number of distinctions among the psychological origins of delinquent acts. First, we can recognize *normal* or casual delinquent behavior. Individually, probably every six- or seven-year-old does a certain amount of experimental stealing from his mother's pocketbook. This is not serious and will usually be outgrown without any special measures. In the gang, especially the boy gang, there is usually a certain amount of prankishness which often has a superficially delinquent character. In addition, boys are expected to do a certain amount of street fighting to prove their mettle. These manifestations again are not serious, and most children develop their own inhibitions and controls without any action by the authorities.

Second, there is what we may term *sub-cultural* [18] (sometimes called *socialized* [19]) delinquency. This is the most common kind. It is characteristic of the lower-class child who, having suffered some hurt or frustration at the hands of middle-class society, turns to a ready-made delinquent culture within his own society. This is primarily gang delinquency, although it may be the breeding ground for later individual criminality. The important thing to recognize about sub-cultural delinquency is that, psychologically, it is not delinquency at all. It is only delinquency in terms of middle-class mores, which do not apply. The gang member is behaving in ways sanctioned by the culture he belongs to, and need feel absolutely no guilt. Indeed, to question the mores of the gang would be far more likely to make him feel guilty than almost any "delinquent" act he might perform. Sub-cultural delinquency, insofar as it is a gang enterprise, is more likely to be male than female. However, as we pointed out earlier, girl fighting gangs are becoming more common. In addition, girls may be accepted into boy gangs, where they play the roll of "moll." Most female delinquency, though, including sexual delinquency, is likely to be of the neurotic or the acting-out type described below.

Third, there is *neurotic* delinquency. This usually takes the form of stealing from his parents (or sometimes a teacher) by a child who feels isolated. Such stealing is often symbolic: the child is not interested in the money as such (he may even throw it away, or lose it, or simply forget what he did with it), but is, in effect, stealing the love he feels his parents will not give him. Or he may, unconsciously, steal as a way of punishing his parents for not loving him. He may steal in ways that seem to insure his being caught, as though seeking punishment to relieve some unconscious guilt. In some cases, children use the money they steal to buy favor with their peers, status they are otherwise denied. Obviously, neurotic delinquency does not call for punishment but for treatment. To avoid confusion, however, let us point out that neurotic delinquency is not a *neurosis,* a state of internal conflict which inhibits action and is expressed in particular symptoms such as diffuse anxiety, compulsive rituals, or somatic complaints. We call this delinquency neurotic because it is an *indirect* expression of an unformulated need or wish.

The fourth type of delinquency, *acting-out* delinquency, where the individual acts out his neurotic fantasies, particularly hostile ones, has something in common with all the others. Acting-out refers to the free, deliberate, and often malicious indulgence of impulse, particularly in the sphere of aggression but also in other areas of delinquency. It is essentially a form of revolt, analogous to the negative revolt described in Chapter 11, though it need not take the extreme forms described there. Like sub-cultural delinquency, it may be more or less consciously directed against the middle-class morality. Unlike sub-cultural delinquency, it may be more an individual matter requiring less sanction from group mores. Furthermore, the acting-out delinquent may himself come from the middle or upper classes. Like neurotic delinquency, it may express unformulated needs that have nothing to do with the specific acts committed. In common with psychopathic behavior, to be described below, acting-out delinquency may betray a brutal disregard for other people's feelings. Unlike the psychopath, however, for whom other people's feelings simply do not count, the actor-out may quite consciously want to inflict pain, even though he may not know why. Like the psychopath, the actor-out is dangerous, but he may be far more amenable than the psychopath to psychiatric help. He may well be a relatively gifted and strong individual, caught up in a pattern of resentments and unstructured cravings and impulses, who needs help in finding ways to use his gifts in socially constructive ways.

Fifth and finally, there is *psychopathic* delinquency. Psychopathy certainly begins very early in life. Indeed, some authors still speak of "constitutional [that is, hereditary or "built-in"] psychopathic personality." The consensus seems now to be that psychopathy represents a failure of the basic identification process in the first five years of life, so that the individual becomes incapable of true feelings for others.[20] This failure can in some cases be traced to a disruption of normal family relationships. However, it is worth noting that the psychopath has an essentially intact personality, but lacks strong emotional ties to reality. The psychopath is remarkable for his emotional blandness, particularly in regard to actions that would profoundly shock the normal individual. He is virtually lacking in conscience or superego, although he professes a recognition of and can speak smoothly in terms of devotion to accepted values. He makes glib promises and resolutions, but meanwhile may be picking the pocket of the person he is talking to. He can never quite see his own responsibility for anything that goes wrong. The psychopath's intelligence is within the normal range but essentially superficial and external. In spite of ability to learn things, he does not profit by the lessons of his own experience, so that his behavior is out of keeping with what he abstractly knows. In fact, he not only seems indifferent to the consequences for other people of what he does, he does not seem concerned about the almost certainly unfortunate consequences for himself—he is incurably, unrealistically optimistic.

The psychopath steals even when he is sure to be caught. He lies even when there is no earthly reason for lying. He may be assaultive or even murderous—although many psychopaths are not at all physically aggressive—but even his violence or sadism has a shallow, unfeeling quality quite unlike that of the child who has a chip on his shoulder. He does physical harm as casually and unthinkingly as he lies or steals. Because he can learn the formulas to which other people respond, he can manipulate people until they come to detect the meaninglessness of what he says. It is not that he specifically wishes people ill, but only that their needs and feelings have no immediacy for him. His own needs and wishes are paramount and absolute. Because he is normally intelligent, he can undertake elaborate plans for getting what he wants, but his thinking, which does not take full account of other people's views, is likely to go awry, and his schemes to collapse. Childhood psychopaths supply the bulk of the adult criminal population, but not all of them end up as criminals. Some simply become unpleasant characters who exploit and betray their friends and families but stay within the law. Some become drifters or marginal personalities. Some settle down to shallow respectability on a low socio-economic level. A few, turning their talents into socially acceptable channels, become financial successes, but it is doubtful that they are able to establish satisfactory personal relationships. Because of the psychopath's lack of strong feeling, punishment does not change his ways, he is extremely hard to deal with in psychotherapy, and we cannot be hopeful about those who are already among us. In terms of prevention, considering the apparent origins of psychopathy in a disturbance of early emotional relationships, we can only point to all the things we have said so far about sound emotional relationships in infancy and early childhood.

Adolescence

The excesses of normal adolescent behavior, like normal preschool behavior, often reach emotional extremes that might lead some people to conclude that adolescence itself sometimes seems a form of insanity. We hope we have made clear that such is not the case. Nevertheless, adolescence is a vulnerable period, both in terms of the painful problems the adolescent has to face and of the reawakening of past developmental issues that were only partially resolved. It is during adolescence that a true *schizophrenic breakdown* may first occur; indeed, schizophrenia used to be known as *dementia praecox,* insanity of the young. Many normal adolescent traits in their extreme forms approximate schizophrenic behavior. Too persistent feelings of dislocation and estrangement, total docility or exaggerated rebelliousness, emotional volatility, feelings that everybody is against one, talk of suicide, and even idealism that seems to be a denial of reality may all have a schizophrenic flavor. Needless to say, most adolescents have developed a tough core of security and an anchorage in reality that permit them to withstand and thrive on the stresses of this period. Since, however, a few do break down, we should attempt to see the form that break-downs are most likely to take.

Schizophrenia is actually a label that embraces several psychoses. All of these have in common a distortion of normal emotional responses and include ideas or feelings about reality which are incompatible with normal views. Ordinarily, the whole of reality is reshaped in keeping with a central conflict within the schizophrenic. This reshaping may take the form of *delusions,* unfounded but no less serious beliefs to the effect that people are trying to poison the individual, that they are accusing him of depraved practices or inviting him to engage in them, or that he has been endowed with special powers and dispensations. Schizophrenics may have delusions about their own bodies: that they are corrupted by strange diseases, that they are being controlled by malignant forces, that they are sensitive to radio waves, that their bodies contain various kinds of machines. Sometimes beliefs of this sort take the more concrete form of *hallucinations,* imaginary but nevertheless vivid experiences where the individual hears voices talking to him or about him, sees visions, or smells strange or disagreeable odors. Schizophrenia does not always take such elaborate or explicit forms, however. Sometimes it is expressed in total apathy and inactivity, sometimes in grossly inappropriate emotional responses to standard reality: the individual may be quite unfeeling about something that is of vital importance to him, he may giggle foolishly in response to almost anything that happens, or he may fly into a rage over trifling setbacks. Some schizophrenics seem to be contented in their fantasy worlds, some seem to lack any emotion, while some are at constant war with their surroundings. They may feel harried by their enemies, they may be verbally abusive, they may take satisfaction in behaving outrageously, or they may be assaultive, self-destructive, or murderous. Quite frequently, the central conflict of schizophrenia is a sexual one, although often heavily disguised. Conflicts over homosexual cravings, feelings of uncleanness, feelings of lack of control, a sense of being unwanted, a sense of vulnerability—all may enter into the schizophrenic pattern. We might also add that males are more prone than females to schizophrenia (as to most forms of emotional disturbance), but that some schizophrenic girls and women show this disorder in its most virulent forms. One hears schizophrenia spoken of as incurable. This is not necessarily the case. Some schizophrenics recover spontaneously from psychotic episodes, temporarily or permanently. Some can live comfortably as long as they remain in the sheltered environment of a hospital or even in a community that understands their weaknesses and needs. A gratifying number show improvement in response to a number of treatments used singly or in combination: tranquilizing drugs, electric shock therapy, insulin therapy, and individual and group psychotherapy, among others.

There is a great gulf between the legal and the practical view of what constitutes *sexual delinquency* in boys (see page 312). For girls, the discrepancy is not so great, particularly if a girl incurs the biological penalty of becoming pregnant. For this reason, and because the adolescent girl may use sexual promiscuity as a weapon of revolt, sex offenses make up a very sizable proportion of delinquent behavior in girls. Psychologically, as we might expect from what was said in Chapter 11 about female sexuality, sexually delinquent behavior in girls often seems to have non-sexual origins. We have just pointed out that it may be an expression of adolescent revolt. It is rather often associated with feeble-mindedness and a passive inclination to do what other people say. It may express a need for affection, for emotional contact and support in girls who lack warm attachments. In some cases, and under certain kinds of pressures, it appears to stem from a need to conform to group mores, from the threat of exile if one does not do as the others do. In general, sex delinquency in girls is often symptomatic of a deeper emotional disturbance or of personal inadequacy. Punitive measures are of little help and may only force a girl into a life of prostitution. Sympathetic case work, however, which can help the girl make practical adjustments, often accomplishes a rapid change.

Sexual deviations may appear in adolescence, although less commonly than the other phenomena we have been discussing. In girls, homosexuality as a fixed pattern, although less frequent than in boys, is probably the form which sexual deviation most often takes. There appear to be two main motivations behind female homosexuality. The first is deep-rooted hostility toward or fear of males. The second is psychological masculinity, a wish to assume the male role—this often extends beyond sexual practices to such matters as dress, mannerisms, speech, and so forth. In the latter case, men are viewed not as enemies but as competitors.

In boys, there are several forms of sexual deviation which may become serious problems during adolescence. It should be noted, however, that all these deviations may play a part in adolescent fantasies, and that some of them may actually be practiced experimentally, without their having any abnormal significance. Rape, which normal boys may fantasy but are extremely unlikely to execute, is ordinarily a part of sub-cultural delinquency, acting-out delinquency, or psychopathy, and does not require further discussion here. Closely allied to rape is sexual sadism. As we know, sex and violence do often become interwoven, and for certain unstable personalities may be interchangeable. Much of the cheap literature addressed to late-school-age and adolescent boys is a thorough and revolting compound of sex and sadism. Occasionally, indeed, it may reach extremes where even libertarian opinions on the desirability of censorship begin to waver. For some normal children, such literature may even serve a positive function by reassuring them that their fantasies are shared by other people. For a few near-psychotic or psychopathic children, however, such literature can be pernicious, supplying a prototype for acting-out behavior. For yet others, likewise unstable but less inclined to act out, it can serve further to confuse their own feelings and attitudes.

A more common form of deviation in adolescence, although still rare, is homosexuality. As in the case of female homosexuality, male homosexuality as a permanent adjustment often reflects fear or hatred of the opposite sex, or else a psychological identification with it. Negative feelings toward girls may be expressed as frank disgust or constant disparagement. Identification with the female role leads to conscious imitation of feminine ways. Homosexuality may also go along with a schizoid (schizophrenic-like but still non-psychotic) alienation from experience, so that the individual needs some extraordinary stimulus, perhaps with elements of revulsion, to arouse him sexually. Yet another form of deviation is voyeurism, or Peeping Tom behavior. All youngsters, to satisfy their curiosity, do a certain amount of peeping and spying. However, when sexual spectacles become an end in themselves rather than a source of knowledge or stimulation, it is apparent that the individual's normal sexual orientation has been lost. Voyeurism may be' associated with feelings of sexual inadequacy, with a guilt about sexual feelings that can be appeased as long as sex is enjoyed only at a distance, or with more serious and generalized personality disturbances. In practice, the adult homosexual or voyeur can often lead an outwardly normal life. It is obvious, however, that his personality organization is to some degree warped and so unsatisfactory. In addition, he lives in constant danger of detection, which would lead, at best, to public shame and hostility, and, at worst, to imprisonment or mandatory hospitalization. Because such deviations are usually deeply embedded in

the individual's character structure, they require prolonged psychotherapy aimed at a general revision of personality.

Although neurotic traits may appear earlier, it is ordinarily in adolescence or after, when the individual's ideal self has become differentiated
from his other selves, that he is capable of full-blown *neurosis,* a state
of conflict between antagonistic and often unformulated inner tendencies that drains his energies and hampers his functioning. As we mentioned previously, the neurotic individual's inner conflicts are seldom
expressed directly. Basically, the neurotic person, unlike the psychotic
or the psychopathic one, recognizes that he is blocked or ineffective
by reason of characteristics within himself but beyond his voluntary
control. The source of the neurosis is usually anxiety or guilt, against
which the neurotic erects defenses which themselves impede his functioning. His tensions and defenses constitute the neurotic symptoms.
Sometimes we find diffuse, "free-floating" anxiety ready to attach to any
situation. However, the anxiety itself may be a defense against something else, such as pervasive but unacknowledged hostility. In some
neurotics, the symptoms take more explicit, often symbolically meaningful, forms, such as specific fears or phobias; ritualized, compulsive behavior; inability to make decisions (*abulia*); or a general sense of
inadequacy, impotence, or worthlessness. These symptoms may affect
only one sharply circumscribed area of functioning, or they may cripple
the neurotic in all his activities.

Perhaps the most common form of neurosis in adolescence is *hysteria,* inner conflict expressed usually through somatic symptoms. One
form of hysterical behavior, now relatively rare (there are fashions in
psychological disorders as in other things), is somatic dysfunction:
hysterical blindness, deafness, paralysis, and so forth, where, although
the affected organ is in good anatomical and physiological working
order, the individual cannot use it. Such manifestations often seem to
be a denial of the organ in an attempt to repudiate what it has experienced or done (a paralyzed hand, for instance, may serve to deny
masturbation), to protect it from harm, to prevent its doing something
in the future, or to justify the individual's helplessness—somatic dys-
functions are not uncommon among soldiers who would rather not
fight, but they are wholly unconscious and so different from deliberate
shirking. Hysterical adjustment may take the form of hypochondria, a
constant inventory of the body to see what has gone wrong, and a tendency to interpret normal and usually unnoticed body sensations as warn-

ings of some dread disease process. We can see how adolescents, with their heightened body awareness, might be prone to hypochondriacal symptoms; almost all adolescents have spells of hypochondria and almost all outgrow it. Yet another hysterical manifestation, and a more serious one, is the unsuccessful suicide. This must be distinguished from the genuine suicide attempt, whether successful or not, which stems from a profound sense of despair or accompanies a psychotic breakdown. The hysterical gesture of suicide is usually an appeal for attention and affection and a means of reproaching an unsympathetic world. Even in cases where the danger of actual suicide is slight, suicidal gestures indicate emotional disturbance serious enough to call for professional help.

Hysteria often blends into *psychosomatic disorders,* where the body undergoes actual pathological changes as a result of corrosion by chronic conflicting emotions. On the borderline between hysteria and psychosomatic disorders, there are manifestations such as fainting, where the physical changes that go with emotion interfere with the blood supply to the brain. Another borderline phenomenon, usually beginning in adolescence, is *anorexia nervosa,* a condition in which the individual finds food, or most foods, inedible or revolting. Anorexia nervosa seems to occur most often in girls, and, according to one interpretation, seems to be an unconscious expression of fear of sexuality, where anything taken into the body connotes, symbolically, sexual penetration. Although anorexia nervosa does not lead directly to physiological disorders, its victims may become badly emaciated and suffer tissue damage due to malnutrition. They generally survive on small quantities of a few selected foods, but they may have to be hospitalized and fed intravenously. At the opposite pole from anorexia stands the far more common condition of *bulimia,* or compulsive overeating. Bulimia may begin long before adolescence, and appears to be an infantile oral character trait. It often is a symbolic expression of a hunger for love and support. It has psychosomatic consequences in obesity and metabolic changes. Other more directly psychosomatic disorders, such as gastric ulcers, migraine, and so forth, are unusual prior to adulthood and so lie outside the scope of this book. It is worth mentioning, however, that such somatic afflictions as eczema and asthma can be made worse or may be triggered off by psychological upsets even in infancy.

We might also say a word about individual differences in psychosomatic reactions. All strong emotions entail clear-cut body changes. And, provided emotions are not so strong as to be disruptive, different emotions seem to entail different patterns of physiological change. But within this general framework, Lacey, Wenger, and others have demonstrated that individuals have their own characteristic ways of reacting to a variety of emotional situations.[21] It can easily be observed that some people react with their mucous membranes, becoming all stuffed up; some with their tear ducts; some react with their skins, flushing or paling; in some, blood pressure goes up, in others down; some react with their muscles, tensing up; some with their digestive tracts, losing appetite or needing to eliminate. We are thus in a position to conjecture that the particular psychosomatic symptom that appears in individuals who live under prolonged emotional strains, and whose tissues break down before their personality organization, is a product of the particular chronic emotion which is at work within the person, of his idiosyncratic form of emotional response, and of tissue vulnerabilities such as a tendency to eczema or asthma. As we can see, the adolescent has moved into a stage of individualized complexity where, like most adults, he is a mixture of normal and abnormal, of strengths and weaknesses, of virtues and faults.

Help for Exceptional Children

Discussion of morbid conditions such as those described in this chapter may lead to certain anxieties, and we feel some obligation to try to put this discussion in its proper perspective. It is obvious that all the "abnormal" psychological symptoms we have described crop up in the most normal of people. It does not necessarily follow that because a child shows some sign of psychopathology he is mentally ill. In the first place, his behavior may be a way of coping with essentially abnormal and stressful living conditions; in such cases, it is the environment that needs attention, and not the child. Furthermore, these symptoms by themselves do not indicate abnormal functioning. They express normal human potentialities shared by everybody. It is only when they begin to dominate the scene and interfere with effective living that they become abnormal and require special attention—which may occasionally consist of nothing more than the familiar prescription of a change of scene for a few weeks. At the other extreme, special attention may consist of prolonged psychotherapy. It should also be obvious that we are at a loss to explain in terms of situational influences many abnormalities thought to be psychological rather than organic, and we may need to give more consideration to constitutional strengths, weaknesses, capacities, and vulnerabilities. Some children survive objectively appalling childhoods without visible ill effects, while others seem to break down under apparently trifling stresses. Some break down or get off to a poor start and then recover with very little outside help, while others may spend a lifetime trying to find a personality they can call their own. Until the conditions of mental health and illness have been better defined, we can only offer the prescription that we have repeated throughout this book: love, emotional warmth, self-confidence and confidence .in the child, solid but not overwhelming authority, enjoyment, opportunity for sound identifications, and encouragement—without coercion —to mental growth and independence.

Meanwhile, some few children do have physical disabilities serious enough to affect their psychological functioning, and others do develop psychopathology. Fortunately, we live in an era when we can face such problems and try to deal with them realistically, instead of locking the child in a closet, castigating ourselves with guilt feelings, rattling family skeletons, and otherwise wasting valuable energies. It is hard for us to realize now that half a generation ago people could not bring themselves to speak publicly of tuberculosis, cancer, or venereal disease, which, thanks largely to publicity by special interest groups, have been brought out into the open, where they can be dealt with. In the same way, we are now coming to acknowledge and attack such problems as emotional disturbance, schizophrenia, mental deficiency, epilepsy, cerebral palsy, and so forth. Possibly the most important effect of campaigns designed to focus public attention on these problems is that they have enabled parents to continue to be parents even when their children were severely disabled; they have made parents aware that children continue to be children in spite of disabilities, that they need the same basic emotional support that other children do.

Children with physical disabilities and severely disturbed children need outside professional help. Whether this kind of help is indicated for the child with emotional disturbances of slight or intermediate severity must be a matter for individual decision. Psychotherapy can help, but it cannot guarantee to do so. Furthermore it costs heavily, in terms both of money and psychic strain, and parents must weigh its possible benefits against its costs to them and to the child. And when they do elect psychotherapy—which often means psychotherapy for the entire family—they must be prepared to follow through wherever it leads. Sometimes, of course, less drastic measures than psychotherapy can be of therapeutic benefit. A good school or teacher, for instance, or participation in a recreation group, can often help a child immensely. Nevertheless, a professional opinion as to the most advisable measures is often helpful. Unfortunately, for those who need and want professional help, there are not enough facilities to go around. The great middle classes are at a particular disadvantage when it comes to finding professional services. The well-to-do can pay for help, and there are many private and public agencies prepared to serve those with limited funds. However, for those readers who are seeking professional help, certain guidelines may be in order. Various professional specialties are licensed or certified by various accrediting agencies, but the individual's best assurance of qualified help is to obtain information from a reliable source. To find out where reputable psychiatric or psychological services can be obtained, the individual can apply to his pediatrician or family doctor, to the medical society of the county where he lives, to the nearest mental health clinic, to his county or local welfare agency, to the psychological association in his state, to the American Psychological Association, or to the psychology department or clinic of a college or university. For vocational guidance, a roster of qualified counselors is maintained by the National Vocational Guidance Association. In the case of particular disabilities, parent or citizen groups have been set up to provide services or maintain a directory of where services are available. Among these are the United Cerebral Palsy Association, the National Association for Retarded Children, the National Society for Crippled Children and Adults, the American Foundation for the Blind, the American Speech and Hearing Association, and the League for Emotionally Disturbed Children, plus, of course, many more. Many organizations have branch offices and clinics around the country, and application for help can be made directly to these. Otherwise, the national headquarters can direct applicants to the nearest facilities.

Pathology of the Environment

We have been talking thus far of problems which, regardless of their sources in the family or the social environment, are essentially problems of individual psychopathology or near-pathology. These problems fall within the province of psychiatry and psychology. We should like to close our discussion of abnormalities of development with a discussion of the so-called sociopathies, pathologies of society, social organization, and family structure which may have deleterious effects on personality development. Obviously, we have taken some incidental account of these throughout this book, and in the present chapter in references to mothering and to delinquency. We have implied earlier that intellectually sterile, unstimulating, and overrigid patterns of schooling may well stifle or deform personal creativity and development. The even more damaging effects of the usual sorts of institutionalization have also been alluded to. Now we should like to give more attention to problems which are the province of social work, the field of child welfare, and, in terms of academic disciplines, of sociology.

Family Pathology

We should note that psychology and sociology are not exclusive disciplines. Their domains inevitably overlap a great deal. However, their emphases are quite different—so different, at times, that the same terms may have quite different meanings in the two disciplines. Sociologically, for instance, a "broken home" is one in which the parents are divorced or separated, or one or both parents dead, regardless of how successfully the remaining members live together as a family unit. Psychologically, on the other hand, a broken home is one in which life is made difficult either by the loss or absence of a parent or by inter-personal strife, even though all the family members are present to participate in it. We shall feel free to use this and other terms in a way biased toward psychology, simply because psychology is our business.

The most immediately important sociopathies, from the standpoint of child development, are those having to do with the family structure, particularly those disruptions which are called broken homes. Until thirty or forty years ago, most such homes were broken up as a result of the death of one or both parents. The efforts of those who attempted to help the survivors of broken homes were largely aimed at placing the children, usually in orphanages. The orphanage is now a vanishing institution, for two reasons. First of all, parents live longer—especially mothers, for whom childbirth is now rarely a hazard. Second, there has been a general recognition that the usual form of group care provided in orphanages leaves much to be desired. As substitutes for orphanages there have now been developed programs to place children without parents in private homes, and to enable a surviving parent to keep his or her family together. Instead of going to institutions, many homeless children are placed in foster homes (temporary placements, with the child's keep paid for by the public or private agency in whose legal custody he remains) or adoptive homes (permanent placements, with the child becoming a legal member of the family). The second substitute for orphanages is the provision through various state agencies and the federal social security system of subsidies for widows and their dependent children, enabling them to keep their families together. Certain flaws have appeared in the foster care and adoptive placement programs. One is that it is hard to find enough foster homes. Another shortcoming is apparent in the case of children who have had to move repeatedly from one foster home to another, because of incompatibility or changed circumstances; such children develop a sense of repeated loss and rejection, and often become victims of psychopathology. Yet another flaw lies in the implicit assumption that any foster home is better than any institution. Some people have moved to improve institutional care instead of scrapping it. By raising the quality, psychological warmth, understanding, and training of personnel, by providing continuity of attachment between a child and a particular person responsible for his care, and by organizing children into *small* groups on a family plan, a number of institutions have improved to the point where they may provide the best solution for children with special kinds of emotional disturbance that prevent their forming attachments to a foster family, and for children past the early school years.

Illegitimacy was at one time an unfavorable circumstance for child and mother alike. We have now come to realize that the child and his mother—often a confused adolescent—are people in need of help rather than punishment. It is not usually feasible for an unmarried mother to keep her child, but an adoptive home can readily be found for him. Adoptive placement, too, at one time carried its risks—as it still may for babies adopted through black or gray market channels. Adoption agencies, however, have now set standards for adoptive families which help insure favorable environments for children. At times, indeed, these standards have been too inflexible, meaning that children have had to spend long waiting periods in the limbo of an agency, sometimes until they were too old to be good adoption risks. There has recently been an attempt to make standards more flexible and still insure a healthful home atmosphere. It has also become accepted practice to let adopted children know early that they are adopted, that they are, in fact, chosen, as a safeguard against their learning the fact accidentally and being overcome by the uncertainty and, perhaps, sense of rejection of not being with their own parents. Adoption agencies have also shown a greater willingness to place flawed babies with families who want them; such babies are often in demand by adoptive parents who would not otherwise be eligible or who are themselves handicapped in some way.

Nowadays, of course, although children less often have to face the problems of being orphaned or branded as illegitimate, they still are confronted with the problems of homes broken by marital discord. In the lowest stratum of society there are many families where intermittent or changing fathers are the rule, where the children's only tie, if any, is to the mother. Such families are particularly likely to breed feelings of isolation and rejection, hostility against society, delinquency, and a gang orientation. Interestingly enough, a certain segment of upper-class society displays a similar pattern of multiple divorce (in the lowest-class families, of course, neither the marriage nor the divorce may be formalized), where there may be a tie with one parent but no clear-cut, sustained family structure. For the children of such families, the boarding school may play the psychological role of orphanage and may be the only stable factor in the child's life. In a sense even more disruptive is divorce in the middle-class family, founded as it is on a more definite assumption of permanence. Sometimes, of course, divorce seems to be the only answer. A family atmosphere of psychological divorce, permeated by coldness or open antagonism, may be even worse for the children. Divorce is simply an explicit acknowledgment that a marriage has failed, and, if anything, may have a stabilizing effect. Needless to say, even a badly spoiled marriage can sometimes be salvaged by putting it on a new footing, where the parents' immaturities will not be in the forefront, and when this can be done—by family counseling, by psychotherapy, or otherwise—it is certainly preferable to divorce. Divorce entails many secondary problems, of course, and these have to be met. Among the psychologically most important ones are those having to do with the children's divided loyalties and how their time is to be apportioned between the two parents. Some divorced parents work severe hardships on their children by trying to win their exclusive affection, by using them as a weapon against the other parent, by trying to justify their own point of view, and even by treating children as substitute spouses. Traumatic as divorce can be, there is general agreement that it is better than trying to maintain a pretense "for the children's sake." The children can more easily understand and accept a real break than deceptions which do not deceive but only baffle and disturb.

Home conditions of poverty and economic deprivation or uncertainty can expose the child to ills ranging from malnutrition to extremes of psychopathology. Although the acceptance of the principle of the welfare state has eliminated many of the conditions Dickens wrote about, we can still find nests of squalor on tenant farms, in migrant labor camps, and in the tenements of every city. Economic poverty may remove the child from the culture at large and deprive him of all the stimulation to growth that is the lot of most children. Some families, of course, maintain their group and individual integrity in the face of the most grinding poverty. On the other hand, it may take more than economic relief to lift other families from a pattern of irresponsibility or depravity. The social agencies in every community know certain families that can be counted on to produce more than their share of school failures, truancy, delinquency, sexual deviation, drunkenness and disorderliness, and disease, and of inadequate personalities who become the parents of other inadequate personalities in a recurring sequence that led early geneticists to talk of hereditary (rather than self-renewing) social incompetence. Recently, social agencies have been experimenting with a co-operative total rehabilitation of such families, instead of the former piecemeal cleaning up of each problem as it arose. Such approaches have met with encouraging success, and may presage a wholly new concept in welfare work.

Agencies and counselors, however, must take account of the possibly devastating effects of conflicts in cultural values. This danger is brought sharply to our attention in Hunt's study of the ecology of mental disease.[22] It came to Hunt's attention that a surprisingly large number of boys who had belonged to the same group in a depressed section of Washington developed some form of psychopathology. Investigating further, he found that those boys who had often taken part in the gang's sexual perversions *and* who had participated in neighborhood religious revivals were the ones who broke down. It was only when sexual perversion was joined to religion in the same individual, implying a state of severe conflict, that psychopathology resulted.

Disaster and Social Disruption

Finally, we should point out that in recent years social scientists have begun to gather and organize information about what happens to children in times of major social crisis due to man-made or natural disasters: war, flood, earthquake, windstorm, panic. It has always been obvious that children suffer from such crises, but now we are beginning to see more precisely what they suffer and how, and what sort of psychological safety precautions can be incorporated in disaster preparations.

The growth of our civilization has produced two parallel trends. First, we are able to create disasters on a gigantic scale, in the form of saturation bombing, concentration camps, forced migrations, and genocide. Second, we have become able to stand apart from our acts of mass destruction, assess them, and plan against the day when we turn our destructive forces against ourselves. Needless to say, we shall reach real social maturity only when such assessments and planning are no longer necessary.

Studies of adult morale have shown that panic is most likely to occur when the individual feels cut loose from his moorings in the group and does not have clear-cut tasks to perform. For the child, at least up to age ten and probably beyond, the essential moorings are in family ties. As we have said previously, it was found that, in general, children evacuated to safety from the threat of aerial bombardment, but removed from their parents, suffered far greater psychological strain than those who remained with their parents even in the face of actual danger.[23] At one time, disaster rescue and relief workers had as their first instinctive impulse the need to collect children and take them to a safe place where they could be cared for in groups. In the Dutch flood disasters of a few years ago, by contrast, a deliberate attempt was made to take account of World War II experience and keep children with their families, or at least their mothers and siblings—fathers, for the most part, being required to take part in emergency operations.

American investigators, studying children's recovery from the psychological effects of such disasters as floods and tornadoes, found that those children who had to step in and take over the functions and responsibilities of a dead or incapacitated parent or older sibling, and those who had the greatest opportunity to discuss and ventilate their experiences, were the first to recover.[24] Ironically enough, "better-off" middle-class families, in which there was less likely to be a clear-cut role for a child to assume, and which protectively tried to keep children from talking about the awful events they had witnessed, were likely to prevent children from discharging their accumulated feelings and thus helped perpetuate them. It should be noted, however, that adults are likely to misperceive the way children experience disaster; a superlative literary example of this is given in the novel *A High Wind in Jamaica*. Following a severe hurricane that demolished the family plantation, the mother observes:

> "That awful night!" said Mrs. Thornton, once, when discussing their plan of sending [the children] home to school: "Oh, my dear, what the

poor little things must have suffered! Think how much more acute Fear is to a child! And they were so brave, so English. . . . You know, I am terribly afraid what permanent, *inward* effect a shock like that may have on them. Have you noticed they never so much as mention it? . . ."

Meanwhile, the children, accepting the new life as a matter of course, were thoroughly enjoying it.[25]

We might mention in passing the nomadic societies of children that sprang up in southern and eastern Europe following World Wars I and II. Children separated from their parents formed roving, predatory bands which developed their own cultures of a highly psychopathic turn. Again there is a literary depiction of such behavior in *Lord of the Flies,* which describes in harrowing detail the sociology of a group of castaway children.[26]

Studies on the effects of major social upheavals are, of course, only at the beginning, but their findings are important and dependable enough to make a vital difference in the thinking of those charged with planning for civil defense and disaster relief. Meanwhile, we can see that we have our work cut out for us to provide a world fit for our children to grow up in.

NOTES (Starred items are recommended as further readings.)

[1] Sarason, S. B., *Psychological Problems in Mental Deficiency,* New York: Harper, second edition 1953, pp. 101-133.

[2] "Retarded infants," *Time,* August 13, 1956, p. 34.

[3] Haeussermann, Else, "Estimating developmental potential of pre-school children with brain lesions," *American Journal of Mental Deficiency,* 1956, 61, 170-180.

[4] Stone, L. J., and Fine, C. G., *The Effects of a Revised Preschool Program on the Personality Development and Communication Efficiency of Young Deaf Children.* (Monograph in preparation)

[5] Griffiths, Ciwa, *The Utilization of Individual Hearing Aids on Young Deaf Children.* Unpublished Ed.D. dissertation, University of Southern California, 1955; Hardy, W. G., "Hearing aids for deaf children?" A panel discussion, *Volta Review,* 1954, 56; Fry, D. B., and Whetnall, Edith, "The auditory approach in the training of deaf children," *Lancet,* March 20, 1954.

[6] Recent studies by L. P. Strean and L. A. Peer suggest that cleft palate is a result of prenatal influence (see pages 20-23), specifically of severe emotional or physiological stress between the eighth and twelfth weeks of pregnancy. Cleft palate was induced experimentally in mice by injecting the mother with hydrocortisone at an analogous point in prenatal development. *New York Times,* September 5, 1956.

[7] Meyerson, Lee, "Somatopsychology of physical disability," in Cruickshank, W. M., *Psychology of Exceptional Children and Youth*, Englewood Cliffs: Prentice-Hall, 1955, pp. 1-60.

[8] Spitz, R. A., "The psychogenic diseases in infancy: An attempt at their etiologic classification," *Psychoanalytic Study of the Child*, 1951, 6, 255-275.

[9] Kanner, Leo, "Early infantile autism," *Journal of Pediatrics*, 1944, 25, 211-217.

[10] Eisenberg, Leon, and Kanner, Leo, "Early infantile autism, 1943-55," *American Journal of Orthopsychiatry*, 1956, 27, 556-566.

[11] Levy, D. M., "Psychic trauma of operations in children and a note on combat neurosis," *American Journal of Diseases of Children*, 1945, 49, 7-25.

[12] An account of one such program may be found in Hunt, A. D., and Trussell, R. E., "They let parents help in children's care," *The Modern Hospital*, September, 1955.

[13] Lee, B. S., "Artificial stutter," *Journal of Speech and Hearing Disorders*, 1951, 16, 53-55.

[14] Johnson, Wendell, et al., "A study of the onset and development of stuttering," *Journal of Speech and Hearing Disorders*, 1942, 7, 251-257.

[15] A survey of theories of reading disability may be found in Robinson, H. M., *Why Pupils Fail in Reading*, Chicago: University of Chicago Press, 1946.

[16] Papanek, Ernst, Lecture, Vassar College, 1956.

[17] Freud, Anna, and Burlingham, D. T., *War and Children*, New York: International Universities Press, 1943, p. 75.

[18] Cohen, A. K., *Delinquent Boys: The Culture of the Gang*, Glencoe, Ill.: The Free Press, 1955.

[19] Bloch, H. A., and Flynn, F. T., *Delinquency*, New York: Random House, 1956, pp. 171-174.

[20] Bowlby, John, "Forty-four juvenile thieves: Their characters and home life," *International Journal of Psycho-Analysis*, 1944, 25, 19-53, 122, 154-178.

[21] Lacey, John I., Bateman, D. E., and Van Lehn, Ruth, "Autonomic response specificity: An experimental study," *Psychosomatic Medicine*, 1953, 15, 8-21; Wenger, M. A., "The measurement of individual differences in autonomic balance," *Psychosomatic Medicine*, 1941, 3, 427-434.

[22] Hunt, J. McV., "An instance of the social origin of conflict resulting in psychoses," *American Journal of Orthopsychiatry*, 1938, 8, 158-164. Also in Kluckhohn, Clyde, Murray, H. A., and Schneider, D. M. (eds.), *Personality in Nature, Society, and Culture*, New York: Knopf, 1953, pp. 456-463.

[23] Freud and Burlingham, *War and Children*.

[24] Perry, S. E., Silber, E., and Bloch, D. A., *The Child and His Family in Disaster*, Washington: National Research Council, Committee on Disaster Studies Monograph Series, #5, 1956; Perry, H. S. and S. E., *Operation Schoolhouse: A Preliminary Report*. Unpublished report to Committee on Disaster Studies, National Research Council, 1956.

*[25] Hughes, *A High Wind in Jamaica*, New York: The Modern Library, p. 64.

*[26] Golding, William, *Lord of the Flies*, New York: Coward-McCann, 1954.

FOR FURTHER READING

Murphy, G., and Bachrach, A. J. (eds.), *An Outline of Abnormal Psychology,* New York: The Modern Library, revised edition 1954. See especially sections on childhood and adolescence, pp. 3-341, and on prevention, pp. 536-589.

Hartley, Birch, and Hartley, *Outside Readings in Psychology.* See especially chapters 22 (hysterical blindness), 29 (hallucinations), 42 (reading disabilities), 49 (amnesia), 62 (psychosomatics), 65 (mental deficiency), and 76 (schizophrenic logic); and Section XV, "Personality and its disorders."

Barker, R. G., Wright, B. A., Meyerson, L., and Gonick, M. R., *Adjustment to Physical Handicap and Illness: A Survey of the Social Psychology of Physique and Disability,* New York: Social Science Research Council, 1953.

Benda, C. E., "Psychopathology of childhood," in Carmichael, *Manual of Child Psychology,* pp. 1115-1161. A highly condensed, somewhat technical survey of many varieties of psychopathology, organic and functional.

CHAPTER 14

The Study of Children

In this chapter, we want to shift our attention from the child himself to the people who study him. Specifically, we want to define the field of child study and how it has evolved, the methods used to find out about children, some of the theoretical issues and formulations that have arisen in this area, and some of the problems that lie ahead for students of childhood.

The Field of Child Study

Child study as a field of specialized interest has emerged at the junction of a great many other disciplines. Its early origins lie in philosophy, education, and natural history. More recently, it has been fed by such sources as experimental psychology, clinical psychology, psychiatry, medicine, physiology, sociology, anthropology, and linguistics. In spite of its mixed ancestry, it is generally thought of as a semi-independent field of study. However, its boundaries remain somewhat indefinite, and its goals and emphases diverse. Let us make explicit three splits of emphasis which, while by no means absolute, will provide a framework for the various activities that go on in the field. First, there can be emphasis either on *research* or on *application,* on finding out how children operate and how they grow, or on doing things to and for children. Child study finds its applications in the psychiatric and psychological clinic, in the schools, in welfare agencies, in the juvenile court, in the doctor's office and the hospital, and in programs of parent and family education. Second, there can be an emphasis on either the *normal* or the *abnormal,* on the usual course of development or on what can go wrong. Finally,

386

there can be an emphasis on the *child himself* and his inner workings or on the *child's environment* and how it affects his behavior and development. Regardless of emphasis, however, the concern is always with *finding out*.

Now let us look at some of the different kinds of things that people who study children are interested in finding out about. Some people are interested in children—*as children*—as a sub-species separate from adults, in the characteristic ways all children, or children at a particular age, or children of a particular type, or children living under particular conditions, function. This interest is reflected, e.g., in such studies as Woodcock's *Life and Ways of the Two-Year-Old;* Biber, Murphy, Woodcock, and Black's *Child Life in School;* and Gesell's cross-sectional studies of particular ages. For some students, the concern is less with how the child operates at any one time than with how he changes. The concern with developmental change may be focused on physical changes, as in the Fels Growth Studies; on intellectual development, as in the work of Piaget; or on total development, as in the writings of Gordon Allport or in Gesell's or Bühler's[1] studies of growth sequences. Some students are interested in the growth process itself, more or less independent of what is growing, be it child, animal, the phylogenetic series, or civilization. We find this interest most clearly embodied in Werner's *Comparative Psychology of Mental Development*. Then we should mention those students who are interested in single children and how they function and develop, either for purposes of clinical diagnosis or for research on the varieties of personality and on personality development and dynamics. Research on single individuals is exemplified by L. B. Murphy's current study of "coping patterns" in young children, the resources and skills they use in dealing with their environments.[2] Finally, we should point to research which only incidentally—or accidentally—deals with children and which does not properly fall within the area of child study. In such research, children are used as experimental subjects, not because the experimenter is interested in finding out about children, but because children are ready at hand to serve as experimental subjects, as specimens of human beings in general. Prominent among such studies are many of the experiments on the learning process, both in the laboratory and in the classroom, which seek to define the external conditions of learning and could as easily use adults or white rats for subjects. We should point out, however, that even studies that do not tell us anything about children as such may still have practical implications for teachers or parents. Studies on the relative merits of spaced and massed practice in learning, for instance, can be quite important for teaching methods.

As we can see, child study is many different things to many different people. It is not yet a field in its own right—nowhere, for instance, can one earn a doctoral degree in child study. Nevertheless, as we shall see, the boundaries between disciplines and schools of thought are gradually being subordinated to a common concern with childhood, and people sharing this concern feel part of a common field.

The Methods of Child Study

It is not our purpose in this chapter to offer a detailed exposition of research methodology, but to point to some of the key techniques and methodological concepts that have emerged as the special tools of child study.[3] These tools are a legacy from the several eras and viewpoints of child study, and can perhaps best be seen in the light of the problems and assumptions that produced them—that is, in historical perspective. In this survey, we are indebted to the historical and theoretical summaries of such writers as L. K. Frank, Gardner Murphy, and J. E. Anderson.[4] We should further make clear that this presentation will be biased in selection and emphasis by the authors' vantage point in psychology, particularly the psychology of personality development.

The most basic tools whose development we shall be tracing are *observation methods, laboratory techniques, tests and measurements,* and *clinical methods.* Each of these arose in an era and has survived, in modified forms, down to the present. The four overlapping eras in the study of the child, corresponding to the four basic tools, are the *naturalist era,* beginning in the eighteenth century and reaching its culmination in the mid-nineteenth century; the *era of early experimental psychology,* at its peak in the last quarter of the nineteenth century; the *era of "individual differences,"* most prominent in the first third of the present century; and the *era of personality study,* covering the past twenty years. This historical division is based on a changing concept of the individual, which will become apparent in the discussion that follows.

The Naturalist Era

As we have pointed out in past chapters, childhood has been a concern throughout recorded history. For the most part, however, this concern has been expressed in maxims and prescriptions, such as the biblical proverbs about sparing the rod, the educational theories proposed in Plato's *Republic* and in the writings of Rousseau, and Cotton Mather's views on child rearing. It did not occur to most writers on childhood to question either what children are like or what, empirically, would work. There were, of course, a few exceptions. We have already mentioned Salimbene's account of an ill-fated experiment by Frederick II, designed to find out what language children would speak spontaneously; a similar experiment conducted in ancient Egypt is reported by Herodotus. Rousseau's *Confessions* is an insightful account of his own childhood, anticipating many of Freud's formulations. The naturalist era began in earnest with the work of Pestalozzi and of Tiedemann, who in the eighteenth century published biographical accounts of infant development, based on extended observation.[5] In the nineteenth century, similar baby biographies were published by Darwin, Preyer, Shinn, and many others.[6] The day-by-day recording of development practiced by these authors became known as the *diary method*. The flavor of such accounts can be gained from the quotation on page 186 from the Scupins' study of their son Bubi.

It is important to note that although these reports were based on the study of single individuals, they were in no way studies of individuality in the modern sense. The early students of childhood were in search of *the* "universal child," and were not at all concerned with the ways one child differed from another.

The naturalists, like the great nineteenth-century naturalists in biology, had as their basic method *observation,* a detailed record of what the child did *in his natural setting* and in the course of his normal day's activities. By and large, they made no attempt to analyze or manipulate variables in the child's situation with a view to studying either particular kinds of responses or influences on development. Another aspect of the naturalist method is that it was *longitudinal*—that is, it consisted of repeated observations of the *same* individual. (The longitudinal approach is usually contrasted with the *cross-sectional,* where development is studied by comparing *different* children of different ages. We shall have more to say about these approaches later.) Nowadays, many of the early naturalist observations are likely to appear hopelessly naïve. Since they lacked comparisons among children, among situations, among conditions of development, and among observers, they were wholly uncontrolled. The observers, for the most part, did not hesitate to impose their own subjective feelings and interpretations on what they saw. Nevertheless, these early records are still a rich source of factual material on child development.

The naturalist method, of course, continued into the era of early experimental psychology and, in altered form, as we shall see, down to the present day. The early psychologists with an interest in children were primarily naturalistic in their approach, but they had already begun to adapt the old methods to the experimental approach. G. Stanley Hall, for instance, worked largely with the new tool of *questionnaires,* where attention is focused on specific areas of children's functioning, and where the investigator relies on the child's own account of what he does and thinks. The questionnaire method meant both that data could be quantified and that they were collected under controlled conditions rather than under natural field conditions.

The Era of Early Experimental Psychology

Unlike the naturalists, who were concerned with the total functioning of the child—but always of *The* Child—the early experimental psychologists were largely concerned with *part-functions:* seeing, hearing, remembering, thinking, and so forth. Like the naturalists, though, they were in search of the *universal* forms of these "pure" functions. In their search for universality and purity, they moved out of the field and into the laboratory, where the complications of everyday life could be weeded out. In the laboratory, they could use the methods of *psychophysics,* varying conditions systematically and one at a time. To make conditions even purer, they stripped stimuli—insofar as this was possible—of all meaning, as in Ebbinghaus's famous nonsense syllables.[7] In their pursuit of the universal, they regarded individual differences in response as an experimental nuisance, and they used repeated measurements to give them averages and smooth curves. In the same way, variations due to developmental differences were unwelcome—the early experimentalists were for the most part interested only in the pure, universal part-functions of the adult. Consequently, there was little laboratory experimentation done with children in the early psychophysical era. Later on, laboratory psychologists did become interested in developmental variations, and studies were made of changes with age in such aspects and kinds of behavior as the reminiscence effect (the tendency to recall more memorized items after a lapse of time than immediately after memorization), reaction time (the interval required to respond to a signal), and problem-solving. Gradually, the psychophysicists abandoned their search for pure functions, recognizing that the person and his sub-systems always had to have some sort of object to behave *toward*—a person does not merely remember in the abstract, he remembers *something*. With this change from an absolute to a relative orientation, it became possible to compare, for instance, the retention of meaningful and meaningless material, or the thresholds at which these are perceived. In addition, the experimental methods of the laboratory became applicable to a wide variety of problems outside the laboratory, where the immediate and long-range effects of more complex conditions—authoritarian versus democratic versus *laissez-faire* leadership, for instance, or the sight method versus the phonics method of teaching reading—could be studied. In effect, the basic method of *experiment* which we have inherited from the psychophysicists demands only that we control our conditions and make comparisons between them.

The Era of "Individual Differences"

Early in the twentieth century, a new concern arose in scientific psychology, a two-faceted concern with seeing people in terms of "complex traits" like intelligence and in terms of how these traits are distributed in the population at large. The emphasis now was not on the nature of single mental functions or operations but on *how much* or *how well* (expressed in terms of deviation up or down from the average of other people). It was still not on individuality as such. The battle cry of the day was that "everything that exists, exists in some measurable degree." We should point out that this attitude for quite a while produced not a search for ways of measuring what was most important, but a preoccupation with those things that could be most readily measured. It was at this time that the tool of *testing* (at first of intelligence, to be followed later by tests of more specialized abilities such as mechanical aptitude, musical ability, and so forth) became of primary concern. Among the pioneers in the testing movement were Galton, Cattell, Thorndike, Thurstone, Terman, Spearman, and later many others. The mental measurements (also known as *psychometrics*) movement was for a long time largely an American phenomenon, but its key figure was probably the Frenchman Alfred Binet—although for him the devising of the famous intelligence test bearing his name was only a side issue. Binet is responsible for the concept of *mental age,* level of achievement in terms of the average scored on an intelligence test by children of a given chronological age. The principle of age-scaling introduced by Binet was later applied to measures yielding such indices as "social age," "reading age," "bone age," and so forth. It is important to see that trait measurements on age or any other scales are always relative to the population at large. Nevertheless, they have often been treated as though they were *absolute* measures, expressing the actual "quantity" of intelligence—or whatever—that an individual possessed.

We should point out that the announced concern of the early psychometricians with "individual differences" was really a concern with *group variation* in respect to one trait at a time, and not with the way one individual differs from another. Nevertheless, mental measurements were applied to individuals for purposes of educational and vocational placement—Binet's test was intended specifically as an aid in estimating an individual's ability to learn, and in distinguishing between the inadequate and the lazy. Going further, a number of psychometricians sought to arrive at an overall assessment of the individual by determining his score on series of tests designed to measure different traits. Although this approach enabled the tester to make a number of separate statements about the individual under consideration, it did not provide any rationale for how these sundry traits were related to each other. Often, the psychometricians seemed to concentrate on the measuring devices themselves, and on generalizing patterns of group variation in terms of the normal distribution curve, to the neglect of the individuals —or even the traits—under study. Although children were extensively used as subjects in preparing and applying tests, the original interest of the testing movement was not in the nature of children. More recently, tests have come into use that reveal more clearly the individual patterns of functioning underlying the total score; testers themselves have become more flexible in interpreting test results; and tests have become an indispensable instrument for studying individual children.

Two concepts that became prominent in the psychometric age are *reliability* and *validity*. Reliability in a test means that it gives essentially the same results from one use to the next, that it provides a stable, dependable measure. The problem of test reliability has been pretty well solved (at least over short periods, while the individual remains much the same), although a certain amount of variability cannot be avoided. Validity, on the other hand, means that a test measures what it is supposed to measure. In theory, a reliable test should also be valid —it is obvious that, since it always comes up with more or less the same results, it must be measuring something. The problem is to know *what* it is measuring. The customary way of validating a test is against some other manifestation of the trait it is measuring. An intelligence test, for instance, should predict how well a child does in school. Unfortunately, judgments as to a child's school performance are not very reliable, quite apart from the fact that school performance is influenced, as we have seen, by a number of factors other than intelligence. In point of fact, intelligence test results do correlate reasonably well with school achievement—that is, *in general,* those who score high on intelligence tests do well in school, and those who score low do poorly. But there are numerous individual exceptions, and we cannot be sure whether these are due to misjudgments by teachers, to the operation of factors other than intelligence, or to the tests themselves. Test-makers have worried a great deal about validity, but have not come up with any satisfactory solution. As often as not, a test is validated by comparing it with other tests of the same thing. The important lesson here is that tests are objective as measuring instruments, but that their validity— the *meaning* of the scores they yield—and, hence, their utility depends as much on subjective judgments as does any other psychological procedure.

It should not be supposed that tests were the only new tools produced during the mental measurements era. The observation methods of the naturalists were also being given a quantifiable form. Two new techniques, especially, were coming into widespread use, the *rating scale* and the *time sample.* Only the second of these was devised expressly for use with children, but both have found many applications in child study. The rating scale is a device by which a judge assigns an individual a score with respect to one or more traits, such as honesty, diligence, co-operativeness, etc. The rating can be relative to other members of the same group, in terms of descriptive categories, or simply a quantitative approximation of the judge's subjective feeling: "Very much," "Slightly," "Not at all." Ratings may be based on specially made observations of specific behavior or specific situations, or on long-standing acquaintance—as by a parent or teacher—with the child. By comparing ratings of the same child on the same trait at different times or by different judges, one can arrive at a measure of how reliable the ratings are. With reliability established, ratings permit comparisons between individuals, between groups, or between conditions—such as teaching methods—affecting individuals or groups. Ratings can be applied to things as well as to people, and are used for such purposes as judging the quality of children's drawings produced under different conditions. Ratings of intelligence have been one of the favorite devices used in validating intelligence tests—although the tests, of course, were meant to supplant such highly subjective methods. The chief problem in using rating scales is to define the traits to be rated in such a way that they can meaningfully be applied to all children.

The time sample is a method of observation which focuses the observer's attention on the occurrence (or non-occurrence) of certain predetermined forms of behavior, which are taken as representative of some trait being studied. Observations are made of a fixed number of children over pre-selected brief time segments, giving a *sampling* of the child's activity regardless of such transient influences as mood, particular events, and so forth. Time sampling has been used to study, for instance, the relationship between having few or many toys to play with and frequency of aggressive outbursts, and the prevalence at various ages or under different conditions of such traits as nervousness and sociability. Much of our knowledge of neonatal functioning comes from the time sample observations made by Pratt, Nelson, and Sun. It is important to see how the time-sampling method was intended to restrict and objectify the free-flowing, qualitative (and, by implication, subjective) diary method of the naturalists. By focusing attention on specific *acts,* which either do or do not occur, and whose occurrence has only to be checked off in the appropriate space on a record, this method relieves the observer of any need to interpret what he sees. On the other hand, this method puts a heavy onus on the person defining the behavior categories that are included on the record sheet, since he has to find objective acts that stand in a fixed relation to the trait being studied; nose-picking, for instance, is often a symptom of nervousness, but many children also pick their noses simply because they have not graduated to handkerchiefs. It appears that time-sampling methods work best when a certain amount of leeway is left to the observer so that he can judge "subjectively" whether or not a given act merits inclusion in his record.

Another trend in the psychometric era, foreshadowing the concern with individuality of the era that was to follow, was the initiation of a number of *longitudinal* studies. As we have said, the early naturalist studies were predominantly longitudinal, but, beginning with the work of G. Stanley Hall, the bulk of research in child development was *cross-sectional,* comparing different children of different ages. The cross-sectional method raised the grave methodological problem of whether a description of growth processes that was based on data from different individuals could properly be considered a description of growth. The longitudinal studies set out to answer this question by mapping the growth of the same individuals from birth onward. They demonstrated, indeed, that the growth curves of individuals differed significantly from the smooth curves based on group averages. We are indebted to the longitudinal studies for our knowledge of latencies and asynchronies in growth, and of the typical growth paths followed by different individuals, patterns that had been totally obscured by the earlier methods of study. In spite of their focus on individual development, the growth studies were largely conceived within the measurements framework, and concentrated on psychometric techniques or measurements of physical traits. Nowadays we cannot help regretting that certain developmental problems that currently seem more urgent were not selected for study. However, every age tends to disparage the contributions of the preceding one, failing to recognize that we cannot always plunge straight to the heart of a matter, and what seems a burning issue today may tomorrow be obsolete. The catalogues of abilities compiled in the classic psychometric age do not today strike us as very compelling, but if the psychometricians had not done their job, we should probably not be able to see the issues that now impress us as crucial. Moreover, as it has turned out, psychometric instruments often do not serve the purposes they were originally meant to, but have become very useful for other purposes.

The Era of Personality Study

Psychology has always been interested in how people operate. The early scientific psychologists and psychometricians, though, were primarily concerned with the technical problem of how human functioning could be taken apart for easy study. By the mid-1930's, there was a growing sensitivity to the complaint from various sources that the person had been reduced to too many bits and pieces, that he had been sacrified to a particular conception of scientific method, and that it was time to try putting him back together again. For when the human being is considered part by part, the special human qualities that belong to his total functioning tend to disappear: his feelings, his purposes, and his personal, idiosyncratic style. The individual is not a simple bundle of traits which he possesses in greater or lesser amounts. His various traits are functionally subordinated in an organized pattern to his peculiarly human concerns, and whatever traits he has in common with other people take on their own peculiar, individual meaning in the context of his specific kind of human functioning. Under the influence both of Gestalt psychology and of psychoanalysis, psychologists were becoming concerned with the concept and the study of personality, of how people are organized—in effect, with the nature of individuality. Whereas the early psychophysicists had sought to measure *pure* functions independent of meanings, and the early psychometricians had sought to measure *pure* intelligence independent of past experience and of other traits like emotionality, the new generation wanted to give all these intrusive nuisances full play, to see the whole person interacting with his real surroundings. In this sense, the new era was a return to naturalism. But unlike naturalism, there was now a concern with the individual, the unique, and the deviant, as well as with the universal.

Indeed, the qualitative diary records of the naturalists underwent a considerable revival in new and more sophisticated forms known as *refined diary methods.* It was established that qualitative records could have a high degree of reliability—in fact, that judges could agree more easily on the qualitative, meaningful aspects of behavior than on the specific, "objective" acts that took place.[7a] This reliability is, however, contingent on training in how children function and in how their functioning is revealed in their behavior. The observer must learn how to remain simultaneously detached, so that his feelings do not become confused with what he perceives, and responsive, so that the meaning and feeling tone of a child's behavior are not lost—to be objective does not mean to reduce one's human subject to a mere object. Among the specific varieties of the refined diary method, in the terminology we have adopted, are *running records,* detailed, minute-by-minute accounts of an event or an action; *impression records,* designed to record a first, overall sense of a group or an individual's functioning; and *anecdotal records,* often based on recall, describing some significant piece of behavior.[7b] Such records are useful both for the study of individual children and for research on group characteristics. The data of refined diary records can be categorized and quantified in the same way as the behavior on which they are based. Indeed, one form of time sampling, instead of providing specific items of behavior to be checked off, requires that the observer make a running record of the child's behavior during each time-sampling unit. By using the same number of time samples for two groups, the groups can be compared with respect to any kind of behavior occurring in the records.

Again in the naturalist tradition, field studies—now mostly of children in the slightly artificial natural habitat of the nursery school— were once more in order. Research by Biber, Woodcock, and other members of what is now the Bank Street College of Education was conducted primarily in the form of field studies. The studies on leadership by Lewin and his associates attempted to set up experimentally a more or less natural environment for the subjects, and used field observation methods. Later on, the ecological studies by Barker and his collaborators, designed to record precisely how and where children spend their time, and what parts of their surroundings are a part of their functional world, were conducted as field studies.[8]

But the really new methods of this era were what Allport has called the *idiographic* techniques, those designed to reveal individual uniqueness, as opposed to *nomothetic* devices aimed at the discovery of general laws.[9] Chief among the idiographic techniques were the *projective methods,* which owe their name and a rationale to L. K. Frank.[10] A projective technique confronts the individual with a largely unstructured or ambiguous situation, to which he is encouraged to respond in any way he wants. The specific meanings he attaches to the situation are deemed significant of *him* and of *his* way of perceiving the world. The best-known projective techniques are probably the *Rorschach,* where the shapes and qualities and meanings that an individual attributes to a series of ink blots reveal the structure of his private world; Murray's *Thematic Apperception Test,* where the stories a subject makes up about a series of pictures tell us about his feelings and attitudes toward certain central dynamic concerns; and Jung's *Word Association Test,* where the individual's reactions to a list of stimulus words point to stressful areas in his life. While these techniques can be used to a certain extent with children, a number of special child-oriented projective techniques (particularly the projective play techniques) have been devised. Some of the stimulus materials used in these techniques are: a heterogeneous assortment of toys representing people and both commonplace and exotic animals and objects (as in Murphy's Miniature Life Toys); a roomful of balloons which the child is allowed to play with—and break; and pictures of children or animals designed to elicit personally toned narratives. There are also continuing attempts to extend the applicability of such techniques as the Rorschach chronologically downward, as in the work of Ford,[11] and of Klopfer and Anna Schachtel with Murphy, Stone, and members of the Sarah Lawrence project.[12] Unlike most experimental and psychometric devices, which demand a particular kind of response, the projective methods give maximum scope to the individual's own response inclinations. They reveal the *what* and the *why* and the *how* of the individual's experience and activity, rather than the *how much* or the *how well.* There are no right and wrong responses to a projective situation, every response being "right," since it tells us something of how the individual sees his world, of how he as a person organizes his perceptions, his wishes, and his values. The projective technique can reveal an individual's inner organization without putting him on trial or making him feel exposed to public view, unlike the questionnaire, whose items he may be unable or unwilling to complete accurately. In short, the projective technique is a device that permits the individual to "reveal himself without committing himself."

The projective techniques were originally intended as diagnostic and therapeutic devices, but have now become firmly entrenched as tools for studying normal personality development. They played an important role in such research as the Sarah Lawrence College studies of normal development and Murphy's continuation of these as studies of "coping patterns." Projective techniques have been used to study personality differences between children of high and low socio-economic standing.[13] A longitudinal study employing the Rorschach test has found a striking group correspondence—with individual exceptions—between peaks of anxiety as indicated by certain test indicators and crises in psychosexual development as defined by Freudian theory.[14] Apart from such personality-centered research, projective tests have been found to be useful instruments for the study of perceptual processes.[15]

Scientists bred in the psychometric tradition have often been disturbed by the problems of reliability and validity in projective methods. It is possible that the concept of reliability is irrelevant to what is an essentially idiographic method, although, in point of fact, the same individual does show consistency in his responses to repeated use of the same instrument. The problem of validity—which hinges about interpretations of projective data rather than the tests' ability to measure any one thing—is still unsolved (just as with psychometric devices), although a number of people are working hard at it. One widely used approach, devised by P. E. Vernon, is the *matching method,* which requires judges to say which of a collection of behavior samples (including performances in projective situations) belong to the same individuals; the judges' success in matching behavior samples can then be evaluated statistically.[16] This method is akin to Cronbach's proposal that validity can best be shown by an interpreter's ability to make real-life inferences from projective data.[17] This is not as easy as it sounds. For one thing, very few psychologists would pretend to be able to know an individual thoroughly from a single test of any sort. Particularly with children, it seems expedient to use a *battery* of projective and other methods, and, wherever possible, to repeat the tests at intervals of a few weeks or months in order to distinguish between stable aspects of behavior and the accidental ones that might affect a single testing. In practice, most studies of individuals involve, over and above projective data, observations made in real-life situations, interview material, biographical information, and perhaps medical and psychometric evaluations. These various kinds of information are then usually integrated in terms of some theory of personality. Furthermore, the very purpose of projective techniques is to get at factors in the individual which would not become evident in most real-life situations—if they did, there would be no need for projective methods. Finally, to know what an individual is going to do in real life requires that one know what kinds of situations he is going to encounter, since he obviously is not going to behave the same way under all circumstances. Meanwhile, the most successful interpretations seem to rest on elusive qualitative cues, but there are earnest efforts under way to try to isolate and identify these cues.

During this same period, there was increasing reliance on the "natural experiment," the method used in such fields as astronomy, sociology, and medicine, or wherever the conditions to be studied are beyond the researcher's control (for either ethical or practical reasons), and he is obliged to wait for them to appear naturally. Studies of the effects of brain damage in human beings are necessarily of this kind. So are studies such as Spitz's on the effects of early isolation on babies. So are studies such as Anna Freud's and the National Research Council's on psychological effects of disasters. In the same way, anyone interested in abnormal development is obliged to deal with those cases he encounters. He cannot manipulate pathogenic conditions except statistically, after the fact. He can, of course, study animals, with which he has greater latitude than with human subjects, and it is worth noting that some of the strongest support for concepts in child psychology comes from the findings of animal psychology—we might mention the studies by Liddell and others with sheep and goats on mother-child relationships and on experimental neurosis—and from the branch of zoology known as *ethology*. The natural experiment is also the method of the clinical psychologist or psychiatrist who wants to make a study of a single individual, as an exercise in idiographic reporting, or because he is interested in the effects of particular conditions, or for research in personality differences or on therapeutic methods. The natural experiment is likewise the method of anthropological research, of which we shall say more later.

As we have seen, then, the four basic methods of child study— observation, experiment, tests and measurements, and clinical techniques—arose successively out of differing orientations and concerns. But all of them have proven their usefulness for a variety of purposes far exceeding their original applications. Not all methods are equally valid for all purposes, of course, but all are valid for particular purposes, and together they form an indispensable armamentarium.

As a footnote, we might add a fifth "method" of child study, fictional treatments of children. Thanks partly to the influence of Freud, and in keeping with the temper of the times, writers of fiction have become increasingly concerned with children as characters. Moreover, there has been a marked shift in how children are viewed. Writers have become aware in a new way of the subjective life of children and of their motivational dynamics. In addition, adult characters in fiction nowadays tend to be accounted for as the products of their childhood in a way that was impossible in the nineteenth century. So far, the communication between scientific child study and literature has been largely in one direction—that is, the novelists and short story writers and essayists have profited from child psychology, but we have failed to take sufficient advantage of their insights. We should like to suggest that the perceptiveness of fictional studies often surpasses anything child study proper has to offer. As a means of becoming oriented to the nature of children, the student could not do better than to look into the literature of childhood. Furthermore, an historical review of such literature from Lamb and Dickens to Joyce and Salinger will bring home to the student with considerable impact just how radically and how rapidly our concepts of childhood have changed.

Trends and Influences in Child Study

In the last section, we presented a view of how the methods of child study evolved. This account was tied to our interest in the various ways of viewing the person, to the concern or lack of concern with individuality. There were, of course, other central themes around which to organize our review of developments in this field of study. We have referred to several of these in passing, and we shall now turn back to two major topics, the heredity-environment controversy, and the several theoretical viewpoints that were important in child study.

Heredity and Environment

Prior to the age of Darwin, people tended to think of behavior and development now as the expression of inborn tendencies, now as the product of environmental influences for good or bad, now in terms of free will. The interconnections among these were left obscure. Thanks to Darwin's theory of evolution, however, man's biological nature suddenly became all-important. Most of the early naturalists were influenced by Darwin, and their chief concern became to understand the unfolding of innate processes in the individual. For the Darwinians, the environment was important, but only as it perpetuated or suppressed hereditary variations by favoring or killing off their carriers. Quantities of data were becoming available from anthropological studies on ways of life totally unlike our own, but these were treated as manifestations of racial differences or of intermediate stages in human evolution. Preyer's observations of children were directed toward a catalogue of instincts and reflexes. G. Stanley Hall was pursuing his notion of recapitulation, so that playing Indians was seen as passing through a biological stage of evolution, and even one's religious beliefs became a matter of biological determination. Indeed, a vast number of things which we now take for granted as learned behavior, culturally and environmentally determined, were, half a century ago, taken just as much for granted as being biologically determined. Much of the early work in the field of psychometrics was a search for biologically given variation—it was an astonishingly long time before anyone appreciated the inappropriateness of giving, say, a Navaho child an intelligence test which required him to identify an automobile and a telephone. When, after a few years, the environment came back into the spotlight, there was an epidemic of studies designed to answer such problems as the relative potential impact of heredity and environment (or "nature" and "nurture") on particular traits; which traits were to be accounted for in terms of heredity and which in terms of environment; and the nature and extent of racial differences in intelligence and other traits. The *co-twin control* studies carried on by Gesell,[18] McGraw,[19] and others, in which the effects of different kinds of training upon two individuals of identical heredity could be assessed, were a reflection of this trend. Between 1910 and 1930, there was a movement of total environmental determinism spearheaded by Watson's behaviorism; Watson held that he could shape a child to any desired pattern merely by controlling his learning experiences in the first few years (see page 67). Watson reversed the emphasis in research away from preoccupation with capacities to a new concern with learning, particularly learning conceived of as a patterning of conditioned stimuli and responses, in keeping with the formulations of Pavlov. But the split between the biological determinists and the environmentalists spread far beyond the laboratory and into the realm of political and social ideology. The hereditarians were the conservatives, the supporters of the status quo, who saw the entire social order built upon biologically given distinctions. The environmentalists were the radicals, for whom there were no biologically given differences and for whom everything was the product of learning.

We hope that our discussion throughout this book has made it clear how obsolete such problems have become today. On the biological level, we know that the organism has to exist in a field, that it has no traits except as these are nourished on the environment in which it is embedded, that its hereditary endowment defines the framework of what it can become, and that within these limits the environment acts to shape it. On the psychological level, we have come to realize that all human behavior is both hereditary and learned, that we must take account of the cultural environment as well as the physical one, and that the problem is one of defining the ways in which a growing person with his own characteristics incorporates a body of values, attitudes, beliefs, knowledge, and practices, making them his own and at the same time being transformed by them. Now we are inclined to realize that each individual incorporates and views his culture in his own idiosyncratic way, but that he would be a very different person growing up in another culture.

Theoretical Influences

In what we have said so far, we have necessarily made some reference to theoretical schools, such as behaviorism and psychoanalysis, that have made contributions to child study. Now let us bring a few of these into the foreground, concentrating on those that are most influential today.

PSYCHOANALYTIC THEORIES Perhaps the most potent single influence on thinking about child development has been the psychoanalytic movement, in all its variants and derivatives, which first pointed to the crucial importance of childhood experiences for later development. It is not our intention here to introduce psychoanalytic theories (they play a prominent part in earlier chapters) or to elaborate them at length. We do, however, want to point to their place in child study. For one thing, psychoanalysis has made us aware of the sometimes indirect relationship between overt behavior and underlying psychological state, so that the same behavior in different people may mean different things, and quite different behaviors can mean the same thing. At the same time, it has provided a rationale by which underlying forces can be deduced from surface behavior, normal or abnormal. This conception of behavior has put a different complexion on many research problems. For one thing, it has directed attention away from capacities and toward the meaning of behavior. It is worth noting that Freud himself was hardly an experimental psychologist, but based his formulations of psychoanalytic theory upon clinical observations. Nevertheless, his speculations have stimulated a great deal of experimental research. The great array of studies on frustration and aggression, for example, stem directly from Freudian doctrines, as do a number of concepts that are currently the object of experimental attack: repression, regression, selective perception, and so on. Similarly, Levy's studies on the sucking response, the numerous studies reported by Sears,[20] and a number of anthropological investigations have been designed explicitly to test hypotheses drawn from psychoanalytic theory. We should further point out that Freud, in the naturalist tradition, was most interested in the *general* laws that governed all human behavior, and that it is only in recent years that psychoanalysts have become primarily concerned about the differences between individuals.

Although psychoanalytic theories are in large part developmental, the founders of the psychoanalytic movement had little to do with children. Their theories of development were based on inferences from the recollections of adult neurotic patients, and not on direct observation of children. It remained for subsequent generations of psychoanalysts— Anna Freud (Sigmund Freud's daughter), Erikson, Klein, Levy, and others—to investigate childhood at first hand. The primary technique of psychoanalysis, of course, is *free association,* encouraging the patient to say whatever comes into his head and to pursue his ideas wherever they lead. A second technique is to have the patient report his *dreams,* which are taken as symbolic representations of his unconscious conflicts. Neither of these techniques works too well with young children. The psychoanalytic workers mentioned above, in their search for a substitute for the free association and dream interpretation techniques for use with children, developed the therapeutic play techniques which in turn influenced the development of many of the projective play techniques used in research with children. Similarly, adult projective techniques, such as the Word Association Test, the Rorschach, and the Thematic Apperception Test, were developed within the framework of psychoanalysis, the first by Jung, the second by a psychiatrist much influenced by Jung, and the third by a follower of Freud.

Psychoanalysis brought to the attention of psychology at large the unconscious, irrational, selfish, and archaic—but nevertheless lawful— forces at work in human behavior. Perhaps because of the need to convince people that these forces really existed—we must remember the bitter indignation and skepticism with which Freud's ideas were first greeted—the early psychoanalysts may have overstressed them in their early formulations. Now that psychoanalysis has been to some extent accepted into the body of psychology at large, and has in turn been influenced by the concepts and concerns of workers in other areas, the psychoanalysts have restored reason, altruism, and a measure of self-determination to a major place in the human economy. Those psychoanalysts who are most concerned with cognitive functions are called *ego-psychologists.* Among the ego-psychologists who have done most with developmental problems are Hartmann, Kris, Rapaport, K. Wolf, and Escalona.

GESTALT AND FIELD THEORIES   Gestalt theory has always been primarily concerned with the study of perception rather than personality (except for some investigations by Wertheimer and by such students of his as Arnheim and Wolff). But, as we have said, its teachings lent support to those who felt that the person must be studied as a whole, and that the single traits studied by the psychometrician, as though they were simply a matter of more or less from one person to the next, in fact exist in the context of an integrated individual and so are qualitatively different from one person to the next.

Perhaps most influential in bringing the Gestalt view to child study (insofar as we may designate him a Gestalt psychologist) was Kurt Lewin, the founder of one type of field theory. Lewin not only produced brilliantly conceived experimental studies, but was responsible for such useful notions as the *life space,* a way of stating the individual's relationship to an environment which functionally was not separate from his own personality.[21] The individual, that is, carries around with him his own view of reality, his effective psychological life space, which in Lewin's and Koffka's[22] view may be quite different from the geographical and social reality he objectively occupies. Lewin's notion of the life space is not unlike Frank's concept of the "private world," except that Lewin applied a system of notation based on topological and vector mathematics to his ideas, and was more concerned with the general properties of life spaces than with their individual varieties. For Lewin, objects are defined not in terms of their physical characteristics but in terms of their positive or negative *valences,* their force of attraction or repulsion for the organism. In short, Lewin's field theory says that the organism must be understood in terms of the environment it occupies, and the environment in terms of how it appears to the organism. In line with his interest in the psychological environment, Lewin was more concerned with the effect of particular situations on behavior than with the general course of development or with the nature of the individual, and many of his and his followers' studies of child behavior tell us more about general human reactions than about the way children see the world.[23]

GENETIC PSYCHOLOGY The school of genetic (that is, developmental) psychology, represented by Werner, Piaget, Goldstein, Scheerer, and a number of other European and American scholars, has inherited from the naturalists an interest in how people develop as a whole. Some genetic psychologists apply developmental principles of organization not only to normal behavior and development but to our knowledge of primitive cultures, of psychopathology, brain damage, and old age. The genetic viewpoint appears in this book in the use of such terms as functional subordination, abstract and concrete behavior, and egocentrism, and hence does not need further elaboration here. It is enough to say that the genetic psychologists, as opposed to psychoanalysts, place greater emphasis on the structure of consciousness and less on unconscious dynamics, although there is no necessary incompatibility between the two schools of thought. The genetic viewpoint has been very fertile of research, and currently studies are being conducted, many of them with children, on the development of word meanings, on the relationships between sense modalities, and on orientation in space.

LEARNING THEORY Learning is an ancient psychological concept, but learning theory, in the sense of a systematic conceptualization of all of psychology in terms of learning, is a fairly recent development. Present-day learning theory is the heir of behaviorism, a behaviorism enriched by what it has assimilated from psychoanalysis and other sources, and by a more flexible and sophisticated methodology. Modern learning theory stems most directly from Hull's laboratory at Yale, and is represented by such people as Marquis, Sears, Mowrer, Dollard, N. E. Miller, Spence, and others. Unlike Watson, modern learning theorists are willing to grapple with a wide variety of psychological phenomena, rather than to exclude everything that cannot be reported and measured according to certain narrow rules. Like Watson, it seeks to explain these phenomena in terms of the laws of learning, conceived of as a complex organization of stimulus-response connections. Whereas psychoanalysis dominates the field of *applied* child psychology, learning theory, in one form or another, is probably the prevailing theoretical trend in most American colleges, universities, and research centers for psychology, including child psychology. Although hardly as extreme as early behaviorism, learning theory is still more preoccupied with the pattern of acquisition than with what is acquired, and more with the external conditions of learning than with how people are fitted together internally. It sees the higher and more complex human functions as posing an essentially semantic obstacle, so that the problem is to re-phrase them in terms of units of learning. The learning theory view of human behavior thus is fundamentally not only mechanistic but atom-istic and reductionist. Instead of dealing with emergent levels of activ-ity, it sees the human organism primarily in terms of its nervous system, a nervous system composed of separate bits organized like a piece of machinery, or, more recently, on the model of an electronic computer.

From the authors' viewpoint, this is an uncongenial level on which to deal with human functioning, because it does not deal with what the authors conceive of as the central problem of psychology, the person living in his human world. Although learning theory has a program that includes an attack on the problems of practical human functioning, and has stated in general terms how it plans to handle them, they remain a future concern. This is, in effect, a disagreement as to the proper business of psychology. Despite this disagreement, the authors are keenly aware that learning theorists are producing highly ingenious stud-ies with findings of importance for psychologists of all persuasions.

ANTHROPOLOGY   Anthropology, of course, is not a theory within psychology but an independent discipline with its own theoretical his-tory, some of it parallel to that of psychology. Nevertheless, anthropol-ogy has contributed a great deal of information and not a few theoretical elaborations to the field of child study. Just as psychoanalysis con-fronted psychology with the fact of unconscious motivation, anthropol-ogy has confronted it with varieties of human behavior that do not readily fit into some of the older psychological schemes. Not only does anthropology bring facts to be accounted for, but it can test psychological formulations made on the basis of observations of children in our cul-ture to see if they apply—as they must in order to have general validity —to children in other cultures as well. Among the anthropologists who have given special attention to patterns of development in primitive societies and in sub-groups in Western society are Mead, to whose work we have referred several times, Kluckhohn, Bateson, Benedict, Linton, D. D. Lee, and others. We should add to this list the names of several sociologists who have been concerned with developmental problems and family relationships: the Lynds, Havighurst, Hollingshead, Riesman, Bossard, Folsom, and others. There has been a marked trend toward collaboration between anthropologists and psychoanalysts and psychologists, as exemplified by the work of Kardiner and by current research on the relationship between linguistic structures and perception. Anthropologists have also begun to exploit the possibilities of projective techniques for use with primitive peoples, enriching both anthropology and psychology with their findings.

The Formalization of Child Study

Despite what we have had to say in this chapter so far, child study has not emerged solely as a product of scientific zeal directed toward an understanding of a newly discovered sub-species. In addition, its existence is a product of a demand by society at large for practical information. Parents, educators, doctors, criminologists, government officials, all needed facts on which to base programs of action. This public need found tangible expression in large sums of money made available for the establishment of public health programs directed toward children, child guidance clinics, and nursery schools, and for the support of research centers and research programs as well. The first of many psychological clinics in the country had been founded by Witmer at the University of Pennsylvania in 1896. Probably the first chair of genetic psychology was established at Clark University to perpetuate the interests of G. Stanley Hall. In 1918 generous grants for research in the area of child study and parent education were made available by the now-defunct Laura Spelman Rockefeller Memorial, administered by Beardsley Ruml and L. K. Frank, and by the Commonwealth Fund. With the help since then of these and other foundations, a number of research centers (sometimes named "research stations" or "child welfare institutes") were set up around the country, either as independent units or as parts of colleges and universities. These centers were often interdisciplinary organizations; sometimes they were under medical or home economics or educational or psychological auspices. Some of the better known of the currently active centers are at Iowa University, the University of Minnesota, Cornell, Yale, Ohio State University, the University of California, the University of Colorado, Western Reserve University, the University of Toronto, the Fels Institute, and the Merrill-Palmer School. Stanford University and the University of Kansas also have flourishing programs of research in child development. Programs of child study, as distinct from education or child psychology, were established here and there at the undergraduate level, too, as at Vassar College, where the authors teach. At the undergraduate level, unfortunately, study in this field is available for the most part only to women. One of the effects of foundation support was to make possible the large-scale longitudinal studies of development, which could not be undertaken without the assurance of continued funds. Outstanding longitudinal studies include those by Terman at Stanford on gifted children; several at the University of California, by the Joneses, Bayley, and Macfarlane; at Minnesota by Shirley and Boyd; and at Harvard, the Brush Foundation at Western Reserve, the Fels Institute, and the University of Colorado.

A number of publications oriented to the area of child study began to appear. The first of these was the *Pedagogical Seminary* (now the *Journal of Genetic Psychology*), founded by G. Stanley Hall in 1891. The roster now includes *Child Development, Child Study, Child Development Monographs, Child Development Abstracts,* the annual *Psychoanalytic Study of the Child,* and *Children,* not to mention educational journals, pediatric journals, clinically oriented publications such as the *American Journal of Orthopsychiatry,* and a number of other journals in which articles relevant to the field of child study appear.

The growth of the field of child study is reflected likewise in lay and professional societies. Organizations of parents and citizens, such as the Child Study Association and the National Congress of Parents and Teachers, date from the late nineteenth century. The Child Study Association is currently conducting a program of research aimed at ways of communicating scientific findings to parents. In 1909, G. Stanley Hall tried to form an association of child psychologists, but failed. However, since the American Psychological Association adopted a divisional structure, it has had a Division of Childhood and Adolescence (now called the Division on Developmental Psychology). In 1920, under the leadership of R. S. Woodworth, who was not a child psychologist but who nevertheless played an important role in the field, a Committee on Child Development was set up in the National Research Council. This Committee later became the Society for Research in Child Development, which is the chief inter-professional organization in this field. In the field of clinical work with children, the leading organization is the American Orthopsychiatric Association. The federal government has likewise played a part in fostering the development of child study, through a number of White House Conferences on childhood; through the Children's Bureau, long in the Department of Labor and now in the Department of Health, Education, and Welfare; and, more recently, through treatment and research centers, and through research grants, both administered by the Public Health Service.

Responsibilities in Working with Children

Research with children is a way of contributing to the whole body of social science. It is an essentially humanistic enterprise, oriented to human goals. Above all, it deals with human subjects—and human subjects who, as we know, are more vulnerable than adults. For this reason, research with children imposes special responsibilities upon the researcher. His long-range goals, no matter how important, are not as important in the ethical scheme as a single one of his subjects. Both for humane and practical reasons, children as research subjects cannot be treated as interchangeable units, but must be dealt with individually, on a personal level of friendliness, respect, and understanding. Whenever any research procedure is in the least bit disturbing, the experimenter must be sensitive to the fact and be prepared to help the child regain his equilibrium, if necessary discontinuing the experiment. Probably this is evident to the investigator working on problems of stress or frustration or failure, who will realize his obligation to reassure the child about his own adequacy. But it should be emphasized that it is exactly those procedures where the child's dynamic processes are not at stake, where the experimenter is interested only in some such psychologically peripheral function as critical flicker fusion or rate of oxygen consumption, that may be most strange or threatening or disturbing for the child, and in which the experimenter is most likely to assume that he can merely turn the child loose at the end of the session. When dealing with children, it is not enough to formulate a neat and ingenious experimental design. In addition, one must design experiments in a way that takes due account of the needs and sensitivities of children.

Apart from research, the field of child study has a responsibility for training people in professional work with children. We feel that knowledge of child development is desirable for all psychologists, and certainly for all clinical psychologists, whether they plan to work with children or adults. It is possible that special qualifications of knowledge and of training and experience with children should be laid down for clinical child psychologists, as is being done in the field of child psychiatry. In any event, the clinical child psychologist needs a chance to work with children. Moreover, he should have a chance to work not only with abnormal children in the clinic, but with normal children in a normal setting. There is much to be said for the potential clinical psychologist's spending a few months as assistant in a nursery school and having an opportunity as well for the systematic observation of older children. Research child psychologists, too, might well benefit from a requirement that they work with and know children in settings such as a nursery school, instead of merely using the nursery school as a convenient pool from which to draw experimental subjects.

It is apparent that the field of child study is still in flux, a flux which we should like to interpret as a creative ferment. Certainly this field has its place in the era of self-conscious parenthood, in a time that has been dubbed the Century of the Child. Children are our link to the future, and it is they who are going to shape whatever brave new worlds come into being. We have a responsibility to them and to the world they are going to live in to make sure that child study, both as the art of dealing practically with children's needs and as a humane science, is based on our best knowledge and our wisest judgment.

NOTES   (Starred items are recommended as further readings.)

[1] Bühler, Charlotte, *The First Year of Life,* New York: John Day, 1930.

[2] Unpublished data.

*[3] An extended account of research methodology with children will be found in Anderson, J. E., "Methods of child psychology," in Carmichael, *Manual of Child Psychology,* pp. 1-59.

[4] Frank, L. K., *Projective Methods,* Springfield, Ill.: Charles C Thomas, 1948; Murphy, G., *Historical Introduction to Modern Psychology,* New York: Harcourt, Brace, revised edition 1949, Chapter 26; Anderson, J. E., "Child development: An historical perspective," *Child Development,* 1956, **27**, 181-196.

[5] Pestalozzi, Johann, *How Father Pestalozzi Educated and Observed His Three-and-a-Half-Year-Old Son,* 1774; Tiedemann, D., *Beobachtung über die Entwicklung der Seelenfähigkeiten bei Kindern,* 1787.

*[6] Darwin, C., "A biographical sketch of an infant," *Mind,* 1877, **2**, 285-294; Preyer, W., *Die Seele des Kindes,* 1882; Shinn, M. W., *Biography of a Baby,* Boston: Houghton Mifflin, 1900.

[7] Ebbinghaus, H., *Memory: A Contribution to Experimental Psychology,* New York: Bureau of Publications, Teachers College, Columbia University, 1913.

[7a] Biber, Murphy, Woodcock, and

Black, *Child Life in School,* pp. 48-54.

[7b] Hartley, Frank, and Goldenson, *Understanding Children's Play,* pp. 341-345. (Adapted from mimeographed course materials from the Dept. of Child Study, Vassar College.)

[8] Barker, R. G., and Wright, H. F., *One Boy's Day,* New York: Harper, 1951; *Midwest and Its Children,* Evanston: Row, Peterson, 1955.

[9] Allport, G. W., "The psychologist's frame of reference," *Psychological Bulletin,* 1940, 37, 1-28. Allport in turn attributes the idiographic-nomothetic distinction to Windelband, W., *Geschichte und Naturwissenschaft,* 1904. See also Allport, G. W., and Vernon, P. E., *Studies in Expressive Movement,* New York: Macmillan, 1933.

[10] *Op. cit.,* fn. 4.

[11] Ford, Mary, *The Application of the Rorschach Test to Young Children,* Minneapolis: University of Minnesota Press, 1946.

[12] Murphy, L. B., *Personality in Young Children,* New York: Basic Books, 1956; Klopfer, B., "Personality diagnosis in early childhood: Application of the Rorschach method at the preschool level," *Psychological Bulletin,* 1939, 36; Schachtel, A. H., "The Rorschach test with young children," *American Journal of Orthopsychiatry,* 1944, 14, 1-9.

[13] Fiedler, M. F., and Stone, L. J., "The Rorschachs of selected groups of children in comparison with published norms. II: The effect of socioeconomic status on Rorschach performance," *Journal of Projective Techniques,* 1956, 20, 276-279.

[14] Benjamin, J. D., and Hilden, A. H., "Infantile anxiety in the Rorschach Test." (Paper presented at meeting of Society for Research in Child Development, 1948.)

[15] Hemmendinger, L., *A Genetic Study of Structural Aspects of Perception as Reflected in Rorschach Test Performance.* Unpublished Ph.D. dissertation, Clark University, 1951.

[16] Vernon, P. E., "The matching method applied to investigations of personality," *Psychological Bulletin,* 1936, 33, 149-177.

[17] Cronbach, L. J., "Statistical methods applied to Rorschach scores: A review," *Psychological Bulletin,* 1949, 46, 393-429; "A validation design for qualitative studies in personality," *Journal of Consulting Psychology,* 1948, 12, 365-374.

[18] Gesell, A., and Thompson, H., "Twins T and C from infancy to adolescence. A biogenetic study of individual differences by the method of co-twin control," *Genetic Psychology Monographs,* 1941, 24, 3-121.

[19] McGraw, M. B., *Growth: A Study of Johnny and Jimmy,* New York: Appleton-Century, 1935. McGraw's study was handicapped by the fact that Johnny and Jimmy proved, in the course of development, not to be identical twins.

[20] Sears, R. R., *Survey of Objective Studies of Psychoanalytic Concepts,* New York: Social Science Research Council, 1943.

[21] For a concise statement of Lewin's theoretical position, see Lewin, K., "Behavior and development as a function of the total situation," in Carmichael, *Manual of Child Psychology,* pp. 918-970.

[22] Koffka, K., *Principles of Gestalt Psychology,* New York: Harcourt, Brace, 1935.

[23] Escalona, Sibylle, "An addendum [to Lewin, fn. 21]—The influence of topological and vector psychology upon current research in child development," in Carmichael, *Manual of Child Psychology,* pp. 971-983.

FOR FURTHER READING

Dennis, W., "Historical beginnings of child psychology," *Psychological Bulletin,* 1949, 46, 224-235.

Woodworth, R. S., *Contemporary* *Schools of Psychology,* New York: Ronald, revised edition 1948. A concise, readable survey of current theoretical orientations.

A Brief Note on Films in Child Study

In their teaching, the authors find it profitable to make generous use of films on infant and child behavior. Even when students have access to real live children, films serve a number of important functions. They provide common, repeatable situations for practice in observing, recording, and interpreting behavior. They can demonstrate particular kinds and aspects of behavior that students might spend precious and fruitless hours waiting to catch. They permit an acquaintance with children of an age (notably early infancy), of a type (emotionally disturbed children, for instance), or in situations (such as faraway lands, institutions, and so forth) which are not ordinarily available to students. However, we have found it necessary to relate films closely to issues being discussed in class, lest they form merely an interlude between discussions. And because students readily fall into the passive set that goes with watching pictures in a darkened room, merely allowing entertainment to flow over them, it is important to help them see a film as an opportunity for critical observation, and to urge them to question its assumptions just as they would those of a written article.

The Vassar series, *Studies of Normal Personality Development,* distributed by the New York University Film Library, comprises a group of films with much the same systematic approach to childhood as this book:

A Long Time to Grow:
    PART I. *Two- and Three-Year-Olds in School*
    PART II. *Four- and Five-Year-Olds in School*
    PART III. *Six-, Seven-, and Eight-Year-Olds—Society of Children.*
    (To be released August 1, 1957.)

Preschool Incidents (A series of films designed to stimulate discussion. The problems raised are left unanswered. The solutions are to come about through discussion within the group.)
    When Should Grownups Help?
    When Should Grownups Stop Fights?
    . . . And Then Ice Cream

This Is Robert (Case study of a child with normal emotional problems. Focuses on the preschool years, with supplementary material on prior and subsequent development. Projective methods are used extensively.)

413

Meeting Emotional Needs in Childhood: The Groundwork of Democracy (How parents and schools contribute to mental health, with special attention to the middle years of childhood.)

Understanding Children's Play (Produced by the Caroline Zachry Institute of Human Development; now distributed as part of the Vassar series.)

Pay Attention (Problems and education of hard-of-hearing children.)

Learning Is Searching: A Third Grade Studies Man's Early Tools (An example of liberal education in the primary grades.)

The use of projective techniques in the study of normal personality development:

> **Finger Painting** (Although not usually thought of as a projective method, finger painting gives the child wide scope for behavior expressive of personality.)
>
> **Balloons: Aggression and Destruction Games** (L. J. Stone)
> **Frustration Play Techniques** (Eugene Lerner)

There are, in addition, a number of Vassar films which have not yet been released for general distribution, although they have been shown on special occasions, such as a meeting of the World Federation for Mental Health. Among these are **Abby, A Backward Look** (development of a child during the first two years, shown in chronologically reversed sequence); **Viki** (an account of the visit of the Hayeses' home-reared chimpanzee to the Vassar laboratory); and **Marvin Cooking** (developing self-expression in an over-inhibited child during a year at nursery school).

We have also used to good advantage a number of films not of our own making. The following selection is not exhaustive; it consists of some of the films we have found most applicable to our own teaching and which are therefore relevant to teaching based on this text.

Birth and the First Fifteen Minutes of Life (René A. Spitz; one of a series produced by the Psychoanalytic Research Project on Problems in Infancy.)

Some Basic Differences in Newborn Infants During the Lying-In Period (One of a series produced by Margaret E. Fries and Paul J. Woolf.)

Life Begins (Arnold Gesell; the pattern of normal development from birth to eighteen months; one of a series.)

Grief (Part of the series produced by Spitz; the effects of separation from the mother during infancy.)

Maternal Deprivation in Young Children (Jenny Aubry and Genevieve Appell; one of a series sponsored by the *Centre Internationale de l'Enfance*. Effects of psychotherapeutic treatment on mother-deprived children.)

Smile of the Baby (Part of the Spitz series; the development of the smiling response.)

Karba's First Years (Gregory Bateson and Margaret Mead; one of a series on Character Formation in Different Cultures. Development in a Balinese child.)

A Child Went Forth (Produced by Joseph Losey and John Ferno. Two-to-seven-year-olds in a summer nursery camp.)

A Two-Year-Old Goes to Hospital (James Robertson; sponsored by the British National Health Service and the World Health Organization. Effects of hospital experience, including separation from her mother, on a two-year-old.)

Angry Boy (Alexander Hammid and Irving Jacoby; one of a series sponsored by the Mental Health Film Board. Genesis and treatment of a behavior problem.)

There are many other fine films in the field. The best sources for locating these are the Children's Bureau list, the State Department list, the World Federation for Mental Health list, current listings in *Contemporary Psychology* and *Psychological Abstracts,* and the Educational Film Library Association. Perhaps the most inclusive source is the H. W. Wilson Company's *Educational Film Guide,* with annual supplements, which lists virtually all 16-millimeter productions.

Bibliography

Adler, Alfred, *The Practice and Theory of Individual Psychology,* New York: Harcourt, Brace, 1923.

Adorno, T. W., Frenkel-Brunswik, E., Levinson, D. J., Sanford, R. N., *The Authoritarian Personality,* New York: Harper, 1950.

Aldrich, C. A. and M. M., *Babies Are Human Beings,* New York: Macmillan, 1941.

Allport, G. W., "Eidetic imagery," *British Journal of Psychology,* 1924, **15,** 99-120.

Allport, G. W., "The psychologist's frame of reference," *Psychological Bulletin,* 1940, **37,** 1-28.

Allport, G. W., *The Use of Personal Documents in Psychological Science,* New York: Social Science Research Council, 1942.

Allport, G. W., *Becoming,* New Haven: Yale, 1955.

Allport, G. W., and Vernon, P. E., *Studies in Expressive Movement,* New York: Macmillan, 1933.

Alschuler, Rose H., and Hattwick, LaB. W., *Painting and Personality,* 2 vols., Chicago: University of Chicago Press, 1947.

Ames, L. B., "The development of the sense of time in the young child," *Journal of Genetic Psychology,* 1946, **68,** 97-125.

Ames, L. B., "The sense of self of nursery school children as manifested by their verbal behavior," *Journal of Genetic Psychology,* 1952, **81,** 193-232.

Ames, L. B., and Learned, Janet, "Imaginary companions and related phenomena," *Journal of Genetic Psychology,* 1946, **69,** 147-167.

Ames, L. B., Learned, Janet, Métraux, R. W., and Walker, R. N., *Child Rorschach Responses,* New York: Hoeber, 1952.

Anastasi, Anne, and Foley, J. P., Jr., *Differential Psychology: Individual and Group Differences in Behavior,* New York: Macmillan, 1949.

Anderson, J. E., "Personality organization in children," *American Psychologist,* 1948, **3,** 409-416.

Anderson, J. E., "Methods of child psychology," in Carmichael, *Manual of Child Psychology* (q.v.), pp. 1-59.

Anderson, J. E., "Child development: An historical perspective," *Child Development,* 1956, **27,** 181-196.

Ansbacher, H. L. and R. R., *The Individual Psychology of Alfred Adler,* New York: Basic Books, 1956.

Asch, S. E., "Studies in the principles of judgments and attitudes: II. Determination of judgments by group and ego standards," *Journal of Social Psychology,* 1940, **12,** 433-465.

Aubry, J. (Roudinesco) "Severe maternal deprivation and personality development in early childhood," *Understanding the Child,* 1952, **21,** 104-108.

Baldwin, J. M., *Mental Development in the Child and in the Race: Methods and Processes,* New York: Macmillan, 1895.

417

Balint, Alice, *The Early Years of Life,* New York: Basic Books, 1955.

Barker, R., Dembo, T., and Lewin, K., *Studies in Topological and Vector Psychology: II. Frustration and Regression,* Iowa City: University of Iowa Press, University of Iowa Studies in Child Welfare, 1, No. 1, 1941.

Barker, R. G., Kounin, J. S., and Wright, H. F. (eds.), *Child Behavior and Development,* New York: McGraw-Hill, 1943.

Barker, R. G., and Wright, H. F., *One Boy's Day,* New York: Harper, 1951.

Barker, R. G., and Wright, H. F., *Midwest and Its Children,* Evanston: Row, Peterson, 1955.

Barker, R. G., Wright, B. A., Meyerson, L., and Gonick, M. R., *Adjustment to Physical Handicap and Illness: A Survey of the Social Psychology of Physique and Disability,* New York: Social Science Research Council, 1953.

Bartlett, F. C., *Remembering: A Study in Experimental and Social Psychology,* New York: Macmillan, 1932.

Baruch, Dorothy, *One Little Boy,* New York: Julian Press, 1952.

Bassett, L. B., *A Study of Some Concepts of Physical Relationships Found in Preschool Children.* Senior thesis, Vassar College, 1956.

Bateson, Gregory, and Mead, M., *Balinese Character,* New York: New York Academy of Sciences, 1942.

Bayley, Nancy, "Consistency and variability in the growth of intelligence from birth to eighteen years," *Journal of Genetic Psychology,* 1949, **75,** 165-196.

Bayley, N., "On the growth of intelligence," *American Psychologist,* 1955, **10,** 805-818.

Bayley, N., "Individual patterns of development," *Child Development,* 1956, **27,** 45-74.

Bayley, N., and Jones, H. E., "Environmental correlates of mental and motor development: A cumulative study from infancy to six years," *Child Development,* 1937, **8,** 329-341.

Beach, F. A., and Jaynes, Julian, "Effects of early experience upon the behavior of animals," *Psychological Bulletin,* 1954, **51,** 239-263.

Benda, C. E., "Psychopathology of childhood," in Carmichael, *Manual of Child Psychology* (q.v.), pp. 1115-1161.

Bender, L., and Vogel, F., "Imaginary companions of children," *American Journal of Orthopsychiatry,* 1941, **11,** 56-66.

Bender, L., *Psychopathology of Children with Organic Brain Disorders,* Springfield, Ill.: Charles C Thomas, 1956.

Benedict, Ruth, "Continuities and discontinuities in cultural conditioning," *Psychiatry,* 1938, **1,** 161-167.

Benedict, Ruth, "Child rearing in certain European countries," *American Journal of Orthopsychiatry,* 1949, **19,** 342-350.

Benjamin, J. D., and Hilden, A. H., "Infantile anxiety in the Rorschach test." (Paper presented before the Society for Research in Child Development, 1948.)

Bertalanffy, L. v., "Some considerations on growth in its physical and mental aspects," *Merrill-Palmer Quarterly,* 1956, **3,** 13-23.

Bettelheim, Bruno, *Love Is Not Enough,* Glencoe, Ill.: The Free Press, 1950.

Bexton, W. H., Heron, W., and Scott, T. H., "Effects of decreased variation in the sensory environment," *Cana-*

dian *Journal of Psychology,* 1954, **8,** 70-76.

Biber, B., Murphy, L. B., Woodcock, L. P., and Black, I. S., *Child Life in School: A Study of a Seven-Year-Old Group,* New York: Dutton, 1942.

Blachowski, S., "The magical behavior of children in relation to school," *American Journal of Psychology,* 1937, **50,** 347-361.

Blauvelt, Helen, "Dynamics of the mother-newborn relationship in goats," in Schaffner, Bertram (ed.), *Group Processes: Transactions of the First Conference,* New York: Josiah Macy, Jr. Foundation, 1955.

Bloch, H. A., and Flynn, F. T., *Delinquency,* New York: Random House, 1956.

Bowlby, John, "Forty-four juvenile thieves: Their characters and home life," *International Journal of Psycho-Analysis,* 1944, **25,** 19-53, 122, 154-178.

Bowlby, John, *Maternal Care and Infant Health,* Geneva: World Health Organization, 1951.

Bowlby, John, *Child Care and the Growth of Love,* London: Pelican, 1953.

Boyd, Elizabeth, *Children's Concepts of God,* Senior thesis, Vassar College, 1955.

Bradley, N. C., "The growth of the knowledge of time in children of school-age," *British Journal of Psychology,* 1947, **38,** 67-78.

Bridges, K. M. B., "Emotional development in early infancy," *Child Development,* 1932, **3,** 324-341.

Bühler, Charlotte, *The First Year of Life,* New York: John Day, 1930.

Bühler, C., *The Child and His Family,* New York: Harper, 1939.

Bühler, Karl, "Les lois générales d'évolution dans le langage de l'enfant," *Journal de Psychologie Normale et Pathologique,* 1926, **23,** 597-607.

Buros, O. K. (ed.), *The Fourth Mental Measurements Yearbook,* Highland Park, N. J.: The Gryphon Press, 1953.

Cannon, W. B., *Bodily Changes in Pain, Hunger, Fear, and Rage,* New York: Appleton-Century, second edition 1929.

Cannon, W. B., *Wisdom of the Body,* New York: Norton, 1939.

Carmichael, Leonard (ed.), *Manual of Child Psychology,* New York: Wiley, second edition 1954.

Carmichael, L., "The onset and early development of behavior," in Carmichael, *Manual of Child Psychology* (q.v.), pp. 60-185.

Cary, Joyce, *A House of Children,* New York: Harper, 1956.

Cassirer, Ernst, "Le langage et la construction du monde des objets," *Journal de Psychologie Normale et Pathologique,* 1933, **30,** 18-44.

Cassirer, Ernst, *An Essay on Man,* New York: Doubleday, Anchor, 1954.

Champion, R., and Ottey, M., "Children's performance on the Vigotsky Test." Unpublished data, Vassar College.

Child Study Association of America, *Facts of Life for Children,* New York: Bobbs-Merrill, 1954.

Christie, Richard, and Jahoda, Marie, *Studies in the Scope and Method of "The Authoritarian Personality,"* Glencoe, Ill.: The Free Press, 1954.

Clemens, Samuel L., *The Adventures of Huckleberry Finn,* 1884.

Cohen, A. K., *Delinquent Boys: The Culture of the Gang,* Glencoe, Ill.: The Free Press, 1955.

Colin, E. C., *Elements of Genetics,* New York: Blakiston Division, Mc-Graw-Hill, 1941.

Conel, L. J., *The Postnatal Development of the Human Cerebral Cortex,* Cambridge: Harvard, Vol. III, 1947.

Conn, J. H., and Kanner, L., "Children's awareness of sex differences," *Journal of Child Psychiatry,* 1947, 1, 3-57.

Cronbach, L. J., "A validation design for qualitative studies in personality," *Journal of Consulting Psychology,* 1948, 12, 365-374.

Cronbach, L. J., "Statistical methods applied to Rorschach scores: A review," *Psychological Bulletin,* 1949, 46, 393-429.

Cruickshank, W. M., *Psychology of Exceptional Children and Youth,* Englewood Cliffs: Prentice-Hall, 1955.

Culotta, D., and Giorgio, S., *Catholic and Protestant Children's Conceptions of God.* Senior thesis, Vassar College, 1956.

Darwin, Charles, "A biographical sketch of an infant," *Mind,* 1877, 2, 285-294.

Davis, C. M., "Results of the self-selection of diets by young children," *Canadian Medical Association Journal,* 1939, 41, 257-261.

Davis, H. V., Sears, R. R., Miller, H. C., and Brodbeck, A. J., "Effects of cup, bottle, and breast feeding on oral activities of newborn infants," *Pediatrics,* November, 1948, 549-558.

Davis, W. A., and Havighurst, R. J., "Social class and color differences in child rearing," *American Sociological Review,* 1946, 11, 698-710.

Davis, W. A., and Havighurst, R. J., *Father of the Man,* Boston: Houghton Mifflin, 1947.

Dawe, H. C., "An analysis of two hun-

dred quarrels of preschool children," *Child Development,* 1934, 5, 139-157.

Dennis, Wayne, "Infant development under conditions of restricted practice and of minimum social stimulation," *Genetic Psychology Monographs,* 1941, 23, 143-190.

Dennis, W., "Historical beginnings of child psychology," *Psychological Bulletin,* 1949, 46, 224-235.

Dennis, W., "Piaget's questions applied to a child of known environment," *Journal of Genetic Psychology,* 1942, 60, 307-320.

Deutsch, Albert, *Our Rejected Children,* Boston: Little, Brown, 1950.

Deutsche, J. M., *The Development of Children's Concepts of Causal Relations,* Minneapolis: University of Minnesota Press, 1937.

Dickinson, R. L., and Belskie, Abram, *Birth Atlas,* New York: Maternity Center Association, 1940.

Dillon, M. S., "Attitudes of children toward their own bodies and those of other children," *Child Development,* 1935, 5, 165-176.

Dollard, John, Doob, L. W., Miller, N. E., Mowrer, O. H., Sears, R. R., et al., *Frustration and Aggression,* New Haven: Yale, 1939.

Du Bois, Cora, "The Alorese," in Kardiner, *The Psychological Frontiers of Society* (q.v.), pp. 101-145.

Dunn, H. Lincoln, *Thumb-Sucking.* (Unpublished manuscript)

Dunn, L. C., and Dobzhansky, Th., *Heredity, Race and Society,* New York: Mentor, revised edition 1952.

Eastman, N. J., *Expectant Motherhood,* Boston: Little, Brown, second edition 1947.

Ebbinghaus, H., *Memory: A Contribution to Experimental Psychology,* New York: Bureau of Publications,

Teachers College, Columbia University, 1913.

Eisenberg, Leon, and Kanner, Leo, "Early infantile autism, 1943-55," *American Journal of Orthopsychiatry,* 1956, **27**, 556-566.

Eisenberg, P., and Lazarsfeld, P. F., "The psychological effects of unemployment," *Psychological Bulletin,* 1938, **35**, 358-390.

Erikson, E. H., "Studies in the interpretation of play," *Genetic Psychology Monographs,* 1940, **22**, 557-671.

Erikson, E. H., *Childhood and Society,* New York: Norton, 1951.

Escalona, Sibylle, "The use of infant tests for predictive purposes," *Bulletin of the Menninger Clinic,* 1950, **14**, 117-128.

Escalona, S., "An addendum—the influence of topological and vector psychology upon current research in child development," in Carmichael, *Manual of Child Psychology* (q.v.), pp. 971-983.

Farnham, M. F., *The Adolescent,* New York: Harper, 1951.

Favez-Boutonier, J., "Child development patterns in France (I)," in Soddy, *Mental Health and Infant Development* (q.v.), Vol. 1, pp. 15-24.

Fiedler, M. F., *Deaf Children in a Hearing World,* New York: Ronald, 1952.

Fiedler, M. F., and Stone, L. J., "The Rorschachs of selected groups of children in comparison with published norms: II. The effects of socioeconomic status on Rorschach performance," *Journal of Projective Techniques,* 1956, **20**, 276-279.

Fisher, Mary S., "Language patterns of preschool children," *Child Development Monographs,* 1934, **15**.

Flory, C. D., "Osseous development of the hand as an index of skeletal development," *Monographs of the Society for Research in Child Development,* 1936, **1**.

Ford, Mary, *The Application of the Rorschach Test to Young Children,* Minneapolis: University of Minnesota Press, 1946.

Forty-Third Yearbook of the National Society for the Study of Education, Part I, Adolescence, 1944.

Frank, L. K., "The fundamental needs of the child," *Mental Hygiene,* July, 1938, pp. 353-379.

Frank, L. K., *Projective Methods,* Springfield, Ill.: Charles C Thomas, 1948.

Freud, Anna, and Burlingham, D., *War and Children,* New York: International Universities Press, 1943.

Freud, A., and Burlingham, D., *Infants without Families,* New York: International Universities Press, 1944.

Freud, A., and Dann, Sophie, "An experiment in group upbringing," *Psychoanalytic Study of the Child,* 1951, **6**, 127-168.

Freud, Sigmund, *A General Introduction to Psychoanalysis,* New York: Liveright, 1935.

Freud, S., *Collected Papers,* London: Hogarth.

Fries, M. E., "Factors in character development, neuroses, psychoses, and delinquency," *American Journal of Orthopsychiatry,* 1937, **7**, 142-181.

Fromm, Erich, *Escape from Freedom,* New York: Farrar & Rinehart, 1941.

Fry, D. B., and Whetnall, Edith, "The auditory approach in the training of deaf children," *Lancet,* March 20, 1954.

Gesell, Arnold, *The Embryology of Behavior*, New York: Harper, 1945.

Gesell, A., "The ontogenesis of infant behavior," in Carmichael, *Manual of Child Psychology* (q.v.), pp. 335-374.

Gesell, A., and Amatruda, C. S., *Developmental Diagnosis*, New York: Hoeber, second edition 1947.

Gesell, A., and Halverson, H. M., "The daily maturation of infant behavior: A cinema study of postures, movements, and laterality," *Journal of Genetic Psychology*, 1942, **61**, 3-32.

Gesell, A., and Ilg, F. L., *Infant and Child in the Culture of Today*, New York: Harper, 1943.

Gesell, A., and Thompson, Helen, *Infant Behavior*, New York: McGraw-Hill, 1934.

Gesell, A., and Thompson, H., "Twins T and C from infancy to adolescence: A biogenetic study of individual differences by the method of co-twin control," *Genetic Psychology Monographs*, 1941, **24**, 3-121.

Gilbert, M. S., *Biography of the Unborn*, Baltimore: Williams and Wilkins, 1938.

Glueck, Sheldon and E. T., *One Thousand Juvenile Delinquents*, Cambridge: Harvard, 1934.

Goethe, J. W. v., *Leiden des jungen Werthers*, 1795.

Goldfarb, William, "Psychological privation in infancy and subsequent adjustment," *American Journal of Orthopsychiatry*, 1945, **15**, 247-255.

Golding, William, *Lord of the Flies*, New York: Coward-McCann, 1954.

Goldstein, Kurt, *The Organism*, New York: American Book Co., 1939.

Goldstein, Kurt, and Scheerer, Martin, "Abstract and concrete behavior," *Psychological Monographs*, 1941, **53**, No. 2.

Goodenough, F. L., and Anderson, J. E., "Psychology and anthropology: Some problems of joint import for the two fields," *Southwestern Journal of Anthropology*, 1947, **3**, 5-14.

Griffiths, Ciwa, *The Utilization of Individual Hearing Aids on Young Deaf Children*. Unpublished Ed.D. dissertation, University of Southern California, 1955.

Griffiths, Ruth, *A Study of Imagination in Early Childhood*, London: Kegan Paul, 1935.

Griffiths, Ruth, *The Abilities of Babies*, New York: McGraw-Hill, 1954.

Gruenberg, S. M., *The Encyclopedia of Child Care and Guidance*, New York: Doubleday, 1954.

Guillaume, Paul, "Les débuts de la phrase dans le langage de l'enfant," *Journal de Psychologie Normale et Pathologique*, 1927, **24**, 203-229.

Haeussermann, Else, "Estimating developmental potential of pre-school children with brain lesions," *American Journal of Mental Deficiency*, 1956, **61**, 170-180.

Hall, C. S., "The inheritance of emotionality," *Sigma Xi Quarterly*, 1938, **26**, 17-27, 37.

Hall, C. S., *A Primer of Freudian Psychology*, Cleveland: World, 1954.

Hall, G. Stanley, *Adolescence: Its Psychology and Its Relations to Physiology, Anthropology, Sociology, Sex, Crime, Religion, and Education*, 2 vols., New York: Appleton, 1904.

Halpern, Florence, *A Clinical Approach to Children's Rorschachs*, New York: Grune & Stratton, 1953.

Hardy, W. G., "Hearing aids for deaf children? A panel discussion," *Volta Review*, 1954, **56**.

Harris, D. B., "The socialization of the delinquent," *Child Development*, 1948, **19**, 143-153.

Harris, D. B., "How children learn interests, motives, and attitudes," *Forty-Ninth Yearbook of the National Society for the Study of Education,* 1950, Part I, pp. 129-155.

Harsh, C. M., and Schrickel, H. G., *Personality: Development and Assessment,* New York: Ronald, 1950.

Hartley, E. L., Birch, H. G., and Hartley, R. E., *Outside Readings in Psychology,* New York: Crowell, 1950.

Hartley, R. E., *Growing Through Play,* New York: Columbia, 1952.

Hartley, R. E., Frank, L. K., and Goldenson, R. M., *New Play Experiences for Children,* New York: Columbia, 1952.

Hartley, R. E., Frank, L. K., and Goldenson, R. M., *Understanding Children's Play,* New York: Columbia, 1952.

Havighurst, R. J., and Taba, H., *Adolescent Character and Personality,* New York: Wiley, 1949.

Hayes, Cathy, *The Ape in Our House,* New York: Harper, 1951.

Hazlitt, V., "Children's thinking," *British Journal of Psychology,* 1930, **20,** 354-361.

Hebb, D. O., "Heredity and environment in mammalian behaviour," *British Journal of Animal Behaviour,* 1953, **1,** 43-47.

Hechinger, F. M., *An Adventure in Education,* New York: Macmillan, 1956.

Heidbreder, Edna. (Studies in concept formation and thinking; for complete bibliography, see Russell, *Children's Thinking*)

Hemmendinger, L., *A Genetic Study of Structural Aspects of Perception as Reflected in Rorschach Test Performance.* Unpublished Ph.D. dissertation, Clark University, 1951.

Hendry, C. E., Lippitt, R., and Zander, A., *Reality Practice as Educational Method,* New York: Beacon House, Psychodrama Monographs No. 9, 1944.

Heron, W., Doane, B. K., and Scott, T. H., "Visual disturbances after prolonged perceptual isolation," *Canadian Journal of Psychology,* 1956, **10,** 13-18.

Hildreth, G. H., *Educating Gifted Children,* New York: Harper, 1952.

Hilgard, E. R., *Theories of Learning,* New York: Appleton-Century-Crofts, second edition 1956.

Hollingshead, A. B., *Elmtown's Youth,* New York: Wiley, 1949.

Honzik, M. P., Macfarlane, J. W., and Allen, L., "The stability of mental test performance between two and eighteen years," *Journal of Experimental Education,* December, 1948, 309-324.

Horney, Karen, *New Ways in Psychoanalysis,* New York: Norton, 1939.

Horowitz, E. L. and R. E., "Development of social attitudes in children," *Sociometry,* 1938, **1,** 301-338.

Horowitz, R. E., "Spatial localization of the self," *Journal of Social Psychology,* 1935, **6,** 379-387.

Horrocks, J. E., *The Psychology of Adolescence,* Boston: Houghton Mifflin, 1951.

Horrocks, J. E., "The adolescent," in Carmichael, *Manual of Child Psychology* (q.v.), pp. 697-734.

Hsu, C. Y., "Influence of temperature on rat embryos," *Anatomical Research,* 1948, **100,** 79-90.

Huang, I., "Children's conception of physical causality: A critical summary," *Journal of Genetic Psychology,* 1943, **63,** 71-121.

Hughes, Richard, *A High Wind in Jamaica* (1929), New York: The Modern Library.

Hunt, A. D., and Trussell, R. E., "They let parents help in children's care," *The Modern Hospital*, September, 1955.

Hunt, J. McV., "An instance of the social origin of conflict resulting in psychoses," *American Journal of Orthopsychiatry*, 1938, 8, 158-164.

Hunt, J. McV. (ed.), *Personality and the Behavior Disorders*, 2 vols., New York: Ronald, 1944.

Hunton, Vera D., "The recognition of inverted pictures by children," *Journal of Genetic Psychology*, 1955, 86, 281-288.

Huschka, Mabel, "The incidence and character of masturbation threats in a group of problem children," *Psychoanalytic Quarterly*, 1938, 7, 338-356.

Huschka, M., "The child's response to coercive bowel training," *Psychosomatic Medicine*, 1942, 4, 301-308.

Irwin, O. C., and Weiss, A. P., "A note on mass activity in newborn infants," *Journal of Genetic Psychology*, 1930, 38, 20-30.

Isaacs, Susan, *Intellectual Growth in Young Children*, London: Routledge, 1930.

Isaacs, Susan, *Social Development in Young Children*, London: Routledge, 1933.

Jackson, Edith B., "The old way is new: Rooming-in," *Vassar Alumnae Magazine*, December, 1948, pp. 7-11.

Jersild, A. T., *Child Psychology*, New York: Prentice-Hall, fourth edition 1954.

Jersild, A. T., and Holmes, F. B., *Children's Fears*, New York: Bureau of Publications, Teachers College, Columbia University, 1935.

Jersild, A. T., Markey, F. V., and Jersild, C. L., *Children's Fears, Dreams, Wishes, Daydreams, Likes, Dislikes, Pleasant and Unpleasant Memories*, New York: Bureau of Publications, Teachers College, Columbia University, 1933.

Johnson, Harriet M., *Children in the Nursery School*, New York: John Day, 1928.

Johnson, Wendell, et al., "A study of the onset and development of stuttering," *Journal of Speech and Hearing Disorders*, 1942, 7, 251-257.

Jones, H. E., *Motor Performance and Growth*, Berkeley: University of California Press, 1949.

Jones, H. E. and M. C., "Fear," *Childhood Education*, 1928, 5, 136-143.

Jones, M. C., and Bayley, Nancy, "Physical maturing among boys as related to behavior," *Journal of Educational Psychology*, 1950, 41, 129-148.

Kanner, Leo, "Early infantile autism," *Journal of Pediatrics*, 1944, 25, 211-217.

Kardiner, Abram, *The Individual and His Society*, New York: Columbia, 1939.

Kardiner, Abram, and associates, *The Psychological Frontiers of Society*, New York: Columbia, 1945.

Katcher, Allan, "The discrimination of sex differences by young children," *Journal of Genetic Psychology*, 1955, 87, 131-143.

Kelly, E. L., "Consistency of the adult personality," *American Psychologist*, 1955, 10, 659-681.

Kenyon, J. H., *Healthy Babies Are Happy Babies*, Boston: Little, Brown, 1935.

Kidd, Dudley, *Savage Childhood: A Study of Kafir Children*, London: Black, 1906.

Kinsey, A. C., and associates, *Sexual Behavior in the Human Male,* Philadelphia: Saunders, 1948.

Kinsey, A. C., and associates, *Sexual Behavior in the Human Female,* Philadelphia: Saunders, 1953.

Klebanoff, S. G., Singer, J. L., and Wilensky, H., "Psychological consequences of brain lesions and ablations," *Psychological Bulletin,* 1954, 51, 1-41.

Klopfer, Bruno, "Personality diagnosis in early childhood: Application of the Rorschach method at the preschool level," *Psychological Bulletin,* 1939, 36.

Klopfer, Bruno, et al., *Developments in the Rorschach Technique,* 2 vols., Yonkers-on-Hudson: World Book Co., 1954 and 1956.

Kluckhohn, Clyde, Murray, H. A., and Schneider, D. M. (eds.), *Personality in Nature, Society, and Culture,* New York: Knopf, 1953.

Klüver, H., "Eidetic imagery," in Murchison, Carl, *Handbook of Child Psychology,* Worcester: Clark University Press, second edition 1933, pp. 699-722.

Koffka, Kurt, *Principles of Gestalt Psychology,* New York: Harcourt, Brace, 1935.

Kreezer, G., and Dallenbach, K. M., "Learning the relation of opposition," *American Journal of Psychology,* 1929, 41, 432-441.

Krogman, W. M., "Trend in the study of physical growth in children," *Child Development,* 1940, 11, 279-284.

Kuenne, M. R., "Experimental investigation of the relation of language to transposition behavior in young children," *Journal of Experimental Psychology,* 1946, 36, 471-490.

Kuhlen, R. G., and Lee, B. J., "Personality characteristics and social acceptability in adolescence," *Journal of Educational Psychology,* 1943, 34, 321-340.

Kuhlen, R. G., and Thompson, G. G., *Psychological Studies of Human Development,* New York: Appleton-Century-Crofts, 1952.

Lacey, John I., Bateman, D. E., and Van Lehn, Ruth, "Autonomic response specificity: An experimental study," *Psychosomatic Medicine,* 1953, 15, 8-21.

Lacey, J. I., and Dallenbach, K. M., "Acquisition by children of the cause-effect relationship," *American Journal of Psychology,* 1939, 52, 103-110.

Lasker, Bruno, *Race Attitudes in Children,* New York: Holt, 1929.

Lazarsfeld, Paul F., Jahoda, M., and Zeisl, H., *Die Arbeitslosen von Marienthal,* Leipzig: S. Hirzel, 1933.

Lazarus, R. S., and McCleary, R. A., "Autonomic discrimination without awareness: A study of subception," *Psychological Review,* 1951, 58, 113-122.

Lee, B. S., "Artificial stutter," *Journal of Speech and Hearing Disorders,* 1951, 16, 53-55.

Lee, Dorothy, "Lineal and nonlineal codifications of reality," *Psychosomatic Medicine,* 1950, 12, 89-97.

Leopold, W. F., *Speech Development of a Bilingual Child,* 4 vols., Evanston-Chicago: Northwestern University Studies in the Humanities, 6, 1939-1949.

Leopold, W. F., *Bibliography of Child Language,* Evanston: Northwestern University Press, 1952.

Lerner, Eugene, "The problem of perspective in moral reasoning," *American Journal of Sociology,* 1937, 43, 249-269.

Lerner, Eugene, and Murphy, L. B. (eds.), "Methods for the study of personality in young children," *Monographs of the Society for Research in Child Development,* 1941, 6, No. 4.

Levy, D. M., "Experiments on the sucking reflex and social behavior in dogs," *American Journal of Orthopsychiatry,* 1934, 4, 203-224.

Levy, D. M., "Studies in sibling rivalry," *Research Monographs of the American Orthopsychiatric Association,* 1937, 2.

Levy, D. M., "On instinct-satiation: an experiment on the pecking behavior of chickens," *Journal of Genetic Psychology,* 1938, 18, 327-348.

Levy, D. M., *Maternal Overprotection,* New York: Columbia, 1943.

Levy, D. M., "Psychic trauma of operations in children and a note on combat neurosis," *American Journal of Diseases of Children,* 1945, 49, 7-25.

Levy, D. M., "The relation of animal psychology to psychiatry," *Medicine and Science,* 1954, 16, 44-75.

Levy, John, and Munroe, Ruth, *The Happy Family,* New York: Knopf, 1938.

Lewin, Kurt, "Behavior and development as a function of the total situation," in Carmichael, *Handbook of Child Psychology* (q.v.), pp. 918-970.

Lewin, K., Lippitt, R., and White, R., "Patterns of aggressive behavior in experimentally created 'social climates,'" *Journal of Social Psychology,* 1939, 10, 271-299.

Lewis, Claudia, *Children of the Cumberland,* New York: Columbia, 1946.

Liddell, H. S., "Conditioning and the emotions," in *Twentieth-Century Bestiary,* New York: Simon and Schuster, 1955, pp. 189-208.

Lindner, R. M., *Rebel Without a Cause,* New York: Grune & Stratton, 1944.

Lippitt, R., and White, R., "The 'social climate' of children's groups," in Barker, R., Kounin, J. S., and Wright, H. F. (eds.), *Child Behavior and Development,* New York: McGraw-Hill, 1943, pp. 485-508.

Long, L., and Welch, L., "The development of the ability to discriminate and match numbers," *Journal of Genetic Psychology,* 1941, 59, 377-387.

Long, L., and Welch, L. (Studies in concept formation; for complete bibliography, see Russell, *Children's Thinking.*)

Lorenz, K. Z., *King Solomon's Ring,* New York: Crowell, 1952.

Lowenfeld, Margaret, "The nature and use of the Lowenfeld world technique in work with children and adults," *Journal of Psychology,* 1950, 30, 325-331.

Lowenfeld, Viktor, *Creative and Mental Growth,* New York: Macmillan, revised edition 1952.

Lynd, H. M., "Identifications and the growth of personal identity," *Merrill-Palmer Quarterly,* 1956, 3, 2-12.

Lynd, R. S. and H. M., *Middletown in Transition,* New York: Harcourt, Brace, 1937.

Maccoby, E. E., Gibbs, P. K., et al., "Methods of child-rearing in two social classes," in Martin and Stendler, *Readings in Child Development* (q.v.), pp. 380-396.

MacCracken, H. N., *The Family on Gramercy Park,* New York: Scribner's, 1949.

MacRae, Duncan, "A test of Piaget's theories of moral development," *Journal of Abnormal and Social Psychology,* 1954, 49, 14-18.

MacRae, John M., "Retests of children given mental tests as infants," *Journal of Genetic Psychology*, 1955, **87**, 111-119.

Maier, N. R. F., "Reasoning in children," *Journal of Comparative Psychology*, 1936, **21**, 357-366.

Mann, Thomas, *Stories of Three Decades*, New York: Knopf, 1936.

Martin, W. E., and Stendler, C. B., *Readings in Child Development*, New York: Harcourt, Brace, 1954.

Maslow, A. H., "Self-actualizing people: A study of psychological health," *Personality Symposia*, 1950, **1**, 11-34.

McCandless, Boyd, "Environment and intelligence," *American Journal of Mental Deficiency*, 1952, **56**, 596-597.

McCarthy, Dorothea, "Language development in children," in Carmichael, *Manual of Child Psychology* (q.v.), pp. 492-630.

McGinley, Phyllis, The Love Letters of, New York: Viking, 1954.

McGraw, M. B., *Growth: A Study of Johnny and Jimmy*, New York: Appleton-Century, 1935.

Mead, Margaret, *From the South Seas*, New York: Morrow, 1939.

Mead, Margaret, *And Keep Your Powder Dry*, New York: Morrow, 1942.

Mead, Margaret, "When do Americans fight?" *Nation*, October 17, 1942, pp. 368-371.

Mead, Margaret, "Age patterning in personality development," *American Journal of Orthopsychiatry*, 1947, **17**, 231-240.

Mead, Margaret, *Male and Female*, New York: Morrow, 1949.

Mead, Margaret, *New Lives for Old*, New York: Morrow, 1956.

Mead, M., and Macgregor, F. C., *Growth and Culture: A Photographic Study of Balinese Childhood*, New York: Putnam, 1951.

Mead, M., and Wolfenstein, Martha (eds.), *Childhood in Contemporary Cultures*, Chicago: University of Chicago Press, 1955.

Merleau-Ponty, M., *Phénoménologie de la Perception*, Paris: NRF, 1945.

Meyer, Edith, "Comprehension of spatial relations in preschool children," *Journal of Genetic Psychology*, 1940, **57**, 119-151.

Meyerson, Lee, "Somatopsychology of physical disability," in Cruickshank, *Psychology of Exceptional Children and Youth* (q.v.), pp. 1-60.

Miller, N. E., "The perception of children," *Journal of Genetic Psychology*, 1934, **44**, 321-339.

Mills, Dorothy, and Bishop, M., "Onward and upward with the arts: Songs of innocence," *New Yorker*, November 13, 1937, pp. 32-42.

Montagu, M. F. A., "Adolescent sterility," *Quarterly Review of Biology*, 1939, **14**, 13-34 and 192-219.

Montagu, M. F. A., "Constitutional and prenatal factors in infant and child health," in Martin and Stendler, *Readings in Child Development* (q.v.), pp. 15-29.

Montagu, M. F. A., *The Direction of Human Development*, New York: Harper, 1955.

Moore, E. C., *Fifty Years of American Education*, Boston: Ginn and Co., 1917.

Mowrer, O. H., "The psychologist looks at language," *American Psychologist*, 1954, **9**, 660-694.

Mowrer, O. H. and W. M., "Enuresis—A method for its study and treatment," *American Journal of Orthopsychiatry*, 1938, **8**, 436-459.

Munn, N. L., *The Evolution and Growth of Human Behavior,* Boston: Houghton Mifflin, 1955.

Murphy, Gardner, *Personality: A Biosocial Approach to Origins and Structures,* New York: Harper, 1947.

Murphy, G., *Historical Introduction to Modern Psychology,* New York: Harcourt, Brace, revised edition 1949.

Murphy, G., and Bachrach, A. J. (eds.), *An Outline of Abnormal Psychology,* New York: The Modern Library, revised edition 1954.

Murphy, G., Murphy, L. B., and Newcomb, T. M., *Experimental Social Psychology,* New York: Harper, revised edition 1937.

Murphy, L. B., *Social Behavior and Child Personality,* New York: Columbia, 1937.

Murphy, L. B., and associates, *Personality in Young Children,* New York: Basic Books, 1956.

Nash, Ogden, *The Ogden Nash Pocket Book,* New York: Pocket Books, 1944.

Neilon, Patricia, "Shirley's babies after fifteen years: A personality study," *Journal of Genetic Psychology,* 1948, 73, 175-186.

Neisser, E. G., *Brothers and Sisters,* New York: Harper, 1951.

Newman, H. H., Freeman, R. N., and Holzinger, K. J., *Twins: A Study of Heredity and Environment,* Chicago: University of Chicago Press, 1937.

Nicolson, A. B., and Hanley, Charles, "Indices of physiological maturity: derivation and interrelationships," *Child Development,* 1953, 24, 3-38.

Olson, W. C., and Hughes, B. O., "The concept of organismic age," *Journal of Educational Research,* 1942, 36, 525-527.

Orlansky, Harold, "Infant care and personality," *Psychological Bulletin,* 1949, 46, 1-48.

Perry, H. S. and S. E., *Operation Schoolhouse: A Preliminary Report.* Unpublished report to Committee on Disaster Studies, National Research Council, 1956.

Perry, S. E., Silber, E., and Bloch, D. A., *The Child and His Family in Disaster,* Washington: National Research Council, Committee on Disaster Studies Monograph Series, #5, 1956.

Pestalozzi, Johann, *How Father Pestalozzi Educated and Observed His Three-and-a-Half-Year-Old Son,* 1774.

Piaget, Jean, *Judgment and Reasoning in the Child,* New York: Harcourt, Brace, 1928.

Piaget, Jean, *The Child's Conception of the World,* New York: Harcourt, Brace, 1929.

Piaget, Jean, *The Moral Judgment of the Child,* New York: Harcourt, Brace, 1932.

Piaget, Jean, "How children form mathematical concepts," *Scientific American,* November, 1953, 74-79.

Piaget, Jean, *The Construction of Reality in the Child,* New York: Basic Books, 1954.

Pinneau, S. R., "A critique on the articles by Margaret Ribble," *Child Development,* 1950, 21, 203-228.

Pinneau, S. R., "The infantile disorders of hospitalism and anaclitic depression," *Psychological Bulletin,* 1955, 52, 429-452.

Pintner, R., and Lev, Joseph, "Worries of school children," *Journal of Genetic Psychology,* 1940, 56, 67-76.

Plant, J. S., *Personality and the Cultural Pattern,* New York: The Commonwealth Fund, 1937.

Pratt, K. C., "The neonate," in Carmichael, *Manual of Child Psychology* (q.v.), pp. 215-291.

Pratt, K. C., Nelson, A. K., and Sun, K. H., "The behavior of the newborn infant," *Ohio State University Studies, Contributions to Psychology*, 1930, 10.

Preyer, W., *Die Seele des Kindes*, 1882.

Rabban, Meyer, "Sex-role identification in young children in two diverse social groups," *Genetic Psychology Monographs*, 1950, 42, 81-158.

Radke, M. J., and Trager, H. G., "Children's perceptions of the social roles of Negroes and whites," *Journal of Psychology*, 1950, 29, 3-33.

Radke, M. J., Trager, H. G., and Davis, H., "Social perceptions and attitudes of children," *Genetic Psychology Monographs*, 1949, 40, 327-447.

Rapaport, David (ed.), *Organization and Pathology of Thought*, New York: Columbia, 1951.

Read, Katherine, *The Nursery School*, Philadelphia: Saunders, 1950.

Redl, Fritz, and Wineman, D., *Children Who Hate*, Glencoe, Ill.: The Free Press, 1951.

Redl, Fritz, and Wineman, D., *Controls from Within*, Glencoe, Ill.: The Free Press, 1952.

Reynolds, M. M., *Negativism of Preschool Children*, New York: Bureau of Publications, Teachers College, Columbia University, 1928.

Reynolds, M. M., and Mallay, H., "Sleep of young children," *Journal of Genetic Psychology*, 1933, 43, 322-351.

Rheingold, H. L., "The modification of social responsiveness in institutional babies." *Monographs of the Society for Research in Child Development*, 1956, 21, No. 2.

Ribble, M. A., *The Rights of Infants*, New York: Columbia, 1943.

Richards, T. W., Newbery, H., and Fallgatter, R., "Studies in fetal behavior: II. Activity of the human fetus *in utero* and its relation to other prenatal conditions, particularly the mother's metabolic rate," *Child Development*, 1938, 9, 69-78.

Riesen, A. H., "The development of visual perception in man and chimpanzee," *Science*, 1947, 106, 107-108.

Riesman, David, *The Lonely Crowd*, New Haven: Yale, 1950.

Riess, B. F., "Genetic changes in semantic conditioning," *Journal of Experimental Psychology*, 1946, 36, 143-152.

Roberts, K. E., and Schoellkopf, J. A., "Eating, sleeping, and elimination practices of a group of two-and-one-half-year-old children," *American Journal of Diseases of Children*, 1951, 82, 121-152.

Robinowitz, Ralph, "Learning the relation of opposition as related to scores on the Wechsler Intelligence Scale for Children," *Journal of Genetic Psychology*, 1956, 88, 25-30.

Robinson, H. M., *Why Pupils Fail in Reading*, Chicago: University of Chicago Press, 1946.

Ross, J. B., and McLaughlin, M. M. (eds.), *A Portable Medieval Reader*, New York: Viking, 1949.

Roudinesco, J. (See Aubry, J.)

Russell, D. H., *Children's Thinking*, Boston: Ginn and Co., 1956.

Salinger, J. D., *The Catcher in the Rye*, Boston: Little, Brown, 1951.

Sarason, S. B., *Psychological Problems in Mental Deficiency*, New York: Harper, second edition 1953.

Sargent, S. S., and Smith, M. W. (eds.), *Culture and Personality,* New York: The Viking Fund, 1949.

Schachtel, Anna H., "The Rorschach test with young children," *American Journal of Orthopsychiatry,* 1944, **14,** 1-9.

Scheerer, Martin, "Cognitive theory," in Lindzey, G. (ed.), *Handbook of Social Psychology,* Cambridge: Addison-Wesley Publishing Co., 1954, Vol. 1, pp. 91-142.

Scheinfeld, Amram, *The New You and Heredity,* Philadelphia: Lippincott, 1950.

Schilder, Paul, *Psychoanalysis, Man, and Society,* New York: Norton, 1951.

Scupin, E. and G., *Bubis erste Kindheit,* Leipzig: Grieben, 1907.

Sears, R. R., *Survey of Objective Studies of Psychoanalytic Concepts,* New York: Social Science Research Council, 1943.

Sears, R. R., and Wise, G. W., "Relation of cup feeding in infancy to thumb-sucking and the oral drive," *American Journal of Orthopsychiatry,* 1950, **20,** 123-138.

Seeley, J. R., Sim, R. A., and Loosley, E. W., *Crestwood Heights,* New York: Basic Books, 1956.

Seidman, J. M. (ed.), *The Adolescent: A Book of Readings,* New York: Dryden, 1953.

Senn, M. J. E. (ed.), *Symposium on the Healthy Personality,* New York: Josiah Macy, Jr., Foundation, 1950.

Sherman, M., "The differentiation of emotional responses in infants: I. Judgments of emotional responses from motion-picture views and from actual observation," *Journal of Comparative Psychology,* 1927, **7,** 265-284.

Sherman, M., "The differentiation of emotional responses in infants: II. The ability of observers to judge the emotional characteristics of the crying of infants and of the voice of the adult," *Journal of Comparative Psychology,* 1927, **7,** 335-351.

Shevrin, Howard. Unpublished Ph.D. dissertation, Cornell University, 1954.

Shinn, M. W., *Biography of a Baby,* Boston: Houghton Mifflin, 1900.

Shirley, M. M., *The First Two Years, A Study of Twenty-Five Babies,* Minneapolis: University of Minnesota Press, 3 vols., 1931-1933.

Shuttleworth, F. K., "The physical and mental growth of girls and boys age six to nineteen in relation to age at maximum growth," *Monographs of the Society for Research in Child Development,* 1939, **4, 3.**

Shuttleworth, F. K., "The adolescent period: A graphic atlas," *Monographs of the Society for Research in Child Development,* 1949, **14, 1.**

Shuttleworth, F. K., "The adolescent period: A pictorial atlas," *Monographs of the Society for Research in Child Development,* 1949, **14, 2.**

Soddy, Kenneth (ed.), *Mental Health and Infant Development,* 2 vols., New York: Basic Books, 1956.

Sollenberger, R. T., "Some relationships between the urinary excretion of male hormone by maturing boys and their expressed interests and attitudes," *Journal of Psychology,* 1940, **9,** 179-189.

Sontag, L. W., "The significance of fetal environmental differences," *American Journal of Obstetrics and Gynecology,* 1941, **42,** 996-1003.

Sontag, L. W., "Differences in modifiability of fetal behavior and physiology," *Psychosomatic Medicine,* 1944, **6,** 151-154.

Sontag, L. W., and Reynolds, E. L., "The Fels composite sheet: I. A practical method for analyzing growth progress," *Journal of Pediatrics,* 1945, 26, 327-335.

Spearman, C. E., *The Creative Mind,* New York: Appleton, 1931.

Spence, K. W., "Theoretical interpretations of learning," in Stevens, S. S. (ed.), *Handbook of Experimental Psychology,* New York: Wiley, 1951, pp. 690-729.

Spiro, M. E., "Culture and personality: The natural history of a false dichotomy," *Psychiatry,* 1951, 14, 19-46.

Spitz, René A., "Diacritic and coenesthetic organizations," *Psychoanalytic Review,* 1945, 32, 146-162.

Spitz, René A., "Hospitalism. An inquiry into the genesis of psychiatric conditions in early childhood," *Psychoanalytic Study of the Child,* 1945, 1, 53-74.

Spitz, René A., "Hospitalism: A follow-up report," *Psychoanalytic Study of the Child,* 1946, 2, 113-117.

Spitz, René A., "Anaclitic depression," *Psychoanalytic Study of the Child,* 1946, 2, 313-342.

Spitz, René A., "The psychogenic diseases in infancy: An attempt at their etiologic classification," *Psychoanalytic Study of the Child,* 1951, 6, 255-275.

Spock, Benjamin, *The Common-Sense Book of Baby and Child Care,* New York: Duell, Sloan and Pearce, 1946.

Springer, Doris, "Development in young children of an understanding of time and the clock," *Journal of Genetic Psychology,* 1952, 80, 83-96.

Stolz, H. R. and L. M., *Somatic Development of Adolescent Boys,* New York: Macmillan, 1951.

Stolz, L. M., and collaborators, *Father Relations of War-Born Children,* Stanford: Stanford University Press, 1954.

Stone, C. P., and Barker, R. G., "The attitudes and interests of pre-menarcheal and post-menarcheal girls," *Journal of Genetic Psychology,* 1939, 54, 27-71.

Stone, L. J., "Experiments in group play and readiness for destruction," in Lerner and Murphy (eds.) (q.v.), pp. 101-155.

Stone, L. J., *Finger Painting: Children's Use of Plastic Materials. A Guide to the Film,* New York: New York University Film Library, 1944.

Stone, L. J., "Some problems of filming children's behavior: A discussion based on experience in the production of 'Studies of Normal Personality Development,'" *Child Development,* 1952, 23, 227-233.

Stone, L. J., "A critique of studies of infant isolation," *Child Development,* 1954, 25, 9-20.

Stone, L. J., "He still learns through his plays," in *Childcraft.* Chicago: Field Enterprises, 1954, Vol. 13, pp. 151-161.

Stone, L. J., and Fine, C. G., *The Effects of a Revised Preschool Program on the Personality Development and Communication Efficiency of Young Deaf Children.* (Monograph in preparation)

Strauss, A. L., "The development of conceptions of rules in children," *Child Development,* 1954, 25, 193-208.

Sullivan, H. S., *The Interpersonal Theory of Psychiatry,* New York: Norton, 1953.

Swan, C., "Rubella in pregnancy as an aetiological factor in congenital malformation, stillbirth, miscarriage, and abortion," *Journal of Obstetrics and Gynaecology of the British Empire,* 1949, **56**, 341-363 and 591-605.

Symonds, P. M., *The Dynamics of Parent-Child Relationships,* New York: Bureau of Publications, Teachers College, Columbia University, 1949.

Teachers for Tomorrow, New York: Fund for the Advancement of Education, Bulletin No. 2, 1955.

Terman, L. M., et al., *Genetic Studies of Genius,* Stanford: Stanford University Press, 1925, Vol. 1.

Terman, L. M., and Tyler, L. E., "Psychological sex differences," in Carmichael, *Manual of Child Psychology* (q.v.), pp. 1064-1114.

Thomas, D. S., *Some New Techniques for Studying Social Behavior,* New York: Bureau of Publications, Teachers College, Columbia University, 1929.

Thompson, Clara (ed.), *An Outline of Psychoanalysis,* New York: The Modern Library, 1955.

Thompson, W. R., "Early environment —its importance for later behavior." (Paper delivered before the American Psychopathological Association, June, 1954)

Thompson, W. R., and Heron, W., "The effects of restricting early experience on the problem-solving capacity of dogs," *Canadian Journal of Psychology,* 1954, **8**, 17-31.

Tiedemann, D., *Beobachtung über die Entwicklung der Seelenfähigkeiten bei Kindern,* 1787.

Todd, T. W., "The roentgenographic appraisement of skeletal differentiation," *Child Development,* 1930, **1**, 298-310.

Trager, H. G., and Radke, M. Y., *They Learn What They Live,* New York: Harper, 1952.

Tryon, C. M., "The adolescent peer culture," *Forty-Third Yearbook of the National Society for the Study of Education,* Part I, 1944, pp. 217-239.

Tryon, R. C., "Genetic differences in maze-learning ability in rats," *Thirty-Ninth Yearbook of the National Society for the Study of Education,* 1940, 111-119.

U. S. Bureau of the Census, *Statistical Abstract of the United States,* Washington 25: U. S. Government Printing Office, 1955.

U. S. Children's Bureau, *Prenatal Care,* Washington 25: U. S. Government Printing Office (periodically revised).

U. S. Children's Bureau, *Infant Care,* Washington 25: U. S. Government Printing Office (periodically revised).

U. S. Children's Bureau, *Your Child from One to Six,* Washington 25: U. S. Government Printing Office (periodically revised).

U. S. Children's Bureau, *Your Child from Six to Twelve,* Washington 25: U. S. Government Printing Office (periodically revised).

U. S. Children's Bureau, *The Adolescent in Your Family,* Washington 25: U. S. Government Printing Office (periodically revised).

Valentine, C. W., *The Normal Child: And Some of His Abnormalities,* Baltimore: Penguin, 1956.

Vernon, P. E., "The biosocial nature of the personality trait," *Psychological Review,* 1933, **40**, 533-548.

Vernon, P. E., "The matching method applied to investigations of personality," *Psychological Bulletin,* 1936, **33**, 149-177.

Warfield, Frances, *Cotton in My Ears,* New York: Viking, 1948.

Washburn, R. W., *Children Have Their Reasons,* New York: Appleton-Century, 1942.

Watson, J. B., *Psychological Care of Infant and Child,* New York: Norton, 1928.

Weaver, Warren, "Information theory: 1. Information theory to 1951—a non-technical review," *Journal of Speech and Hearing Disorders,* 1952, 17, 166-174.

Weininger, Otto, "Mortality of albino rats under stress as a function of early handling," *Canadian Journal of Psychology,* 1953, 7, 111-114.

Welch, L., and Long, L. (Studies in concept formation; for complete bibliography, see Russell, *Children's Thinking*)

Wenger, M. A., "The measurement of individual differences in autonomic balance," *Psychosomatic Medicine,* 1941, 3, 427-434.

Werner, Heinz, *Einführing in die Entwicklungspsychologie,* Leipzig: Barth, 1933.

Werner, Heinz, *Comparative Psychology of Mental Development,* Chicago: Follett, revised edition 1948.

Werner, Heinz, Freud, A., Sears, R. R., and Frank, L. K., *Symposium on Genetic Psychology,* Worcester: Department of Psychology, Clark University, 1950.

Werner, Heinz, "Microgenesis and aphasia," *Journal of Abnormal and Social Psychology,* 1956, 52, 347-353.

Werner, Heinz, and Kaplan, Edith, "The acquisition of word meanings: A developmental study," *Monographs*

of the Society for Research in Child Development, 1950, 15.

White, R. W., *The Abnormal Personality,* New York: Ronald, 1948.

Whiting, J. W. M., and Child, I. L., *Child Training and Personality,* New Haven: Yale, 1953.

Wilkinson, F. R., and Cargill, D. W., "Repression elicited by story material based on the Oedipus complex," *Journal of Social Psychology,* 1955, 42, 209-214.

Withers, Carl, *A Rocket in My Pocket,* New York: Holt, 1948.

Witmer, H. L., and Kotinsky, R., *Personality in the Making,* New York: Harper, 1952.

Wolff, Werner, *The Personality of the Preschool Child,* New York: Grune & Stratton, 1946.

Woodcock, Louise P., *Life and Ways of the Two-Year-Old,* New York: Dutton, 1941.

Woodworth, R. S., *Contemporary Schools of Psychology,* New York: Ronald, revised edition 1948.

Yarrow, Leon J., "The development of object relationships during infancy, and the effects of disruption of early mother-child relationships." (Paper delivered before the American Psychological Association, September, 1956)

Zachry, Caroline, *Emotion and Conduct in Adolescence,* New York: Appleton-Century, 1940.

Index

A

Achievements tests, 229, 258.

Absolutism, 211, 213, 221, 242.

Abstract space, 185, 186.

Abstraction, 242, 361, 405. *See also* Concepts, Generalization.

Abulia, 373.

Acting-out behavior, 367, 372.

Acting-out delinquency, 367.

Action-objects, action-space, 88, 90, 185.

Active dominance, 87, 155, 230.

Activity preferences. *See* Interests.

Activity rate. *See* Tempo, personal.

Active language, 118.

Activity, as characteristic of organism, 32.

Addison's disease, 75.

Adjustment, 318.

ADLER, ALFRED, 132, 139.

Adolescence: defined, 269; cultural nature of, 271; changing character of, 294-295; end of, 322; social provisions for, 331-334.

Adolescent rebellion, 294, 317, 367, 371.

Adolescent sterility, 300, 318.

Adoption, 378, 379.

Adrenals. *See* Endocrines.

Adult-child relationships: toddler, 110; preschool child, 145, 152-153, 160; middle years child, 214-215, 225, 233, 265; adolescent, 289, 290, 305, 322. *See also* Education, School.

Adulthood, symbols of, 272, 322.

Affection, 175. *See also* Emotion.

Affiliation, 217.

Afterbirth, 24.

Age scales, 391. *See also* Growth age.

Aggression, 147, 149.

ALDRICH, C. A., 83.

ALDRICH, M. M., 83.

Alice, 152, 179.

Allergy, 21.

ALLPORT, GORDON, 345, 387, 411.

Alor, 79, 94.

AMATRUDA, CATHERINE S., 82, 117.

Ambiguity, tolerance of, 339, 340.

Ambivalence, 98, 166, 307, 314, 319, 324. *See also* Dual ambivalence, Growth ambivalence.

AMES, LOUISE B., 139, 173, 184, 201.

Amnion, 14.

Anal character, 130.

Anal stage, 113, 130, 166.

ANDERSON, J. E., 388, 410.

B

H